Online Auctions at eBay

2nd Edition

**Bid with Confidence,
Sell with Success**

Send Us Your Comments

To comment on this book or any other PRIMA TECH title, visit PRIMA TECH's reader response page on the Web at **www.prima-tech.com/comments**.

How to Order

For information on quantity discounts, contact the publisher: Prima Publishing, P.O. Box 1260BK, Rocklin, CA 95677-1260; (916) 632-4400. On your letterhead, include information concerning the intended use of the books and the number of books you wish to purchase. For individual orders, visit PRIMA TECH's Web site at **www.prima-tech.com**.

Online Auctions at eBay

2nd Edition

Bid with Confidence, Sell with Success

Dennis L. Prince

A DIVISION OF PRIMA PUBLISHING

A Division of Prima Publishing

Prima Publishing and colophon are registered trademarks of Prima Communications, Inc., Rocklin, California 95765.

Publisher: Stacy L. Hiquet

Associate Publisher: Nancy Stevenson

Marketing Manager: Judi Taylor

Managing Editor: Dan J. Foster

Senior Acquisitions Editor: Deborah F. Abshier

Senior Editor: Kim V. Benbow

Technical Reviewers: Chris Aloia

Copy Editor: Hilary Powers

Interior Design: Scribe Tribe

Interior Layout: Marian Hartsough

Cover Design: Prima Design Team

Indexer: Sharon Hilgenberg

This book is not authorized, sponsored by, or affiliated with eBay Inc. Microsoft, Windows, and Notepad are trademarks or registered trademarks of Microsoft Corporation. Netscape, Netscape Navigator, and Netscape Communicator are trademarks or registered trademarks of Netscape Communications Corporation.

Important: Prima Publishing cannot provide software support. Please contact the appropriate software manufacturer's technical support line or Web site for assistance.

Prima Publishing and the author have attempted throughout this book to distinguish proprietary trademarks from descriptive terms by following the capitalization style used by the manufacturer.

Online auctioning has certain inherent risks. Readers who engage in online auctioning do so at their own risk, and the use of the information or techniques discussed in this book will not guarantee any particular financial performance or success. The author and publisher therefore disclaim any liability, loss or risk, personal or otherwise, which is incurred as a consequence, directly or indirectly, of the use and application of information contained in this book.

Information contained in this book has been obtained by Prima Publishing from sources believed to be reliable. However, because of the possibility of human or mechanical error by our sources, Prima Publishing, or others, the Publisher does not guarantee the accuracy, adequacy, or completeness of any information and is not responsible for any errors or omissions or the results obtained from the use of such information. Readers should be particularly aware of the fact that the Internet is an ever-changing entity. Some facts may have changed since this book went to press.

ISBN: 0-7615-2414-2
Library of Congress Catalog Card Number: 99-65391
Printed in the United States of America

00 01 02 03 DD 10 9 8 7 6 5 4 3

For my family.
Thank you for putting up with my hours online,
bidding, selling, and writing. I'm lucky to have you.

Preface

In December 1995, I stumbled across a unique little Web site called AuctionWeb. A clever innovation in online buying and selling, it was a public meeting place to swap goods, adding an enticing auction format that gave more thrill to the chase and more excitement to the climax. I loved it and became fully engrossed, absorbing every nuance of the site and every aspect of conducting auctions on the Internet. Of course, the name AuctionWeb has since been retired; it is now known the world over as the online phenomenon eBay.

In November 1998, I approached Prima Publishing with the idea for a book that would detail what I've learned and achieved at eBay. Since I was already accustomed to explaining eBay to friends, family, and online cyberpals, writing it all down as a source of easy reference seemed natural. The first edition of Online Auctions at eBay: Bid With Confidence, Sell With Success, was published in April 1999. In three short months, a new edition was needed. Quick! Someone print some more.

But before the presses could start rolling again, I saw that eBay, a perpetual "work in progress," was on the move, growing and changing to keep pace with its swelling community and their increasing auction needs. Therefore, reprinting the first edition was not the answer. A revised and expanded second edition—that's what was needed, and that's what you're reading today. It has everything the first edition had and more, bringing you up to date with the latest developments at eBay.

As a bonus, I'm happy to announce a new Web site, **www.prima-tech.com /auctionfun**, has been developed to act as a companion to this edition. Check the site frequently—I'll be posting useful tools and updated information as eBay continues to grow and change. My goal is to help anyone interested in eBay to become a confident and successful member of the auction community.

So, thanks for picking up this new edition of Online Auctions at eBay. I hope you'll enjoy what you're about to read and find answers to the questions you may have. More than that, I hope you'll find the same fun and fascination as I have, making the most of everything the site and its resident community has to offer. There's a good time waiting for you at eBay. I'll look forward to meeting you there.

— Dennis L. Prince
September 1999

Acknowledgments

As with any book, there are always so many people to thank, so I better get started.

First, thanks to Pierre Omidyar and his original vision for eBay. Thanks to his efforts and belief that online trading could be successful, none of this would have been possible.

Next, thanks to my literary agent, Laura Belt. You were tireless, patient, and always there to answer my questions. I'm glad we got to work together on this (again!).

Then, my thanks to the team of folks who read my early treatments of this book and made comments and suggestions that helped add more polish and fun to the final product. My superb technical editor, Chris Aloia and my copy editor, the incredible Hilary Powers. Thanks for taking this second edition around the test track, effectively kicking the tires and adding more spark to the plugs. By this time, I hope your committed eBay lifers!

Of course, a huge round of applause for the fine team at Prima Publishing. You folks really know how to get a book on the shelves. Thanks to Stacy Hiquet and Nancy Stevenson, my publishers, Debbie Abshier, my acquisitions editor, Dan Foster, the managing editor, Jose Ramirez and Mike Tanamachi for a terrific cover design, Danielle Foster for the great interior design (and a sturdy soapbox), Marian Hartsough for the smooth interior layout, and Sharon Hilgenberg for the fine indexing work.

Special "thank yous" go to Prima's Kim Benbow, my project editor, and Judi Taylor, the marketing manager; your enthusiasm and belief in this book has made this the most fun an author could have at work. Thanks for staying the course with me; I know it hasn't always been easy, and I appreciate your extra efforts and enthusiasm.

Of course, there are more behind-the-scenes people at Prima who were involved and instrumental in making this book a reality. My warm and sincere thanks to each of you.

Last, but certainly not least, I must acknowledge the eBay community. I'm glad to have dealt with so many of you over the years. Your spirit, convictions, and love of the auction are what caused me to write this book in the first place. Thanks to all of you who wrote so many nice letters in response to the first edition. I promise to continue to answer all questions that come my way. I salute you all and look forward to even more great fun in the years to come.

About the Author

Dennis L. Prince has been an active member of the eBay community since 1996. He has participated in hundreds of auctions as both buyer and seller. He has literally exchanged thousands of dollars in transactions and has achieved a very respectable eBay community rating. As a seasoned hobbyist and collector, he has worked with long-distance business transactions (businesses and person-to-person) for over 20 years.

Contents

Introduction

When was the last time you had fun shopping? I don't mean just finding satisfaction with a particular purchase you might have made. I mean fun *shopping*—no traffic, no crowded parking lots, and absolutely no long lines of other impatient shoppers slowly inching toward some horribly understaffed checkout counter.

When was the last time you went on a treasure hunt? Have you experienced the adventure of seeking some fabled relic, searching high and low using only scant clues, your personal determination, and a bit of good old-fashioned luck? Do you believe such treasure exists?

When was the last time you found yourself in the enviable possession of some item that embodied true scarcity and desire? Have you had people beating down your door lately hoping to persuade you to let go of that treasured possession, offering you riches beyond your wildest expectation? Would you even know if you own such an item today?

And when was the last time you played a good game of chase? A game full of fun, excitement, challenge, and wits? Have you pitted yourself against the wiles and cunning of another player in an arena charged with energy, craftiness, and a bit of the unexpected?

Did you know you can do all of this and more on the Internet? Well, you can. There's an incredibly fascinating feature that the Internet has been serving up: online auctions. I suspect you've heard of them. They're those places where people are flocking to do some serious online shopping, searching for lost treasures, offering items of desire, and playing a great game of buy and sell.

If you listen to the news, read online commentary, or watch the stock market, you'll know there is an undeniable avenue to all of this activity and excitement: *eBay, Your Personal Trading Community*. This book is about online auctions, eBay style. You'll find a new hobby in eBay, or perhaps strengthen and advance an existing hobby. eBay has something to offer everyone, and, as you'll learn in this book, it's a place to have some fun, meet some great people, find that certain item that has been missing from your life—and possibly offer up such an item to fulfill the desires of another.

Or maybe you just want to know more about the whole eBay thing to see what all the commotion is about. Fair 'nuff.

Why This Book?

eBay is the single most successful person-to-person online auction site on the Internet today. Many people have used it, but many more still have not. I've been using eBay for years now, and I find that I'm continually answering some of the same questions from others eager to find out what eBay's all about.

- How do you find what you're looking for on eBay?
- How do you know what to sell?
- When's the best time to bid?
- How do you make sure you don't get ripped off?
- How do you keep up with the other buyers and sellers?
- Is it legal?

Well, of course it's all legal, and it's all fun. Do I mind answering these questions? Absolutely not. But I've realized there's a real need for a resource that eBay users can turn to for answers to their questions and for insight and advice about how to make the most of what eBay has to offer.

As with anything new, the more you practice, the more you learn and improve. I've been an active member of eBay since 1996, and, believe me, I've learned a lot and have honed my skills as I work the auctions. I've successfully bought and sold hundreds upon hundreds of items. The eBay Web site itself has improved since my first days using it. It has undergone many changes since its first appearance, and I have learned and grown right along with it.

Every month, I see new users come into the eBay community. In earlier days, new eBay users would be somewhat wide-eyed at the events occurring all around. I recall my own first experiences, where many of us new users would meet each other rather informally (maybe we were bidding on the same or similar items), and we would share experiences and methods with one another quite freely. The community was small then, and it was easy to strike up electronic friendships as we each worked to make more of the eBay experience. We users learned with each other and from each other.

However, as Internet usage continues to grow at exponential rates each year, and eBay itself finds its user community in the midst of a population explosion, it's simply not as easy for newer users to come into the virtual auction place and quickly find the help they want or the advice they need. In fact, subcommunities have formed in which the very seasoned users converse among themselves, discussing auction activities, issues, and tactics. It's not any sort of cyber-clique, but it is difficult for a new user to get into the fold as easily as in days gone by.

So I write this book to help you. In my years of working on eBay, I've learned—as you will—that eBay is more than just a Web site. Beyond the extensive item listings and the furious mouse clicking as bids are placed, there is more to what makes the auction successful. I've learned much about the actual *business* of an auction. In fact, once the auction has ended, the business has really only just begun. My goal with this book is to help you understand the depth of the auction, and what you'll be signing up for when you decide to join in. You'll need to bring commitment and consistency to the auction party if you want to make the most of the online auction experience. Don't misunderstand me—it's not drudgery by any means. However, you'll want to be knowledgeable enough to know how the whole process works so your participation can be fruitful and enjoyable.

What's New in This Edition?

A lot, actually. eBay is growing by leaps and bounds. Since the first edition of this book was published, the number of registered eBay users has almost doubled (that's right, *doubled*). There's been a constantly growing swarm of activity at eBay which, quite frankly, even seems to have taken the good folks at eBay by surprise. So, to respond to the increased demand of the site's resources as well as to acknowledge the needs, wants, and desires of the growing eBay community, the eBay site has undergone some significant changes and improvements.

First of all, you'll notice the eBay site design has changed, as reflected in the pages of this revised edition. eBay went to considerable lengths to make sure the new site design—called the revised *Information Architecture*—would be more user friendly and easier to navigate. It employed the talents of a focused team of site designers, eBay's own *Human Interface Group*, plus lots of direct user surveys and one-on-one tests with established eBay users as well as folks who had never used the site at all. The outcome, I have to say, is a credit to the effort invested. To the users who have commented on a beta (test) version of the new design, it has come as a most welcome change.

But besides the new site design, this edition also includes in-depth explanations of many of the site's new features and programs. New search tools, safer bidding screens, increased customer safety programs, and a few whiz-bang thingies that are pretty cool and really help make eBay more reliable and more fun.

And, if you like facts and figures, rest assured that I'll be bringing those up to snuff, too. The e-commerce (electronic commerce) landscape has changed dramatically in recent months and the new reports and statistics are showing some staggering facts. You'll see for yourself a little later in the book. The numbers are impressive and the results of some of the recent Internet studies are real eye-poppers.

Plus, I get to go shopping again (oh, woe is me). That's right. To properly show you how the new site design and features work, I'll need to jump into the trenches to bid on and sell all kinds of interesting, fun, and often funky little goodies. I had some fun stuff to work with in the first edition of this book, and I look forward to having just as much fun (or more) doing it all over again. It's all in the name of frontline research, and it must be done. Don't cry for me, though. I'd be in there buying and selling anyway. I'll just let you peer over my shoulder while I do it.

Who Are You?

Well, I don't know you personally, but I can tell you who I think you are and, if I'm correct, why this is the sort of book you've been looking for. Anyone who has heard about the rampant success of eBay and wants to find out what all the buzz is about should read this book. Perhaps you're completely new to the Wonderful Webbed World and you're looking for a fun place to hang out. *That's great.* Or, maybe you're a bona fide Web rat who's thinking this eBay-babble is worth a second look. *Cool.* Perhaps you've been searching for some rare and treasured item and have heard that eBay hosts over two million live auctions daily—increasing your odds of finding that elusive artifact. *Oh, do press on.* Or maybe you just have an attic, garage, or basement full of your kids' old stuff and, since they've gone off to college and left you with the mess, you might like to turn that clutter into some valuable auction fodder. *(Just don't tell your kids I gave you the idea, OK?)* Well, eBay is the place. Whatever your motivation, think about how you might answer the following questions:

- Have you heard about eBay, and want to know how to get into the game?

- Are you looking for some unique item that will make your collection complete, but having no luck finding it?

- Do you have a collection that you want to sell, and want to be sure you can find the largest group of potential buyers that will increase your chance of selling at higher prices?

- Are you in the business of selling merchandise, and want to migrate from conventional methods to an online auction?

- Are you curious about the present value of items in an open, active marketplace subject to real-time ebbs and flows?

- Are you looking for an alternative to the regular 9-to-5 daily grind where you'll be free to unleash your entrepreneurial drive?

- Do you want to find a fun Web site where you'll see nothing short of raw, in-your-face capitalism at its finest?

- Do you have gobs of money and don't know what to buy with it?

- Do you have gobs of time and don't know how to spend it?

- Or, are you "just browsing, thank you"?

If you answered yes to any of these questions, then certainly this book has something useful and fun in store for you.

What You Will Find in This Book

In this book, I'll help you understand more about auctions in general—what they are, how they started, and how they've changed—particularly as they've migrated from the traditional auction house to the virtual auction block. You'll find, as I did, that understanding more about auctions themselves will help you feel immediately knowledgeable as you enter eBay. You'll learn how the Internet has affected auction traditions and rules, and how this unique form of e-commerce is making such a pronounced impact on online merchandising.

When you're ready to start, I'll take you through a highly detailed tour and tutorial of buying and selling at eBay. I'll show you how to view what eBay has to offer, how to find the items you desire, how to join in the bidding, and (hopefully) how to win an auction without losing the farm.

If selling's your bag, then I'll tutor you on how to determine what's best to sell on eBay, how to list your items, how to draw attention and bids to your wares, and how to best ensure your auction is a success. If you think you have a lot to sell, then eBay is the place to sell a lot of what you have.

Most important, I'll show you what to do *after* the auction. Understand that what you are engaging in here is online business. Although it's a lot of fun, it's not just a game. There's a real world full of real people that you'll inevitably be dealing with. To most new users (and even some of the experienced ones), this can be the most intimidating area of auction transactions: actually closing the deal. It's at the post-auction point that you internalize the idea that you're performing a true business transaction. But, don't let this concern intimidate or overwhelm you. I'll show you how to close your deal, as buyer or seller, with confidence and ease. It's done more than a million times every day by people just like you. If they can do it, you can, too.

And as the Internet continues to permeate our culture today, I would be remiss if I didn't spend a reasonable amount of time discussing the evolution of online interactions and etiquette that are absolutely necessary to be successful in this evolving market. So in this book I will share my best experiences, my good experiences, and a few of my not-so-good experiences as I've dealt in this unique buy-and-sell arena. I'll show you how good doses of respect, understanding, and humor will benefit you in your auction adventures as well as your overall online travels. And by helping you use an appropriate amount of professional style, I'll show you how to get the results you want and deserve.

You'll find all of this and more in the pages of this book, plus I take just a little space to share some of the neat items I'm buying and selling at eBay. I've had a great time at eBay and have no plans to stop any time soon. It really all boils down to a good attitude and fun-loving approach. I'll give you the benefit of looking into my exploits over the past several years, showing you the good times to be found and giving you a head start that I never had.

What You Won't Find in This Book

This book will *not* elevate you to the status of a self-made millionaire overnight. You're not going to immediately strike it rich and an armored car is not going to be dropping by your house as some karmic result of having read this book. If you're looking for the secret methods that will make you insanely successful and perversely rich from eBay auctions, or you seek some coveted sleight-of-hand tricks that will make you *the* master auctioneer to be reckoned with, you'll need to continue in your quest.

This book is not an infomercial in sheep's clothing—it takes a reasonable approach to the eBay experience that all can enjoy. Yes, some individuals have been successful on eBay. Some users have acquired huge profits and are happily self-employed through this unique medium. However, in this book, I want to make you comfortable in your use of eBay, confident in your online skills, and, even further, successful in your interactions with others in ways that will yield the most pleasurable transactions with virtually zero stress. Yes, by your own diligent efforts, you *might* be one of the few that can amass tremendous wealth from the online auction place. But don't quit your day job just yet.

How This Book Is Organized

I've written this book with a key purpose: to ease your mind and bolster your enthusiasm for the fantastic fun you will find at eBay. "*Ease my mind?*" you ask. Is eBay so intimidating? Well, no, but as with so many new tools or business ventures, there is a degree of uncertainty at the outset.

I've designed this book to help you find the information you need quickly and directly. It's divided into five major parts, each providing a generous serving of the details you'll need. You'll find the answers to your questions and will learn more about the situations you'll encounter at eBay.

Part 1: Understanding Auctions and the Internet

A good background of understanding is always helpful. In this first part, I'll tell you about auctions in general to make you familiar with the overall development of eBay's intent and style. I'll lead you through a discussion of why auctions can be a preferred method of buying and selling goods, and how an auction can provide immediate benefits to a newcomer. I'll teach you about the migration of auctions to the World Wide Web. You'll learn about the formation of eBay, how it started and how it has come to be the most successful online person-to-person auction, hands down. I'll also tell you how I got started with eBay and why it has become my favorite online site. Since you'll be working on the Internet, I'll give you some guidance and tips about online security and privacy as well. I won't attempt to "boil the ocean" or bore you with a seemingly endless harangue of tech-facts. Rather, I'll give you some basic information as well as my personal insight of Internet safety based on real statistics coupled with my personal experiences. I'll explain Internet safety in terms you can understand as well as show you specific ways in which safety is being seriously promoted at eBay.

Part 2: Get Started and Join the Fun

Here's where you roll up your sleeves and get yourself going. In this part, I'll first help you assess your readiness to participate by evaluating your present hardware, software, and online tool set. You want to be sure you have the goods to play the game, and I'll show you the simple components you'll need (plus a few extras you might want) to be sure your online experience is not fraught with technical setbacks. Then I'll acquaint you with eBay's auction site and introduce you to the plethora of auction categories and items that you'll find every time you visit. I'll show you how you can become a member of eBay's trading community, how to start finding those lost or forgotten treasures you've been searching for, and how you can make your presence known by raising your virtual bidder's paddle. As you will be embarking on a new adventure in e-commerce, I'll give you some advice and pointers about the auction marketplace that will help you understand each participant's role in the process and even how emotionally charged the whole experience can be (winners rejoice and losers lament).

Part 3: Becoming a Savvy Bidder

By this time, you'll be hooked. No doubt about it, bidding in auctions is a pleasantly addictive new hobby. Since you've played the game and are learning what eBay's community has to offer, it's time to start honing your skills. In this part, I'll teach you what I now know about bidding in auctions and how you can stand a better chance to win the item you covet without draining your wallet. I'll show you how to become quickly informed about the items you wish to bid on, and how to tell if you're falling into a bidding war that you needn't fight. I'll explain the different types of auction formats you'll see on eBay, and how the bidding styles will change for each auction variation. Then I'll show you how to use the tactics that most bidders employ to emerge victorious in their pursuits. And to keep you from becoming overwhelmed by the details of each auction you participate in, I'll give you some simple methods to manage your bidding activity and track auctions in which you've bid.

Part 4: You Are the Auctioneer

Step up to the podium and take hold of the auctioneer's gavel. In this part, you'll learn the role of being the seller, parading your wares in front of almost six million potential bidders across the globe. I'll show you how to determine what's worthy of selling at auction (and you'll be surprised to see what sells). I'll help you survey your potential buying public and figure out when it's time to put your treasures on the auction block. To help you be successful, I'll show you the options you have when you list your special item, from simple auction pages to more elaborate item advertisements. I'll actually teach you some HTML (HyperText Markup Language) coding that you can use to make truly eye-catching auction listings. If you've never written a line of code before, rest assured; I'll provide some HTML templates that you can cut and paste to use immediately and repeatedly. And before I leave this part of the book, I'll take some time to discuss the basic principles of managing your auctions and providing outstanding customer service. Regardless of all your skills, technical aptitude, and sought-after merchandise, customer service is always the most prized commodity you'll have to offer. Use it well, and you'll be sure to increase your sales.

Part 5: After the Auction

After the thrill of the final bids and the revealing of the high bidder, then what? This is the part of the book that will shed much-needed light on how the auction concludes with the actual exchange between the seller and buyer. I'll show you the best methods of communicating in ways that will build immediate trust between you and the people you'll be dealing with. I'll discuss the dos and don'ts of payment, including tips about the different payment methods available. If you're sending money for an item you've won, will it be a matter of holding your breath and taking a leap of faith? No, not really. I'll show you how you can protect yourself as you send your hard-earned dollars to the item's proprietor and how you can best determine the honorable intentions of said proprietor. And if you are said proprietor and wondering how to deal with your high bidder, then I'll show you how to track your completed auctions, collect your monies due, and please your high-bidding customer with an item that will exceed expectations. This includes best tips for packaging your items and shipping them so they'll reach their new owner safely. If you follow the guidelines I describe in this part of the book, then you're sure to establish yourself well in the auction community and further develop a reputation that your own mother would be proud of. Isn't that special?

Each part of this book, you'll see, has been presented in a way that its content can stand on its own. If you want to immediately learn more about the best bidding methods, then jump to Part 3. If you're new to auctions and the Internet, start with Part 1. If you have to ship an item and don't know the best way to package it up, Part 5 is where you want to be. You get the idea. The overall flow of information in this book is presented to logically build your evolving set of auction skills. Each new chapter you read will build on the information of preceding chapters. But you're free to skip around and refer back to certain parts however you like—you'll never feel lost or that you've just come in at the punch line. I've designed this book to serve as a constant and easy-to-use reference. Whether you're a beginner or a more seasoned Net surfer and auction-player, this book has much to offer anyone who chooses to get involved. Its design is simple: learn where to play, how to play, and make sure the play is fair and fun.

Extra Special Features

Just as I'm going to show you how to add pizzazz to an auction listing, I'll add some extra touches in this book as you read through it. These will be fun little icons that call your attention to elements and ideas that I think you should pay special attention to:

Hey! Pictures!! Everyone loves pictures, and I'll scatter some through these pages where you can better see what I'm trying to explain at any given time, like the one in Figure IN-1. You might find a picture of an eBay screen, you

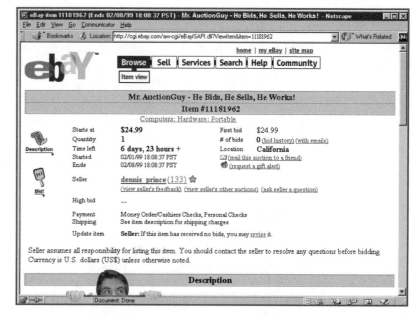

figure IN-1

Mr. AuctionGuy, huh? Sounds intriguing.

might find a picture of some cool item bought off the auction, you might find just about anything.

NOTE This "handy" note is offered to give you a bit more background information or perspective or just some FYI tidbits as you read along.

TIP When you see the light bulb light up, you'll know I've got a useful tip for you— some pearls of wisdom that will be keys to your success at eBay, helping you avoid potential snares and cut some corners along the way.

ALERT Hit the brakes! Alerts tell you to stop, look, and listen during a particular point of discussion. As with any business transaction or online experience, there always tend to be some "gotchas" lurking out there. I'll try to expose some that you're likely to encounter, helping you to avoid them altogether.

SOAPBOX When you see this soapbox, you'll know I'm stepping up on high and getting ready to speak freely. I've learned a lot about eBay, auctions, and business deals over the years. I'm afraid I just can't keep from sharing some of my biases with you. I'll try not to rant, but I think I can give you good food for thought as I discuss some of the more sensitive and sometimes controversial issues you'll find in the wonderful world of buying and selling.

These special elements will work as your signposts along the way. They'll break up discussion at just the right times to help you internalize the ideas, tools, or strategies that are being presented. They'll help keep you on the right path as I guide you through the auction landscape.

Find It on the Web

Another new feature that coincides with this edition is a special online spot at the Prima Tech Website. As a time-saver to you, I've uploaded the templates you'll find in this book: HTML code, form letters, miscellaneous examples, and more. Just go to

www.prima-tech.com/auctionfun

I invite you to visit the site and freely download anything you think will help you in your auction exploits.

What Do You Need Before You Start?

Obviously, having a PC or access to one is a real big help. There's not a whole lot to do online otherwise. Most home PCs you'll find today are designed with the Internet clearly in mind. If you have recently purchased a PC, I'll get you up to speed and ready to go to eBay in no time. If you're not certain about what kind of PC or software you might need, I've included a brief rundown of that in Chapter 5.

I'll assume you know what the Internet is as well as the World Wide Web (they're two different things, by the way). You don't have to be the Big Kahuna of Internet surfers to make use of what you'll learn here. The discussion is designed to help Web users of all skill levels.

And, at its core, this book is firmly centered on the aspects of the auction itself—what it is, how it works, and how to play. The electronic aspect is just a different take on the concept of buying and selling in an enthusiastic environment. If you have the desire to learn more about online auctions and have enough enthusiasm to bring to the party, those are really the key ingredients that will make this adventure rich and rewarding for you.

By the way, how fast are you at clicking your mouse? The bidding gets pretty exciting out there and you're sure to become part of a cyber-shootout at some point. Think you've got what it takes? Good! That's the spirit!

Tell Me How You're Doing

My main goal in writing this book is to help others join in the fun to be found at eBay. In these pages, you'll find much of what I've learned over the past years. For sure, I can't guarantee you'll be a raving success at eBay, nor can I assure you that doing everything I suggest will make you an auction god. My real hope is that you'll find answers to your questions—even those questions you haven't thought of yet—that will help you to have a better time at eBay and be as successful as possible in the auctions. But I might not get to everything that you could encounter. Knowing that eBay is an ever-changing, ever-improving site, I realize you may find that something minor has changed from how I've described it. Whatever the case, I invite you, my fellow eBay community member, to drop me a line and ask me any other questions you might have or tell me about any potential snags you might run up against. You can reach me at the following e-mail address:

dlprince@bigfoot.com

Yes, this invitation does result in quite a bit of mail flowing into my e-mail account. I've heard from many readers of the first edition of this book already. I've been diligent enough to respond to each person who's written to me, and I've enjoyed the conversations. It's all in the spirit of helping, and I'll continue to do my very best to answer all questions I receive as quickly and completely as possible.

Even if you don't have a specific question, if this book helps you get involved or helps sharpen your skills at eBay, I encourage you to let me know. I always enjoy hearing from other users, especially those with whom I might share a common interest. Don't be shy. We're all friends here.

But now it's time to jump into the fun of online auctions at eBay.

part 1

Understanding Auctions
and the Internet

chapter 1

The History of the Auction

It seems practically every time I describe eBay to friends and acquaintances, encouraging them to get involved, their response is, "*Well, how do auctions work?*" A good question, and one that bears explanation. Even though I am discussing a newly developed form of commerce—relatively speaking—it's important to remember that the heart of this topic is *the auction*. Although online auctions are still an emerging and evolving economy in their own right, auctions themselves are quite a bit older than you might expect.

Yes, this is going to be a history lesson of sorts. You might wonder why auction history matters to you. But you should understand that auctions account for multiple billions of dollars of revenue in our world and you'll benefit from understanding more about how auctions work and how they serve as a key method to manage the exchange of goods the world over. Auctions have been going on for a long time, and their rules and methods have been set so solidly that if you don't understand the format of an auction, you're already in the dark. And some auction masters, you'll find, are all too eager to take advantage of you if you don't understand the basic concepts and strategies.

This chapter will give you background on the origin of the auction—what an auction really is and where the first recorded auctions began. You'll learn that there are many different types of auctions and that each has its own unique purpose. And, as with most anything humans touch, you'll see there are cheaters in the midst of it all, looking to exploit an unfair advantage. Alas, such is fate, but the discussion in this chapter will expose the methods of history's Dishonest Johns, some of which are still practiced today.

What Exactly Is an Auction, Anyway?

Most people believe they understand auctions quite well already. Nothing to it, right? Someone has something to sell, asks for an opening bid, and the bidders battle it out.

Auctioneer: *I have two thousand dollars. Who'll make it twenty-two fifty? Twenty-two fifty in the back. Who'll give me twenty-five hundred? Twenty-five hundred dollars. Who'll give me twenty-seven fifty for this exquisite piece? Twenty-seven fifty. Who'll make it three thousand? I have three thousand dollars. Who'll make it thirty-two fifty? Thirty-two fifty, anyone? Three thousand two hundred and fifty dollars for this rare find?*

The high bid is three thousand. Three thousand dollars going once…three thousand dollars going twice…fair warning…SOLD to the gentleman in the back for three thousand dollars!

Looks easy, right? This is how auctions have been shown in film, television, and popular writing. When all bidding is complete, the gaunt, suit-clad auctioneer surveys the bidding parlor once more, bangs his gavel, and announces the winning bidder. The crowd murmurs softly, with satisfaction or frustration.

Although this is the traditional understanding of an auction, it really isn't the complete truth. The word "auction" stems from the Latin root *auctio*, which means "an increase." But in this oldest definition, the meaning can be misleading. Did you know that some auctions are not based on increasing prices but rather on decreasing prices? Some auctions don't even involve the interaction of bidders and an auctioneer. And some auctions aren't for the sale of a single, unique item but are for the sale of multiple units of the same item.

Simply put, an auction is a way to sell something when the true value is unknown to the seller. When an item or group of items is auctioned, the seller presents the goods to a group of potential buyers who will offer their personal belief of the value. The auction helps the seller who is not sure how much an item or commodity ought to bring in.

And you'd be amazed at what is bought and sold at auction. While the first images that come to mind feature the renowned British auction houses where rare and treasured works of art are put on the block in front of a parlor of astute art connoisseurs, auctions are also used daily for the sale and purchase of land, fish and game, flowers, wine, cars, construction contracts, stock, and more. The U.S. government uses auctions to *sell* the national debt, in the form of securities (treasury bills, bonds, and notes), in which bidders (institutions) will bid a price for a number of securities they believe will have the best future yield. Much of what you and I buy each day has been affected by auctioning: the price on offer is directly influenced by what the seller paid at an auction to get hold of the commodity.

Auctions are also used to insert a bit of objective mediation in the distribution of goods or such. An auction was once held, it's reported, to allocate something as whimsical yet desirable as "window offices" at the Arizona State College of Business. This approach let the school allocate the limited number of prime offices available in a fair manner, and kept the staff from taking issue with the way the offices were eventually assigned. The burden was actually passed on directly to those who desired the offices, leaving it up to each of them to determine how much the offices were really worth.

So, in essence, the auction is used to buy or sell goods of undetermined value while also establishing a fair and objective manner of distribution. A buyer may be looking for a good deal or for an item or commodity that isn't available via conventional means. A seller may be looking to make the highest profit possible on an item that clearly has some distinct value, but may have even higher value when put to the test of competitive bidding.

Where Did Auctions First Start?

OK, so here's the history lesson I promised you. Did you know that history records the earliest auctions in Babylon dating back to 500 B.C.? It is believed that, at that time, annual auctions were held to distribute women

who were eligible for marriage. In fact, it was conditional that the high bidders would marry the woman they "won." As with any "commodity," some items were more desirable than others—the most beautiful of women inspired lively bidding whereas those less graced might have to pay a dowry to be accepted into an auction.

SOAPBOX Please, please, please don't write to me angrily about this information I share. I'm not in any way saying I condone it. I'm only reporting what I've learned. We can't change history; we can only learn from it.

Further, history reveals that auctions were quite common in ancient Rome. There, you would find the *atrium auctionarium,* which was the primary place to stage auctions. In Rome, the auctions were quite well designed and organized. Four representatives participated in an auction: the *dominus* was the actual owner of the goods, such as property; the *argentarius* was responsible for organizing, monitoring, and maybe financing the sale; the *praeco* promoted the auction, and the *emptor,* or buyer, was the auction's high bidder.

TIP Hey! Here's a phrase you're almost certain to be familiar with: *caveat emptor,* or *let the buyer beware.* Now you know where to trace the origins of that phrase. I suspect most people learned about this phrase, not from historical research, but from television's Greg and Peter Brady. Oh well, at least there's something to learn from TV. This, and the fact that "Mom always says, 'Don't play ball in the house.'"

Usually, Roman auctions would occur after military victories in which soldiers would claim the site of the victory as theirs and then sell it at public auction. In fact, auctions were such a staple of Roman society, it is believed that Roman businessmen might have even accompanied soldiers into battle in hopes of managing a potential sale. Isn't it nice to know that ruthless opportunists existed long before our current state of capitalistic practice?

History even tells us that the entire Roman Empire was auctioned at one time. When Emperor Pertinax was killed, the empire was auctioned. The high bidder was a fellow by the name of Didius Julianus, who instantly became the new emperor, of course. A short time later, though, he was beheaded when Septimus Severus conquered Rome. There's a concept called *winner's curse*, which you'll learn about later; old Julianus certainly fell victim to this one. Later, the empire was returned to the people. I'm not sure what happened to the head.

History also notes that auctions were held in ancient Buddhist temples as a key money-raising activity. And in the early seventeenth century, the belongings of deceased monks were auctioned off. Is nothing sacred?

Auctions came to Great Britain possibly as early as 1595, but most documented activities occurred in the seventeenth century. At that time, auctions were generally held in taverns and coffeehouses, with artwork being the primary commodity. But it was in 1744 that Sotheby's was established, with Christie's being founded later in 1766. These two primary auction houses have been the making of the auction's great history. Both houses are, of course, still in operation today, and both have made the migration to the Internet in addition to their traditional, in-house auctions.

The auction found its way to America soon after it appeared in Great Britain and has been well practiced in this nation, largely for the liquidation of goods or for the sale of otherwise nonvalued goods unmarketable via conventional methods.

Why Auction?

Auctions provide value to both buyers and sellers, and some of the history you've just learned shows how auctions can be used to sell and buy goods of many sorts. But let me further elaborate on the use of the auction.

From the first, auctioning goods has been a way to achieve a price when the relative value is not firmly established or shared by others. This is true when an item is of *potential value* but that value is not yet proven.

For example, a wine dealer might have an extensive inventory of vintage wines, but perhaps hasn't yet sampled each to personally know the makeup and worth of every bottle in stock. An auction allows the potential buyers to help determine that worth, within reason usually, as each vintage will probably have a specialized group of buyers who would be pleased to have it for their own collection.

The same goes for items of historic value. A rare artifact might not have a known value among other such documented discoveries. However, an auctioneer can establish an association of the new find to more widely known artifacts, especially if the new find can spark interest and speculation as to the rarest of the rare or the key to finding other, still hidden treasures. You've surely heard tales where treasure maps to untold riches are highly coveted. The treasure might not actually exist, but there is enough value in the potential of finding such treasure that the map will create undeniable interest and desire for exclusive ownership.

The treasure map analogy also leads to another reason for auctioning goods: making scarce, sometimes one-of-a-kind goods *available* to a group of buyers. Allow me to veer off a bit to give you a fictional example that might better explain this theory. To have a little fun, assume you have the original undergarment worn by Darth Vader during the destruction of the Death Star (Episode IV, right?). If this were the case, then you would have a rare item, indeed. Star Wars *completists* (that is, people who must own absolutely everything associated with a topic) would probably claw at one another to own and proudly display the Evil Lord's briefs. These are probably one-of-a-kind (I suppose) and such a unique item as this would be worth whatever price paid simply for pride of ownership.

 SOAPBOX This is actually a concept that I readily embrace, as buyer and seller. No, I don't want Darth's undies, but there is much to be said about auctions as an opportunity to bid for items otherwise not readily available. Sometimes, the appearance of an item in an auction is more of an *opportunity to own* the item at all, as opposed to being an outright bargain hunt. I often auction items with the expectation that buyers will jump at the chance to own such a unique piece and not that they'll be able to pick it up for a song, so to speak. In all fairness, I also abide by this sentiment when I'm the buyer, too. I'll discuss this idea at length in Parts 3 and 4 of this book.

So, working from this aspect of item scarcity, the prop man who ran off with the Dark Lord's white cottons might not know what price he could get for them. A member of the Society of Collectors of Celebrity Undergarments might try to offer him a mere pittance, thinking the prop man has no clue how precious the underpants really are. But the seller might find overwhelming response if he makes the fearsome Fruit-of-the-Looms publicly available to anyone who cares to bid on them. Although I don't mean to derail this concept with the unusual analogy I'm using, I think you can see the point I'm making. An item's value is largely determined by how available the item is, how *many* are available, and, bottom line (no pun intended), how much someone is willing to pay for the right of ownership.

A final point to make that supports the reason for auctions has to do with distribution. As with the window offices at the Arizona State College of Business, auctions are often a fair way to mediate the distribution of items in short supply and high demand.

One of the first auctions I ever attended was at, of all places, a comic book shop. The shop's owner had a really cool promotional lobby display for a then-popular film. He was constantly being hounded by patrons asking whether he'd sell the display and at what price; I was one of the hounds. After several weeks of distraction, the owner decided to auction it off at a given time on a given date. He knew if he just sold it outright to one of the people who had been pestering him, he would draw scowls of discontent from the other wannabe-possessors. Since many of these would-be buyers were customers, he didn't want to take the chance of alienating any of them and possibly losing their future business. His decision: let 'em fight it out among themselves. And fight we did. I'm happy to report that I did not end up owning the display. No big deal. There would just not be any good place for me to put that bulky, gaudy, overvalued hunk of cardboard anyway. Besides, the guy who did get it probably paid too much. What a dope. (I'll discuss auction losers and the *sour grapes* attitude later.)

But the key point is that the owner took himself out of the spotlight, not having to be responsible for the feelings or attitudes of the item's bidders. He made the item available and the captive marketplace (those of us in attendance) was responsible for the outcome ourselves. Equally, if the eventual owner ever felt he paid too much for the item, that buyer only had himself to blame; the shop owner wasn't involved with establishing the final sale price. Smart move on the owner's part, wouldn't you agree? In the end, the owner made a tidy profit from the sale of the item, auctioned many other items the same night, and decided to hold weekly in-store auctions as a regular business practice.

Of course, there are variations on the themes presented here, but now you can see the key reasons why an auction can be the ideal manner of selling goods. The auction can benefit both buyers and sellers in a variety of ways, all dependent upon the will, intent, and desire of those involved.

Different Types of Auctions

As there are different reasons for conducting auctions, so there are different types of auctions. Although you won't find some of the auction types discussed here available for use at eBay, you can learn a lot about how auction styles were developed and why.

But before you think about the different kinds of auctions, it's first a good idea to be clear about why you will be participating in an auction. Personal expectations are a big factor in determining which auctions are best to get what you want. First, you may be motivated to join in an auction because there's something you want for your own use—acquiring a certain work of art or a special collectible that will complete your personal collection. If this is your intent, you will have your own idea of how valuable the item is *to you;* no one else will know how much you personally value the item nor how much you are willing to pay. In essence, you set your own spending limit. Although you compete with the self-imposed spending limits of others, you still have control over how much you are willing to spend. You can set your limit as high as you like, determined by how badly you want the item in question.

By contrast, you might be joining in an auction on speculation—you are looking to purchase items at low prices and resell them at a decent profit. In this case, your spending limit would probably be less than if the item was for yourself—you need to build in room for profit by your knowledge of a price you could hope to resell for.

The way you bid in auctions will be largely affected by the reason you've chosen for participation. If the goods are for yourself, you might be willing to pay more; if the goods are for resale, then you will need to pay less to ensure a better future profit. Once your expectations are clear, then you can determine which sort of auction might help you get what you want at a price that you can live with.

The English Auction

The most common type of auction—and the type you're most likely to encounter on eBay—is the *English auction*. This is the well-known auction method of bidders increasing the price of an item until the final bid is cast without further increase. This is also known as the *Ascending-Price* auction or the *Open-Outcry* auction. Its format is simple: the auctioneer starts the auction at an enticingly low level, bidders increase the price during the course of the auction, and when the room falls silent, the item is sold to the highest bidder. This is the kind of auction you might join in when you find that item you've *always been looking for* and in which you might bid higher to gather the item into your own collection. And, if you're the high bidder, you've succeeded in your quest.

Well, the highest bidder doesn't necessarily *always* win the goods. If the auction never reaches its lowest acceptable price, the item might not be sold at all. How can this be? Well, there is a variation of the English auction known as the *Reserve Price auction*. In this variation, the auctioneer establishes a reserve price—that is, the lowest acceptable selling price for the item—before the auction begins. Sometimes this reserve price is the opening bid asking price, but sometimes it's not. Often, opening bids are accepted lower than an item's reserve price just to stimulate bidder activity. If the bidding meets or exceeds the reserve price, the item is sold. If the reserve price is not met, the auctioneer is not required to sell the item even at the highest bid received. You'll find the Reserve Price auction is quite popular on eBay, and you'll learn more about the mechanics of it in Parts 3 and 4 of this book.

Other variations of the English auction include different methods of placing bids. Suitable only to a live auction parlor, auctioneers might determine that bids are to be placed by way of hand motions or other such signals—tugging an ear, raising a bidding paddle, or laying a finger alongside your nose.

Tip *Never* take small children to a signaling auction. They have their own variation of the finger-*alongside*-the-nose technique, which they use quite often.

In all seriousness, *signaling* in an auction is very beneficial to bidders, especially those who want to remain anonymous during the course of the bidding. For example, it's common for the presence of renowned bidders—maybe fine art appraisers or collectors—to affect the behavior of others in the bidding parlor. Frequently, the other bidders will listen for the *expert bidder* to place a bid, then follow in a flurry of their own bidding, believing the expert knows something about the particular item's worth. This, of course, completely ruins the expert bidder's chance of getting a good price. By using bid signaling, the expert bidder is less noticeable and can bid somewhat more freely. The type of bidding you'll find online at eBay allows some anonymity of sorts, which you'll learn about later. Bidding anonymity often allows you to pick up some personally desirable treasure at a lower cost when no one else is looking.

The Dutch Auction

Then there is the *Dutch auction*. This auction is quite a bit more complex than the more common English auction. A Dutch auction is particularly useful when multiple units of a single item are available for sale. In this sort of auction, the seller will establish the size of the batch of identical items and state the amount of the opening bid for each item. Bidders then bid on one or more of the items, up to the total quantity available, stating the most they are willing to pay for each item—this may be more than the seller's opening bid price.

For example, say you have 10 copies of a desirable lithograph depicting five bulldogs playing poker. You list the opening bid at $10. The bidders come—and who wouldn't with an item of this caliber?—and a total of 9 of the 10 lithographs receive a bid. This could be 9 different bidders each wanting a single copy, or any combination of bidders and quantities that equal the 9 lithos that have been bid upon. OK, assume the auction ends and each bidder had bid the opening price of $10. In this case, each bidder is awarded a litho at $10. Simple, right? Well, here's where it gets more interesting: now assume that 12 bidders had placed bids of varying amounts—some bid $10, but two bid $12 and one bid $14. Since there are 12 bidders and only 10 lithos, who gets a litho when the auction ends? In a Dutch auction, the highest bidders always get the quantity they bid for (they could have bid for more than one), but they only pay the lowest winning bid.

Now follow me here: in this scenario, three bidders bid more than the opening bid and they will receive rights to one each of the lithos. The other seven lithos available are awarded to the first seven bidders who entered their bids of $10. The guys who don't get the lithos are the last two to have bid in the $10 range. Then, when the winning bidders are announced, *all bidders* are only required to pay the lowest successful bid amount realized during the auction: $10. This is because, while three were bid above the opening bid price, seven more were still available *at* the opening bid price. The three top bidders' higher bids actually secured them rights to one of the lithos—bumping off the unfortunate two who didn't make the cut—but the three still got the benefit of getting the lithos for less than their high bid price.

The price of an item in a Dutch auction only advances higher than the opening bid price when all items available have been bid for at higher-than-opening-bid prices. So, in the previous scenario, assume all lithos were bid for at various prices by 25 bidders, all of whom wanted one copy each. At the auction's end, the top 10 bidders would have rights to claim one of the lithos and, again, would only pay the final price of the lowest winning bid.

TIP When you win in a Dutch auction, be sure you are only being asked to pay the lowest winning bid value. A seller who asks you to pay your *high bid* value in a scenario like the litho auction is simply confused. The only time you'd pay your actual bid amount regardless of the lowest winning bid is in a variation known as the *Yankee auction*. In the Yankee auction, all the final qualifying high bidders are required to pay their high bid values.

Whew! That's a bit to chew and swallow, huh? However, apart from their inherent complexity, Dutch auctions can be very useful if you're looking to acquire multiple items at potentially low prices. It all depends on how high the opening bid price is, how many items were bid on, and at what bid value. If you're a seller, the Dutch auction helps you quickly unload an inventory of the same item, such as those boxes of *The Executive* trench coats your Dad's been storing in his garage all these years. On eBay, you'll find the Dutch auction available for your use.

Other Auction Types

Although the English auction and Dutch auction are the two most common types of auctions you'll encounter on eBay, I will briefly share details of a few more auction types or variations you might encounter outside of eBay.

The Silent Auction

This is a public auction in which items are posted for bid on a sheet of paper. Bidders write their names and high bids on the paper. All bids are visible for other bidders to see. When new bids are entered, those bids must be higher than the previous high bids. This auction might run for a period of days or weeks or whatever. All bids must be entered before the official end of the auction—which means there could be a flurry of last-minute bids just before the auction closes. At the end of the auction, the high bidder wins. I've seen this auction style used often in fundraising activities in which bidders are encouraged to bid higher in the name of a recipient charity or other nonprofit organization.

The First-Price, Sealed-Bid Auction

In this auction, bidders will write their bid amount for an item or items on a piece of paper and seal that paper in an envelope. This sort of bidding can take place over an extended period of time. When the end of the auction is reached, all submitted envelopes are opened to determine the final selling price. In this type of auction, the winning bidder pays exactly the price proposed in the bid. A variation of this theme occurs when multiple quantities of an item are available. In this case, the highest bidders are chosen as winners in a descending manner—high bids descending to low bids—until all available items are won. Then, the high bidders pay exactly the price each had written on their paper. Yes, this means the high bidders can all be paying different prices for the same item, depending on their bid amounts.

That's the Yankee auction format, remember? This type of auction has been used for the purposes of refinancing credit and foreign exchange.

Phone Auctions

This sort of auction should be quite familiar. Although not truly a different auction type (they usually follow the rules of the English auction), phone auctions have been used successfully by public television as another means for raising broadcasting funds. The phone is really the only difference: it allows bidders to call in their bids while they watch the auction activity on TV.

Phone auctions are also used in the collectibles market. Private individuals list ads in trade papers describing their goods up for auction, as well as the date and time the auction closes. I've been involved in many of these auctions. The auctioneer will typically not close the auction until five minutes after the final bid is received. If another bid comes in within the five-minute period, the auction end time is extended for another five minutes. This affects all items in the auction, usually, and can literally add a couple of additional hours to an auction's actual closing time. Why the five-minute window? Easy. The auctioneer usually only has one or two phone lines available for use during the auction. The five-minute window helps the auctioneer allow for a busy line as bidders struggle to get in their final bids.

Mail Auctions

This is an auction variation akin to the First-Price, Sealed-Bid auction. The main difference is the use of a postal system for the delivery of bids to the auctioneer. Bidders might be limited to only one bid, but that depends on the rules set by the auctioneer. This is a simple way to conduct an auction and doesn't require a lot of overhead for staging the auction or calculating the result.

There are many other auction types in existence, each with a different spin on the method of determining winners or placing and receiving bids. If you want to learn more about the intrinsic details of auctions, you might wish to read some of the auction references you'll find in Appendix A at the back of this book.

Traditional Trickery and Other Unfair Acts

Every scoundrel seeks a sucker; every cheater chouses a chump. Alas, it is the human condition that, at one time or another, some are tempted with the promise of ill-gotten gain or unfair action. Auctions, being a way to make gains, are subject to undesirables who wish to tilt the scales in their favor at the expense of others.

Over the history of the auction, several methods have come into play that offer unfair advantage to some. Among those methods are the following nasty little acts.

Collusion

This is actually a general term that describes any act where several individuals band together, typically in secret, to unfairly affect the outcome of the auction. *Collusion* can be defined as secret agreement or cooperation for a fraudulent or deceitful purpose. Read on and you'll understand what I mean.

Auction Rings

These are a common occurrence and are the most practiced form of collusion. In an auction ring, a group of bidders meet secretly and decide to win a particular auction item but not to outbid one other during the auction, regardless of which member of the ring really wants the item. Because each member of the ring refuses to bid their true belief of the item's value, the item is often sold at a lower price than could otherwise be realized in a fair auction. After the auction, the ring will again auction that item among themselves. From the proceeds of the private auction, the member of the ring who publicly won the auction is reimbursed the value of the original winning bid, and the balance of the private auction proceeds is evenly divided among the members of the ring.

To illustrate, say a ring consisting of 10 members has its collective eye on a new High-Definition TV being sold at auction. Through their collusive actions, they get the unit for a mere $7,000 as opposed to the approximate $15,000 the set should command. Rick was the designated bidder (and winner) in the ring, and the others were sure not to outbid him—but Mike is the one who really wants the set. After the auction, the ring holds its own private auction. Mike, who wants the set most, ends up bidding $13,000 for it and wins. Of the $13,000 high bid, Rick is reimbursed his public bid of $7,000. Then, with the balance of $6,000, each member of the ring—even Mike and Rick—receives an equally distributed $600. The end result: each member of the ring makes $600 on the deal. Mike gets the set for only $12,400 when it is really valued at a current market price of $15,000. In their wicked delight, the ring members decide that Mike will host this year's Super Bowl party. This system, of course, works best among a limited number of bidders in a public auction where the majority of bidders present are members of the auction ring.

Predetermined Signaling to the Auctioneer

This one's quite simple and straightforward: a bidder might actually be in collusion with the auctioneer, arranging a method to bid without being noticed by the rest of the parlor. In some cases, this might not actually be unfair. If you'll recall the example of the expert bidder who didn't want to be seen bidding on the item, the prearrangement to cast bids without revealing who was bidding might work to keep interest in the item down, allowing the bidder to purchase the item at a much lower price than otherwise possible. While not directly cheating, the bidder and auctioneer have deprived the seller—if one is being represented by the auctioneer—of a potentially higher profit for the item. At the same time, the bidder could argue that the system just levels the playing field, allowing even competition against a similar but unknown expert who might pursue the same item.

Thievery

I've read of occurrences in which auction bidders might arrange to steal an item from an auction lot prior to the auction's start. For example, a thief might lift a soup spoon from an otherwise complete set of vintage silverware. After the auction is over, the thief might approach the winner and offer a single soup spoon of the same vintage—which the winner's set seems to be missing. The thief will sell the soup spoon to the winner to complete the prized silverware set. Too bad. The winner already had rightful owner-ship of the missing spoon. This concept also works in another way: two auc-tioneers might be in cahoots with one another where one auctioneer might offer the silverware set, minus the soup spoon. After the win, the high bid-der is contacted by the first auctioneer's partner. The partner just happens to have the single missing spoon and will offer to sell it to *help* the high bid-der complete the set. In some cases, the partner might actually pose as one of the bidders in the original auction, thus believably being in the know about the winner's recent acquisition.

Shill Bidders

Shills are prearranged bidders who, with no intention to buy an item, will bid on it to artificially raise the final selling price. This tactic is often employed when a seller fears the profits for an item won't reach hoped-for levels. The shill gets called in to bring the price up in the hope that a legit-imate bidder will outbid the shill. If the shill bidder ends up with the high-est bid, the auctioneer will simply resell the item later. A few people I've talked with believe that the auctioneer might actually be acting as a shill bid-der in the case of phone auctions. At any time, the auctioneer could falsely report that more bids have been received for an item, causing a legitimate bidder to have to bid more to acquire the piece.

Afterword

There are many different ways that auctions can be defrauded. It seems that every time a new safeguard is put in place, a new end-run is developed for unfair purposes. I don't intend to suggest that *all* auctions are crooked or are being defrauded in some manner. It would be unnecessary for you to assume the worst of an auction, auctioneer, or other bidders. The great majority of auctions, I believe, are legitimate and trustworthy. This information has simply been presented for your information. It's better to be aware than to be a victim.

chapter 2

The Benefits of an Auction

I used to really dislike auctions. I guess I almost hated them. I would cringe at the thought of having to *enlist* in the rank-and-file competing for a scarce item. I saw auctions as a way for greedy sellers to exploit me—dangling some item I desired in front of me and many others, taunting us to bid higher and higher and higher. The seller would be wringing his hands gleefully, mocking us bidders as we desperately offered all we could in the hopes of owning the coveted object of our blind desire. I didn't need this grief at all.

I was wrong. After years of participating in auctions, I've come to see them differently. They present opportunities I had never considered, especially when I learned just how many auction styles there really are. Since I spend most of my time pursuing various collectibles and cultural oddities, I have seen how auctions of various forms have become quite popular. So popular, in fact, that the auctioneers are faced with competition among their own. The ebb and flow of buyers, sellers, and market tolerance strikes a balance that makes the auction a benefit to practically all players.

In this chapter, I'll show you how the auction can benefit you. In a world of balance, I'll explain how auctions provide a self-correcting marketplace. The online auctions of eBay have come to change the way things are bought and sold. The scales are no longer as weighted in favor of one party, and the once exploited can now find justice and fairness. I see this as a win-win situation. Sellers win. Buyers win. Everyone wins—usually. I think you'll see this, too.

Sellers Find More Buyers

"It's only worth as much as someone is willing to pay." How many times have you heard this? Probably too many times, but maybe because it's a universal truth in the marketplace. When you have something to sell, you need to find someone who'll buy. Is it a special item you're selling that requires a special buyer? Is it a common item you're selling that has mass appeal? Is it a twisted combination of both? Whatever the circumstance, you've got some wares, and you need to peddle them. So, start peddling.

Auctions, you'll find, are a great way to gather many potential buyers to a single event. Many people are looking for a bargain, while some are looking for the opportunity to own something they might not otherwise find. But, most prominently, just about everyone is curious enough to stop and look. Rubbernecking is a national pastime. Whether it's motorists slowing to check the gore-factor of a highway accident, or looky-loos who want to poke and peek in every cupboard when you're trying to sell your home, people just can't help wanting to look. If you have something to sell, the more free lookers you can attract, the more opportunity you have to entice those lookers into becoming buyers.

In direct regard to eBay, the current pool of almost six million registered users is enough to tell you that you'll be up to your neck in potential buyers. But wait, that's only the *registered users.* Although people have to register with eBay in order to bid, anyone can visit the Web site for free without being a registered user (as with most other Web sites). Nonregistered *lookers* are free to roam the auction listings, and they constantly do so as they learn about eBay. When they see some item they absolutely must have (hopefully your item), they'll usually register and get into the bidding. That's how I got hooked. Maybe that's how you will, too.

So consider the sheer numbers: you have the whole Web-surfing populace out there as your potential customer base. Remember, too, this includes international users. You have the attention of Web-heads around the world. Some sellers choose to limit their sales to domestic (those in the United States) bidders only. Why?! The international market is full of lively bidders, many of whom pay top dollar—and beyond—for items only marketed or otherwise available in the West. Not to be corny, but you really do have the whole world in your hands. That's more than any trade show, phone auction, or personal Web page could ever claim to deliver.

Buyers Find More Items

Now, switch roles. *You're* the buyer. What is it you're looking for? Imagine you have spent years looking for that elusive premium ring of *Hamburger Hungry*, the little burger-character from the now defunct Red Barn restaurant chain. The last time you saw yours was back in third grade—1972. It was in your sock drawer, but like many a stray sock, the ring disappeared. You know you never would have willingly gotten rid of it. But, alas, the ring has been gone for more than a quarter of a century.

It's such a stupid little trinket, but you just can't seem to live without it. You've asked at trade shows: nothing. You've searched the trade papers: still nothing. You've looked for years and have never been able to turn one up. With a sigh of resignation, you finally gave up, saddened at the thought that this plastic piece of time that holds such a warm place in your heart is gone forever.

One day you search eBay. "Red barn" is your search criterion. And . . . nothing. That's it. Game over. It simply doesn't exist anymore. But never say never. Another day, a couple of years later, you run a frivolous search for "red barn" and . . . bingo!! The little bugger's there! Trumpets go off in your head. You do a little dance. You're fulfilled. There's Hamburger Hungry, and he's still *mint in the package!!!* Somehow, this whimsical piece of plastic that occupies no more than one square inch of space on the Earth has resurfaced. Without a doubt, you win this auction. The ring is once again yours. You tell a close friend about your adventure, about how the ring has so eluded you, and how you have been victorious in reclaiming a small piece of time from your past. Your friend tells you to get a life.

Get the picture? You'll find that auctions can be the venue of choice that can reunite you with long-lost treasures, make you familiar with treasures you've

figure 2-1

The Hamburger Hungry premium ring from Red Barn Restaurant. It's so good to have you back again.

heard of but never actually seen for yourself, or even guide you to discover treasures you'd never known existed and that you simply cannot live without. As silly as it might sound, that Hamburger Hungry ring is something I pined after for years and years. For you, it might be a scarce coin, a rare piece of carnival glass, an autograph, a trading card, a book, a Beanie Baby, or anything. Whatever your passion, you just might learn that the *impossible to find* . . . isn't.

How does this vast serving of auctionable goods help you? Easy. Now you have power—purchasing power, but not of the monetary sort that often comes to mind first. The auction, with its ever-changing potpourri of wares, gives you the power to pick and choose among offerings from literally millions of peddlers. Think of the antique shows, collectible conventions, estate sales, and trade paper advertisements: you have typically found a decent assortment of available items, yet limited to what can be found in that particular venue.

I've been to many collectible and advertising shows over the years and, though I have found some great items, most of my purchases at these sorts of gatherings were made at some of the first shows I ever attended. To my growing disappointment, I found that at each new show, I either kept seeing the same old items I had seen before or I'd be drowning in a glut of whatever was the current trend or rage. When the Star Wars trilogy was rereleased in 1997, I was at first amazed but soon annoyed that *everyone* was pushing Star Wars stuff. Granted, in mass marketing it makes sense that you'll be bombarded with promotional items and gimmicks designed to generate interest and sell the public on such events as the newly revised *Star Wars* and its companion films. But on the trade circuit, the various dealers and collectors are pushing the same product. Why? Plain and simple: hype. The first rare, mail-away Han Solo figure in Stormtrooper regalia I saw was interesting, but when I saw fifteen more at the same show I realized there would be no unique finds that day. Now, with the release of *Episode I: The Phantom Menace,* you can only imagine how much Darth Maul and Jar Jar Binks stuff you'll be wading through. Ho-hum.

But my point is that, with venues such as eBay, private individuals are able and eager to get involved, selling their curiosities. At eBay, unlike the local collectibles show or antiques fair, you're likely to see just about anything up for auction, and your chances of finding some odd little piece that maybe only you can appreciate are much greater than at those mainstream collector shows. And, remember, the eBay experience not only extends the width and breadth of this continent, but also crosses oceans to incorporate the wares of international sellers. Tapping the international supply is often how you'll find items that have been scarce in your local region or nation.

And, lastly, what this all boils down to is selection. With so many people adding their items for sale on eBay, your ability to shop and choose increases in a way probably not otherwise possible. As a buyer, that's what it's all about: you can be more successful when you have a better selection. In a market typically dominated by dealers or resellers, who among us at one time or another hasn't heard something like, "*Oh, these are incredibly tough to come by. If you want one, you'd better buy this one now. I'll probably never get another.*" That's fine. When you find two more on your own, you can contact that dealer and offer your extra for sale. After all, they're practically impossible to find. . . .

Timing

Timing is everything, right? A stand-up comic delivers each punch line at the precise moment to get the biggest guffaws possible. The space shuttle initiates its lift-off countdown at just the right time to reach an orbit that will get it where the pilot wants to go. A lawyer presents the key piece of evidence at the moment that will leave an indelible and undeniable impact on the scrutinizing jury. Well, believe it or not, auctions also work best when properly timed—sellers find the greatest reward by properly timing the appearance of their auction, and buyers are best served by timing their bidding as well.

I'll look at the sellers first. If you're planning on selling an item at auction, you'll want to do your best to offer it at a time when it will receive the most attention and, preferably, be in highest demand. For instance, when New Line Cinema released its big-screen rendition of *Lost in Space* in 1998, general interest in the subject grew tremendously. *Lost in Space,* the classic television series from the 1960s, has been a perennial favorite among collectors. In fact, it's seemingly more popular today in its syndicated form than it was during its first network run. If you had vintage *Lost in Space* memorabilia to sell, you were relatively assured that you'd find a buyer willing to pay hefty prices. Then, along comes a highly marketed film version, and *Lost in Space* merchandise becomes even hotter than ever. Major media events such as this will rejuvenate interest in a topic while also generating new interest among individuals previously unfamiliar with the subject matter. The hype for the subject builds to feverish heights (thanks to well-timed marketing campaigns), and *Lost in Space* items are being successfully sold at eBay faster than you can say "Aolis 14 Umbra" (brush up on your *Lost in Space* trivia if this one shot past you).

If you had vintage *Lost in Space* merchandise to sell from January 1998 through May 1998, you would most likely have seen a handsome return for your efforts. Moreover, the line of new *Lost in Space* items manufactured and marketed in 1998 saw such demand that they were immediately auctioned at eBay, drawing bids well in excess of their current retail values. The demand for the items was so high, thanks to the level of marketing hype, that they were being sold out as soon as they hit store shelves. If you were able to buy these items at retail, you could immediately list and sell them on eBay at double (or more) what you originally paid.

NOTE Timing is key to maximizing your investment. I was fortunate enough to key in on one of the classic remote control robot toys from the series. As soon as they were released for retail sale in 1998, a rumor spread around eBay that manufacture of the new toy had, for some unknown reason, already been discontinued; the initial shipment that made it to retail outlets was all that would be seen. Instantly, this became a high-demand collectible! I was lucky enough to find a few of them at my local Toys R Us. Retail price was about $15, but I was able to auction them for $30 and above. I never found out how the rumor originated, but it seems to have been untrue in the end. In the coming months, the robots were quite available in the retail market. You couldn't even recover your retail investment now if you were to attempt to auction one.

The *Lost in Space* example I've chosen to use here is only one case (see Figure 2-2). Consider the popularity of baseball memorabilia during the playoffs and World Series. How about the potential demand for original Austin Powers memorabilia now that the new film is such a wild hit (oh behaaave)?

figure 2-2

The remote-controlled *Lost in Space* robot caused a flurry of activity upon a rumor that production had ceased after the first shipment of units.

Easily, consider the demand for *any* Beanie Baby as soon as it is retired—or what if someone gets clever and decides to *impeach* a Beanie? You get the idea. The auction provides you with a wide market at your disposal when hype is at its highest. Use it well and use it often.

But how about buyers? How does a buyer benefit from aspects of timing at eBay? After all, if the hype is on, aren't you destined, as a buyer, to pay top dollar to get those hard-to-find items? Maybe, but maybe not.

For the buyer, timing allows you the opportunity to contend for any particular item. In traditional methods of buying and selling scarce items, it has always been the rule of "first come, first served." If you weren't first to an item, you might as well have been last. This is especially annoying when your inquiry about something is met with, "Gee, I just sold that five minutes before you called. Sorry." I hate when that happens.

When you see an item listed for auction on eBay, it's listed for a run of three, five, seven, or ten days. You don't have to be first to the item, you just have to get to it before the auction ends. This helps you take a more relaxed approach to your hunt. If you're a collector, you're probably familiar with the various trade papers that serve your particular collecting interest. How many times have you bothered the newsstand attendant or bookstore employee, asking about when the new issue of the journal would arrive? When it does arrive, how many times have you hastily purchased a copy, raced home to search the listings and, almost in a froth, made phone calls to the sellers in hopes that *you would be first?* It's a pain, believe me. In fact, it takes much of the fun out of buying for a collection or otherwise.

In the auction environment, however, you have time—time to find your item, time to evaluate it, and time to decide if, when, and how much you will bid for it. This leads to the second point of how auction timing benefits the buyer: the freedom from having to make snap decisions and rush into a purchase. At the auction, you can leisurely review an item up for bid. If you have specific questions, you can e-mail the seller to get the information you need. You then have time for further research, especially if the item is advertised as being rare, one of a kind, or of a limited edition. You'll have time to research other auctions for similar items and their current bids. Or you can perform searches on the Internet using any of the powerful search engines, looking for more information about the item. You'll be surprised how much you can learn on the Internet—oftentimes, you can find entire Web sites devoted to a single item or a series of related items.

More important, you'll have time to fully consider your true desire for an item up for bid. Rather than make an impulse buy because the seller is pressuring you by saying, "If I don't sell it to you now, I'll probably raise the price and sell it at a show next week," you'll have time to see if the purchase really fits into your financial capabilities. Or you may find the same item in another auction but in better condition or more complete, or you may find an entirely different item you would much rather spend your money on. The benefit to you, the buyer, is that you have time to consider all of these things before you commit to buy.

NOTE Since bidding and selling timing is such a critical factor to success, you'll be glad to know I've devoted all of Chapter 17 to the topic.

Leveling the Playing Field

There's often a disadvantage to both sellers and buyers when they are negotiating a deal: if one person is truly skilled at negotiating, or knows more about an item than the other, someone might end up holding the less-sanitary end of the stick after the deal's been made. A seller might have a true golden treasure (without realizing it), and a more informed buyer might take advantage of that seller's lack of knowledge. A buyer, on the other hand, might be easily duped into believing an item is rare and of great investment potential, later to find out that it's a common piece or, even worse, it's a reproduction of some sort! Both sellers and buyers are susceptible to unsavory conditions. To correct this, you need an objective third party to get involved as a form of mediation. That third party can very well be the auction forum.

The auction provides balance to the valuation of items up for sale. When two individuals privately negotiate a sale, only they are involved and they must rely on their own knowledge, skill, and cunning when striking a deal. At eBay, however, the sale is visible to all who choose to look. Each bidder shares knowledge about an item's value or desirability simply by way of placing bids. Spirited bidding is usually an indicator that the item is in some demand, whereas stale or no bidding might indicate a dead item. The bidding *market* helps set the ultimate value of the item, and frees buyers from being ripped off or sellers from being taken to the cleaners.

Now consider each party in the sale individually. The seller in an auction is typically under considerable scrutiny. They've placed their item up for bid, hoping that they'll attract buyers who will be interested enough to bid for the item and even compete for it. The seller, being visible to the entire eBay bidding community (as well as to other sellers), will need to be straightforward, honest, and accurate in describing the item for sale. The potential buyers can confer among themselves to develop *their* opinion of an item's integrity and value. In fact, the eBay community has become so viable a unit that it can, in extreme cases, cry "Foul!" at the sight of grossly misrepresented or unlawful items, thus invoking the powers at eBay to summarily shut down the auction and even suspend or expel the offending seller. It's a virtual better business bureau.

But the seller has advantages as well as controls in the auction market. An auction can help the honest, community-minded seller find a good return on items that might otherwise have been undervalued. Remember the discussion from Chapter 1—auctions are terrific for sellers who have items of unknown value. Place the item up for bid, and let the bidders do the rest. As a seller, you really needn't worry about getting the reasonable sale value for your items. It's rare that you'll take it in the shorts when your item has the potential to be viewed by almost six million sets of eyes!

Now consider the buyer. The auction helps you buy items at prices that the market will truly bear. If someone tries to sell you a current Beanie Baby at an inflated price, you can counter by pointing out that this Beanie is worth no more than retail price because there's a plethora of them to be found at eBay as well as in the retail mainstream. The buyer now has the power of knowing the marketable value of an item, thanks to the millions of "market analysts" that are using eBay. As noted earlier, the power of time is on the buyer's side. You have time to consider your intent to purchase, gather information about an item, and decide how much you really want to spend.

 SOAPBOX In regard to collectibles, I believe there has been an absolute glut of *Limited Edition, Collector's Edition,* and other such promoted items. The various manufacturers of goods have seen how labeling items in this way can generate more sales these days than ever before. However, these "limited editions" are being manufactured by the tens and hundreds of thousands. Someone please define *limited!* With eBay, though, it becomes easy for buyers to see that "limited" items, although maybe temporarily unavailable in their geographic region, are quite plentiful elsewhere and available at a reasonable price. I believe the geographic span that eBay reaches will help bring the market back into balance and restore the fun of hunting for and finding items that are truly limited or scarce.

If you are a buyer and you're looking for a real steal, you might be hard-pressed to find one on a desirable item at eBay. Some buyers prefer one-on-one deals to increase their chances of getting a great deal on an item. Although the sellers benefit from having six million sets of eyes seeing their items, this is often a curse to buyers. It's pretty difficult to snag an item cheap when so many other folks have the same intentions as you. It doesn't mean that you can't find some great values and often overlooked treasures at eBay, but don't expect to find an autographed Babe Ruth baseball card without others seeing it as well.

As a final perspective, the buyer is also under scrutiny at eBay. Have you ever had something to sell, found your buyer, and then waited endlessly for the payment to arrive? How many times have you *held* an item for a buyer, turning down subsequent offers as a matter of keeping your word, only to find the buyer never intended to pay or dropped the idea and didn't bother to let you know? It's bad news when this happens. Naturally, in face-to-face deals, a buyer will typically pay up on the spot (just watch out for bad checks). On eBay, however, bad buyers (a.k.a. *deadbeat bidders*) become known quite quickly. As a buyer, take care when you bid: your bid is a commitment to buy. As eBay states, some failures to buy might even be prosecutable. Now, before you get in a huff and call your lawyer, the point is just that you should honor your bids as you hope a bidder for your item might do. And, here again, through the auction community, the seller is protected from flaky would-be buyers.

For the Benefit of a Benefit

eBay also works to benefit people who aren't even involved in the online buying and selling at all. Within the framework of all the auction activity, it is only natural that eBay can be leveraged to raise money for and donate to charitable causes. I think everybody has heard of charity auctions. eBay, through the strength of its online community, has seen this opportunity and made good use of it.

eBay created the *eBay Foundation* in June 1998. This is a charitable fund that was originally established through a donation of more than 107,000 shares of eBay's common stock to the Community Foundation Silicon Valley (CFSV), which is a tax-exempt public charity devoted to the ongoing support and furtherance of philanthropic interests and the building of a stronger community. The CFSV works with donors to identify the best recipients of donations, making grants to numerous nonprofit organizations.

The eBay Foundation is governed by eBay employees who support a basic philosophy of helping others help themselves. They strive to seek out organizations that will help individuals more fully develop their own skills and aptitudes. The foundation's belief is that, by helping individuals recognize their own potential, they will inspire those individuals to contribute to their own communities in a positive manner. As eBay's founder, Pierre Omidyar, puts it, "Personally, I have always believed in helping people to become the best they can be."

Already, the eBay Foundation has made grants to organizations that have a long-running vision to help build their communities. Recent grant recipients include Friends of Farm Drive, CHAMPS (a San Jose State University mentoring program), Home Care Companions, and Project H.E.L.P., among many others. The eBay Foundation continues to solicit suggestions for the furtherance of the foundation's impact and seeks out additional organizations that might benefit from an eBay grant.

Besides the eBay Foundation, the site has also been effective in hosting special charity auctions by other means. In a national television appearance, eBay founder Pierre Omidyar visited NBC's *Today Show* to talk about eBay and demonstrate its use. During the appearance, Pierre encouraged the show to donate an official *Today Show* leather jacket, which was then autographed by the show's cast. The item was listed on live television and immediately received a remarkable number of bids. This auction ran for five days and realized a final high bid of $11,400. The money was donated to a charitable cause.

More recently, eBay was put to similar use on the *Rosie O'Donnell Show*. In January 1999, Rosie, who gave Tickle-Me Elmo his thrust into sales superstardom after featuring the wiggling, giggling critter on her show, initiated an eBay auction for memorabilia autographed by guest John Travolta (see Figure 2-3). The auction, which consisted of a vintage Travolta teen mag and *Welcome Back Kotter* bubble-gum card pack, brought in a final high bid of $2,075. Rosie donated the proceeds to the For All Kids Foundation. Rosie, by the way, *is* a registered eBay user and an active auctioneer as well.

figure 2-3

Vinnie Barbarino apparently hasn't lost his charm among bidders.

Further, actor/director Ron Howard has conducted several charity auctions on eBay, *People* magazine auctions autographed celebrity photos for charitable causes, and Athlete Direct auctions private collections from some of the world's greatest athletes, with all money being donated to a deserving cause.

chapter 3

The Birth of eBay

Now the discussion turns to the online realm known as the Internet. The expanse of the Internet's cyberspace is linked by a continuum of electronic pointers—or addresses—affectionately known as the World Wide Web. It has become everybody's virtual window to the cybernetic cosmos, providing myriad paths and destinations. It's easy to get lost on the Web, but it's somewhat of an adventure to find out what lies ahead, just around the next hyperlink.

As you read this, I'm assuming you're familiar with the Web and aware of its impact on our world today. If you're not, I'd be interested in learning how you've managed to avoid running into it.... Talk of surfing the Net is everywhere today. Some years ago, the Web was considered something of a hangout where a silent subculture was congregating, discussing the next generation of chip designs, planning a Doom Deathmatch, or enjoying a virtual latte in an online chat room. Once the mystery of the Net was brought into better light and made more accessible, hundreds of thousands of new surfers found the electronic wave and they loved it. And when something is this popular, you can bet there are minds at work thinking of the potential earning power just waiting to be harnessed.

Today, the Internet is a marketing paradise. Being online is the best place to be. Unlock your mind. Unlock your inhibition. Unlock your wallet. There's a whole new way to find, learn, meet, and *shop*, and you're gonna love it. Don't fight the wave, ride it.

This chapter briefly explores the Internet explosion and brings light to the newest raves in e-commerce. It's a free world out there, and entrepreneurial minds are hard at work, thinking of new ways to fill voids and satisfy niches. And it is in this spirit of creative problem solving and risk taking that eBay was born.

The Internet Revolution

The Internet is here to stay. That's undeniable. It seems every day someone announces new advances in Internet technology and new applications for its use. The World Wide Web, which is the road map into the Internet, is arguably the most comprehensive and convenient method for accessing the Internet's information warehouse. Armed with their favorite browser (such as Netscape Navigator or Internet Explorer), Web users are able to find whole libraries of information through a few simple mouse clicks and keystrokes.

It's been reported that roughly 90 percent of Web users access news online. With over 2,700 newspapers to be found online, it's no wonder. The ability to search, click, and read news stories from a browser window makes conventional newspapers almost obsolete—and you won't get ink on your fingers.

Published statistics have reported that from 1994 to 1998 Internet use increased from 3 million users (mostly in the United States) to an estimated 102 million worldwide. A report published in January 1999 updated the number of users to 151 million. The numbers of users are expected to reach 477 million by 2002 and continue on to the 1 billion mark shortly thereafter. The reason for the rapid and nonstop increase is the number of sites and services to be found on the Net. Commercial Web sites, those selling products or services from a *.com* address, numbered around 24,000 in 1995. A January 1997 report quickly updated the number of .com sites to the neighborhood of 650,000. As of this writing, that number is estimated to have reached well over 3 million commercial sites. Hey, surf's up!

So there's more than just information to be found on the Net. In the decade of the 90s, Internet e-commerce—sometimes also referred to as *i-commerce*—has become a phenomenon to behold. Online shopping is a plain and simple success, undoubtedly. Online merchants, many of whom have migrated from conventional retail stores to establish their own dazzling Web presence, are finding a multitude of online shoppers who are spending literally billions of dollars in cyberspace. During the 1998 holiday shopping season, it was estimated that festive bargain surfers would spend close to a record $13 billion online, an anticipated increase of 230 percent over 1997 figures. In the final tally, the actual figure reported on January 14, 1999 amounted to only $8.2 billion in online holiday sales, though (did I say *only*??). If you think that's impressive, consider the results of a June 1999 report released by the University of Texas. That report concluded that the total revenue generated in the United States as a result of online commerce was over $300 billion. That included not only revenue from online sales but also revenue that was generated as a result of businesses investing in hardware, software, and consulting services to guide online business success.

Why is e-commerce so popular? Many Web surfers credit the success to the basic human desire to sit around in your PJs, slippers, or whatever and shop till you drop (or click till you're sick). Others mention the sheer convenience of shopping whenever you choose. Web business sites are typically up and running 24 hours a day, seven days a week. In fact, most sites report that their busiest periods of online sales occur between the hours of 10 P.M. and 10 A.M. It makes sense that, if you have a regular day job, you rarely have time to run necessary (let alone frivolous) errands, and your weekends are probably filled mowing the lawn and cleaning out the garage. Thanks to online shopping, though, you have free access to the wares whenever you choose regardless of peak highway traffic periods or the varied operating hours of brick-and-mortar business places. Add the fact that you can almost effortlessly comparison shop online by way of a few simple mouse clicks and it becomes a real no-brainer why e-commerce has made its unmistakable impact.

A Different Form of E-Commerce

As the consumer culture quickly becomes accustomed to online sales, online sales sites need to vie for attention—and money—even quicker. Web sites include eye-catching banners to attract would-be buyers, providing a quick and easy link to the enticing site. Promotions are run and advertised from launching pad sites such as Yahoo!, Lycos, and Excite. You'd even find enough intelligence in the searches you conduct that result in banners appearing for advertisers pushing goods that are closely related to the topic of your information search.

The interesting question to some merchants is how to make shopping more fun and even exciting. Web sites offer a multitude of graphics, banners, and scrolling marquees. Some offer interesting scavenger hunts and trivia contests. But the truly interesting site would be one that requires the interaction of a shopper in a way that makes a purchase more of a quest, more of a game, than a simple surrendering of some specified price. The online auction is the answer.

Online auctions allow shoppers a different kind of consumer experience. Usually, an auction site will lure potential bidders in with incredibly low opening bids for brand name merchandise such as computers, home audio, or home video products. Believing there's a deal—or steal—to be had, a shopper will stake a claim on the item, hoping to find a final price that even the "sales associates" at the local electronics superstore would envy. The appeal of the online auction is very similar to that of regular online sales—shoppers can bid and buy from the privacy of their own home any time of the day or night. The added bonus—the *game* element—is that the auction offers the sport of competition between bidders. Each will place escalating bids, hoping to outbid the others while still ending up with a bargain. The auction format feeds the competitive spirit in many people, and it's just plain fun. In this shopping experience, you don't just buy an item, you *win* it.

The first online auction, Onsale (**www.onsale.com**) appeared as far back as 1994. Since then, many other auction sites have appeared on the Web. Many of them have offered branded goods like electronics and sports equipment from well-known manufacturers. Ridiculously low opening bids like $2 for a home audio system would be more than enough to lure bidders. The bids, of course, would only increase as more people visited the sites and found equal interest in items up for auction. As mentioned in Chapter 2, an auction will simulate the marketplace. The price for an item is usually comparable to the known retail value—sometimes a little higher and sometimes a little lower. Although a type of item, say a 19" television set, might sell for a variety of prices, the average high bid price is typically similar to what can be found through direct purchase methods. But the fun is still to try to win the TV for a rock-bottom bid.

Auction sites like Onsale have seen great success in their sales of durable goods—these days just about everybody needs a computer, television, DVD player, or whatever. Moreover, these days, everyone's looking for a bargain. In fact, thanks to the Internet and the huge popularity of online auctions, some analysts ponder whether consumers will be willing to pay fixed prices for very much longer. As more and more people turn to the auction for better deals, consumer attitudes are changing. Many online retailers are wondering if they'll need to continually offer some sort of dynamic and highly competitive pricing scheme. The jury's still out on this one, but it's a compelling argument.

But although auction sites dealing in durable goods have delivered what the mainstream consumer was looking for, something was still missing. What was a person to do if he or she were trying to find the hard-to-find? What if a person owned the hard-to-find, and wanted to dispose of it at a good and reasonable price? What then?

eBay Goes Live

Pierre Omidyar, an Internet enthusiast, was having a discussion with his girlfriend, Linda, one day. Linda was a collector, and held a particular passion for PEZ figures—you know, those little dime store candy dispensers with flip-back character heads that reveal a compact sugar ingot. As Linda was building her collection, she had mentioned to Pierre that she wished there were a good way for her to further her collection and meet other collectors over the wide-reaching Internet. This desire made perfect sense to Pierre, and he quickly determined that such a method could be quite useful and popular, existing as a sort of electronic marketplace and forum where people could meet and swap goods among themselves. A virtual online flea market could be established—without the dusty air, greasy corn dogs, and lousy beer.

On September 5, 1995—Labor Day—Pierre Omidyar officially launched eBay to the online world. Originally named *Auction Web,* it surfaced as the Internet's first person-to-person trading post, providing private buyers and sellers a place to spend money and make money without significant overhead. eBay operated simply: it worked as an impartial third party that offered a common meeting ground for individuals, supporting itself mainly on commissions received from successful auction sales. Sellers would pay a small listing fee to advertise their items. Then, after the auction was over, and providing an item actually sold, the seller would pay a very small percentage of the final proceeds to eBay. If the item wasn't bid on, the seller paid no commission (except the nonrefundable listing fee).

 SOAPBOX You might be thinking what I was thinking when I first surfed around eBay—"*Oh, sure. It costs money to buy and sell here. No thanks.*" I'll admit, at first I believed that listing fees and sales commissions would chew up my profits. Actually, I found it not to be so bad after all. When I learned how many bidders were using eBay to find items—even in the early days shortly after eBay's startup—I saw the commission was peanuts compared to the sales potential I could—and did—find at the site. Even after paying the commission and listing fee, I was still getting higher profits than I could from conventional methods of selling my junk. Incidentally, you'll learn more about how listing fees and final bid commissions are calculated in Chapter 20.

The Growth of eBay

Since Labor Day '95, eBay has grown steadily in acceptance and popularity. As of this writing, eBay has more than 5.6 million users registered to participate in bidding or selling. During 1997, eBay added more than 30,000 new registered users per week to its ranks. As previously mentioned, the more users involved, the better your chances of finding a particular item for sale or of finding the price you want for an item you're selling.

If you're really into statistics, here are some more for you: as of this writing, there have been more than 50 million auctions held with over 200 million bids having been placed. eBay now receives over 1.5 *billion* page hits per month, features more than two million active auctions on any given day, and has more than 200,000 new items added daily in over sixteen hundred different categories. That's enough to leave you pop-eyed. These are statistics that have been updated significantly since the first edition of this book was prepared and will most assuredly continue to increase each day.

eBay clearly is the largest person-to-person online auction site on the Web today. eBay had been achieving a sort of cult acceptance and approval among newly inducted and self-proclaimed *auction addicts.* News of a good thing travels fast along the Web, but eBay truly found high visibility on September 24, 1998. In what was to be the stock market's first initial public offering (IPO) since August 1998, eBay began trading shares of common stock under the symbol *EBAY.* eBay offered 3.5 million shares of its stock at an introductory price of $18 per share. The offering was made to raise $63 million for the company, allowing for the payment of debts and further investment in business development and general corporate purposes.

To the befuddlement of most stock analysts, eBay stock took off skyward with no attention to traditional trading performance or analyst predictions. Within weeks, the stock was selling near $80 per share. It broke the $100 ceiling without so much as a stutter, and kept rocketing ahead. By December 1998, it handily broke the $200-per-share point without looking back. Before 1998 ended, eBay stock reached a high of $321 per share. To the market's amazement, eBay announced a 3-for-1 stock split on March 1, 1999. Within only weeks afterward, it was already showing a 50 percent growth per newly valued share. eBay has been included in *The Motley Fool's* "Rule Breaker" stock portfolio. Who knows what's in store for this hot ticket stock?

With this incredible stock market ride, eBay has drawn the attention of the nation and the world. All major news services, periodicals, trade journals, and business analysts found they had to acknowledge the existence of eBay. Back in December 1998, eBay was reported to have a market value of nearly $12 billion, which was noted as higher than consumer products mainstay Clorox and about three times higher than Apple Computer.

Moving into the second quarter of 1999, eBay remained strong in the stock market and even stronger on the Web. It is still the hottest auction site online for person-to-person trading and shows no sign of slowing. A report prepared by Media Metrix on January 29, 1999, announced eBay as the second most popular Web site on the Internet in terms of user minutes spent at the site (Yahoo! came in first). The same report went on to list eBay as the Number 3 site for online shopping and Number 20 of the most visited Web sites on the Internet. Of course, those statistics became quickly outdated. In May 1999, eBay was reported of having a market capitalization valued at $25 billion. eBay is now ranked the third most popular Web site online and is the third most recognized brand name in e-commerce.

eBay, in response to its success, continues to further develop its site, adding new features in advance of and at the request of the eBay community of users. The site has been the talk of the economic industry for some time now and all eyes seem to be fixed to the auction giant to see what it will (or won't) do next.

Secondary and Tertiary Markets

Besides being the virtual trading post of our future, what else has eBay shown it serves in our current culture? I've already talked about eBay's being the place to find the hard-to-find, but that generally applies to nostalgic items from the past. What about the hard-to-find of the present? Does eBay play a part in fulfilling certain retail shortages? You bet.

If you were one of the stressed soldiers from recent holiday seasons, you would have been glad to know that eBay was among the very few sources that could fill an empty spot under your Christmas tree. In 1996, Tyco's Tickle-Me Elmo sent frantic shoppers to the tinsel-laden wasteland of Yuletime toys. Like warriors off to battle, these desperate retail runners armed themselves with their own wits and determination, fortified by wobbly wheeled steel-mesh combat vehicles to bring their men—or Muppets— back to their own home bases. There were casualties. From the less aggressive shopper to the innocent store clerk, people got hurt during the course of battle. During many of the incidents, though, no actual Elmos were sighted. Elmo was apparently so loved that he was hated. What a mess.

eBay had Elmo, and, for prices into the hundreds of dollars, you could have him, too. Some of the lucky among us found Elmo through normal retail outlets, buying him at an acceptable price. Did all of these Elmos make it under Christmas trees, though? No way. Many found their way onto eBay instead. It was a classic story of the *haves* and the *have-nots*. Elmo was auctioned to record numbers of bidders. If you had Elmo, all you needed to do was add your auction listing, then sit back and smile at the thought that the proceeds would pay a large chunk of your holiday bills. But what if you were the one who sorely needed Elmo? eBay was the place to find him. While some might lament the fact that this appeared to be some form of pure capitalistic exploitation, if someone really needed one, eBay had the cure to the ill.

The same situation held true in Christmases to follow. In 1997 it was Tyco's Sing-and-Snore Ernie and Tamagotchis. In 1998 Furby fever captured the holiday masses' wild-eyed desire. Now, it's Pokemon and Star Wars stuff. For each shortage you'd find at the usual retail outlets, you'd find the highly valued supply on eBay. The point is that eBay was the island in the storm. Although you would expect to see significantly high prices for rave items in high demand and low supply, the point is that you could be 99 percent assured that you would find the item up for bid at eBay. It just comes down to asking yourself, "How bad do I need it?"

These are what I call the online secondary and tertiary markets. The secondary market is where an item, after being bought through normal retail channels, is in turn sold again, usually between two private parties. That's a lot of the activity on eBay. It's perfectly legal as long as the goods aren't stolen or otherwise restricted in an area. The tertiary market, I believe, comes about when the item is sold again for a third time—and even beyond—and typically still at a reasonable profit. Some items can change hands so many times that it's possible for you to buy back something you once sold, it having changed many hands since you last saw it. In fact, I have sold items at eBay and later either found them up for bid again or featured on an individual's Web site, but rarely by the same individual with whom I had made the original transaction.

How I Got Hooked on eBay

I found eBay practically by accident. As a collector, I saw the new online medium as a major advance that would help me find those items for which I had long been searching. I started on the USENET, where you'll find a plethora of specialized newsgroups dedicated to anything from Barney hate mail to discussions of rare medical anomalies. In late 1995, I found the group **rec.collecting** and spent a lot of time reading the "For Sale" listings while posting a few inquiries of my own.

As I became a regular on this newsgroup, I kept seeing postings about auctions. As I explained before, the word *auction* might just as well have consisted of four letters in my mind. But some of the items were compelling enough to me that I just had to read about them. Many of these listings were no more than an individual calling for direct e-mail bids on an item, up through a certain day and time when the owner would determine the lucky winner-buyer. That was pretty straightforward. However, many other postings told of a Web site to visit where the individual's item was "up for bid." It was something called AuctionWeb found at a URL of **www.ebay.com/ auctionweb**. So, I went there, and I've never left.

eBay—or AuctionWeb at that time—was a veritable playground for finding rare, not-so-rare, and generally curious items. It was a unique format, quite active, and just downright different enough to make me want to get involved. Being a collector of toys and such, I found a category for Games and Hobbies. I was amazed by the hundreds of listings. I saw items I recognized. I saw items I'd only heard of. I saw items I had never heard of. But when I came across a listing for the *Poppin' Hoppies* game, I practically fell off my chair.

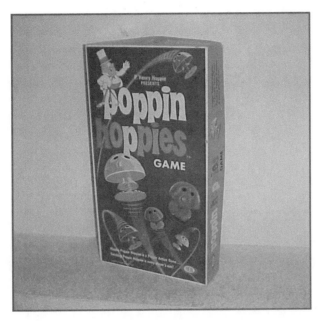

figure 3-1

From 1968, the seldom seen Poppin' Hoppies game. What a great time to be a kid.

Poppin' Hoppies was a cute little game from 1968 in which you and an opponent would work with a collection of little suction-cupped, spring-loaded critters. The goal: be the first to get all your critters secured in a "suctioned" position. It was harder than it sounds. Those things would pop off all over the place as you scrambled to get them all suctioned for at least a split second to claim your win. I was six years old, but I still remember the Christmas I got this game. My Grandpa Dave and I played and laughed for hours. As my Grandpa has long since passed away, this is perhaps the most vivid memory I have of spending time with him. And here was that game on eBay. I got registered and won that game.

Since that first auction, I've been a steady user of eBay and have bought many items from many people. It wasn't until I saw a unique California Raisins item that I turned my attention to selling.

Del Monte, who used the irresistible Claymation figures to promote raisins to greater heights of popularity, licensed a unique premium that consisted of three PVC raisin figures, perched atop a musical sandwich that played

chapter 3

The Birth of eBay

figure 3-2

Del Monte's musical (and profitable) raisins. They earned it through the grapevine.

"Heard It Through the Grapevine." I saw one of these listed for auction in the rec.collecting newsgroup, and remembered that I also had one. At that time, I decided to post it for sale directly on the newsgroup. I decided to ask $55 for it (the one at auction was up to a present bid of $62). One individual contacted me and offered $45 for it. I discovered that she was bidding on California Raisin items at eBay. I thought her offer was low, and instead decided to list it on eBay. The final result: I received a high bid of $79. Not bad for a first-time auctioneer. Since then, I've been an avid seller on eBay.

You'll probably have similar stories to tell. In late 1997, a statistic was published revealing that the average eBay user was spending about 23 minutes per day on eBay. In early 1999, that statistic has been revised and reports the new average use time is 126 minutes. Your actual time may vary. Just the day before writing this, I spent *hours* on eBay—listing new items for sale, bidding on a couple of great finds, and interacting with others via e-mail. Don't get me wrong: I *do* have a life. But I also have found a lot of enjoyment through eBay, especially having been able to grow with the site, building good relations with practically all of my buyers and sellers. I've learned that you can get as much out of it as you're willing to put into it. As with any venture or hobby, you'll just want to use good judgment, common sense, and moderation.

chapter 4

Is It Safe?

Safety on the Internet. It's a big deal and something that concerns people every day of their lives. Everybody is looking for safety, whether driving a vehicle, letting the kids play down the street, or sharing personal information online. There are no guarantees in life—except death, taxes, and trash day, and even trash day falls through sometimes when the guys go on strike—but you should strive to maintain as much control of your personal information as you can while you surf and shop online. Some say it's anal; I say, "So what?"

Safety in e-commerce is of particular concern to everyone. How secure is that "secure" Web site anyway? If I give my credit card number online, can someone intercept it and use it falsely? How do I know when I'm dealing with a trustworthy individual or reputable business when I can't even see a face on the other side? What if I run into problems or unsatisfactory goods and services while online? Is there a virtual complaint desk I can go to for help and satisfaction? These are the sorts of questions many struggle with as they turn to this new way of buying and selling.

Maybe you're familiar with the Net and don't have significant safety concerns or have already taken care of your personal online security. But did you realize that less than half the population of the United States has ever been on the Internet? If you're new to the Net, that's OK—you're not alone. This is the time for you to understand the basic steps you can take to feel comfortable in your online travels. And you'll see that there are others out there who are taking action for you to make your journeys through *Cyburbia* pleasant, hoping that you'll come back to visit again and again.

General Concerns About the Internet

The Internet has raised a whole new debate—and distrust—about privacy and safety on the cybernetic landscape. No doubt you've heard accounts of how your personal information is often freely available online. You're told how you must watch over your information yourself, being careful never to divulge anything of a private nature online. Protect your personal statistics, your private affairs, your medical records from becoming the indulgence of online cybersnoops and Web-weevils. In fact, protecting this sort of information has become enough of a scare that the mere concern has been keeping millions of individuals from ever accessing the Internet. The only problem, though, is that an awful lot of your personal information is *already* online whether you access the Net or not.

Huge databases exist that contain your personal information: your name, telephone number, address, directions to your house, even your shopping habits can all be found online. Research firms and marketing analysts study this information continually to better understand you and how you might be best served by (or sold on) a product or service. If you've ever responded to junk mail you've received in your mailbox—snail mail or electronic mail—then you've provided information that tells the sender something of your interests. You'll probably be receiving more mail of a similar nature any day now. Is this dangerous? Probably not. Is it annoying? Maybe. Can you do anything about it? Sure. Request that your name be removed from the mailing list—electronic or otherwise—and your wishes are respected 99.9 percent of the time. That's a start.

 TIP A good place to begin is at the Direct Marketing Association (**www. thedma.org**). There, you'll find the information and forms needed to remove your name from national mailing and telemarketing lists. Try it! You'll like it!

So what about all that other information about you that's available online? Should you start a personal campaign to have yourself removed from all databases and literally disappear from the electronic environment and become a veritable Orwellian unperson? Good luck. As I said, there are thousands of databases with so much of your information already on them that you'll never catch them all. Even before the electronic age, this information about you was available. Sure, it wasn't as easy to get to, but it was still there, available to most anyone who might have a penchant for finding out as much as possible about people.

SOAPBOX Leapin' Lizards! Does free access to your personal information make you a target for unpleasant online acts? In my opinion, no. Millions of us surf about on the Net, chatting, inquiring, shopping, and just hanging out. With so much activity online, I really maintain that you and I are small potatoes. Hackers and other Net-nerds are probably more interested in breaking into bank systems and such; you and I are just traffic on the line. But if you're not convinced, I invite you to further investigate this matter on your own. Refer to Appendix A of this book for additional resources about Internet safety and privacy. You should do whatever you feel is appropriate to make your online experience most comfortable for you.

Take Care of Yourself

While there are many organizations online concerned with your personal safety, the bottom line is that it's really up to you to be your own watchdog. You need to understand where you're surfing, what you're doing on various sites of interest, and whether any of your personal information is being shared during your visits. It's really quite easy to safeguard yourself online, and it's a practice you'll want to develop into a regular habit.

Whenever you visit a Web site for business transactions or whatever, determine if you'll need to register to participate (at most sites, you will). Before you register, check to see if the site has a published *privacy statement*—it will tell you what information the site collects during your visits and how it uses

that information. If you can't find a privacy statement, e-mail the site directly to request it. If you can't get a straight answer, head straight out of that site and off to a more secure one instead.

In some cases, sites will pass along some of the information you provide to marketing firms and such to feed those databases I already told you about— *if you allow it.* That's right—a well-developed, well-protected site will allow you to *opt out* from having your personal information or site activities shared with other businesses or research firms. It's not a bad idea to simply say, "*No, thank you*" when you see the opportunity to opt out (usually, it will be a check box on a site's registration form or order form that asks if you permit the sharing of your information).

If you like the idea of opting out, take it a step further by requesting the major credit reporting agencies (Equifax [**www.equifax.com**], Experian [**www.experian.com**], and Trans Union [**www.transunion.com**]) not share your personal information with marketing and research firms. Yes, you need to request they *not* share your information, otherwise, it's assumed you don't mind. Well, *do* you mind?

These are just a few examples. Really, it comes down to the fact that you need to be eternally vigilant of what you share about yourself while online. You shouldn't quiver with debilitating apprehension, but you should be responsible and know that you are the best gatekeeper of your personal data.

Majority Rules

All right, but what about the other people out there? Face it. When you step into cyberspace, you're stepping into a whole new world, often much different from the physical world you already know. It's like visiting another country. There are different people there, and they have their own culture, style, and rules. You know the old adage, "When in Rome...." That same principle pertains to the Internet as well. The way you behave will quickly let others know whether you're a good witch or a bad witch.

When the Internet first got rolling, it was largely populated with computer geeks and machine heads (two terms that I can rightfully use since I've joined the ranks of those who wear them). It was a place where people literally spoke a different language. You'd encounter so many cyberterms and acronyms (shorthand in which letters represent whole words, such as ASAP for As Soon As Possible) that you could find yourself witnessing conversations that didn't seem to make much sense but were obviously perfectly clear to those engaged in the bizarre babble.

When you first enter cyberspace, you'll probably be somewhat overwhelmed and ignorant about the ways of the cybercommunity. In fact, you'll be regarded as a *newbie*—someone who is new to the landscape. Like it or not, there is something of a class or ranking system that quietly works online. Everybody has to start somewhere, but soon you'll be as fluent as the next guy. Pocket protectors are optional.

But aside from the learning curve you'll need to cope with, you can typically find that most people online are friendly and helpful. Even though those geeks seemed to create an environment geared toward confusing the rest of the world, by and large, they exercised the basic tenets of the Golden Rule: do unto others as you would have them do unto you. Sure, interactions could get spirited at times (you don't have to be online for that), but the basic Net culture was built on a reasonable amount of respect.

How, then, do you ensure you are gaining the personal respect you want and deserve online? Simple: exercise the Golden Rule in everything you do. Although I maintain that it is the exception in relational terms, there are some people who get online and behave in ways they might never dare in the physical world. Why? No one can see them. No one really knows who they are, right? Online, people can assume any identity, history, or passion that might serve them best or amuse them most at a given time. They can say what they choose in any way that they choose. They are free to indulge themselves in any way they like, regardless of who might get hurt in the process. This is another reason why so many people are still resistant to the Net—they aren't certain about the people they'll be interacting with.

SOAPBOX Well, gee, that's scary. I could be dealing with some psycho or mass-murderer out there. Let me out! I say, what's the difference between online interactions and personal interactions? Yes, it is true that you have the element of physical visibility in the real world, but aside from that, anybody can assume any identity upon first meeting. Call me naive, but I've met more nice people than not in my lifetime. In my opinion, you can partially thank the media (film, news, television) for society's distaste, distrust, and discontentment. But there might be someone as nice as your blue-haired grandmother out there, and she may even give you cookies and milk. Be aware, be cautious, but don't be paranoid.

OK, you can assume that if there is some cybercreep out there, he probably won't hang around very long, especially if he (or she) is not getting the kind of reaction or response he was hoping to arouse. He'll get bored or paranoid himself for fear that he'll be discovered. But most of all, he'll not want to play by the online culture's rules and will tire of fighting against them. His actions may even invite the retaliation of others who simply won't tolerate a bully or a troublemaker.

To you, this means you will follow the rules, too. They're easy to follow and you probably won't even think of them as rules after a short time online. They're just simple standards of human conduct, well within reach of everybody. If you're new to the area, just relax and ask questions. Most people will help you out, remembering when they were newbies. In turn, once you've become at ease online, you'll be able to pass on the favor to some other newbie. Remember the feeling of when you were new, and do what you can to make another newbie's experience even easier than yours. What a wonderful world this could be....

Community Minded

There is definitely strength in numbers, and part of your cyber experience will be in one or more *virtual communities*. As stated before, the Internet is like a whole new country—in fact, eBay alone has a larger population than many actual cities and towns—and you will be meeting a lot of people as you make your way about. It's much like physically moving into a new community—you'll want to find out what services are available to you, what clubs or interest groups exist that appeal to you, and where you might go if you need help. You'll find all this and more online.

On the Net, you can find many Web sites that support your interests. If you're into quilting, perform a search on "quilts" from any search engine. You'll probably find a variety of commercial, organizational, and personal Web pages that discuss quilting. And, just as you were attracted to quilting, you're bound to find others with your same interests as well. It's said that people of similar interests often share similar philosophies—not always, but often. There's probably a friend out there waiting for you to meet them just as that person could be sitting next to you if you attended a workshop on quilting techniques.

As I've already mentioned, I am an avid collector of all kinds of stuff. I have made many good friends online just by sharing maybe one common interest. The interesting thing I've repeatedly found is that when a collector meets another collector, they often want to offer more to one another in terms of information and help than might have initially been expected. They're just as happy to have made a new friend as you are. And, in contrast to what you've just read about creeps and kooks on the Net, you'll typically find that most people online are *very* polite. When you return their virtual handshake, it's the making of a great friendship.

So the aspect of community comes into play when the people you meet begin to introduce you to others they know who also share the common interest. I once met a fellow online when I was posting to an autograph-related newsgroup. He offered me some help within the newsgroup, and we soon took our discussions off the newsgroup and into direct e-mail communication. I believed it safe to have direct conversations with him because I had watched him conduct himself within the public forum. He was just as pleasant in our direct communication, and, after a short time, he felt comfortable with me.

 Tip Remember, online *you're* just as much a stranger to others as they are to you.

So, upon developing mutual trust, my new autograph buddy asked if I would be interested in participating in a private e-mail distribution list with other autograph collectors. He explained the group was centered on sharing stories of acquiring celebrity autographs as well as sharing tips with one another about the best sources of autographs and the proper etiquette to use when asking for in-person autographs. Membership in the distribution list was only offered via recommendation from an existing, trusted member. Before I knew it, I was involved in sharing my autograph stories with about 30 other pleasant and friendly people. I had become a member of an *online community*.

Still not convinced? Well, there were instances in that autograph community where a couple of people came on board and turned out not to be the Good Sams we hoped they would. The group was very diplomatic. The group's administrator would politely remind the member in question about the group's rules and demeanor. Often, that was enough to straighten the situation out. Other times it wasn't. One individual, bent on fighting for his rights of free speech and method of expression, wouldn't temper himself to censorship of any kind. No way. No how. The community's response to him: See ya! Again, this was a community that practiced respect for one another and the love of a common interest. We all have to temper ourselves in one way or another in life. If you don't think so, just tell your boss how you really feel about those oppressive ways, that imperialist self-righteousness, and that bad breath.

When you restrain yourself with certain individuals in certain situations, then, believe it or not, you're tempering yourself out of respect (or fear) of the other person. Are your rights compromised? I don't think so. You're expecting others to conduct themselves appropriately with you. It's this sort of mutual respect that we all practice in order to get along with one another. I guess it's kind of corny, but I call it *civilization*.

And why does this all matter? It matters because eBay is a large online community. It's made up of individuals from all over the world who share a common interest: they've embraced the Internet and are looking for new ways to trade goods. Within this larger community there are subcommunities where people interested in similar types of goods buy, sell, and chat. When you first join eBay, you agree to conduct yourself responsibly, acknowledging that other community members deserve the same respect as you do. That's your first assurance that eBay will be a place you can go to have safe and supportive interactions with others. Since you all share the common desire to meet in this online marketplace, it's in everyone's best interest that the community functions peacefully in order to keep itself intact and to draw the participation of even more members who will have something positive to add to the overall experience. Just as the community has citizens, so does the Internet have its *netizens.* Be a good netizen, and you'll reap the rewards the community has to offer.

 SOAPBOX OK. Hopefully I haven't gone overboard in my advising, yapping, and preaching about good Net behavior. If I have, I'm sorry. Maybe that's you I hear saying, "*Sheesh! Loosen the bone, Wilma!*" I just believe the Internet is what its users make of it, and you can quickly poison the pond if you're careless.

eBay, of course, has a greater vested interest in the methods of its community than did the autograph distribution list I belonged to. That group, by the way, disbanded after about a year and a half because the administrator was having trouble with some of the members. Nothing serious, but a few more members got on the free speech rant themselves and the hassle was more than the administrator cared to endure. In the end, everyone lost out, including the free speakers, because we lost our unique forum for sharing with one another.

eBay would have much more to lose than a group of autograph swappers. Being a truly viable and profitable online corporation, eBay takes appropriate steps to protect the community it has fostered. Yes, some will gripe about eBay interfering with the rights of its members, but the basic right of *all* members is the right to participate in an online community that is safe and free from unprovoked harassment or persecution. Yeah, this is more than just another Web site; we're talking *grass roots* here. eBay's appeal is that it is an online community full of involvement, recognition, and diversity. You'll meet doctors, lawyers, teachers, artists, authors, moms, dads, and young adults from the world over. It's a melting pot of world society, and it's invigorating. Soon enough, you'll be logged on yourself, and you'll learn what I'm talking about. In my mind, it is truly an opportunity to be cherished and continually nurtured.

Basic Netiquette Tips and Techniques

OK. Real quickly now, I'll run down a list of ways in which you can take action to preserve your personal safety and respect while online. In a subsequent section, I'll share how eBay is working with you (and for you) to the same end.

First, Aretha Franklin knew what she was sounding off about when she sang, "*R-E-S-P-E-C-T.*" If you have respect, both to give and receive, you have the foundation for good online relations. People want to be treated fairly and with dignity. Other people will make mistakes online—as will you—and it's really to no one's benefit to make a spectacle of it or to be made a spectacle yourself. Just remember the Golden Rule and you'll be fine.

Next, don't be afraid to show some trust to others, but just practice a little silent caution. No one wants to deal with a paranoid individual. It prevents normal communication and gets downright annoying in extreme cases. Ninety-nine percent of the time, you can tell someone's intentions within the first few interactions, or by reviewing some of their behavior with others (especially in newsgroups, online chats, or at eBay's Feedback Forum). Don't immediately embrace everyone you meet, but don't be afraid to reach out a bit to acknowledge a nice gesture or good deed that has been done. I've discovered that the people I believe I can trust most are those that understand the sensitivity of the trust issue itself. Most honest people won't ask you to divulge personal or private information just as they wouldn't want the same information about themselves to be divulged. Just use your head and keep a positive outlook.

Third, the Internet's twist on the Golden Rule goes something like this: *Flame not lest ye be flamed.* In the online realm, *flaming* is the act of sending abusive or offensive messages to others. It can also be a way of inciting a response from another individual that will surely lead to confrontation. It's true that we can't see one another online, but that doesn't mean we're completely safe from aggressive behavior or aggravated reprisal. If you get irate with someone online, just take heed: that person might be a bit more clever about this computer stuff than you are. There have been stories of flaming volleys including e-mail bombs (some sort of destructive message or incessant mailing of the same message), public ridicule and embarrassment, and even the ability for some to find your IP address (that's your active Internet connection address) and actually tap into your PC. Again, paranoia should be checked at the door, but just be sure that if you start something, you're ready to finish it.

"Can't we all just get along?"

There are other points to consider for conducting yourself reasonably online. Remember that the majority of what you do will be viewed in a public forum. You might offend someone you didn't even know was there. Do you ever wonder if law enforcement monitors areas of the Internet? They do.

Next, keep your emotions in check. It's easy to strike out against that "faceless monster" who just ticked you off. Maybe they didn't mean to. One undeniable difficulty of cyber communication is the absence of tone or inflection in your words. You might come off as sarcastic or cutting without really meaning to. Take extra steps to ensure your communications can be easily interpreted. Then remember there are real people out there behind those e-mail IDs. They have feelings, just as you do.

And, lastly, exercise a healthy dose of forgiveness. Everybody blunders from time to time, or speaks out of turn when they wish they hadn't. It's the human condition. Turn the other cheek and work for peaceful reconciliation. You might find an equally sincere response on the other end. If you can't resolve an issue, resolve to drop it and move on. Lugging around your personal bag of injustice will only weigh you down.

And what if you need help? Well, there are plenty of places to turn for that. You can easily search the Internet to find Web sites that will help you better understand the ways of cyberspace, Netiquette, and online safety. See Appendix A for a small sampling of some of these helpful sites. And there's always the most powerful tool available to you: your PC's power switch. Just turn if off if something's getting too weird for you. It's doubtful that there will be someone on the other end just waiting for you to return (that would be paranoid, wouldn't it?).

eBay's Increased Efforts for Safe Trading

Well, finally! He's going to talk about eBay again. Oh, happy day. Why all the yakking about general Net safety, Netiquette, and so on? Well, the principles and ideas I've just shared have helped make my eBay experience more enjoyable and positive. I find that the other people I meet at eBay generally share the same principles and ideals as I have expressed. Before you know it, hey, you're in a community of netizens.

 SOAPBOX Before going on, let me explain why I wear such rose-colored glasses when I talk about my good experiences and trust when working at eBay's site: less than 1/100 of 1 percent of the millions of transactions that take place at eBay wind up in some sort of trouble or complaint. That's probably less than what occurs in the physical world. That statistic, coupled with my own good experiences, is why I feel comfortable trading at eBay.

But what about the wolves in sheep's clothing slinking about on eBay? What, specifically, can or is being done to make the actual auction experience better and more trustworthy? Well, besides bringing its users' own respectfulness to the table, eBay has also served up some very useful and effective programs to help everyone out.

Grass Roots, or Power to the People

One of the most effective methods of keeping trouble out of your neighborhood is to form a *neighborhood watch* group. Who would be better suited to recognize trouble or misdeeds than the people themselves? At eBay, the people in the trading community take their pastime activity seriously (especially those who choose to do it full time) and aren't very tolerant of monkey business.

When you become a member of the eBay community, you'll find it's easy to strike up fast friendships. If you're a good citizen, you'll find yourself in the company of other good citizens. But communities watch out for their own, and bad press will travel fast. I was once alerted to a less-than-honorable bidder by another community member; my community friend told me of a fellow that had been placing high bids on items and then never following through. This friend contacted me because he was just stiffed by the no-goodnik. I thanked him for looking out for me. I told then another friend and, as one television commercial puts it, "*and so on, and so on, and so on....*"

 TIP Alerting people about another user's misdeeds can be a touchy subject. eBay could consider this as *auction interference:* a person not actively involved in an auction contacts bidders to warn them of another seller or bidder. If done maliciously, this would indeed be a foul offense, but if there is evidence that warrants the unsolicited notification, I might welcome the insight and experiences of the helpful community member. If in doubt, contact eBay directly for further clarification.

eBay recognizes the power of its community, and fully supports their efforts and hears their concerns. eBay reminds us all that it's a caveat emptor environment we're working in, and we do so by our own choice. However, eBay also recognizes that people desire a place to trade goods in an open forum, and eBay has found remarkable success by providing a safe and supportive meeting place. To this end, eBay has and continues to implement programs, methods, and features that make the community a better place to trade. Read on, and you'll see what I mean.

 NOTE Though eBay strives to make the trading better and more reliable, it must assert that it does not accept absolute liability for business transactions that might go bad. It's a policy that makes sense, and you'll read more about it when I discuss the registration agreement in Chapter 6.

OK. I have to throw in my two cents here. I have heard and read of others who think eBay should bear more liability when deals go bad. To that, I would disagree—people use eBay by their own free choice, and no one can guarantee 100 percent that something will go as expected. That's anywhere. You can get ripped off from infomercials, ads in magazines, classified listings, and so on. In those cases, the "hosting party" provides a disclaimer that it will not be liable for any product defects or misrepresentations. Besides, if eBay were to become involved in liability claims, then it'd probably be swamped with true claims, fabricated claims, and claims from those who couldn't work things out among themselves. This, in my opinion, would quickly dilute the quality of the site and undermine the motivation for some community members to act responsibly. eBay has become the thriving success it is due to the fact that it is the open forum for regular people like you and me to trade our wares without a bunch of bureaucratic meddling or exhaustive red tape.

TRUSTe and eBay's Privacy Policy

TRUSTe is a nonprofit organization that was founded in 1996 to address the rising concerns about Internet privacy. It was a combined effort built and pilot tested by the Electronic Frontier Foundation and CommerceNet. The two organizations were committed to developing awareness of the need for Internet privacy for online users, and looked for some method of providing visible *branding* that would immediately communicate to a user (much like the Underwriter's Laboratory or Good Housekeeping seals). When the TRUSTe program was first introduced, 100 sites participated to offer their input and advice. By mid-1997, TRUSTe was fully staffed. Auditing giants PriceWaterhouseCoopers and KPMG Peat Marwick were participating. The official rollout of TRUSTe was conducted worldwide at the June 10, 1997, Federal Trade Commission online privacy hearings.

The core principles that drive TRUSTe are as follows:

- Users have a right to informed consent.

- No single privacy principle is adequate for all situations.

TRUSTe works with online content providers to review their sites' methods and policies to ensure adherence to the two principles just mentioned. A site's content will be fully reviewed and regularly audited for compliance to the TRUSTe privacy initiatives. Upon approval, the site will have the privilege to display the TRUSTe brand. Since its launch, TRUSTe has endorsed a large list of licensees including C/NET, AOL, Disney.com, and many major search engines like Yahoo!, Lycos, and HotBot. Of course, eBay is fully licensed as well. For more info, visit **www.truste.com**.

SafeHarbor

SafeHarbor was developed by eBay to work as an umbrella of programs that add quality and assurance to the whole eBay experience. It is the visible commitment that eBay wants to preserve trust in the community and, in many cases, some of the methods and programs found within the SafeHarbor program have come about based on requests from eBay community members themselves. See, I told you they get involved.

At the highest level, SafeHarbor incorporates tools and processes that help eBay users be successful in their auction activity (buying and selling). It goes to the extent of working with consumer groups and law enforcement agencies to investigate and severely deal with cybercrooks. Naturally, this is not a hammer that eBay swings carelessly. eBay has staff who review suspicious activity on a case-by-case basis, and it is committed to providing an objective position in cases of dispute.

eBay is really just a place—a *venue*—for buyers and sellers to meet. Having provided the space, eBay has already done a lot for buyers and sellers around the world, giving them a place to meet and trade. However, eBay is committed to retaining its original appeal and attraction as a place for safe trading. The programs within SafeHarbor are evidence of that commitment. In addition, eBay has endorsed the efforts of the Internet Fraud Watch program, which is operated by the National Consumers League.

The Feedback Forum

After just a few months online, eBay's founder, Pierre Omidyar, instituted the eBay *Feedback Forum*. Quite simply, this is a public bulletin board for eBay users to provide feedback about other users they deal with. It's the tried-and-true method of learning more about the people you'll possibly deal with. If you have a pleasant experience with another user—maybe a seller who provided excellent customer service or a buyer who sent a lightning-fast payment—then the Feedback Forum is where such good deeds can be publicly rewarded. With every positive comment received, users gain an incremental *feedback rating* that makes up their overall *feedback profile*. At certain breakpoints in the feedback levels, eBay community members are awarded different colored stars next to their names, visually indicating they are members in good standing. It is a simple reward system, but it really works. Most important, the feedback system allows eBay community members the opportunity to build a good reputation for themselves.

Of course, there is the other side of the Feedback Forum. If you're a not-so-nice person, don't ship items you've sold in a timely manner (or at all), or don't make good on your winning bids, then you can expect to receive feedback for bad behavior as well—still in the public eye. This comes in the form of negative feedback, which leads to deductions from your overall feedback profile rating. Don't think it doesn't matter, either. Many users refuse to deal with others who have negative feedback. Some potential bidders pass on an item posted by a seller with negative feedback. Some sellers will negate the bids of a would-be buyer with negative feedback. And some of eBay's member services are restricted to members who maintain a positive feedback profile. It's all fair and is the purpose of the feedback system. If you have excessive negative feedback, then your eBay feedback rating can go into negative numbers. You won't be getting any stars for this sort of rating and, if you've accomplished an overall feedback rating totaling more than −4, eBay will suspend you from using the site and you will lose your registered status. If you're not registered, you can't play. Pretty simple, huh? And you thought only kindergartners went for that gold star stuff. It still applies, even to big people.

However, the Feedback Forum can be abused. It is possible for dishonest users to attempt to bolster their feedback rating by having friends post positive feedback for them even though a transaction hasn't taken place. Or they can try to register themselves under different user IDs and post their own positive notes for themselves. eBay has gotten wise to this and has developed ways to safeguard against this sort of thing. Today, feedback can be posted in reference to an actual auction that has occurred (citing the auction ID number), thus providing a protected method of ensuring only those involved in the auction can post feedback for one another.

 NOTE Currently, there is a rising sentiment that this should be the *only* way that feedback can be posted on eBay—as a direct result of a legitimate auction that has concluded. For the moment, it is still possible to post feedback for another eBay user without specifying an actual auction (say, when one user helps another user out in a more general sense and the one who received help posts a positive feedback note to acknowledge the good deed), but that policy may change.

Some users have also fallen into feedback wars, posting negative notes about one another in a childish exchange. After the first posting, be it positive or negative, any follow-on postings by the same user ID will not have cumulative effect. And you can't post stacks of positive messages about yourself or have your mother do so in an effort to rack up a high rating.

Sometimes, a deal might go bad, a mistake might be made, or a misunderstanding might occur. Sometimes we act in haste, only to later regret our actions. It is possible to work out a negative situation between community members. If their differences can eventually be resolved, it is possible to reverse a negative feedback note (if one was hastily posted) by having the same user post an offsetting positive note. It won't be possible to gain a positive increment to the user ID in question, but you can negate the effect of the negative note. Hopefully, your dealings won't need to go this route if you remember all I've said (and I've said a lot) about using good judgment and respect in all your online interactions.

 NOTE A recent change implemented by eBay prevents negative feedback from being posted if it is not directly related to an actual transaction (specifying a valid auction ID number).

By and large, the Feedback Forum works very well. Use it appropriately and read what others have posted about other community members. That's why it's there. I'll show you the actual mechanics of the Feedback Forum in Chapter 23.

Suspension and Loss of Registered Status

I've already mentioned that an excessive negative feedback rating will lead to the loss of a user's registered status. Here, though, I just want to add that there are a couple of other reasons for having such action taken against a user.

Shill Bidding

You learned about shill bidding in Chapter 1. eBay is adamantly against this unfair tactic. Taking additional steps to thwart this unacceptable activity—that is, users who have others (friends, accomplices) falsely bid up the price of an item or use multiple identities (eBay IDs) to bid up their items—eBay actively investigates reports of shill bidding. First-time offenders will be suspended for a 30-day period. Do it a second time, and you're suspended indefinitely. End of story.

Bid Shielding

It sounds a little like shill bidding, but it's quite different. Bid shielding is a type of collusion in which someone (or more than one person) places a ridiculously high bid in an auction only as a way of protecting one of the lower bidders. What's that you say? Why would someone do something so bizarre? Well, here's the rest of the story: at a point before the auction ends, the overactive high bidder retracts that high bid, leaving the item available for some designated lower bidder. Remember the discussion about the auction ring in Chapter 1? This is very much the same thing. A pair or group of bidders could find items of interest and designate one of the bidders in the group as the intended winner. That person's bid is placed, then the other group members bid up the item to an insane price to ward off other potential bidders. This action protects the lower bid. If the false high bidders don't retract their bids, they might choose to dishonor their bids after the auction closes. The intent is the seller will work down to the group's designated bidder, who might get the item for the shielded lower bid. Despicable, isn't it? If eBay catches word and concrete evidence that this sort of activity has taken place, those involved will be indefinitely suspended from using the site.

Deadbeat Bidders

The names get more colorful as we go along, but the behavior is still very much *off*-color. This term was actually coined by the eBay community. It describes users who bid on items but do not follow through to honor those bids. It's true that "stuff happens" and sometimes even the best intentions of honoring a high bid can go awry. Understanding these situations, eBay will provide a friendly warning at the first occurrence (that's invoked only if you weren't able to resolve the issue and the seller reported the incident). If you do this a second time, there's reason to suspect a trend, and you'll receive something of a nastygram that sends a more serious warning. Three times, and you will be suspended for 30 days. A fourth offense, and you're outta there.

Escrow Service

Yes, eBay even provides access to an online escrow service. No, don't expect that you'll be able to buy your next house at eBay—although it is now possible at some other sites online, and somebody once sold a mobile home on eBay. However, the escrow service eBay endorses is designed to provide additional assurance to buyers (and sellers) in the case of high-dollar purchases or the purchase of items described as very rare (some antiques or rare memorabilia). The escrow service eBay currently endorses is *i-Escrow*, a third-party organization that can be engaged to hold payment in trust as the seller and buyer conduct their transaction. It's actually quite a clever application of an age-old transaction mediator. The basic steps in conducting an escrow transaction go like this:

- The buyer and seller establish an online escrow transaction at i-Escrow.

- The buyer sends the high bid payment to the escrow service (using check, money order, or credit card).

- The escrow service lets the seller know the buyer's payment is now in the escrow account.

- The seller sends the auctioned item *directly* to the buyer by means of traceable delivery (USPS registered mail, UPS, or some such).

- The seller provides the shipment tracking number to the escrow service for the item shipped.

- The buyer receives the item and accepts it if satisfied.

- Upon buyer's acceptance, the escrow service releases the buyer's payment to the seller.

Pretty cool, huh? This is serious business stuff, and sometimes it makes sense. Say you missed the great Sammy Sosa homerun baseball auction, but someone lists an auction for one of his foul balls. If the bidding goes wild and the final price is hefty, an escrow service might be the safest way to complete the transaction. Both buyer and seller are protected from any situation where more than just the ball might go foul. I'll describe more about how to use i-Escrow in an actual transaction in Chapter 21.

Verified eBay User

This is a new program introduced in the 2.0 version of SafeHarbor. The Verified eBay User program is a planned pilot program in which users will provide additional identifying information in order for them to be visibly classified as "Verified eBay Users." During normal user registration (you'll learn more about registration in Chapter 6) you'll need to provide some basic information that will be validated at that time. The basic information is required for your participation. The new Verified eBay User program—which will be voluntary—requires additional information that can, without a doubt, ensure you are who you say you are. What information? Well, by offering your Social Security number, driver's license number, and date of birth, you will achieve the highest level of eBay user verification, which is denoted by a special icon appearing next to your eBay user ID. Don't get in a huff; remember, this will be a *voluntary* verification. However, to other eBay users, you will be showing your intention to be fully identifiable, hence signaling you wish to conduct honest transactions at eBay.

SOAPBOX Oops! My rose-colored glasses just slipped down my nose a bit. I'm not 100 percent certain about offering this additional information. I've been taught for years to protect my Social Security number—even though it's been passed around quite a bit as I've gone through life. Still, I'll be interested to find out more about what the rest of the eBay community thinks of this suggestion and how it is generally received. As of this writing, the Verified User Program has still not been officially implemented for use.

Trade with Confidence— eBay's New Insurance Feature

This has certainly been one of the biggest hang-ups facing the auction community and one which eBay has struggled to resolve for the users. Since the majority of eBay auctions are conducted by private individuals, there is very little that consumer protection organizations can do to retrieve a buyer's money if some shady seller collects the cash and skips town. It's been enough of a concern to many would-be users that it has prevented them from joining in the bidding. eBay has served up a pretty decent solution to this "perceived" problem in the way of a new buyer insurance program—Trade with Confidence. Backed by insurance giant Lloyd's of London, eBay now offers buyer protection up to $250 (less a $25 deductible) in the case that a buyer gets taken to the cleaners on a purchase. Now, at first glance, you might not think that's much of a deal (especially considering the deductible), but I believe it's quite a generous offer that eBay has served up. Remember, this is a caveat emptor environment we're all working in. eBay, though, has heard its community's voice and has provided a reasonable response.

OK, a couple of thoughts: First, eBay was under heavy scrutiny for the reported incidents of fraud that were seeping out of the auction activity. In fact, the Internet Fraud Watch reported online auctions as the single highest contributor to fraud claims in 1998. Don't let that scare you, though. Airplane crashes get some pretty visible coverage in the media, but air travel is still statistically safer than driving a car—something most people do every day. But eBay needed to respond to the fraud and buyer safety issue, and Trade with Confidence was a good answer (my opinion).

Second, if you ever think of casting stones at eBay's insurance program, don't forget to first gather *all* of the safety programs eBay offers to both buyers and sellers. Each acts as a filtering point that helps eliminate the chance of things going wrong in an auction transaction. These programs, in conjunction with your vigilant efforts to trade safely, should protect you from the foul deeds that might cloud the auction skies. This is not a commercial or paid-for endorsement—it's really what I believe.

Authentication and Grading

Here's another of the newer informational programs eBay has brought to the community. Authentication and grading are key to being most informed about what you are selling or what you intend to buy. You want to be sure you know your item well before you sell it—you'll be better equipped to answer potential bidder questions and set a reasonable value on your item. If you're buying, you'll want to understand what it is that you're planning to buy to be sure what you get is the real deal as opposed to a real drag.

eBay hasn't gotten into the appraisal business directly, but is instead offering directions to organizations that can assist community members in the area of item verification, validation, and condition grading. Currently, eBay users can find their way to the International Society for Appraisers (ISA), Professional Coin Grading Service (PCGS), Professional Sports Authenticator (PSA), and Real Beans (for Beanie Baby authentication) through the links that eBay provides at Safe Harbor.

Better Business Bureau Online

To further prove its commitment to the viability of its business practices and safety for the community members, eBay has become a branded member of the Better Business Bureau (BBB) Online. eBay now sports the visible BBBOnline seal on its home page, demonstrating that eBay has voluntarily become a BBB participant and has met the BBB membership standards. Though this doesn't provide an immediate tool or aid for the community's use, BBBOnline branding does further exemplify eBay's commitment to ensure a safe trading environment for the users. For more info, check out **www.bbbonline.org**.

Legal Buddy

No, this isn't a little lawyer pal you tug around on a leash or keep in your pocket. Legal Buddy is more directly designed for what are known as *content owners*—that is, owners of intellectual property or copyrighted material. There's a big underground market out there in pirated software, audio recordings, designer clothing, and accessories. Dang! There were even counterfeit Furbies changing hands on the black market, and you've just learned how Real Beans helps to sift out bad beanies. eBay does not want any part of commercial bootlegging, and works with companies and other copyright owners to identify and eradicate listings of such bogus booty.

Legal Buddy provides a way for content owners to search eBay listings using tools like an automated keyword search that will do a daily scouring of the various items up for auction. If something shows up that is not authentic, the content provider contacts the eBay Legal Buddy team to investigate the listing. Illegitimate items will be removed from the listings, with notification going to the seller and any current bidders. Repeat offenders (that is, bootleggers) will be suspended from eBay and may even find themselves being contacted by the Federal Trade Commission, the FBI, local attorneys general, or even the Postmaster General. That's a bad bunch of bananas.

So this seems fine for content owners, but is this of any benefit to eBay community? Sure. In the simplest example, you'll be protected from buying your favorite video, CD, or DVD at auction, only to find out it's an inferior copy made in some dude's garage. Rather than have you go through the disappointment of buying copied junk, eBay tries to prevent these auctions from ever completing and money from ever changing hands.

Open Lines of Communication

Not truly a program but still highly effective in keeping the community clean, eBay provides many different methods to contact someone on the eBay staff. You'll find dedicated e-mail addresses that you can use for specific questions about the following eBay elements:

- Customer support and general site usage
- User agreement stipulations
- Site privacy questions
- Charity efforts and the eBay Foundation
- Job openings at eBay

These are just some of the specially designated e-mail boxes for your specific (or not-so-specific) questions for the eBay staff. You'll find these and more e-mail addresses on the eBay Services and Help pages (I'll show those to you in Part 2).

 SOAPBOX Now, before I leave this discussion, I feel I should reiterate the disclaimer that my personal appreciation for eBay's efforts is just that— *my* personal appreciation. I fear that some could think this has been a glowing tribute that might smack of compensation or endorsement by eBay. Nope. It's just my honest assessment and opinion of what eBay has done for the community and how I believe it has had a positive impact on my activities and attitude while working the auctions at eBay. If I didn't believe it, I wouldn't write it—you can quote me on that.

What Do You Think?

Well, that's my experience and insight into safety on the Internet and at eBay. So, now I ask *you*, "Is it safe?" I've given you a lot to think about in terms of general safety and security on the Internet as well as how eBay approaches the same concerns within its own site. Hopefully, you now can see that there are many different programs, organizations, and various tools and tips that will make your online experiences more secure, and your eBay experiences virtually worry-free. Remember to refer to Appendix A for more resources you can check out for information about Internet safety.

part 2

Get Started and Join the Fun

chapter 5

What You Need to Begin

To make sure you'll be able to roll into the auction fun and take advantage of the features of eBay's site, you need to do a bit of advance work. The auction environment you'll soon be in is best experienced with the proper equipment. That's right; you need to be sure you have the right hardware, software, and useful little extras that will put you in the best position to enjoy the sights, sounds, and bidding frenzy that will meet you at eBay's front door.

Don't fret if you're not computer literate or technically suave. Home PCs these days are getting so simple to set up and use that even if you don't own a computer as you read this, you could easily get one, set it up, and get on eBay in no time flat.

Getting the Basics

What's that you say? You don't have a PC and don't foresee having one in the very near future? Does this mean you can't play? Not necessarily. There are ways around this situation. You'll see as you read this chapter that there are less conventional but still plausible ways to get in on the auction action.

Coupled with the hardware, you'll want to be sure you have some of the basic software you'll need (yes, including an Internet browser) to make the most of the time you'll spend at eBay. You'll find that the whole package is becoming quite affordable and practically ready to use. So, let's get cracking, OK?

Hardware That Isn't Soft

The first thing to think about is the PC itself. This is your *box, desktop unit, mini-tower,* or whatever you or the manufacturer choose to call it. This is the brains of the outfit and for ease of discussion, I'll refer to it as your PC. And, just as I've given you several names that it could be called, you'll find even more choices out there regarding the make, style, and content of each. The point in this section is not to go soft on the hardware you choose. You don't need to dole out a fortune to have a good time on the Internet, but the more you can afford, the better time you'll have with it.

If you already have a PC and have it fully tuned, skip over this part. If you don't have a PC or aren't sure if what you have is adequate, look for these common components.

CPU (or Chip) Speed

Someone once said, *"Speed kills."* Well, if you don't have adequate CPU clock speed, you'll definitely be *dying*. Every year (or less) it seems a faster chip is introduced to the PC market, and manufacturers quickly snap 'em up to put into their new PC offerings. The nice thing these days is that you can get good CPU speed for a really reasonable price. You can still get by on that old 486, but only use it if you really have to. The Intel Pentium chips (known as *Pentium I* or *PI*) were pretty much made for the Internet, and you can do reasonably well using one with a speed as low as 133MHz (megahertz). I wouldn't recommend buying a Pentium PC at this time; they're being discontinued by Intel. Intel's Pentium II (*PII*) chips make the Internet experience that much more enjoyable with speeds that reach the 450MHz mark. Still not fast enough? Look into the latest generation of Pentium III Xenon chips, which have been engineered to perform at speeds up to 550MHz. Intel also offers a new Celeron CPU that provides a lower price point since it has no separate cache (which saves you *cash*). It still performs quite well, and the speed is ever increasing with new versions being released. And, not to focus solely on Intel, there are good CPU offerings coming from AMD (the K6 series) and Cyrix (the 6x86 and MII chips). The choice of which CPU to buy depends on how you intend to use your PC—mostly word processing and spreadsheets, lots of Internet surfing and graphics viewing, or gratuitous amounts of gaming? At this time, I recommend at least a Pentium II with a 300MHz clock speed. It will give you good Internet response and download graphics at a nice pace. You'll do fine with this, but aim higher if you can. As for that PC with the 486 chip inside—it'll make a nice planter once you've upgraded.

Modem

The *modem* (modulator-demodulator) does all the talking. This is the communications component that accesses online services via a standard phone line. Although some modems communicate over cable or digital lines (a definite performance boost), you'll find the home PC market generally offers the standard phone line version since it's the most likely to be available in a PC user's home. Again, speed is the determining factor here just as with the CPU. Most common today in the home PC market are modems with speeds of 28.8K, 33.6K, or 56K bps *(bits per second)*. Obviously, the faster speed you can get, the faster you'll see Web pages respond and load when you're online. If you're thinking about the 56K variety, though, check with your ISP to make sure you get one it can talk to.

 Tip A word of clarification: even if you use a modem with a speed of 56K, you might only be able to connect at a maximum communication speed of 33.6K. Why? It all depends on the type of phone line in your home. Standard copper wiring can only support a maximum transfer rate of 33.6K, even if your PC has a 56K modem. If you live in a newer home, you might have fiber-optic lines, which will support the maximum capabilities of the 56K modem. If you're not sure, check with your phone company. They'll tell you the type of wiring available in your area.

You'll also find you can choose from an *internal* modem (it's installed inside the PC) or an *external* modem (it's placed outside the PC—on your desk or wherever). There's no difference in the modem's performance with either installation. Most new PCs have internal modems, so you won't need to muck with it. For some, that's a bonus. Others like the easy access in case they choose to upgrade later. Internal or external—get whichever suits you best.

Memory

Simple. The more internal memory your PC has (described as RAM—*Random Access Memory*), the faster it will perform. The PC can store information in RAM for immediate use as opposed to accessing the disk drive to retrieve the information needed. The current standard for RAM size is 64MB *(megabytes),* but 128MB is fast becoming the more popular configuration. Again, more is better.

Disk Storage

This is the amount of space available for information storage on your PC's internal disk drive, or *hard drive.* A few years back, most disk storage rates were measured in megabytes. Today, we're talking *gigabytes* (GB). A gigabyte is approximately one billion bytes of information. The more disk storage you have in your PC, the better time you'll have while you're logged on. You'll be able to store more applications on your PC's internal drive, avoiding the need to load floppy disks or CD-ROMs. And, as you encounter a lot of multimedia applications on the Internet, you'll need more applications to get the full effect of the great Web designs you'll find out there. The current standard for disk storage today is around 4GB to 6GB, although I see that standard quickly pushing up to the 10GB, 12GB, 14GB, and 16GB ranges. More, more, more.

Video Card

The video card is sometimes overlooked, but it shouldn't be. It's the power behind the graphics you'll see (or won't see) on your PC's monitor. Today, most video cards have some sort of 3-D graphics accelerator; they'll give your CPU a boost when displaying intricate graphics to provide more life-like images. Video cards also sport different amounts of on-board memory to manage different amounts of colors and color depth. The standard is

4MB of video memory, but 8MB cards are fast claiming "standard" status. The most important point in considering the video card is to properly match it to the monitor you will use. Read on.

Monitor

Some people refer to the monitor as the "computer." You know different now, but the monitor can be just as important as the CPU in the overall performance of your home system. You'll find these in a variety of sizes: 15, 17, or 21 inches are the common choices for the home consumer. Understand, though, that the actual screen *viewing area* will be less than the monitor's advertised size—just as with televisions, screen dimensions are reported as a diagonal measurement. A 15" monitor works just fine, and a 17" will give you more on-screen real estate to work with. The 21" monitors can be somewhat overwhelming in their vast size and desk space consumption. The most important aspect of a monitor you'll need to consider is the resolution—the number of *pixels* it will display. A pixel is the individual point of resolution on your monitor. The more pixels you have, the better the resolution the monitor can deliver. For a 17" monitor, look for at least 1024×768 resolution. There's also another detail to consider: refresh rate (the rate at which the monitor continually repaints the display you see on the screen). Look for a refresh rate of at least 75Hz to 85Hz. Anything less and you'll get the flicker effect. Try not to get too cheap when buying your monitor and, by all means, avoid the no-name monitors. A good monitor will last you a long time. Preferably, you would be upgrading your CPU sooner than you would your monitor. And don't forget the important point of matching the monitor capability to the PC's video card capability, and vice versa.

And So On . . .

Of course, you're going to find many other hardware features when you shop for a PC. The points I've listed here are among the most important to consider as you make your decision. A system that follows the recommendations I've made will treat you quite well as you venture onto the Internet and especially as you spend time at eBay. I won't get into all the technically gory details here. If you want more information about choosing a PC and evaluating the different component options available to you, please refer to Appendix A for further resources.

Tip Don't forget Y2K. If you're planning on buying a new PC before the new millennium rolls around, be sure it's certified as "Y2K Compliant." (For that matter, be sure your current PC is set for the switchover.) This could affect operating systems (such as Windows 98), pre-loaded applications, and even CPU and memory specifications. Manufacturers have been working feverishly to ensure that their products will work reliably as the new year rolls in. Most PCs purchased within the past year or two have already been established and marketed as being Y2K compliant. Still, you'll want to be sure. Run a topic search of "Y2K" from any search engine (Yahoo!, Lycos, and so on) to find a wide assortment of Y2K-readiness sites from manufacturers and others, eager to help your PC ring in the new year without leaving you wringing your hands. Cheers!

Software That Isn't Hard

PC software is becoming ever more simple to use and even simpler to install—most of the software you'll need can be found already installed on new PCs, and most of the rest more or less installs itself at the click of a mouse. People have become accustomed to icons, buttons, and application windows. It's a great time to be using a PC because they're mainly designed for average Joes and Janes on the street.

There are tons of different applications out there for you to use and explore, but the ones described in the upcoming sections are likely to do most to enhance your eBay experience.

Operating System

Well, you can't do nuthin' without the operating system. This is the interface that communicates with the files and applications on your PC. You'll be most familiar with Windows 95, Windows 98, or Mac OS. They're all simple to use, and they're pretty much always loaded on a new PC you might purchase. There are too many features to mention here, but you're certain to be satisfied. They're very visual, very intuitive, and kind of fun. Some people prefer to use UNIX or Linux operating systems, which are quite powerful, but for the mainstream user and for the purposes of this book, I'll be showing you examples from a Windows 98 environment.

Word Processor

You'll have a lot to write, so you'll want a good word processing program. You'll need this to prepare any number of documents. For your eBay work, you'll probably need this to prepare templates for your auction listings, which will save you from having to recreate the wheel every time. I'll get more into creating auction listings in Part 4. But you'll probably find some basic word processing application installed on most home PCs today. Their features can be somewhat limited, and you may want to investigate upgrading to another application, available just about anywhere PCs or office supplies are sold. Today, I'm using Microsoft Word, and I'm quite happy with it.

Spreadsheet Application

Just like that bright little guy who kept track of his dad's cows in Lusk, Wyoming, you'll want some sort of spreadsheet tool to keep track of your auction activity. Depending on your anticipated level of activity on eBay, you'll probably want to track all the small but important details of the auctions you bid in and especially those where you are the seller. If you don't already have a spreadsheet application—some new PCs have them preloaded as part of an office suite, some don't—you'll need to go out and find one for yourself. The most common are Microsoft Excel, Corel Quattro Pro, and Lotus 1-2-3. Again, more detail about using spreadsheets for your eBay activity can be found in Part 4.

Image Editing

You don't have to be a graphic artist to make good use of an image editing application. You'll later learn how important images can be to your auction success. Image editors range widely in price, complexity, and capability. You can find very straightforward editors that will cost only about $50. If you're quite the graphic van Gogh, you can spend upwards of $500 on a very robust graphics application. Some new PCs are including copies of Microsoft Picture-It, which is a very direct point-and-click application. It won't do some things the more pricey applications will, but I've found it works just fine in a pinch. Also, you can find numerous image editors for free on the Internet—that is, you have a free trial period to test drive the software. Look for LviewPro or PaintShop Pro. They usually have trial versions (shareware) that you can download and use immediately. More on image editing in Part 4.

Picture This

Having just briefly mentioned image editing software, I should talk a bit about where the image you'll edit is going to come from. A picture is worth a thousand words—and on eBay, it might be worth a thousand bids! Pictures are going to be a key element of your auction success if you choose to sell items. I'll go into all the whys and what-fors in Part 4, but suffice it to say that a picture of an item is going to help potential bidders feel more comfortable with what they're bidding on. Pictures even attract bidders to bid on an item they might otherwise have passed by, and some bidders won't bid on an item at all if there isn't an accompanying picture. This said, you would be well advised to consider investing in some sort of image-capturing device—in simpler terms, a digital camera or a scanner.

It seems digital cameras are all the rage, and some people even wonder if the growing popularity and acceptance of digital cameras will pose a threat to the standard 35mm variety. Digital cameras are easy to use and, much as with image-editing software, you can find digital cameras with a variety of features spanning a wide range of prices. The real bonus of a digital camera is that you can easily photograph an item from any perspective and immediately upload the image to your PC and, ultimately, your eBay auction listing. Using an image editor to clean up the photo of your item, you can quickly and quite easily create some pretty nice auction listings. Digital cameras are being offered by a variety of different manufacturers, and you're certain to find one that fits your budget—figure on an average price of $300 to $500, though.

Another option is to use a scanner. The most common type you'll find today is the flatbed variety—the ones where you place an item on the glass and *scan* an image of it, picking up a digital representation in a process very much like using a conventional photocopier. Scanners often offer clearer images of your item than you can get with a cheap digital camera. Scanners, however, are limited in the size of their scanning area. I've seen many auctions where sellers will politely apologize that their scanner wasn't able to capture the entire item, or that several scans have been made and pasted together to create the representation of the whole item. Scanners are great for capturing high-quality images of flat items such as photos, posters, and so on (again with size being a potential constraint). However, the scanner fails to provide a three-dimensional image of an item. With the advent of the digital camera, image-capturing technology has found better mass market acceptance, making scanning technology cheaper at the same time. You'll be pleased to find scanners have become increasingly affordable. Many of the lower-end models can be found for $100 or less. The better midrange quality scanners can usually be purchased for about $200 to $300.

You can also use PC cameras that are designed to operate from the PC's keyboard and are typically mounted on the top of your monitor. Often, these are designed for telecommuting and video conferencing. However, you can use a PC camera to capture images of items you want to auction. The obvious drawback to this sort of camera is that it's not as portable as a digital camera. I don't find as many PC cameras available as I do digital cameras or scanners. If you want some pricing information, you'd do best to shop around the usual computer outlets or, hey, check the eBay listings.

Personally, I like to use both a digital camera and a scanner. The digital camera provides ease of use, portability, and the convenience of being able to capture images of items from various distances and angles. The scanner is superior to the digital camera for images of flat objects (scanners are really the best choice if you're selling autographs; you'll get the best digital reproduction of a signature that buyers will be able to inspect easily and closely). The ability to switch between the two devices will put you in a position to create and present images of almost any item.

 NOTE Well, at this point I don't expect you'd be eager to put me in the car and take me shopping with you. I realize that, by my recommendations so far, I've potentially spent a lot of your money. Remember, these are just recommendations. You don't need to follow them implicitly. And remember that hardware is getting cheaper by the day. I'll bet you can beat the prices I've noted here and leave me feeling like a high-paying stoop.

Choosing a Browser

No doubt you're quite aware of Web browsers. They're the application that allows you to surf the Web in a friendly, interactive way. The browser is designed to display each Web site you'll encounter in cyberspace. In fact, the Web is really just a series of individual documents, or *Web pages*, all linked together. The browser interprets each page, including any multimedia content such as sound files, images, or animations, and displays the whole thing for you to view as intended by the Web page author.

The two most popular browsers available today are Netscape Navigator and Microsoft Internet Explorer. It's estimated that 90 percent of all Internet users have one of these browsers. Although there is much controversy regarding how one browser might be trying to oust the other or how some users adamantly expound their browser of choice as the superior tool, there's really not much difference between the two. If you can use one, you can pretty much use the other. It's all a matter of personal preference.

Regardless of any struggles for market dominance or the building of cybernetic empires, the nice thing about the two browsers mentioned here is that they're free! You'll find you can get free browser software in several ways: it might come installed on a PC, it might be provided free when you choose an Internet connection service, or you can download it (including subsequent upgrades) from the Netscape and Microsoft Web sites. Not a bad deal. And you're always free to change to a different browser or use both in conjunction with each other. Just tune out the industry chatter and pick the one you like best.

 NOTE For the content of this book, I will be using Netscape Navigator 4.6. Appendix A will direct you to additional resources to help you better understand the use of this browser.

Connect!

Well, if you've been staying with me up to this point and have all your hardware and software in place, you're pretty much all dressed up but with no place to go . . . yet. The final element you'll need for your tour of the Internet and World Wide Web will be the actual connection itself. Once you're connected, a whole new world awaits you on the other side of your monitor screen.

Getting connected to the Internet is truly a simple task. All you need is a regular telephone line and an *Internet service provider* (*ISP*). What's an ISP? This is a company—either national or local—that has a whole series of powerful servers that run day and night to route incoming access requests and data transmissions to and from the Web and your PC. The ISP has to cover the overhead for installing and maintaining these high-powered servers, so it will charge you a regular fee for using its equipment. ISPs can be large national providers (America Online, Prodigy, CompuServe, Microsoft Network) or smaller local providers that you'll find in your local region. The major differences among providers are features offered, price of the service, availability and reliability of the service, and customer support. The biggest key, though, is how you will be charged for Internet access—a flat rate with unlimited usage or a flat rate with metered (incremental cost) usage. If you plan on spending a lot of time online (and it's easier to clock up the hours than you think), you should seek a provider that offers unmetered (unlimited) connection time at a flat rate. With Internet capabilities and use on the rise, most providers offer a flat-rate unmetered service. On average, you can expect to pay about $20 a month for a regular active and unmetered connection to the Internet.

The other key point to consider about the ISP you choose is the phone call you'll make to access its servers. Be certain the connection you make will be a local call—watch out for long-distance calls or toll calls that will make your phone bill go where no bill has gone before. Ask the ISP if it has local numbers for your area. That way, it will be just another local call, avoiding hiked-up charges.

I use a local provider because it's cheap, easy, and meets my needs. Most local providers, being in fierce competition with other providers, offer 30-day money-back trial periods. You can use the service for a month and, if you're not satisfied or just not using the Net the way you thought you might, you can cancel your account with the ISP and receive a refund. This allows you to shop around and test drive the different providers until you find the one that meets your needs. However, if you're on the road a lot and might need to access the Net from a variety of locations—which means you might need to bid on that auction from some hotel room—then you'll be better off subscribing to one of the national providers I mentioned earlier. The national providers will allow you to dial into their servers as a local call from anywhere in the nation whereas dialing into a local ISP from a different geographic area will incur a long-distance charge. (Just to add to the options, some local ISPs offer "roaming" privileges—local numbers in other parts of the country that you can use to access their services. Before you dismiss a local provider because you're planning to travel, see if it will let you dial in from your destination.)

And, to bring your eBay auction concerns into the picture, you'll want to be sure you can find an ISP that is easy to connect to and will provide a reliable connection for you to use. Some ISPs might have too few phone lines connecting to their servers, and you might encounter frequent busy signals if the lines are tied up by other customers. Also, if the service isn't providing some sort of consistent reliability, you might find your connection is dropped (meaning the server disconnects you) without warning. Since the auctions at eBay operate on a time schedule, being unable to access the site or getting dumped off it from a broken connection will surely cause you to miss out on auctions that are ready to close. This makes for a grumpy bidder or seller, so don't be bashful about shopping those ISPs and asking them the tough questions about why they're better than the ISP down the block.

Free Samples

Just like when you walk through those big warehouse stores and sample the munchies from the different vendors, you can also pick up some nice freebies on the Web. Since the Web has become a multimedia paradise, you'll probably want to look into sampling some of the free and trial software that is ready for the taking. Since there are so many free packages for you to try, I won't even begin to list them all. For a good start, visit **www. download.com**, **www.moochers.com**, or **www.tucows.com**. It's OK to download free software provided the programs have been intended as *freeware* or *shareware*. If you're visiting Macks Software Shack at **www.youcantproveit.com**, be careful. If you're offered a fully functional program that usually has to be purchased, and if you're offered a key code to unlock it, it's probably a pirated copy. Beware!

Some of the freebies you'll find might not necessarily enhance your eBay experience, but they're worth mentioning just because they're free!

 NOTE Hey. If you want to find more freebies that aren't just software related, visit **www.free.com**. You'll find tons of free stuff from all over the place. I like free stuff.

Thumbing a Ride Without Thumbing Your Nose

OK, at the beginning of this chapter I promised you alternative ways of connecting to the Net assuming you don't have a PC of your own. You can hitch a free ride on the Net a few different ways. Just because you don't currently own a PC is no reason to pooh-pooh the potential of online auctions or assume you can't still get into the action. Consider some of the following alternatives.

First, if you're a student, your college should have some sort of student union that maintains active access to the Internet. Institutions of higher education have recognized the vast potential for research offered by the Internet, and are therefore ensuring the open availability of PCs that you can use to surf the Web.

Second, you can also check with your local public library. Again, since a library is a repository of knowledge and information, access to the Internet is practically required for the institution to be worthy of its title. Just be sure to keep your outbursts of "I won!" down to a whisper.

Some housing communities and retirement communities might also have a center where open PCs are available for community members' use. You could look there for an opportunity to connect up for free.

How about those cyber cafés where you can get a cup of mocha and download the latest in overdyed hairstyles? These places are becoming quite popular, and you're allowed to do other things besides just downloading dirty pictures from their PCs.

And how about where you work? Most companies today use PCs connected to a local area network (LAN) to allow intracompany communication and electronic business. Chances are, your company's server is connected to the Internet, again due to the vast amounts of useful information it offers. For safety and security reasons, your company's server is probably behind a *firewall*, which is a mechanism that prevents any unauthorized access or content from outside the company (like hackers or spam) from getting in. If a certain kind of activity is off limits to company personnel, the firewall can also prevent undesirable content (like FTP sites or streaming video, which can be real resource hogs or could contain mischievous or inappropriate content) from being accessed, retrieved, and returned to the company's servers. It's like having that *Dating Game* chaperone sitting between you and your date, making sure your requests and advances are noble and condoned. If not, you'll get a slap on the hand.

The other roadblock you might find when using a company's Web server is the proxy server. *Proxies* act as go-between servers that receive Web requests from inside a company and pass them along to the Web. The proxy, being detached from the main company servers, gives the appearance that only a single server is in use within the company. Is that a big deal? Sure. Competitors and others would love to know what a company's infrastructure looks like and possibly what kind of data is on the *real servers*. The proxy server is a facade of sorts that camouflages the real scope of the infrastructure or information used within the company.

Luckily, a site like eBay doesn't end up on company server blacklists and should be accessible. As a word of advice, though—be sure your company allows access to the Net by use of its equipment. Avoid excessive surfing when you should be working and, by all means, stay away from any objectionable or prohibited sites while using company equipment (you know the ones I mean).

These are all methods to cruise the Web and even access eBay without having to invest in your own equipment and connection. The downside of these alternatives, though, is you will need to use the hardware and software configurations that have been established on these PCs. Also, in public places, you might have difficulty getting to use a PC because somebody else got to it first. Again, with the time factor involved in auctions, you might not be able to get in on some bidding if you can't get to a PC when you need to.

How 'Bout My TV?

Yeah, how 'bout that? You've probably heard much about the PC alternative known as *Internet TV*. Can this work for auction action at eBay? Absolutely. In fact, many regular eBay users are using Internet TV services for their auction activity.

Internet TV is an alternative in which you actually use your television set as the monitor and access and surf the Net through a special Internet TV console and keyboard. They're kind of reminiscent of those old Commodore 64 units. (Remember those?)

Internet TV units are currently being served by NetLink, Web-I, and WebTV. They're pretty easy to use. Just connect a couple of wires from the unit to your TV, hook into an available phone jack, and you're ready to go.

There are a few drawbacks in regard to the types of software applications provided with the Internet TV units, so you should fully test a unit at the retailer before you decide to buy. However, you'll find that these units are far less expensive than an actual PC. Just don't tie up the TV when the family wants to watch *Leave It to Beaver* reruns.

A Final Thought

While the recommendations I've suggested here are clearly not top of the line or state of the art, there is a price tag involved. However, it's an investment that is sure to pay off. If not at eBay alone, you'll see the payoff of your investment in other areas of the Web. Only you can decide what will be best for you as only you know how you intend to use the Web and eBay. But don't be surprised if you get in and soon find you're eager to upgrade your equipment. It's happened to all of us. The nice thing, though, is that much of the hardware, software, and other accessories I've mentioned in this chapter can actually be found up for bid at eBay. How convenient, huh? Maybe you can get a good deal.

chapter 6

Welcome to eBay

At last! You're here. Isn't it exciting? Well, maybe not just yet because I haven't shown you around. But take my word for it, it *is* exciting, and I'm excited to tell you about it.

Welcome to eBay—a veritable hub of online excitement. I'll show you around the site's home page so you can become familiar with the look and feel of eBay. I'll teach you about the different areas you can go within eBay, and how to recognize the different icons that will become a mainstay of your continuing eBay experience.

There's really a lot more at eBay than *just* auctions. Wait until you see some of the neat features that are available to registered community members. And, before you're done here, you'll be registered as a full-fledged eBay community member. It's fun, it's easy, and it's the only way to play. Let's go!

Accessing the Web Site

Well, this is pretty straightforward: in your browser's location bar, type in **www.ebay.com**—the URL, or Internet address, for the site. Press Enter, and you'll soon find the browser window's title bar displaying *eBay—Your Personal Trading Community.* You've arrived!

One thing you'll notice about the site is that you don't have to enter a password, enable any special Java scripts, or go through other such delays. eBay is a friendly, easy-to-use site, and it's free for all to drop by and look around. When the page has finished loading, you'll see a display much like the one shown in Figure 6-1.

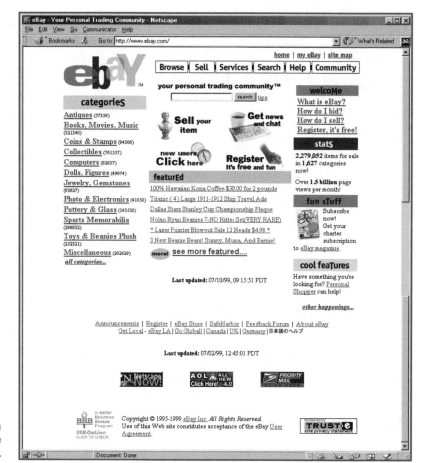

figure 6-1

The eBay home page offers a great layout with easy-to-use icons and navigation bars.

The eBay Home Page

As you look at the eBay home page, you'll see a variety of different displays, icons, and hyperlinked text. It's not uncommon to see the home page content change slightly from visit to visit—maybe some statistics will be updated or a timely topic will be featured to catch your attention. eBay is a dynamic site that strives to keep pace with events online and offline, but the key working elements you'll find on the home page are as follows:

- **Mini Navigation Bar.** A collection of three links at the very top right-hand side of the home page. This mini "navbar" will actually appear on every page within the eBay site to give you fast access to these useful links:

  - *Home.* As the name suggests, this link will take you to the eBay home page, which will look much like what you see in Figure 6-1.

  - *My eBay.* Perhaps one of the most-liked features of the site, *my eBay* is a great tool for users to keep track of their eBay activities such as what they're selling, what they're bidding on, and what is the status of their active eBay account. I'll show you more of *my eBay* a bit later in this chapter.

  - *Site map.* A quick view of the different areas and services available on eBay, all easily accessible through an exhaustive offering of hyperlinks.

- **Main Navigation Bar.** The set of boxlike links at the top of the page just below the mini navigation bar. These are your keys to the site, and you'll see this main navigation bar on every eBay page. Here, you'll find the following quick links:

  - *Browse.* Takes you to the eye-popping assortment of category listings and groupings of items up for auction. If you just want to stroll the virtual aisles to see what catches your eye, this is the link for you.

- *Sell.* Takes you directly to the *Sell Your Item* page where you can begin hawking your treasures to the eBay community.

- *Services.* Takes you to an area where you can learn about eBay's policies and programs that will enable and enhance your buying and selling activities.

- *Search.* Takes you to eBay's powerful site search page where you can look for items in a variety of useful ways.

- *Help.* eBay is big on help, and here you'll find links to specific topics that can and will answer most of your questions.

- *Community.* eBay is a community and provides special areas for community members to learn more about new site developments as well as chat places for members to meet and discuss topics of common interest.

A nice addition to the main navigation bar is the set of *sub-navigation bars* that will appear when you use one of the links just described. Figure 6-2 shows you how the sub-navigation bar can give you further quick access to the eBay features you'll be using time and again.

- **Search Field**. Just below the home page toolbar, you'll see the text box labeled *Search*, and it does just that. From the home page, you can enter an immediate search based on the title of an item you're looking for. You'll be a search expert after you read all the details in Chapter 7.

- **Quick Icons**. Just below the Search field, you'll see a set of four quick icons that you can use to easily branch to high-use site features.

  - *Sell your item.* Takes you to the page where sellers list items that they want to auction.

figure 6-2

Sub-navigation bars offer helpful links related to the eBay feature or service you've chosen.

Browse	Sell	Services	Search	Help	Community

| overview | registration | buying & selling | my eBay | about me | feedback forum | safe harbor |

- *Get news and chat.* Takes you to the same areas that you reach by using the *Community* link from the main navigation bar.

- *New users click here.* Takes you to a help area specially designed to get new users up to speed and in the game. It's an area that's full of links and information designed to help new users learn more about the eBay experience.

- *Register. It's free and fun.* Takes you to eBay's registration page so you can become a full-fledged community member yourself.

■ **Categories**. Well, this is what it's all about: stuff. When you see the *Categories* heading on the home page, it's the launching area to the aggregate groupings of things up for auction. Choose any of the category headings and you'll whisk away to more granular subheadings that help you zero in on what it is you'll want to bid on. By the way, the little number in parentheses you see next to each category subheading is the number of active auctions currently running in that grouping. Pretty impressive, huh?

■ **Featured**. This area lists the featured auctions, of course. Some sellers pay extra to have their items listed in the special Featured category for increased visibility. Items with featured status can be reached from any of the different auction item categories.

■ **Welcome**. Moving over to the right-hand side of the home page, you'll find your red carpet into the eBay site. The links under the *Welcome* banner will get you quick answers to what you want to know. As I said, eBay is big on help and you'll find a big helping of it through the Welcome links.

■ **Stats**. If you like numbers, you'll love these. eBay frequently posts the site statistics for all visitors to see and marvel at. At a glance, you'll see the volume of items up for bid, the total number of bids received since eBay began, and so forth. If you're new to the site, Stats will help you quickly see why eBay is such a desirable place to buy or sell. If you're a long-time community member, it's always fun to see how the site's statistics continue to shoot up and up (and, trust me, they do).

- **Fun Stuff**. This little area calls your attention to special events, offers, or happenings on eBay. You might find holiday activities, charity events, or special deals offered to registered eBay members.

- **Cool Features and Other Happenings**. As you see in Figure 6-1, *Cool Features* is a heading that will call your attention to some of the neat things eBay has to offer, while *Other happenings* will lead you to the rest of eBay's deals and special goodies. Expect to see the features on this right-hand side of the eBay home page change to keep pace with events and features that will be of interest to community members.

- **Additional links**. Below the Featured area, you'll find additional links such as *Announcements, SafeHarbor, About eBay,* and so on. These are just some more useful links to quickly and easily access other areas of interest and information.

- **Endorsed links**. You'll find useful icon links to other organizations that eBay endorses or has partnered with and that are useful to eBay community members.

- **Copyright**. Of course, the eBay site content is fully copyrighted and cannot be used without express permission from eBay. In this copyright area (you're scrolling down, right?), you'll also find a link to the terms of the eBay User Agreement. I'll cover that a little later in this chapter.

 NOTE   Just so you won't think you're going nuts, remember that some of the content on the eBay home page might change each time you visit. The features I've described will be there sometimes; other times they won't. Ahh, variety.

New to eBay?

When you click on the *New users click here* icon from the eBay home page, you'll jump to the *Help Basics* page. Once there, you'll find two particularly useful links: *What is eBay?* and *Welcome Wagon*. The first link explains to newcomers what eBay is all about and shares its community values with those eager to join in the fun. The second link—Welcome Wagon—is where eBay shares more of its goals and philosophies about the site. You will be welcomed to the site and given a quick overview of what's in store.

The Help Basics page goes on to provide a wide assortment of links that explain commonly used terms, answer frequently asked questions (FAQs), provide access to the user help chat areas, and explain the different activities and situations you might encounter when signing up and using eBay. A nice bonus feature is the inclusion of a *help search* field. If you have a specific question and don't know where to find the answer on eBay (perhaps *"What is sniping?"*), use the help search to find the area where eBay has your answer. Further, if you're still not getting the answers you need, eBay invites you to contact its support staff directly via a special link, *Ask eBay*. I told you the folks there were big on help.

The eBay New User Tutorial

Since many people do better with pictures than with words, eBay offers a well-designed new user tutorial that covers the key aspects of using the site. From the *Help Basics* page, you'll find a collection of tutorials that provide screen captures to follow along with as you learn how to use the site (see Figure 6-3).

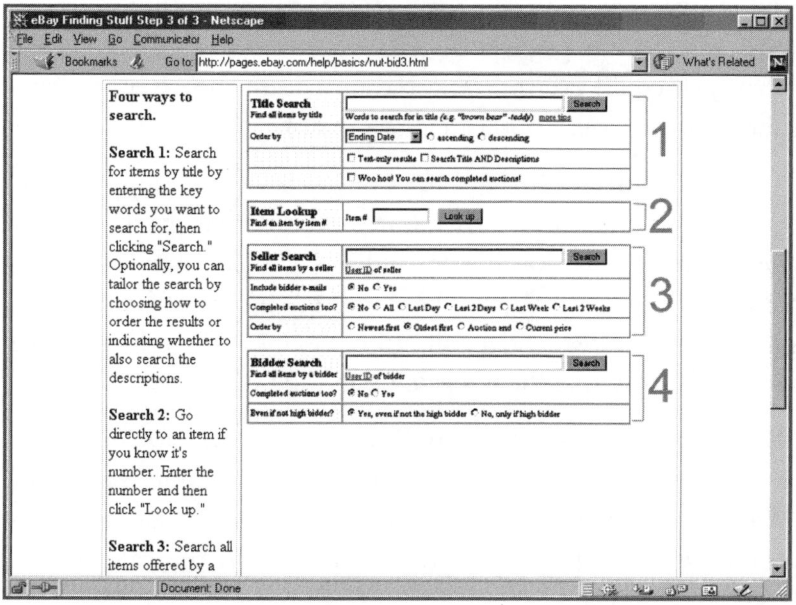

figure 6-3

Here's a tutorial example that shows new users how to search for items up for bid.

eBay's tutorials break down the basics of eBay registering, searching for items, bidding, selling, and using images in auction listings. Each tutorial has screen captures and helpful text describing a different topic of interest. If you go through all the tutorials, you'll have a pretty good idea how to participate in the various eBay auction activities. There is no diploma at the end, but the self-satisfaction you'll have is far more valuable.

ALERT Just like the eBay home page, the rest of the site is continually on the move, and the tutorials don't always keep up. If you go through the eBay tutorial, don't panic if the screen examples you see don't exactly match up to the live screens on the site.

NOTE The information you'll find in the eBay tutorials is already covered in this book. Still, the tutorials are useful and, if you have the time, it's good to go through them.

The Auction Listings

Well, this is pretty much the heart and soul of what eBay is all about: the stuff up for bid. As you read in Part 1, there are more than two million items up for auction at eBay at any given time. That's a bunch of stuff! You'll find more items than you could ever possibly bid on within the extensive categories and subcategories (over 1600 categories in all).

To get started with the auction listings, click on *Browse* from the main navigation bar or click on the home page's *Categories* title bar. Both of these links will take you to the auction listings index page. Give the Categories page a moment or two to load; it's crunching through those 1600 categories, establishing links to nearly two and a half million items. When the page has loaded, you'll see a display like the one shown in Figure 6-4.

Figure 6-4 shows less than half of the 1600-plus categories. You'll need to scroll on down the page to see the complete offerings. Aye Caramba! What a gold mine! Much like the Categories area on the eBay home page, each category on the listings index page notes the total items in the category (in

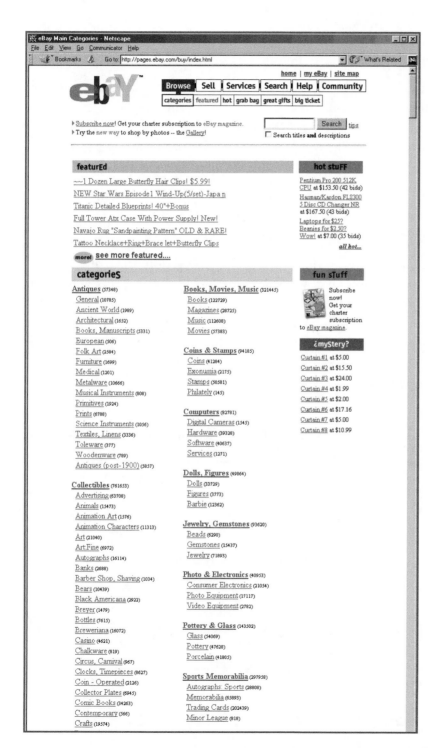

figure 6-4

And there they are: your links to almost 2.5 million items up for bid at eBay—and this is only a portion of the list! Surely you'll find something that interests you.

parentheses to the right of the category title) as well as how many items you can find in each subcategory.

If you want to look at the items up for auction in any subcategory, just click on a link that interests you. How about trying the subcategory *Digital Cameras* within the major category *Computers*? Maybe you can get a good deal on a digital camera. When you choose the Digital Cameras subcategory, you're off to the listings currently available there (see Figure 6-5).

Once in a subcategory, you're free to review the titles of the different items that you might want to bid on. But what is all that information in the listing page? Take a closer look at Figure 6-5.

First, at the top of the page you'll see the eBay navigation bars that appear on every eBay page. Below that, you'll see a handy search field that allows you to search for items with specific words in their title. You can choose to search all of eBay or just the category you are currently sitting in by using the check boxes you saw earlier in the window below the search field. With this search, you can also decide if you want to search item titles or include a search within the item descriptions. More on search methods in Chapter 7.

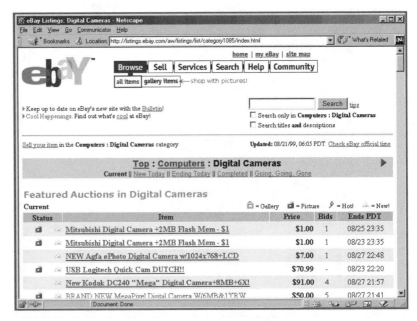

figure 6-5

Each subcategory on eBay shows the individual listings of items currently up for bid in that area.

Do you see the link titled *Sell your item?* This is a quick link for sellers to list an item within this category. It's a fast way to start listing that special item that would do well in the category you're looking at. I'll cover listing and selling in more detail in Part 4.

Next on the page is the category title bar; it tells you which category and subcategory you're reviewing. Below the category title bar are some very useful links that help narrow your view based on current listing status (for example, *New Today, Ending Today,* and so on). This, too, will be explained in Chapter 7.

The next category title bar you'll see tells you what sublisting of items you're viewing. As shown in Figure 6-5, the items you see are in the *Featured Auctions* category. These will be the first items you see in any item category and subcategory. The sellers paid some extra money to have their items classified as "featured," so they get the added benefit of seeing their items show up at the beginning of the category and subcategory pages.

Now look at the elements of each item line. First, you see the *Status* of the item—*Gallery, Hot, Picture,* or *New*—indicated by the cute little icons. If it's a new item (listed within the last 24 hours), then it will be shown with the ☀ icon. If the item has received more than 30 bids, it will be considered a hot item (that is, very popular among bidders) and will have the 🔥 icon displayed with it. If the seller has included a picture with the listing, you'll see the 📷 icon displayed at the far right of the item description. This is a real draw to potential bidders, which I'll explain further in Part 4. Finally, the 📷 indicates the seller chose to have that item featured in eBay's picture gallery (more on that later).

After the fun little icons comes the title of the item. The seller creates the item title, carefully wording it in a way that will draw attention and persuade someone to look and bid. Item descriptions are limited to 45 characters so they'll need to be used wisely.

Still moving along, across to the right, the next information you see is the current high bid for the item, noted as *Price*. To the right of that, you'll see the number of bids that have been placed on an item. Finally, you'll see the ending date and time of the auction. The time is always displayed in Pacific (West Coast) time since eBay is located in California. Cowabunga!

NOTE To be sure your watch is properly synchronized with eBay's clock, click on the text link titled *Check eBay official time* that you'll find at the bottom of every listing page.

TIP Be aware that the high bid and number of bidders shown on the item listing page might be out of date. The listing pages are updated periodically, not instantly. You might see a certain high bid price and number of bids on the listing page and later discover that on the Item Details page the high bid might be higher with more bids actually having been placed.

If you scroll past the featured items in the category you're viewing, you'll find the regular listing of available items under the category heading. For this example, you'll find *Current Items in Digital Cameras*. The listings are always presented in descending date order—that is, you'll find the most recent listings first. The items whose auctions will be closing very soon will be on the last pages of the category listings.

Notice to the right of the *Current Items* heading is a page counter. Figure 6-6 shows the counter for this example.

Use the *Next page* link to view the successive pages of listings available in the category you're browsing. Another way would be to find the page counter at the end of the *Current Items* page you're viewing. It will provide links that allow you to jump anywhere within the collection of listing pages and looks

figure 6-6

For this example, the page counter shows a total of thirty-one pages of digital camera listings to browse through.

eBay Listings: Digital Cameras - Netscape					
File Edit View Go Communicator Help					
Bookmarks Location: http://listings.ebay.com/aw/listings/list/category1085/index.html				What's Related	
Items in Digital Cameras			You are on page **1** of 36. Next Page ►		
Current			= Gallery = Picture = Hot! = New!		
Status	**Item**		**Price**	**Bids**	**Ends PDT**
	Nikon CoolPix 950 New in Box***No Reserve***		$500.00	-	08/24 05:36
	SUPER 3-day Relisys Digital Camera + EXTRAS!!		$1.00	-	08/24 04:25

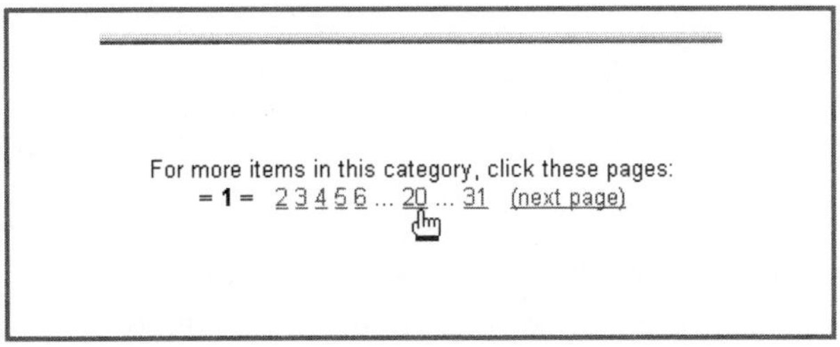

For more items in this category, click these pages:
= 1 = 2 3 4 5 6 ... 20 ... 31 (next page)

figure 6-7

Use these page counter links to randomly jump through the pages of a category listing.

like what you see in Figure 6-7. Often, you'll find some category and sub-category listings that go beyond 100 pages!

TIP Remember, the listings are sorted in descending date order. If you want to quickly get to the listings that are about to close, jump to the last page or two of listings. They're going...going...gone!

Finally, near the end of the first page of a category's listings, you'll find the group of all hot items listed. Because hot items have had more than 30 bids received, they get special recognition on the first page of each category listing.

Now that you know more about what the listings mean as well as how to get to them, feel free to settle back in your chair and start shopping. There's a lot to see, and I can practically guarantee you'll find something you'll want to bid on the first time you use the site.

NOTE In the next chapter, I'll give you some good tips on how to use the auction categories and listing titles to find the things that really interest you. For this chapter, you just need to understand the layout and content of the category and listing pages. Of course, I don't profess to be able to keep you from searching for things right now. It's OK if you do. I'll still be here when you come back.

Get Local or Go Global

Like I said, eBay has become the worldwide meeting place for folks who want to buy and sell just about anything. However, some community members want to "parse the world" a bit as needed. For example, some members would choose to only bid on items that are in their local area, saving postage costs or avoiding currency conversion situations. Some members are looking for worldwide domination with their auctions, but want assistance in reaching the other side of the globe.

eBay has stepped up to the plate for both these scenarios by introducing *regional services* that assist community members wherever they are and wherever they wish to buy and sell. As this book goes to press, eBay has successfully launched and is operating *eBay L.A.,* which is where buyers and sellers from the Los Angeles area can meet and trade within their own geographic community (of course, anyone can pop in to trade there, too).

On the global end, eBay has launched their *Go Global!* initiative, an acknowledgment that eBay has drawn community members from over 50 countries. eBay has successfully started up eBay Canada, eBay U.K., eBay Germany (actually an acquisition of the German *Alando* auction site), and eBay Japan. Again, the expressed goal is to allow community members meet and trade in their particular regions, time zones, and currencies.

If you want to learn more about what eBay is doing to global trading, spend some time at the *Go Global!* page (find it in a link at the bottom of the home page), and open your eyes to world around you.

eBay Extras: Additional User Features

As you can see, eBay has grown to include more than just auction listings. Remember, eBay is very committed to the sense of community at its site. To prove it, eBay has some additional features that help users become more involved in their online community and share their common interests with other community members. You can get to any of the special feature areas by clicking on the *Services* selection from the main navigation bar.

About Me

Actually, it's about *you.* This is a neat feature that eBay has recently added. Each registered eBay user is invited to put together a simple on-site personal Web page. They can share who they are, what hobbies interest them, and maybe what sorts of items they are searching for. eBay provides an easy-to-use form-style setup page to make the creation of About Me pages simple and fun. When an eBay user has completed an About Me page, a special icon will appear next to their name everywhere on the site; it looks like this:

me

My eBay

This is a useful tool to help you review your activity while on eBay. As mentioned before, you can get to it immediately via the link on the mini navbar. With My eBay, you can review the auctions you've bid in as well as the auctions you've conducted yourself. You can choose the period of time you wish to review—you can even choose to see all activity since the time you first joined eBay. This tool also helps you quickly review your feedback rating and individual comments. Many long-time eBay community members swear by this tool—some swear at it when it's not available, which has happened in the recent past: eBay worked frantically to beef up their hardware and software to accommodate the millions of new users frequenting the site. The my eBay function was temporarily disabled leaving many users temporarily dismayed. That situation seems to be resolved now.

Virtual Bulletin Boards

Grab your java and enjoy the chatter. eBay provides a whole host of different bulletin boards for you to read and also post your own messages—they're really chat rooms. You'll find the eBay Cafe (great for idle chit-chat), the eBay Announcements board (learn about the latest developments at the site), the Discuss eBay's Newest Features board (where the discussion gets quite lively) and the Wanted Board (see if someone is hunting for that, er, unique item you're looking to get rid of). These are just some of the bulletin boards and chat rooms you'll find at eBay. There is also an entire series of category-specific chat spaces for community members to swap stories and compare notes specific to their areas of interest. All the bulletin boards can be found under *Community* link from the main navigation bar, then *chat* on the sub-navigation bar.

The eBay Store

If you're one of the proud community members, then you'll want to stop by the eBay Store and buy a few items that show others you're a full-blooded *eBaysian*. You'll find eBay T-shirts, sweatshirts, coffee mugs, and more. Stop by and grab your official eBay garb.

Getting Registered

Well, are you ready to register now? As you can see, eBay has a lot to offer. It's already a fun place, and you haven't even started bidding yet. Of course, before you can bid (or sell) you'll need to get registered. Here's how to do it.

First, it's a good idea to read the eBay User Agreement. You can find it on the home page at the bottom; it's the link labeled *User Agreement*. eBay strongly encourages all users to read and understand the agreement before they register. It's a lot to read, but you'll understand your responsibilities and eBay's responsibilities as you get into the buying and selling activity.

After you've read the User Agreement, read eBay's Privacy Policy. You can find it by clicking on the *Help* link on the main navigation bar, and then choosing Community Standards from the sub-navigation bar—or just click on the TRUSTe link from the bottom of any page. The Privacy Policy explains how eBay uses and does not use the information you provide as an eBay community member. Again, this is good information for you to understand before you register.

Once you've read all the fine print, go back to the eBay home page and click on the *Register. It's free and fun* icon in the middle of the page. This starts your registration process and gets you closer to joining in the auction fun.

The first registration screen you'll see will ask you for the country you live in. Select your country from the list and click on the push button labeled *Begin the registration process now* (see Figure 6-8).

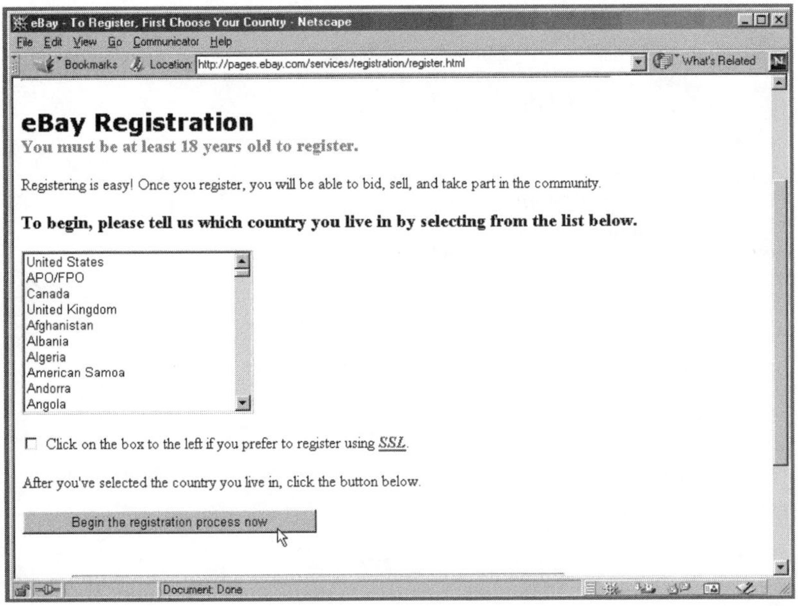
eBay - To Register, First Choose Your Country - Netscape
File Edit View Go Communicator Help
Bookmarks Location: http://pages.ebay.com/services/registration/register.html
What's Related
eBay Registration
You must be at least 18 years old to register.
Registering is easy! Once you register, you will be able to bid, sell, and take part in the community.
To begin, please tell us which country you live in by selecting from the list below.
United States
APO/FPO
Canada
United Kingdom
Afghanistan
Albania
Algeria
American Samoa
Andorra
Angola
Click on the box to the left if you prefer to register using SSL.
After you've selected the country you live in, click the button below.
Begin the registration process now
Document: Done

figure 6-8

The first step to becoming a registered user is to let eBay know what country you're from.

ALERT Present your ID at the door! Remember, by eBay's rules, all users must be at least 18 years old to register.

The next screen you'll see confirms the country you've selected (by a flag icon in the title bar) and gives you an overview of the steps necessary to become registered. Read this information and proceed (see Figure 6-9).

First, fill out the required registration information as prompted in the screen shown in Figure 6-10.

Then, if you choose, you can fill out the optional information form that will help eBay understand a little more about you, your interests, and how you found eBay (see Figure 6-11).

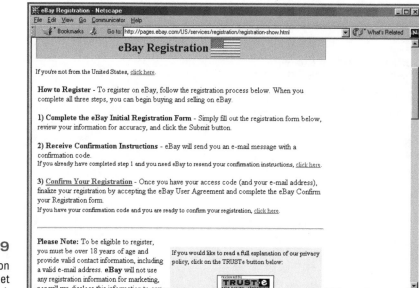

figure 6-9

Read the eBay registration steps and move along to get yourself registered.

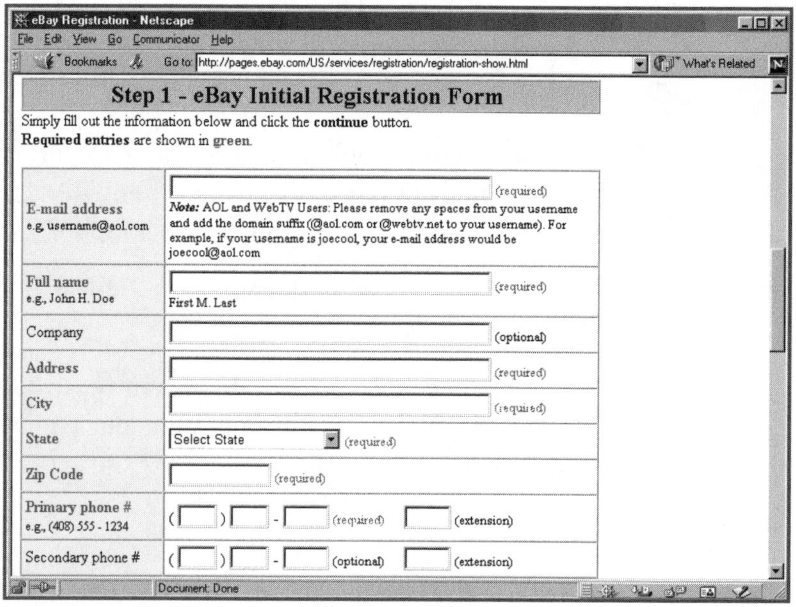

figure 6-10

The required information helps eBay determine who you are and how its staff and other community members will be able to contact you.

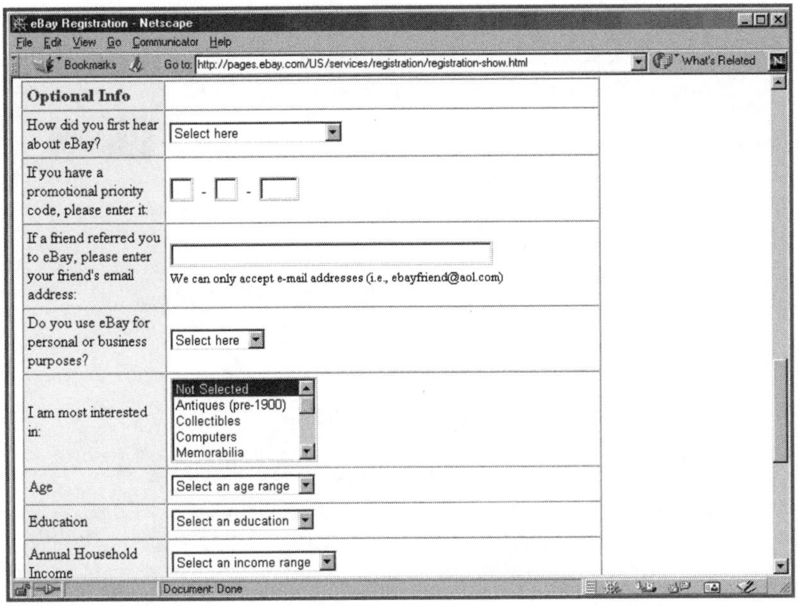

figure 6-11

The optional information is just that—optional. Fill it out if you like, but it's not absolutely necessary.

When all your information has been entered in the initial registration forms, click on the *Continue* button to proceed. From here, eBay will let you confirm the information you provided and submit your initial registration request. Upon doing so, you've completed Step 1 of the registration process.

Notice that it's an *initial* registration request. eBay will validate the information you've sent—mainly to verify the e-mail address and also to assure you're not creating a duplicate registration ID—and will send a confirmation message to the e-mail address you specified. That message will have your personal confirmation code. This is Step 2 of the registration process.

When you receive the confirmation message, return to the eBay Site Map from the mini navigation bar link and click on the *Confirm New Registration* link under the Registration heading. When you do, you'll jump to the *Confirm Your Registration* screen and the eBay *User Agreement* (see Figure 6-12).

Yes, you'll need to give the eBay User Agreement one last read and verification before you take the final steps to becoming registered. Don't scoff. This is what makes the community the well-mannered (mostly) place it is. Read

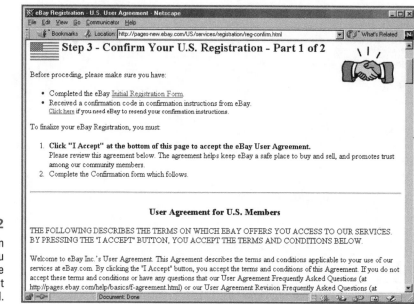

figure 6-12

Confirming your registration is the last step before you become fully signed up. You're getting excited aren't you? But first, some more stuff to read.

the full agreement and click on the *I Accept* button at the bottom of the screen. Of course, if you change your mind at this point, you can click on the *I Decline* button, but why?

And the last screen you'll see, which marks the last step in the registration process, is where you'll establish your official eBay user ID and password (see Figure 6-13).

NOTE The user ID isn't necessary; it's actually a way for you to identify yourself at eBay without using your e-mail address. If you don't choose a user ID, then every time you appear on an eBay auction—buying or selling—you'll be identified by your verified e-mail address. Some people prefer not to have their e-mail address so visible, especially to nonregistered users who are free to drop by the site and look around all they like. eBay created the user ID as a way of helping members protect their e-mail address from every Tom, Dick, and Mary.

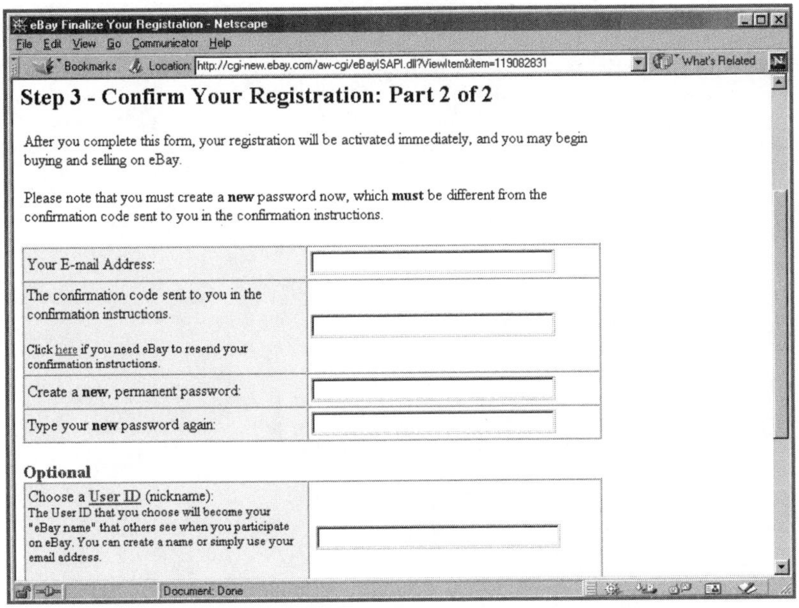

Step 3 - Confirm Your Registration: Part 2 of 2

After you complete this form, your registration will be activated immediately, and you may begin buying and selling on eBay.

Please note that you must create a **new** password now, which **must** be different from the confirmation code sent to you in the confirmation instructions.

Your E-mail Address:	
The confirmation code sent to you in the confirmation instructions. Click here if you need eBay to resend your confirmation instructions.	
Create a **new**, permanent password:	
Type your **new** password again:	

Optional

Choose a User ID (nickname): The User ID that you choose will become your "eBay name" that others see when you participate on eBay. You can create a name or simply use your email address.	

figure 6-13

Create your eBay identity, and you're ready to rock 'n' roll.

All that's left to do is fill out the required fields, the optional user ID field, and click on the *Complete your registration* button. Faster than you can say "I wanna join," you're in and ready to start bidding and selling. Welcome. The community is anxious to meet you.

TIP I know you're eager to get started, and I won't delay you from seeing the eBay sights. However, now that you're a registered user, you should know there are a host of special services and features just for you. Whenever you can tear yourself away from the auction listings, go back to the Site Map and spend some time looking through the many links you'll find there. You'll learn how to manage your registered information (user ID, password, and e-mail address), how to contact other registered users you might want to deal with, and a ton of other useful information that will make your eBay experience all the better.

chapter 7

Searching for Items

Who's up for a treasure hunt?

There are so many items up for auction at eBay that it's really like a virtual treasure hunt. In those millions of active auctions, you're sure to find some peculiar piece that you'd like to claim as your own. And eBay's much like one of those clearance stores around town—the inventory changes every week (well, at eBay it can actually change every day).

The key to unlocking the potential of eBay's auctions is knowing how to find the things you're looking for, and knowing that some things will actually find you. If you're looking for a different kind of online interaction, then this is the place.

For more fun, follow along in the actual eBay site while reading this chapter. If you don't have the hardware or the ISP connection set up yet, that's OK; the pictures in this chapter will show you the on-screen action I'll be describing.

Now it's time to go find some cool stuff.

Viewing Featured Items from the eBay Home Page

I'll start with the most direct way to find items up for auction. On the eBay home page, you saw the title bar *Featured* and a sampling of a few of the featured auctions active on eBay. You can click on any of those items you see listed for more details, or you can click on the *see more featured* link to see even more featured item listings. Trust me; there's a bunch (see Figure 7-1).

 TIP Clicking on the *Featured* title bar from the home page will give the same result as clicking on the *see more featured* link.

When you choose to see the featured listings, eBay will display an amazingly lengthy list of items. Why are these items featured? Because the sellers wanted them to be. Any item can be designated as a featured item at the time the seller lists it for auction. So why aren't all 2.5 million active items featured? Simple. eBay charges an additional $99.95 at the time the seller lists the item to have it located in the featured listings. Yep. It's the old adage of location, location, location, and prime real estate on the eBay site is

figure 7-1

The featured items on the home page are a quick launching pad to sample some of the different sellers' wares.

gonna cost a seller a few extra bones. But it might be a small investment if the seller really has a hot item and can push the profit by having it in a prominent location rather than nestled in one of the many auction categories and subcategories.

In the Featured list, you'll find a whole potpourri of items from all different categories. Most often, you'll find things like computer hardware and software, sports memorabilia, jewelry, and bulk items. Although these might not be the exact things you're immediately interested in, the featured listings give you an opportunity to view some of the selling and bidding trends at eBay. When Michael Jordan announced his retirement, a ton of Jordan items showed up in the featured listings. When *The Phantom Menace* was released to theaters, it was all you could do to keep from tripping over Star Wars stuff. The featured listings are a place to keep a finger on the pulse of the general interests of the eBay community.

Featured listings also exist for each of the different eBay categories. Again, a seller listing items for auction can choose to have a particular item appear in a *category featured listing* rather than in the general featured listings. The difference is that the item doesn't get top-of-page featured status until you enter that category and begin to view the listings there; that's when the featured item will take a prominent place over other, nonfeatured items. The cost: $14.95 to gain the featured location in a particular category.

NOTE   Don't get overly concerned about the listing costs I'm sharing with you here. When it's time for you to list your special item, I'll go over all costs and options at once (see Part 4). For now, I just want you to know there is a premium to getting an item featured, and not just because some sellers have friends at eBay who are pulling strings.

SOAPBOX   So what do I think about featured auctions? I'm glad you asked. Frankly, I tend to skip right past them. They're just a subset of items you can find in other ways on eBay. I don't disagree that having them in the Featured category is a way to draw additional viewers, but when I'm looking for goods, I'll typically go right to the category where the stuff I want is usually located. I encourage you to try all the different item search options available at eBay so you can determine which methods you like best. There, that was diplomatic, huh?

Using the Category Listings

eBay's home page also sports the *Categories* title bar. Below it, you'll see links to the major item categories. This is stuff you first saw in Chapter 6. Here, though, you're going to use the category listings as a funnel to help you narrow your focus on the types of items that interest you. You can click on any of the category titles and jump to the main index page for that category. For now, click on the *Books, Movies, Music* category link on the eBay home page, and you'll jump to the index page for that category, which you can see in Figure 7-2.

The category index pages give you a pleasing view of the whole area. At a glance, you can see all the different subcategories. Remember the number in parentheses to the right of the subcategory title—that's the number of active auction items you'll find when you go there.

The *Featured Auctions* list at the right-hand side of the Books, Movies, & Music index page shows you the featured items that have been listed in this category. That's pretty good visibility. Maybe that online college or high

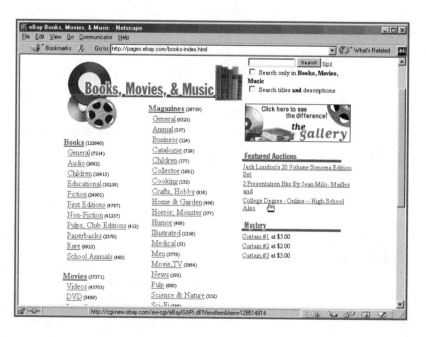

figure 7-2

The index page for the Books, Movies, & Music category helps you narrow your search for the things you want.

school degree you can see in the Featured area is just what you've been needing. Maybe not.

Do you see the *Mystery* heading just below the featured items? That's intriguing. What could be behind curtains #1, #2, or #3? Only one way to find out—click on one. The mystery heading is a fun way to randomly find items in a sort of hide-and-seek manner. It's something eBay does to add some adventure to the listing pages. The sellers' items aren't always hidden like this, though. It's just a random thing to add some more interaction to the Web site. I suppose the only thing missing would be the lovely Carol Merrill, right? I wonder if she uses eBay....

So, when you click on any of those subcategory headings, you'll jump to those item listings. It's just like I showed you in Chapter 6, but I'll show you again. Since I'm a recent DVD convert, and I can see the subcategory link *DVD* has 3,499 items up for bid, that would be a good place for me to start sniffing around. Figure 7-3 shows you some of the listings I found.

Looking at Figure 7-3, you'll see the *Featured Auctions* first. If nothing there struck your fancy, you could scroll down the screen to get to the *Current*

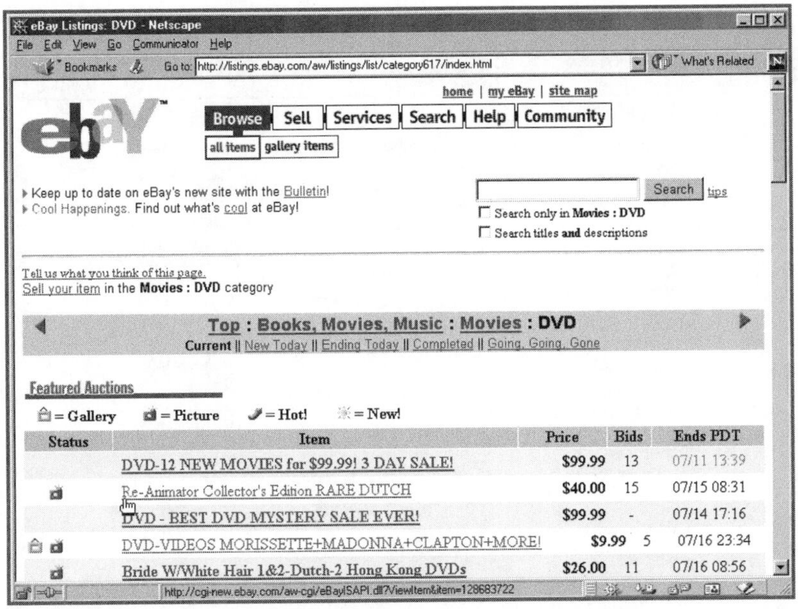

figure 7-3

Hey! The out-of-print *Re-Animator* DVD. That might be one worth coming back to check out.

Items in DVD listings. Remember to use the page counters and associated links to navigate through the pages of listings for the category that interests you (refer back to Figures 6-6 and 6-7).

Another way to view the items in a subcategory is to use this handy little gang of hyperlinks:

Top : Books, Movies, Music : Movies : DVD
Current || New Today || Ending Today || Completed || Going, Going, Gone

Use these links, and they'll do just what they promise. You can view all items in the subcategory that are new for the day, set to end for the day, already ended, or Going, Going, Gone (ending within five hours or less). Pretty convenient, I'd say.

Of course, you always have the option of reviewing *all* the category titles and their major subcategories. If this broader view is what you're looking for, then go back to the eBay home page, click on the *Categories* title bar or the *All categories* link. After a couple of minutes of chugging through the 2.5 million items, you'll see a category overview index like the one shown in Figure 7-4.

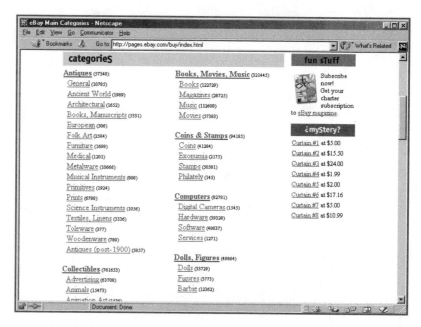

figure 7-4

Remember, this is just a partial view of the eBay category index. Gadzooks, there's a lot to look at!

When you look at Figure 7-4, you'll see the link *Movies* under the category heading *Books, Movies, Music*. Notice, though, that you can't see the sub-headings (such as *DVD*) from this index view. You'll need to click on the *Movies* link to get to a place where you can choose a narrower focus like *DVD*.

Don't forget there are more than 1600 item categories to sift through on eBay. That's why it might take a couple of minutes to load some of the category indexes. Figure that it will take even longer to review all the listings, even if only in a single category or subcategory. Don't expect to do it in a day.

 ALERT   Wait! If I can't view all the items in a day, then how do I keep from missing an auction of something I really want? I hear you, and I share your senti-ment. But the truth is that you just can't see it all. If you're anything like me, though, you probably can't afford it all, either. I'll share more about researching items and planning your bidding in Part 3. Right now, just take in the scenery and get a feel for the kinds of things that lie waiting for you on the auction block.

Looking for Newly Added Items

So, imagine you've stayed up all night scouring the listings of lunchboxes within the *Collectibles* category. You just have to find that rarest-of-rare Hometown Airport lunch pail you had in third grade. You find none—after all, they're really rare. But don't give up. You'll just have to keep checking back to see if someone eventually lists such a treasure. Does this mean that you'll have to go searching through the entire list of 2,100 items and try to determine which are the new items, hoping not to skip by the Hometown Airport box you want so badly? Nope. eBay's gonna give you a little help.

Look back at Figure 7-3. There you'll see the little ☀ icon to the left of some listing titles. This means the listings are new, having been added within the last 24 hours. Very cool. If you're diligent in your quest, repeat-ing your search day after day, you'll be able to take a quick look at the new items that have been listed since your previous visit to the category. That'll make it easier to find out what's new in any category.

When searching through the category listing pages, remember that new items usually appear first in the list, descending by date. So all the new items, marked by the ☀ icon, will rise to the top of the list. As you scroll down through the list and ahead in the following pages, you'll then find the listings for items that have been listed for more than a day, no longer being flagged as new.

ALERT There is an exception to the rule of new items always being at the top of the list. If a new item was added but it has a short auction run time (maybe only three or five days), then you wouldn't see it until you drilled further into the descending pages of items up for auction. Yeah, that makes some new items a bit more difficult to find, but that ☀ icon will still jump out at you as you search deeper into the item listings.

Another way to easily find new listings is to use the hyperlink *New Today* on the item listing page. While you're in an item subcategory listing page, just click on the *New Today* link (you can see an example in Figure 7-3). When you click on the *New Today* link, the listing will be refreshed, and you can quickly review only those items that have been newly listed, again flagged with the ☀ icon. The difference with this search is that eBay will only show you the new listings; you won't see any of the continuing auctions that have been going on for more than a day.

One final point about searching for items using the standard listings: there is a lag time between when a new item is listed and when it actually appears in the listing results. eBay updates the listings with newly added items about once every hour. So it is possible that a new item will be listed and you won't be able to find it via category listings right away. This shouldn't cause any problems, though; it's just something to be aware of.

Using the Search Tools

Working with the listing pages is all fine and dandy, but many people would like a more direct method to cut to the chase. If you're looking for a specific item, maybe a movie or a record, you might be happier if you could search for the title or name of that item rather than sift through the pages of listings in either movies or records. Well, that's easily accomplished.

In many places around eBay, you'll see the useful little search fields. You saw the first one on the eBay home page (look back at Figure 6-1) right near the top of the page. With that search field, you could start looking for a specific item the moment you access the eBay site.

Look also at Figures 7-2 and 7-3; those pages have search fields as well. Whenever you're searching through category listings, you can bail out and go for a direct search instead of thumbing through the listings.

You use the eBay search fields the same as you would if you were searching for Web sites using Yahoo!, Alta Vista, or any other Internet search engine. Click in the search field, and type something. Click on the Search button to the right of the entry field and eBay chugs off looking for items whose titles contain what you've typed. As you can imagine, typing something generic like *book*, *poster*, or *CD* could return a boatload of matching items. Try to type something a bit more specific to what you're looking for.

Let's say you're a big Beatles fan (well, *you're* not big, but your enthusiasm for the Fab Four is). OK, using one of the eBay search fields, type in **Beatles** and click on the Search button. eBay will return a list of matches that contain *Beatles* in the item title. Get more specific: type in **Yellow Submarine,** and eBay will return items with that in the title. You get the idea. Before you know it, you're getting ready to bid on an out-of-print *Yellow Submarine* video, a Corgi Yellow Submarine die-cast toy, and an original *Yellow Submarine* movie poster. You're also getting ready to visit your bank—these Beatles items get awfully expensive. But the key is to type in words that might bring back a list of items that most closely resemble what you're looking for.

This is all very fine, but the search is still too wide open. You want other ways to search for items, and maybe not just by the title of the item. No problem. Wait until you see eBay's exclusive search page. From any of the navigation bars you see listed—on the eBay home page or at the top of most any other eBay page—click on the *Search* link. You'll be taken to a wonderful search page like the one you see in Figures 7-5 and 7-6.

Well, there's certainly a lot more going on at the eBay search page than those simple title searches you've just learned about. For starters, you can see the

fi9ure 7-5

The incredible eBay search
page. It doesn't get much
easier than this.

fi9ure 7-6

Wait! There are more ways to
search on the second half of
the eBay search page.

Title Search is still available on the search page, but now you can specify a dollar range for the items you want your search to return. Maybe you're on a budget. If so, using the dollar range will only show you matching items that are in your price range. No agonizing over great items with stiff prices—you just won't see them. You can also choose how you wish to order your search results—on ascending (lowest to highest) or descending (highest to lowest) order. If you want to keep your search restricted to one country, just make your choice in the area labeled *Country where the item is.* See the *Order by* field that has *Ending Date* filled in? That means the search will order by the auction ending dates of the items your search finds. Click on the little down-arrow next to that field, and you'll find you can also change the Order by criterion to use bid price (the current high bid value) or search ranking (how closely the item matches the keywords you entered) when listing your search results. And you also have a couple of check boxes at your disposal in the Title Search box. *Text-only results* will display search results that are, well, text only. You won't see the usual coloring and font types as you do in a standard listing of items. This saves a bit of processing time, avoiding the additional graphics and such. Then *Search Title AND Description* does what it promises—it searches both the item titles and item descriptions looking for the key words you've entered. Feel like you're getting a bit more control over those 2.5 million auction items, don't you?

Moving on, the next search box, *Item Number Lookup*, lets you perform a direct search using the item number as your search key. Each eBay auction item is assigned a number when it is listed. If you happen to make note of the number of a particular item that interests you, just enter that number here and eBay will go get it for you, post haste. The unique thing about this kind of search is that it takes you directly into the Item Details page, not to a listing title that you'll need to click on to get to the item details. Slick.

For still more ways to skin this cat, take a look at the search box titled *Seller Search.* If there's a particular seller that you find always seems to have the kinds of items you want to bid on, enter that eBay ID here to see your favorite currently has up for auction. The different categories of option buttons within the search box allow you to see the e-mail addresses of the bidders who are bidding on those items. Take a look at the seller's completed auctions from a variety of date ranges, and determine how you want to order the result of the search. Finally, there's a selection field that lets you choose how many rows (items) per displayed page you wish to have eBay show you.

NOTE The Seller Search also comes in handy when you're the seller. You can use this search to call up all your active auction items and quickly see how your stuff is doing.

Further down the Search page, you'll see the next search box, *Bidder Search*. If you're a bidder, this is the best box for you to use. By entering your eBay user ID, you can quickly see the different items you've bid on, how high the current bids for the items have gotten, and whether you're still the high bidder. In this search box, you can review completed auctions in which you've bid, and you can choose whether to see all auctions you've bid on or only those auctions in which you are (or were) the high bidder. This search box also lets you choose the number of items you want displayed on each page of search results. Getting the hang of this?

The last search box is the *Completed Auctions*. It's the least robust of the search tools you'll find on the search page, but it's still quite useful. Why would you want to view completed auctions? After all, it's not like you can still bid on them; they're over and done with! Still, searching completed auctions is an excellent way to do some research at eBay. Maybe you need to see how much you've been spending in bids over the past few weeks. Maybe you want to see what kinds of Beatles items have been up for bid over the past few weeks and what kind of high bids those items got. Research is a big part of being successful at eBay. I'll go into serious depth about this topic in Chapter 11.

Now you're probably just about up to your ears in search methods at this time. But the eBay search page offers one more useful trick—eBay *Search Tips*. eBay, created and supported by some pretty brainy programmers, has heard the cries of the eBay community to enable very sophisticated search methods.

The search methods devised thrust you away from simple text searches to
some downright fancy database extracts. You can get to these super-special
search tips by clicking on the *More tips* link in the Title Search box. When you
do, you'll bounce to a screen like the one shown in Figure 7-7.

By the way, notice the location of the vertical scroll bar in Figure 7-7; what
you see is only the start of all the search hints and rules you'll find. Figure
7-7 is the bare tip of the iceberg of search secrets you'll be able to use. You
can review the search tips yourself on eBay's site. There's a lot of them, so
don't stay up too late into the night studying them.

Exceptions to the Rules

Well, there always has to be some exception to the rules, right? Searching for
stuff on eBay is not 100 percent foolproof. But the key reason for not being
able to find items is such a common one—misspelling! A seller who misspells a word in the item's title is going to be left out of a lot of search results.

And a buyer (or searcher) who misspells a word in a title search is probably not going find much of anything in the results.

Case in point: I've been searching for some original movie memorabilia from 1972's *Poseidon Adventure.* Look at that name, "Poseidon." That's a classic spelling bee minefield. Let's see . . . "i" before "e" except after "c," except for exceptions. Well, this one shoots holes all through that grade-school mantra. And, as luck would have it, I missed out on a great auction for a *Poseidon Adventure* movie poster because the item was listed as *"Poseiden Adventure."* Aaargh! The seller misspelled the simplest part of the word. But you get my point. If your spelling's a bit weak, do something about it. eBay hasn't installed a spelling checker and probably doesn't plan to any time soon.

> **NOTE** I'll talk a whole bunch more about good item titles and descriptions in Chapters 16 and 18.

To the Gallery

One of the newer features used in searching for items at eBay is the new eBay Gallery. This was something eBay started in January 1999, beginning with listings in the area of Antiques. The concept is the same as viewing auction listings by category and subcategory. This format, however, provides a small image (a *thumbnail*) of the item right on the listing page. If the image attracts your attention or raises your curiosity, you can click on the item and review the item details. You can see examples of the Gallery entry page and listing page in Figure 7-8 and 7-9.

How do you get to the Gallery? Simple. At the top of the search page you saw in Figure 7-5, you'll see a sentence, *Try the new way to shop by photos—the Gallery!* Click on the word "gallery" in that sentence—it's a hyperlink that will take you directly to the gallery where you can peruse the tantalizing photos of goodies that might just find their way into your life.

figure 7-8

eBay's Gallery features many categories that provide images of the items up for bid.

figure 7-9

Clicking on *Books, Movies, & Music* and then on *DVD*, I found my way to this Gallery listing of some great films in the exciting DVD format.

TIP Notice from Figure 7-2 that you can also access the Gallery listings for certain categories right on the standard Item Listing page. There's a conspicuous *Gallery* picture link just waiting for you to click on it.

Introducing eBay's Personal Shopper

And what if, after all of these search aids, you're just not finding what you want? Should you go away mad, sad, or generally dejected? You could, or you could decide to put eBay to work for you. The new Personal Shopper has been designed with you in mind, and it will stay up late at night looking for the elusive items you so deeply crave. Here's how it works.

From the main navigation bar, click on *Search*—that will take you to the standard eBay search page. However, in the sub-navigation bar, you'll see a selection titled *Personal Shopper*. Click on it, and you'll jump to the Personal Shopper access page (see Figure 7-10). Enter your user ID and password (enabling the temporary cookie if you like) and click on the *Submit* button.

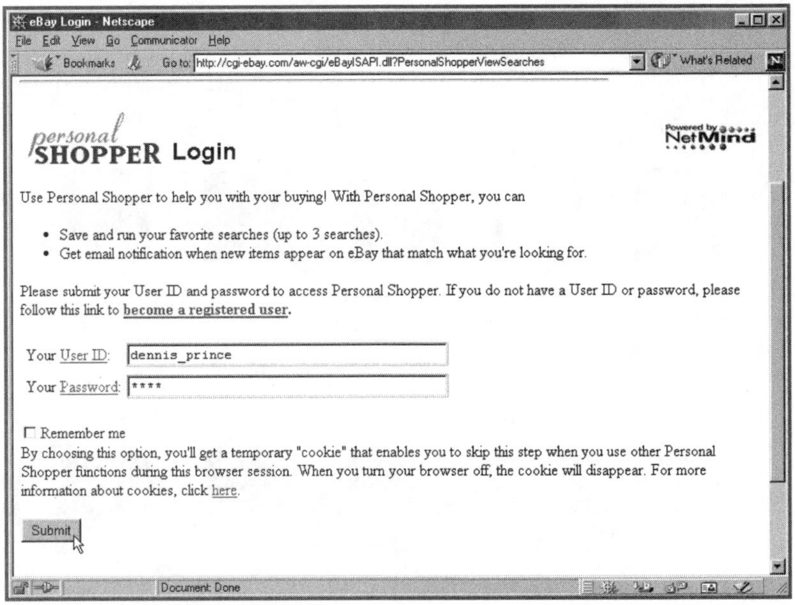

![eBay Personal Shopper Login screenshot. Window title: eBay Login - Netscape. URL: http://cgi-ebay.com/aw-cgi/eBayISAPI.dll?PersonalShopperViewSearches. personal SHOPPER Login. Powered by NetMind. Text reads: Use Personal Shopper to help you with your buying! With Personal Shopper, you can: Save and run your favorite searches (up to 3 searches). Get email notification when new items appear on eBay that match what you're looking for. Please submit your User ID and password to access Personal Shopper. If you do not have a User ID or password, please follow this link to become a registered user. Your User ID: dennis_prince. Your Password: ****. Remember me checkbox. By choosing this option, you'll get a temporary "cookie" that enables you to skip this step when you use other Personal Shopper functions during this browser session. When you turn your browser off, the cookie will disappear. For more information about cookies, click here. Submit button.]

figure 7-10

Access the Personal Shopper tool using your eBay user ID and password.

NOTE The first time you use the Personal Shopper, you'll need to read an agreement and agree to its terms before you can actually use the tool. Personal Shopper is a sublicensed product of NetMind Technologies. Read their Terms & Conditions statement and continue on. You won't be slowed down by it in the future.

Upon successfully accessing the Personal Shopper page, you'll see a display much like that shown in Figure 7-11.

If you want to add some searches for Personal Shopper to run for you (there's a limit of three you can run at any one time), just click on the *Add a New Search* button. Do that, and you'll see a screen like that shown in Figure 7-12—it's where you'll enter the criteria for what you want Personal Shopper to hunt down for you.

Now, the whole deal behind the Personal Shopper is that it will send e-mail messages to you whenever an item shows up on eBay that matches your search criteria. It's pretty straightforward and is just another tool to help you find the things you want most.

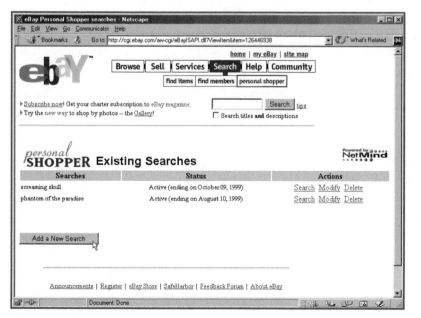

figure 7-11

I've already put the Personal Shopper to work for me, sleuthing and scouring eBay night and day to find the odd little things that make me happy.

Wanted: Sooner Than Later

If you're still not satisfied that all these search tools will turn up that special
something, take the more aggressive approach and post a message to eBay's
Wanted Board. It's one of those chat spaces that you can access via the main
navigation bar—use the links *Community, Chat,* and select *Wanted Board*
under the Chat Rooms heading. As an illustration, I've posted one of my
wants that you can see in Figure 7-13.

Once you've posted your want ad, the rest of the eBay community will be
able to see it. Who knows, maybe someone out there has what you want and
will be putting it up for auction soon.

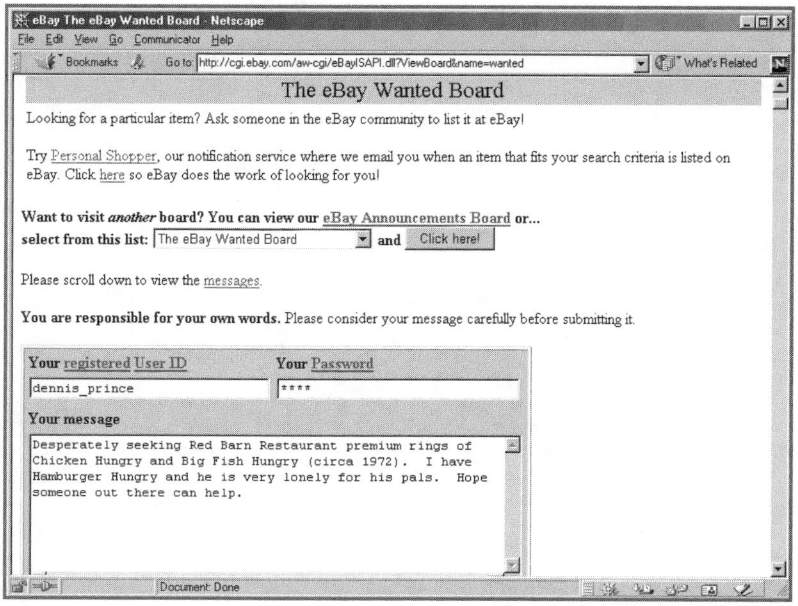

figure 7-13

I guess I'm one of the impatient ones. Let's see if a posting to the Wanted Board will turn up the two Red Barn rings I'm wanting.

And so, as you can plainly see, eBay has a multitude of search tools that help you find items of interest. With all this searching power, and over 2.5 million items to choose from, I'd be surprised if you didn't find something that you simply cannot live without.

chapter 8

Go Ahead, Place Your Bid

By this time I've given you enough information to be dangerous. It's time to dive into the auction mix. You've been wide-eyed with delight looking over all the items up for auction. I'm sure you've done some surfing of the categories and listings on eBay, and I can practically guarantee that you found something you'd like to have. Perfect! That's why you're here.

So how about if we get into this beast and see the nitty-gritty details of things you want to bid on? It's time to let the other bidders know you have arrived.

Bidders, take your mouse. Get set. Bid!

Reviewing the Item You'll Bid On

In Chapter 7 you saw how much there is to bid on at eBay. With 2.5 million items to choose from, you're sure to find that hard-to-find something you've been longing for. To test that theory once more, I did a search for an old illustrated horror magazine, *Vampirella*. That was one of those old horror comics from the late 60s published by Warren Magazines—the folks who gave us those literary monoliths *Creepy* and *Eerie* magazines. I never owned *Vampirella* magazines because Mom said that vampire lady didn't wear enough clothes. My seven-year-old eyes didn't see a problem. At that time, girls were icky and fangs were cool. But I digress.

I want to see if I can find the rare first issue, so I'll perform a search on "warren vampirella 1." Lo and behold, I find exactly what I'm searching for—and two of 'em, to boot! (See Figure 8-1.)

 Tip Even if your search brings back immediately gratifying results, don't forget to try spelling variations and other changes in the description to get the most matches possible for what you're seeking. I got really specific here, but it still paid off. Who knows what else I might have found if I'd left out one of the l's in Vampirella?

You can see that the item titles in Figure 8-1 are the links to view the details of the listings that match your search results. Before I go further, I'm going to make some quick judgments here. First, I'll immediately throw out the third item since it's not exactly the issue I'm looking for, although elements of its description met my search criteria. Now I'm down to the two listings of the first *Vampirella* issue I'm looking for. No rocket science here—I'm going for the issue that has a high bid of $16.50 *and* has a picture included (see the PIC icon). Sorry, but that one with the opening bid of $200 is a bit out of my comfort zone. So I'll click the title of the second item—the details are shown in Figure 8-2.

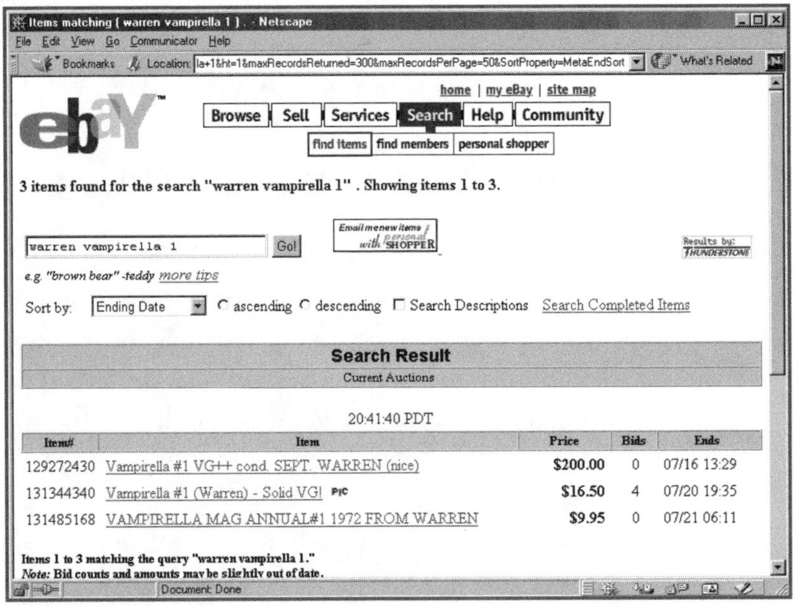

figure 8-1

Your search is their command. I find the exact item I'm looking for with hardly any effort.

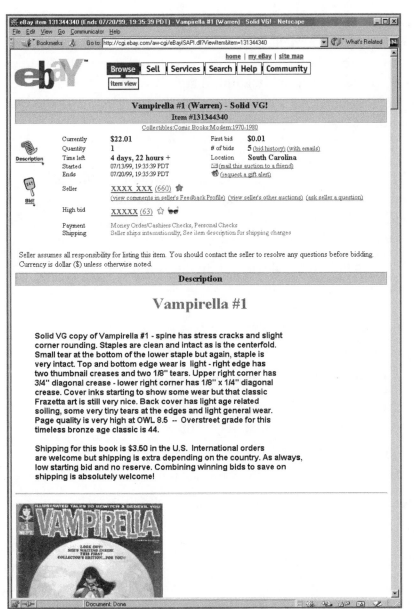

figure 8-2

The item detail screen lets you see all the information about the item you want to bid on.

With Figure 8-2 as your reference, look at the item detail screen and see what you can quickly learn about the item you want to bid on.

First, the title bar in the middle of the screen tells you you're looking at the item described as "Vampirella #1 (Warren)—Solid VG!" Below the description, you see the item's auction identification number—Item #131344340. Below that, you see a link that tells you which listing category this item appears in; it's a link you could use to get immediately back to the item listings.

Over to the right, you see a couple of icons:

This is a link to get to the description area of the listing. In Figure 8-2 you can already see it. However, for normal browser use, you could either scroll down using the side scroll bar or jump down using this icon.

This is a link that will take you to the area where bids are placed. I'll show that to you in just a moment.

Now to riffle through the two columns of information you see in the middle of the details screen:

- **Currently**. Shows the current high bid on the item.

- **Quantity**. Tells you how many are available for auction. Some auctions will be for multiple units. Maybe the seller has two copies of this magazine, but there's only one up for grabs here.

- **Time left**. How much longer will this auction be active?

- **Started**. When did the auction start (date and time)?

- **Ends**. What is the official ending date and time of this auction?

- **Seller**. Who's got this thing for sale, anyway?

Pause here for a moment because there's some useful information for you. The seller's name is a hyperlink. If it is displayed in a standard e-mail address (like name@place.com) then clicking on the link will pop up your browser's e-mail message creation window; you can quickly write an e-mail message to the seller. If the seller's name isn't in e-mail format, then it's an eBay user ID you're looking at—you'll need to go through an extra step to verify your registered status before you'll get this seller's e-mail address. The number in parentheses to the right of the seller's name is the seller's current feedback rating number. The higher this number, the more positive feedback this seller has received. Click on the number in parentheses, and you can read the comments others have left for the seller.

 ALERT Wait a minute! Figure 8-1 shows the high bid as $16.50. Why does Figure 8-2 show $22.01? You're not going nuts, and there isn't a time lapse at work here. Remember, the eBay title listings are often outdated when you're viewing them. If you want to get up-to-the-minute status on an item's true high bid, it's the item details page that will reveal the real skinny.

Now, below the seller's name are three more links: *View seller's feedback* does the same thing as clicking on the feedback number, *View seller's other auctions* lets you see a list of other items the seller is currently auctioning, and *Ask seller a question* will pop up your browser's e-mail creation window so you can ask your question via e-mail. Returning to the screen, you see some more items:

- **High bid**. The eBay ID or e-mail address of the current high bidder. You can send an e-mail if you want (or the seller can) by clicking on the name. You can also read the bidder's feedback comments by clicking on the number in the parentheses.

- **Payment**. The seller's payment requirements might be listed here, chosen from a list of options that eBay provides when the item is listed. The seller might choose to describe payment options in the body of the item's description instead—the seller of the *Vampirella* magazine chose this alternative.

- **Shipping**. Same thing. eBay provides some shipping options a seller can select; those options might appear here or the seller can list shipping instructions in the body of the item's description.

- **First bid**. This was the seller's specified opening bid.

- **# of bids**. Shows you how many bids have been placed on the item. The *Bid history* link to the right of the number lets you view who has bid and when the bids were placed. You won't see the amount of the bids until the auction is over; they're secret. The *with emails* link will show you the other bidders along with their e-mail addresses.

- **Location**. Where is this item physically located? This lets you get an idea of the kind of shipping charges you might need to pay in addition to your high bid price. Oh yes, 99 percent of the time, shipping costs extra. Be ready for that.

Now, the next two elements you see on the item detail screen bear a bit more explanation, and I don't want to just dash through them.

Below *Location* on the item details screen, you see the link *Mail this auction to a friend* with the little 📧 icon. eBay provides this simple and direct way to notify friends, via e-mail, about an auction you think might interest them. When you click on the link, you'll jump to a new window where you'll create your e-mail message to your friends. You can see it in Figure 8-3.

The next link you see below the *Mail this auction to a friend* link is the *Request a gift alert* link with the fun little 🎁 icon. If you're the giving type, this link will let you notify a friend, family member, or whomever that you have just won an auction for them and the item is to be a gift to them. No,

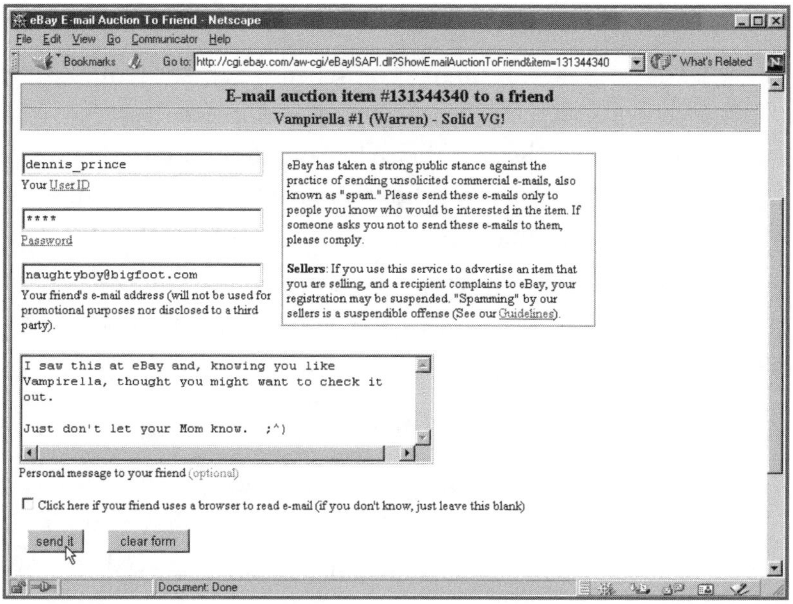

figure 8-3

Tell your friends you saw it at eBay. Watch them spend their money rather than you spending yours.

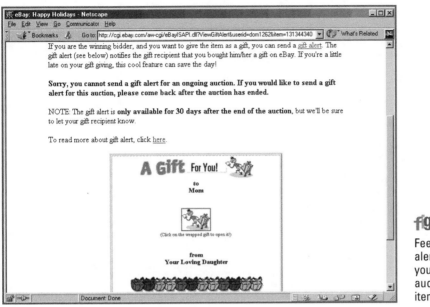

figure 8-4

Feeling generous? Send a gift alert to tell someone dear to you that you just won an auction and they are to be the item's new owner.

really. It's online altruism as you live and breathe. When you click on the icon or the link, you'll jump to the gift alert screen that you see in Figure 8-4.

If you're the high bidder when the auction has ended, you can choose to notify someone that you plan to give the item to them. Click on the *Request a gift alert* button, and you'll jump to the next screen where you'll enter the proper information and send your notice of niceness to the unsuspecting recipient (see Figure 8-5).

When you send a gift alert, the gift recipient will get an e-mail message from eBay telling them about what a swell person you are and where they can go on eBay to see what you won for them (the virtual gift card will show it's *from* you). Of course, it will be up to you to get the item and then ship it to the lucky soul you designated.

ALERT Better get a move on! If you want to send a gift alert to someone, you'll need to do it within 30 days of the auction's end. After that, the listing will be removed, and you'll be out of luck. Also, you can only send a gift alert *after* an auction has closed and if you are the high bidder. You'd feel pretty silly sending a gift alert too soon and then getting outbid. Whoops!

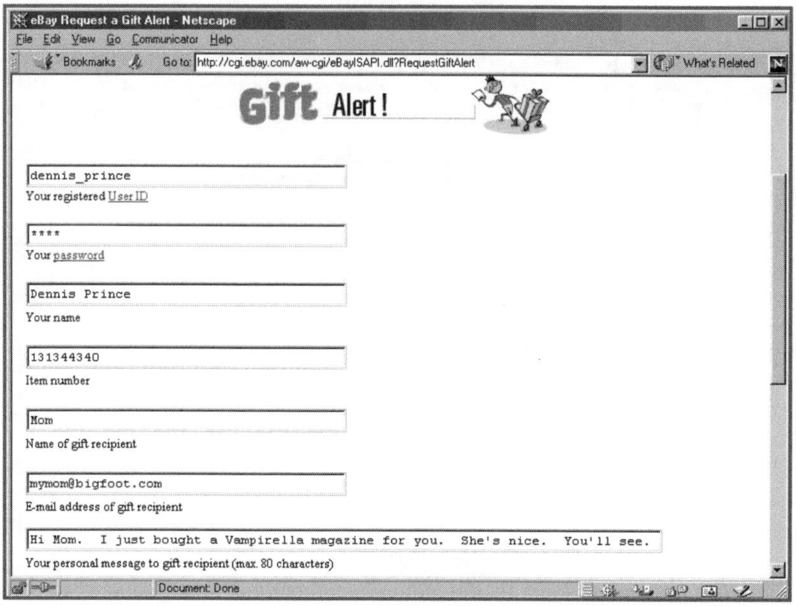

Gift Alert !

dennis_prince
Your registered User ID

****
Your password

Dennis Prince
Your name

131344340
Item number

Mom
Name of gift recipient

mymom@bigfoot.com
E-mail address of gift recipient

Hi Mom. I just bought a Vampirella magazine for you. She's nice. You'll see.
Your personal message to gift recipient (max. 80 characters)

Document: Done

figure 8-5

Plug in the information and
your message of giving is on
its way. What a pleasant
person you are.

Well, back to the auction at hand. About midway through the item details
page, you'll see eBay's text that lets you know both buyer and seller are getting into this potential transaction by their own free will. eBay encourages
both parties to contact each other in case of questions or any other need to
ensure the deal is going to be successful. Really, eBay wants its users to know
there's no reason to be bashful; communication is the key to making good
business transactions.

And, finally, you come to the item description. This is where the seller will
write something to tell you more about the item up for bid. From the example in Figure 8-2, the seller is letting you know about the condition of this
first issue of *Vampirella* magazine (originally published September 1969).
The seller goes into great detail letting potential bidders know what they can
expect if they win this item. That's good! And the seller lets you know it's up
to the buyer to add the price of postage and what that price will be. Finally,
the seller supports international shipments—probably significantly increasing the number of potential bidders who may decide to stake their claim.

So what do you think? You've read the details about this item. Do you have any thoughts or hesitations about proceeding to bid? Have you been able to develop any opinions or intuitions about either the item or the seller? Let me tell you mine.

First, the seller has a high feedback rating—at 660, I'd say this person's been around for quite some time. However, never take the feedback at face value. The real story is in the number of positives and negatives that make up the final count. By reviewing this seller's feedback, I learned he has no negative comments. A real plus!

 SOAPBOX So I should only trust sellers with high feedback, right? Wrong. Even if you come across a seller with very low or even no (zero) feedback, you shouldn't dismiss them so quickly. Remember, when you start selling, you'll have a zero feedback profile yourself. Unless there are many negative feedback messages in a seller's profile, the low rating just means they're new to eBay. If it makes you feel better, send them an e-mail note, ask them some questions, give them a chance. You'll hope someone does the same for you, won't you?

The location specified for the seller and the item is South Carolina. You could easily verify that with eBay's Registered User Information Request (you'll have to be a registered user yourself, of course, before eBay provides this information to you). In this case, I'll give the seller the benefit of the doubt—I feel no need to be suspicious. In Chapter 11 you'll learn how to conduct some deeper investigation about sellers and the things they sell.

Something that's really useful in helping you decide if you want to bid on an item is a picture of the item itself—and this seller has provided one. A lot of people don't like to buy items sight unseen, and get concerned that a seller's grading of Very Good (VG) might not match the buyer's interpretation. Pictures aren't necessary, and many auctions find great final bids without them. However, absence of pictures was more acceptable in the early days of eBay. Today, pictures are becoming more the required fare for a successful auction. As you can see from Figure 8-2, this seller provided one, which I could scroll down to examine further.

NOTE Had this seller not included an image, that wouldn't be cause to believe there's something fishy going on. If you want all the gory details of an item's condition, whether an image is included or not, send an e-mail to the seller. Most are very willing to provide intricate information to help you feel better about your bids. Don't be bashful. Just ask.

You can also see that the item has already received five bids. OK, so you're not the only one interested in this magazine (in reality, *you* probably *aren't* interested in this magazine at all, but it works for this demonstration— please continue to indulge me). How much has that current high bidder bid? You don't know. eBay allows use of a *proxy* system of bidding—you can enter the maximum amount you'd ever be willing to pay for the item, and eBay will only post the highest bid that it takes to keep you as high bidder. If the person who is the high bidder enters a maximum high bid of $35, then when you come along and bid $22.51 in this auction, you'll be immediately outbid by the first bidder's proxy maximum. Make sense? However, if you really needed this magazine to fill that vacant slot in your *Vampirella* collection, it might be worth up to $45 to you. If you bid that as your maximum high bid, you'll be the new high bidder at a high bid of $36. Follow me now: it only took $36 of your maximum bid of $45 to top the other guy's maximum of $35. Each bid placed on an item requires a certain bid increment, determined on the current high bid—in this case, the required bid increment at 22.01 is only $.50. Once you cross the $25 threshold, though, the increment rises to $1 above whatever the current high bid might be. (Psst. There's a chart in Chapter 12 that shows the bid increment ranges.) But if you bid $45, that topped the other guy's $35, and then you needed to beat him by the minimum bid increment of $1. This is all done in a flurry of proxy bidding (your bid, their bid, your bid, their bid, until you top their maximum, then proxy bid once more to meet the minimum increment). Therefore, the new high bid—*your* high bid—is $36, and you have an additional cushion of $9 to protect you from other small-increment bids. If you don't fully understand now, you'll see more in the next section of this chapter.

The Bidding Process

OK, you've learned enough about the item and the Item Details screen. You're ready to bid.

First, click on the bidding paddle *(Bid!)* icon. When you do, the display will immediately scroll down to the bidding area, as shown in Figure 8-6.

In the *Bidding* screen, all you need to do is enter your maximum bid value (remember, it has to be higher than the current bid; eBay tells you the minimum you need to bid). Be sure to scroll down and read the fine print on the screen; it tells you that you're about to enter into a binding contract when you bid, and also explains more about proxy bidding.

Once you've entered your maximum bid value, click on the *Review bid* button. eBay will review the bid information you entered, check to make sure it's higher than the current high bid, then give you a new screen to complete and review before you actually place your bid (see Figure 8-7).

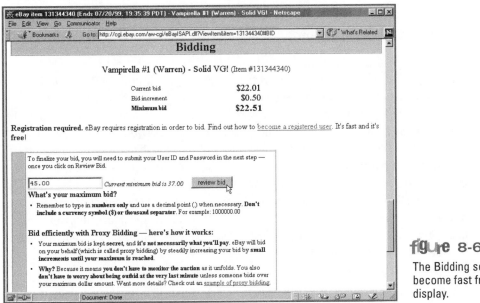

figure 8-6

The Bidding screen. You'll become fast friends with this display.

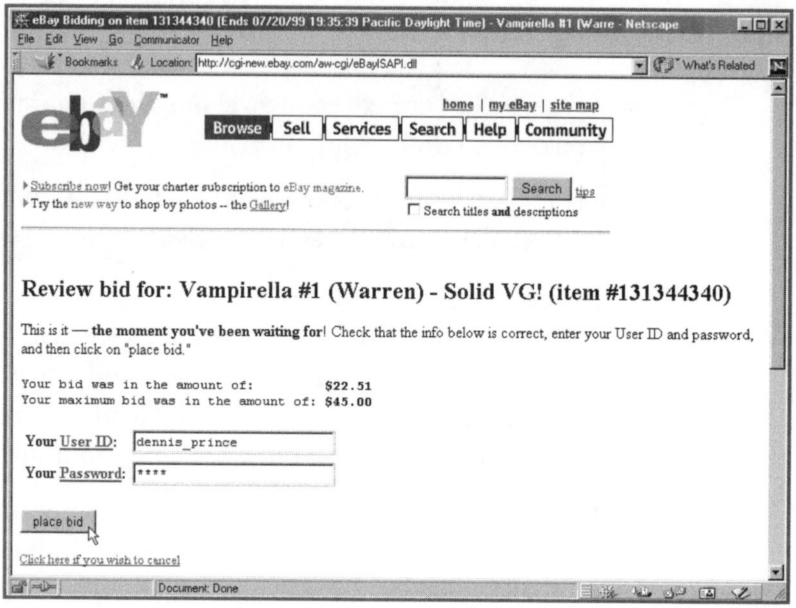

figure 8-7

Enter your user ID, password, and take a last look at what you're planning to bid. If you're sure, place that bid!

In the *Review bid* screen, double-check that your maximum bid is really what you can and will honor if the bids get that high. To let eBay properly process your bid, you'll now need to enter your eBay user ID and password.

NOTE Did you hear the one about the *eBayla Bug*? In March 1999 the bug-busting team at **www.because-we-can.com** found a huge security hole in eBay's bidding process. With the inclusion of a mischievous Java script in an evil-doing seller's auction, eBay bidders were having their user IDs and passwords lifted right out from under their noses. Of course, that allowed the evil seller to then assume the identity of any user who bid on the Java-jaded auction, doing whatever they pleased on eBay under the stolen ID of any unwary bidders. What you see in this bidding demonstration is a change to the eBay bidding process: the input of user ID and password was moved to the second part of the bidding process, protecting the users' information and inoculating them against the ravages of eBayla. It wasn't truly a virus, but it could have left you feeling sick had it ever hit you.

Further, you'll see a *few useful tips* on the Review bid screen that encourage you to review the seller's feedback before you bid, to make sure you understand the conditions of payment and shipping the seller has specified, and even to think about using an escrow service if the item you're bidding on is a big-ticket item. If you don't like the information you see on the Review bid screen or have suddenly changed your mind, bail out! Use the browser's Back arrow or the link on the eBay screen that reads *Click here if you wish to cancel.* You'll leave the *Review bid* screen, and your bid will not be placed. But if you want to go ahead, click on the *Place bid* button.

eBay will calculate your bid information against any other bids that have been received for the item. After it does that, your screen will be refreshed, and you'll quickly find out how your bidding stood up against the other bidders (see Figure 8-8).

If your bid tops the pile, congratulations! eBay announces, *"You are the current high bidder!"* It's OK to be excited. This is the part of the game that I told you about. It's fun. Be sure to read the additional text on your bid confirmation—it lets you know there may be a delay in showing you as the high bidder for the item but that's only on the item listing pages. Rest assured that your bid is officially recorded in the item details, and that's what matters at this point. You'll also read about what to expect when the auction closes. I'll give you more of that detail a bit later in this chapter. But,

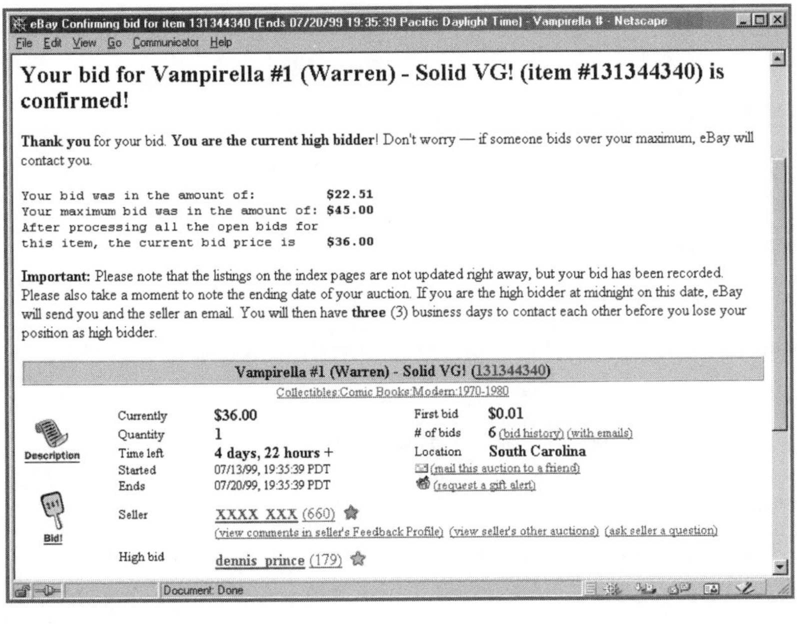

figure 8-8

And just like that, you're the high bidder! Did you hear the money getting sucked out of your wallet when you placed your bid? Don't worry, you'll get used to that sound.

for now, congratulate yourself. You've just become initiated into the world of online auction bidding. Enjoy!

Your Bid Notification and Daily Status

So now you're the Big Bad Bidder in an auction. Now what? Well, first eBay will notify you that you've grabbed the high bidder slot for the item. As a way of notifying you, eBay will send a preformatted e-mail message to you with the details of your recent bid. It's a way to remind you of your recent auction activity while also providing verification that you are who you say you are (via e-mail, anyway). The e-mail message for the *Vampirella* auction looks like this:

• •

```
Subject: eBay Bid Notice—Item 131344340: Vampirella #1 (Warren)—
Solid VG!

From: aw-confirm@ebay.com

To: dlprince@bigfoot.com

Dear dennis_prince,

Here's a quick note to confirm your eBay bid!

Vampirella #1 (Warren)—Solid VG! (item #131344340)

Your bid was in the amount of:         $22.51

Your maximum bid was in the amount of:  $45.00

The auction closes on:                 07/20/99 19:35:39 PDT

Web location used:                     http://www.ebay.com

After processing all open bids for

this item, the current bid price is:   $36.00

http://cgi.ebay.com/aw-cgi/eBayISAPI.dll?ViewItem&item=131344340

*If you placed this bid by mistake, here's what to do:

Check out the information on retracting your bid, which can occa-
sionally be done. You'll find this among the services listed in the
Buyers section.

Best of luck in your bidding—trade on!
```

• •

This e-mail message just restates what you already know: you're the high bidder...for now. Look at the message and notice that the auction still runs for another four days, twenty-two hours (it's past history as you're reading it). This is plenty of time for other bidders to get into the game.

Another nice feature provided to bidders is the eBay daily status report. If you are the high bidder in any auction, eBay will send a daily update message to your e-mail address. It looks something like this:

• •

Subject: eBay Daily Status as of 07/16/99 03:00:27 PST

Date: Fri, 20 Jul 1999 11:25:20 -0500 (EST)

From: aw-confirm@ebay.com

To: dlprince@bigfoot.com

Dear dennis_prince

All information is current as of 07/16/99 03:00:27 PST

Please visit eBay for the latest information.

You are a high bidder on the following auctions:

Vampirella #1 (Warren)—Solid VG! (item #131344340)

Current bid: $36.00

Auction ends on: 07/20/99 19:35:39 PDT

http://cgi.ebay.com/aw-cgi/eBayISAPI.dll?ViewItem&item=131344340

—— End Status ——

Thank you for using eBay! If you have not already done so today, it wouldn't hurt to mention eBay to a few of your friends!

• •

Reviewing Your Bids Online

Besides the daily status report you'll receive in your e-mail, you should do some regular checking of your bid's longevity directly on eBay. There are a couple of methods to achieve this. Use the easy-to-find *my eBay* link in the mini navbar on every eBay page. When prompted, enter your user ID and password. Scroll down to the area of *my eBay* where you'll find the heading *Items I'm Bidding On.* For this demonstration, the result looks like what you see in Figure 8-9.

Alternately, you can use the eBay search page and perform a Bidder Search on your user ID. It's usually a good idea to check the option button labeled *Yes, even if not the high bidder*—it lets you see the items you've bid on that are still active but for which you might not still be the high bidder; I'll show you what to do about that in the next section of this chapter.

When you use the Bidder Search, and you'll see a screen like the one shown in Figure 8-10. Just like the other searches you've learned about, the items that are returned from your search are links to the item detail pages. From the looks of Figures 8-9 and 8-10, your high bid is still standing strong.

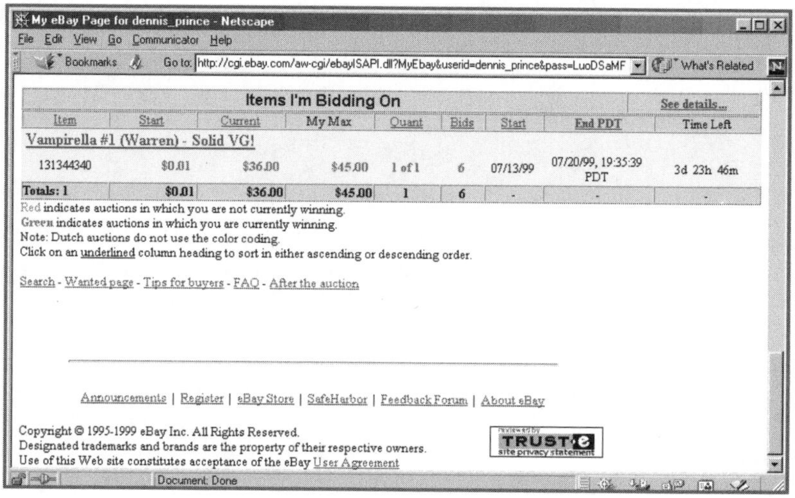

figure 8-9

Use *my eBay* to see how your bids are holding up. Are you still the bidder with the most bite?

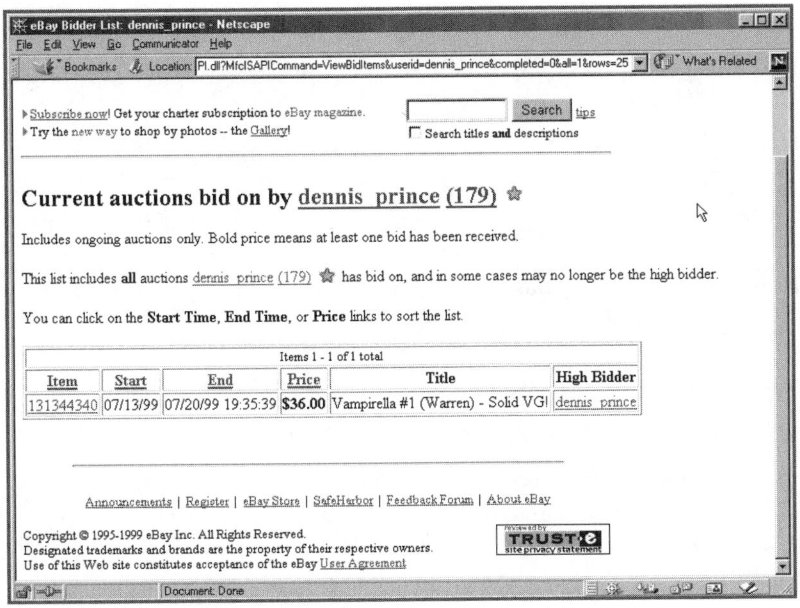

figure 8-10
Use the Bidder Search function as an alternate method to see how well your bid dollars are enduring. Looks like you're still the top dog.

Hey! You Were Outbid!

And then it happens, like a slap upside the head—you've been outbid. *"I what?! But how??"* Well, obviously because someone has more money than you—or more they're willing to part with—and isn't shy about tossing it on the bidding table. Wanna make something of it? Maybe you do.

You can find out about being outbid in an auction a couple of ways. First, suppose later in the day someone comes by and places a bid on that *Vampirella* magazine at a maximum of $47. You know that will beat your maximum bid, and the new bidder will be triumphant. When this happens, eBay will let you know. Much like the daily status report you receive, you'll receive a special *outbid notice* when someone has topped a bid on an item that you previously had locked up in your name. The outbid notice looks like this:

• •

Subject: eBay Outbid Notice—item 131344340: Vampirella #1 (Warren)—Solid VG!

From: aw-confirm@ebay.com

To: dlprince@bigfoot.com

Dear dennis_prince,

Heads up! Another eBay user has outbid you on the following item!

Vampirella #1 (Warren)—Solid VG!

The current bid amount is: $46.00

The auction closes: 07/20/99 19:35:39 PDT

Of course, your existing bid may be reinstated if this competitor's bid falls through. You can keep an eye on things if there's still plenty time before the auction closes. Visit

http://cgi.ebay.com/aw-cgi/eBayISAPI.dll?ViewItem&item=131344340

Otherwise, you can stay in the running and place another bid. Just visit

http://cgi.ebay.com/aw-cgi/eBayISAPI.dll?ViewItem&item=131344340

Safety tip: now that you're no longer the high bidder, you may be contacted by the seller or another person to sell you a similar item without going through eBay. Because this is against eBay rules and we cannot track such transactions, you would not be eligible for eBay's services that protect buyers, such as insurance or mediation.

If you have any questions, be sure to visit our Help section; it's best to email us from there rather than replying to this message, as replies here can't be processed. Just click http://pages.ebay.com/aw/help/help-start.html

Good luck with your bidding!

• •

The other way you'll find out about being outbid is by doing a regular check-up on your bids—use *my eBay* or the Bidder Search. (Remember to check for items in which you might no longer be the high bidder.) In a flash, you'll see if your name still appears in the high bidder slot.

The nerve of somebody to actually think they can outbid you when you've clearly let it be known that you want this item. Deal with it, Bucko. It's all part of the game. Just as you rejoiced when you outbid that last guy, someone's rejoicing that they've just hammered you. Really, though, it's not a personal matter. Don't think anyone's out to outbid you for the fun of it. (They wouldn't do that, would they?) Supply and demand, remember?

Now you have a choice. Do you want to turn away and let the item go, or do you want to get back in the ring and throw a few more punches? If you truly believe you want *that* item, then bid again. You might be able to reclaim your title as exalted high bidder. But just before you do, think about running another search for the item. Who knows, there may be others that have shown up since you first found this one.

Lastly, you must know that there will be times when you're outbid, and you won't be able to do a thing about it. How? Easy. You can be outbid in the final seconds of an auction, and you won't have time to receive an outbid e-mail, perform a bid check, or even attempt to place another bid. When this happens, you've just been struck down by a *sniper*. Snipers wait until the final minutes or seconds of an auction before they strike. Just when you think you're about to walk away the winner, BANG!—you're dead. What can you do? I'll show you in Chapter 13, including how you can become a sniper yourself. Fight fire with fire, right?

eBay Turns the Page

In August 1999, eBay introduced a unique and innovative feature: wireless auction notification. Yes, in a partnership with SkyTel Communications, eBay has served up a method to notify you of auction outcome directly on a pager or PCS (*personal communication system*—a whiz-bang cell phone). They call it *eBay a-go-go*—a rather silly name, but an interesting feature all the same. It's a way to keep track of auctions when you're on the go.

The idea is simple: you can be alerted to auction activity even when you're not monitoring your e-mail or not anywhere near your PC. If you're outbid in an auction, you'll receive a wireless alert. If an auction ends and you're the winner, you'll receive an alert. When an auction you're hosting ends, you'll get another alert. It's a whole new level of auction *alert*ness, and it's available wherever you go.

SOAPBOX Clearly, this isn't a required feature to find fun and success at eBay. Actually, it might be more suitable for those auction addicts who simply *must* know when "anything auction" is going on. But, if you thrive on this sort of real-time information or just love little gadgets dangling and jangling from your belt or purse, then give it a try.

So, how do you join in the James Bondian revelry? Well, if you already have a wireless device and an active account with a wireless service provider (Sky-Tel, AT&T, Motorola, and so on), all you really need to do is sign up at the eBay a-go-go Web page (see Figure 8-11). Use the link, *Other Wireless Users*, and follow the simple three-step instructions.

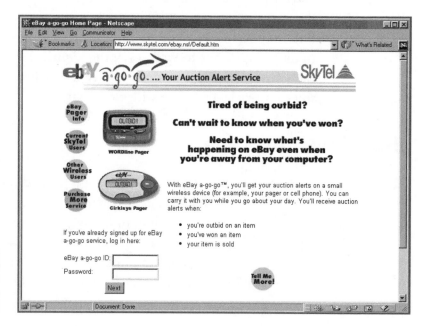

figure 8-11

The eBay a-go-go Web page is your way into the wonderful world of go-anywhere auction awareness. Just don't go in the shower with it—Bzzzzztt!!

Join the eBay a-go-go plan by creating a new account and providing your current wireless information. It's that easy. Before you know it, you'll be receiving auction alerts at any hour wherever you go.

 TIP Be aware that you might need to alter your eBay user ID when you sign up for this service. Your eBay a-go-go ID needs to match exactly to your regular eBay user ID—it's how eBay recognizes and traces who needs to be alerted. If your current user ID doesn't meet the eBay a-go-go ID criteria (review that at the new eBay a-go-go account page), you'll need to make a user ID change. No biggie. Go to *my eBay*, and use the link *Change my User ID*.

But what if you don't already have a wireless device? Maybe you haven't already been blessed with an electronic leash . . . er . . . communication convenience. Not a problem—eBay and SkyTel have designed a special device just for you. Look back at Figure 8-11, and you'll see two branded eBay pagers to choose from—they were made specifically for the eBay community. Just click on the link, *eBay Pager Info*, and learn more about the devices and the services you can purchase. Yes, just as with any other wireless communication service, this costs money. Just as with the major providers, this eBay-SkyTel solution has a list of options and service plans to choose from. Just decide how badly you need this service and to what extent. Then strap one on and join the personal electronics revolution. Yippee-kay-yay!

The End of the Auction

To bring this to a close, assume you were the high bidder for the *Vampirella* magazine at the time the auction ended. Hooray! Now what?

When an auction ends, eBay starts sending e-mail messages again. This time, though, eBay will forward an *end of auction* message to both the buyer and the seller. Assume I actually win this auction. The end of auction message I would receive looks like this:

Subject: eBay End of Auction—Item #131344340 (Vampirella #1 (Warren)—Solid VG!)

From: aw-confirm@ebay.com

To: sellinstuff@aol.com

CC: dlprince@bigfoot.com

Dear sellinstuff and dennis_prince,

DO NOT REPLY TO THIS MESSAGE. PLEASE ADDRESS YOUR MAIL DIRECTLY TO BUYER OR SELLER.

This message is to notify you that the following auction has ended:

Vampirella #1 (Warren)—Solid VG! (Item #131344340)

Final price: 48.00

Auction ended at: 07/20/99 19:35:39 PDT

Total number of bids: 12

Seller User ID: sellinstuff

Seller E-mail: sellinstuff@aol.com

High-bidder User ID: dennis_prince

High-bidder E-mail: dlprince@bigfoot.com

Seller and high bidder should now contact each other to complete the sale.

IMPORTANT: buyer and seller should contact each other within three business days, or risk losing their right to complete this transaction.

The official results of this auction (including e-mail addresses of all bidders) can be found for 30 days after the auction closes at:

http://cgi.ebay.com/aw-cgi/eBayISAPI.dll?ViewItem&item=131344340

If you won an auction in which the seller has at least a positive feedback rating of 10, you can send a gift alert. This is a great feature if you're buying gifts or if you're a little late on your gift-giving. To use this feature, see:

http://cgi3.ebay.com/aw-cgi/eBayISAPI.dll?ViewGiftAlert&item=60211079&userid=dennis_prince

If you have trouble contacting each other via e-mail:

http://pages.ebay.com/aw/user-query.html

Please leave feedback about your transaction:

http://pages.ebay.com/aw/feedback.html

For other valuable "after the auction" needs:

http://pages.ebay.com/aw/postauction.html

****

Thank you for using eBay! If you have not already done so today, it wouldn't hurt to mention eBay to a few of your friends!

http://www.ebay.com

Item Description:

Solid VG copy of Vampirella #1—spine has stress cracks and slight corner rounding. Staples are clean and intact as is the centerfold.

Small tear at the bottom of the lower staple but again, staple is very intact. Top and bottom edge wear is light—right edge has two thumbnail creases and two 1/8" tears. Upper right corner has 3/4" diagonal crease—lower right corner has 1/8" x 1/4" diagonal crease. Cover inks starting to show some wear but that classic Frazetta art is still very nice. Back cover has light age related soiling, some very tiny tears at the edges and light general wear.

Page quality is very high at OWL 8.5—Overstreet grade for this timeless bronze age classic is 44.

Shipping for this book is $3.50 in the U.S. International orders are welcome but shipping is extra depending on the country. As always, low starting bid and no reserve. Combining winning bids to save on shipping is absolutely welcome!

• •

That's quite a document, isn't it? Read it carefully because it's a full-fledged agreement between a buyer and seller. It has all the details of the auction at the time it closed, and it provides the necessary contact information for the buyer and seller to get in touch with one another and close the deal. As you can tell, this is where eBay's job is over. This is also where a lot of eBay users get a bit queasy because suddenly they're on their own and have to deal with a total stranger. Not to worry.

Although you'll read all sorts of details about closing the deal in Part 4 of this book, here it is in a nutshell:

- The seller usually contacts the buyer via e-mail to say the auction has ended and it's time to pay. Payment is usually required in advance and should include the appropriate charges for postage.

- The buyer should reply quickly to the seller to say the message was received and payment is en route. Don't drag your feet on this one, Buyer. If you bid for the item, you promised to pay up—and within a reasonably short time.

- The seller receives the buyer's payment and, depending on what form the payment is in, either ships the item right away (usually for money orders, cashier's checks, or cash) or deposits the buyer's payment, if it's a personal check, and waits for it to clear the bank before shipping the item.

- The seller usually contacts the buyer via e-mail to say the item is on its way and by what plane, train, or slow boat it will be arriving.

- If the item arrives and is satisfactory, the buyer should let the seller know the transaction has come full circle and is now complete. If there's a problem with the item (it's damaged, doesn't match the description originally listed, or whatever), then the buyer and seller should try to resolve the problem as quickly and cleanly as possible. Problems do sometimes arise, but they can practically always be worked out. More on this tender topic in Part 4.

- And, finally, if both buyer and seller are equally pleased with the transaction, they should leave positive notes for one another in eBay's Feedback Forum. That's how the good reputations of community members are built.

And that's how it's done the majority of the time. It's fun, and it's addictive. You're probably itching to do it again. Go ahead. Enjoy yourself. There's still a lot more to tell you about eBay and auctions, but for now get in there and do some bidding.

chapter 9

General Advice and Common Sense

Well this is all pretty cool, isn't it? All these great items to look at, the opportunity to place a bid on any of them, the fun of seeing yourself as the current high bidder, the jubilation of actually winning the auction. What a rush!

By the time you're reading this chapter, I would expect you've become quite a skilled auction hunter. There is so much to see at eBay that the urge to bid is practically irresistible. You'll probably find that looking turns to bidding quite quickly.

It's fun to play at the auction and even easier to bid, but remember that it isn't all just a game. Keep your head when you're out there searching and bidding. Real money and real people come into play at some point, and you'll need to pay the piper. But more than that, there are a few additional things you should think about as you've now become fully initiated in the auction excitement.

So please just push back from the keyboard and free the mouse from your iron-clad grip for a moment. There are a few things you should consider as you embark on auction frenzy.

"No, Beaver, of course you're not in any trouble. I just want to have a talk with you, son."

Whose Market Is It, Anyway?

You've seen some auction action now, and it's time to think about who's really in control out there. When you're searching for neat things, finding obscure items, and being lured by the ever-present *hard-to-find* treasure, remember that the final value of anything is still determined by how much you're willing to pay. If you don't want to pay the price, you don't have to. By this I mean that if an item has a high starting bid or has gotten enough bids to be at a high price, you can decide if you want to play in that particular auction or not.

Remember back in Chapter 2 when I explained how the auction format helps level the playing field between buyers and sellers? Well, seven chapters later, it's still true. Because the auction is a dynamic marketplace and items flow through the Web site like water from a faucet, it's up to *you* to decide when you want to take a drink. You have the power of the bid because without bidders there are no sellers.

You could make the opposite argument that without sellers there would be no auction, period. That makes sense. If there's nothing to buy, there's no reason to visit eBay. So because the sellers bring their items to the auction site and stimulate activity, shouldn't they have some control over how the auction market works? Sometimes, but not always. It's the old *give and take* going on out there. Some auctions are raging successes and some are total flops. The buyers and sellers work together to establish the market tolerance, even without realizing it. I find it fascinating because it's an economy all to itself, and it reflects our consumer attitudes and desires. But since the buyer is the one who brings the money to the auction, the buyer has the ultimate and final say-so.

So who really owns the market? Well, I believe it's the bidders who ultimately determine the success of an auction, but they're often their own worst enemies. Bidders have the power to buy or not buy, that's true. However, in the heat of a bidding war, bidders can send the price of an item so high that it sets a new benchmark for that item's worth. The difference between direct buying (getting an item from a seller one to one) and auction buying is the added element of competition among bidders. The competitive element is usually to blame when an item's price soars and everyone stands around looking dumbfounded, wondering what the big deal is. This comes back to haunt future buyers because now another seller of the same item can use that high price as justification for yet higher price expectations. Drat!

But remember that as buyer you don't *have to* pay outlandish prices if you don't want to. You do, however, need to decide how much the item is worth to you and if you believe you'll see another one any time soon.

SOAPBOX This is the real test of intestinal fortitude within the auction space. Can you say, *"nope, not gonna do it, it's not the prudent thing to do?"* Let me tell you firsthand, it's not an easy thing to do. I've agonized over bidding on a high-priced item right up to the final minutes of an auction. If I turned away, I often second-judged my decision, sometimes kicking myself for chickening out. But, in hindsight, it usually turns out for the best, freeing up funds for something else I want, need, or whatever. Plus, with very rare exceptions, the items I've turned down have shown up again. You'll need to decide for yourself, but try to avoid letting yourself become captive to a pricey auction.

Supply and Demand

Supply and demand?! Wow. This is like Economics 1A, isn't it? All those college courses you sat through listening to theories of aggregate demand and market slopes. What a bunch of junk, right? Well, maybe not. This stuff might have some real-world use after all. Hey, I always thought math was stupid and useless until I learned it helped me count money.

Getting back to a point in the earlier discussion: how much you're willing to pay for an item often depends on how hard you think it will be to find another. You can decide this for yourself based on your experience of how often you find some item for sale. But, many times, there is a hype or mania about any item where others tell you it's the rage of the millennium, a limited edition, or discontinued and out of print. These are warning flags that the Supply and Demand brothers are on the prowl.

On eBay, you'll see a lot of variation in item prices—often for exactly the same item. You'll find an item that is a total sleeper—it's not of terrific interest at first glance. But by the time the auction's getting ready to end, the bids have reached such an incredible level that you're certain it's not just the price that is "high." What are these bidders thinking, or do they know something that you don't?

Some auctions for the simplest-looking items can unexpectedly skyrocket. I recently sold a paperback book that told of the making of the movie *Jaws*—coincidentally, it was called *The Making of the Movie JAWS*. The final bid for the pocket-sized book was $84! The original cover price: $1.50. Does this mean I found a stupid bidder? Not at all. The book, which was popular with about ten bidders, is difficult to find and is about a consistently popular subject—*Jaws.* This book wasn't the best in the world, but it was of a limited run and is rarer than a copy of the novel itself, which was reprinted, and reprinted, and reprinted. You get the picture.

Now, the real goofiness comes into play when you see another seller with the same item up for auction, hoping to ride the coattails of an earlier auction's runaway success. This new auction, though, sputters and stalls. How come? Well, maybe the item that just sold wildly was important to only a couple of bidders. Maybe the appearance of a second, and third, and so on, of the item indicates it's not so rare after all. Maybe there's no explanation at all—it was just a fluke. Getting back to the last soapbox discussion, it's when the demand is down (and so are the prices) that you strike and get your own copy for a fraction of what the earlier frenzied auction took in.

Now consider an item that isn't limited, old, or historic in any way. Can such a thing cause bidders to go on a mad search, paying high prices that seem to have no sense of sensibility? You bet. Ever hear of the Furby? Of course you have.

Take a look at Furby Fever. It captivated our nation during the 1998 holiday season. This talking, squeaking, clicking, burping, bouncing little electronic gizmo took the holiday shoppers hostage, trapping them in crowded store aisles and forcing them to surrender their wallets and purses.

Maybe you first found out about Furby on eBay—I did. What's a Furby, and why are people talking so much about him/it/that? A look at the auction listings showed that this fuzzy little doorstop (retail price $30) was pulling high bids in excess of $100, and he was a brand new item. Quick! Run down to the store and buy some to auction. These people are nuts!

Ahh, but you can't get Furby in stores. He's sold out everywhere you go, and when you ask if there are any in the store, the salespeople just laugh in your face. *"You silly sap. Don't you know Furbies are the hottest thing around? You'll have to go to someplace like eBay if you really want one. Wake up."*

The demand for Furbies was so high that stores were selling every last one they received and still had to turn rampaging shoppers away. If you absolutely had to have one before December 25 rolled around, you'd better have been bidding. If you were one of the lucky ones who bought one at a retail store, then you had the prime opportunity to realize a huge return on your investment, all within the same week you bought the little bugger. During the week of December 7, 1998, a search for "Furby" on eBay brought back over 7,000 of the furry bandits. None of those auctions were about to stall, either.

The point of all this is that supply and demand are key to the success of auctions. It's usually the most obscure item you might think about throwing away that rakes in the most cash. Or it's the hype of some feverish craze that makes bidders see red and bid beyond their own good judgment. Again, this comes back to the personal decisions that buyers need to make for themselves: How much are you willing to pay, and what if you can't find another?

An Item for All Seasons

Some things at eBay will sell well regardless of hype, pitch, or temporary bidder insanity. There are some items out there that will always command a good price and that you'll probably never pick up at any kind of rock-bottom deal. If you're a buyer, you'll need to be on the lookout for hot items that seem to have a low price. If you're a seller, you need to know when you have a hot item and be able to advertise it properly.

Since everyone seems to have some sort of fondness for the entertainment industry—maybe a favorite celebrity, TV show, movie, cartoon, or whatever—you'll usually find certain items in this category are always in big demand. Nostalgia is the in thing these days, and nostalgic entertainment is selling for big bucks. So, if you're collecting movie posters from the films of John Wayne, Clint Eastwood, or James Dean, you can expect that these items will always command a high price.

Sometimes, a topic can be so hot that some buyers are willing to accept poor quality merchandise just for the sake of getting their hands on some original item. The first issue of *Detective Comics* might command a high price even though the cover was once detached and has been taped back into place. It won't get as high a price as a perfect copy, but it's still rare enough and limited enough that it will find a buyer who has some cash to spend.

And the perennial craze that seems to be immune to peaks of popularity is probably known to us all: Beanie Babies. Where they came from, I don't know. The fact is that Beanies are hot, have been hot for a long time, and don't appear to be cooling off any time soon. How come? Beanies have built-in collectibility: they retire. Ty, the manufacturer of Beanie Babies, has cleverly devised a method to ensure the product almost always sells out. After a period of months, some Beanie characters are no longer produced. It's called *retirement,* and it's a form of Beanie birth control. Naturally whenever a desirable item is no longer available, the demand shoots up and takes the prices up with it. The real quest for Beanie collectors is to find out which Beanies are going to be in shortest supply and then stock up on those before forced retirement rolls around. I only wish I could be so desirable when I retire. I'll have to wait and see.

So if you get a good price on a well-known hot item, consider yourself lucky. Chances are, though, that when that hot item shows up on the auction block, you'll be elbowing with other bidders to take a crack at owning the thing, whatever it is. It's all part of the treasure hunt.

Set Realistic Expectations

OK, so maybe I've let a little air out of your balloon. I don't mean to. It's true that the auction is a competitive marketplace. It's true that you'll be matching wits and wallets with a lot of other bidders out there. But people flock to eBay because, despite all this, it's still just downright fun. It all depends on how you approach it and what sorts of expectations you set for yourself.

If you're at eBay doing some bargain hunting, you'll probably find some success. Auctions can be a great way to snag items for practically nothing (don't forget the cost of postage, though). Recall that eBay's search page has a search parameter where you can look for items that are within a particular price (high bid) range. But don't expect to find a rare book, retired Beanie, or obscure promotional item for only a few bucks. Again, it depends on the popularity of an item and how many people it appeals to.

If you're looking for rare items, try to view the auction as your place where you'll actually *find* what you're looking for. Sometimes you'd be willing to pay significant money for some kind of something, but you have to find it first! eBay is the place where you can probably find it.

 SOAPBOX I get an immediate nervous charge in my stomach when I find something that I've spent years and years searching for. Just the find itself generates enough excitement to make the auction worth my time. Then it becomes exciting to find out how many other people might be looking for the same thing. And so actually getting what you've found becomes a thrill and a bit of a mystery; you'll wonder how it will end, what the final price will be, and if you'll be the one who emerges as the high bidder.

Another thing to keep in mind is the condition of the things you'll find on eBay. Hopefully the sellers will be very descriptive and honest when they describe the items they're selling. But if someone's selling an original document signed by Abraham Lincoln, it's probably going to be a bit worn and well traveled. Don't expect perfection if you're looking for and buying items that aren't new. They've been through countless hands, every one adding their bit of wear and tear to the piece. Outside of being completely misled by a deceptive description, be aware that you are buying used goods many times, and many times the goods will appear…used. If you ever have questions about the exact condition of an item, contact the seller well before the auction is due to end. It might save anguish and disappointment later.

Also, remember the key of eBay: it's a *person-to-person* auction place. Most of the time, you'll be dealing with regular Joes and Janes—the men and women on the street. But many of the buyers and sellers at eBay participate in their spare time. They might not always be as professional as you might like or as immediately responsive as you might expect. These are real people living real lives, and occasionally they have other things to do. You won't be calling a customer service desk to raise Cain about the fact that you haven't received a response to the e-mail you sent three hours ago.

Most people I deal with on eBay have regular jobs but typically try to do their best to help out their customers (the bidders). But stuff happens and things come up. So long as you're not being totally ignored, avoided, or abused, allow for a little of that real-life factor to creep in somewhere.

And, lastly, understand that some people using eBay are doing so as their single source of income. That's right; some people are making their living buying and selling on eBay. They might be a little different in the way they manage auction activity. You may, for example, find excelling levels of customer service from these people because they can devote 100 percent of their time to the auction. That's a plus. But they might also be very strict in how much they'll pay or how much they'll accept as payment when they buy and sell. They have to make a profit to stay in business. You might find that dealing with these people is less *familiar*, not as engaging or "chatty" as with less intense eBay participants. They're busy, and they probably have a lot more customers just like you. Don't be offended—they're just doing their job.

Don't Let Your Eyes Be Bigger Than Your Wallet

This is probably the toughest discipline you'll have to deal with. I know it's difficult when someone has a really choice item up for bid, and it's something you simply cannot live without. Everybody experiences that high level of want. But they also experience that low level of cash, too. Especially—and usually—when contending for several items.

There's a false sense of security and even invincibility that you can be lulled into when you bid at eBay. Bidding only requires you enter some dollar amount—your maximum bid—and then you click your mouse and submit your bid. Shazaam! You're the high bidder. It feels so good. You have the power of inexhaustible funds that propel you to the level of King Bidder, watching your collectible empire blossom overnight. But then you have to pay.

This whole area is really the psychology of keeping your head when you bid at an online auction. It's the same as using a credit card to do your shopping. You perform a simple little transaction with some innocuous looking plastic card—or plastic mouse—and you immediately get something you want. Your wallet never came into play and actual cash never appeared during the entire transaction. Cool. You can do it again right now.

At eBay, though, there are no credit card transactions. You don't pay eBay for the item you've won (the way you would at many sites that run wholesaler auctions), you pay the seller directly. You're dealing with real people and promising to pay real money. Sure, many sellers can accept credit card payments (those who operate an established business with a valid merchant account), but many others can't. When the day of reckoning comes along—that is, when the auction ends—you'd better be prepared to make good on your bids with whatever form of funds the seller has specified will be accepted.

It's all too easy to place bids. In a single sitting, you could commit yourself, via your bids placed, to hundreds of dollars in high bids that might come back knocking on your door. There's an interesting phenomenon known as *winner's curse* that I first mentioned in Chapter 1. What is it? Simply enough, winner's curse is the way the jubilation you feel when you've won the auction for some item, clawing and fighting to emerge as the illustrious high bidder, suddenly runs up against the realization that now you have to pay for what you've just won.

"Oh dear. What is to become of me? I don't have $850. Oh the pain, the pain."

Bidding in several auctions simultaneously, which is probably what you'll be doing, has pretty much the same effect as racking up that credit card bill. All at once, more or less, the different sellers contact you and ask for their money. It adds up quick, so be ready for that. If you need to, keep a budget of how much you can afford to spend in a given period of time.

The most difficult part of all this, and where the most discipline is needed, is to resist the temptation of all those wonderful items you'll find every day at eBay. Sometimes, I have had to restrict myself from even logging on to the site. Every time I search the listings, I *always* find something I want. It never fails. I just have to know that going in and also know that I don't *have to* bid on everything I see. It's hard not to, though.

ALERT Guard your auction reputation! If you bid higher than you can afford to pay, you'll be in a real pickle. The seller isn't going to be happy to hear that you really don't have enough money to cover your bid. In a flash, you'll be labeled one of those "deadbeat bidders," and that's a moniker you're not likely to shake off very quickly. Take care how you bid.

If you suspect you'll be an active bidder, my best recommendation to you is that you also become an active seller. Think about it: if you can sell successfully on eBay, you can make money to buy the other things you see up for auction, with the proceeds of your sales funding the cost of your bids. Check into Part 4 for successful sales techniques that will help you develop a way to make the auctioning start to pay for itself.

Get Rich Quick. . .Not!!

Well, this whole section might as well be a soapbox presentation. You will find many tempting offers from eBay sellers that promise to make you masterful at the art of selling on eBay and making *huge* profits. Quit your job. Buy a vacation house. Make a million dollars. You've just found your buried treasure.

Maybe, but maybe not. There are actually many very successful sellers (who are also astute buyers) on eBay, but I believe them to be the minority of the audience. You can make some extra money selling on eBay, but to truly make enough for it to become the sole source of your income, you'd better be really good, really determined, and really ready.

Think about it. If you're going to make a living buying and selling, you'll need to invest in the goods you sell. It can be done, but it's not as simple as stuffing envelopes at your kitchen table or losing 30 pounds while still eating whatever you want.

I admire the sellers who have developed special home-grown software or user handbooks that help other users find ways to make $1,000 a month on eBay. I couldn't live on $1,000 a month, but I wouldn't walk past it if I saw it lying in the street, either. However, when the "how-to" sellers claim they make $1,000 a month, are they doing that selling stuff, or selling their how-to product? I call it the *shovel principle*, and it goes like this: The man who uses a shovel to dig ditches for a living doesn't make near as much money as the man who sells the shovel. It's less tiring and taxing to distribute shovels than it is to get on the other end of them and put them to use.

If you have the motivation and ability to make a living using eBay auctions, then go for it. Just be sure your expectations are well founded—and be prepared to make other arrangements if things don't go as well as you first imagined. And be careful.

Do Things Ever Go Wrong?

Like the present-day adage goes: s*tuff happens* (or some variation of that theme). Things will happen at eBay that neither you or I like, just as things sometimes go wrong everywhere in this mechanized multimedia world.

The people at eBay have been working intensely trying to ensure that their Web site and the hardware servers that run it are able to keep up with the demand the users are putting on it. Remember, the eBay site gets over 1.5 billion hits (surfer visits) each month. The popularity of the site has required eBay to continually improve site flow, functionality, and hardware backup. Unfortunately, some things don't always run as seamlessly as you would like.

Most often, the problem you could encounter at eBay is that the site is running kind of slow. This is especially true during peak times when most users are visiting. I've found 6 P.M. PST to be a pretty busy time during the weekdays—everyone got off work and they're cruising the auctions. It might take some extra time for that listing page or item detail page to load. If you're planning on doing any last-minute bidding, make sure you get a good feel for how fast the site seems to be responding.

On some occasions, eBay has experienced all-out system crashes. This is when the servers, one or more, simply freeze up and stop responding. Obviously, if the system has crashed, you won't be able to get in and bid, sell, or sometimes even look. Although system crashes have been the exception and not the rule, eBay has seen more system crashes or slowdowns this year than anybody there would care to admit. Most notorious was the 22-hour system crash that occurred on June 10, 1999. Like a pileup on an interstate highway, eBay buyers and sellers were held back in an online traffic jam that kept them from accessing the site. It was marked as a major day in online history, and those stranded users weren't one bit happy.

 SOAPBOX   In the '80s, *"I want my MTV"* seemed to be the generation's mantra. Now, it seems *"I gotta eBay today"* is the new outcry. From my observations, people get a bit skittish if they can't get onto eBay daily to check out how their sales are going, how their bids are holding up, or what's new to be had. I'll admit it: I sometimes feel that way myself.

The press was all over eBay during June 1999's major outage, citing this as the most flagrant in a string of recent system crashes that befell the site. eBay has indeed had some problems in the first half of 1999 that have tested the loyalties of even the long-time community members. And while many beefed and belly-ached about the situation, they still came back in droves once the site was back up. Why? Because eBay is still the largest and most widely used online action site today. Wannabe auction contenders love to see the giant stumble, but still can't muster up the same draw that eBay has developed in its short history. And, although growth and proliferation are top goals of the eBay site, the powers that be still seem to remember how their bread is buttered: it's the community that makes them successful.

eBay has recognized the adverse effect of system crashes, and in a very refreshing statement, eBay's CEO (Meg Whitman) and founder (Pierre Omidyar) made a public apology to the eBay community on eBay's Announcements notice board. But, more than just apologizing, Meg and Pierre assured the community that their number one priority would always be to keep the site up and running at acceptable performance levels 24 hours a day, seven days a week. To do that, they recommitted to staff up eBay as needed and to pull up their plans for having a "hot box" ready and waiting—a disaster recovery server that would mirror the activity on the daily use server and be available to provide uninterrupted service in case another server mishap should occur.

Certainly, the events of June 10, 1999, were unique and unheralded. But what about other times when the eBay systems creep along or become unavailable to anxious shoppers and bidders? In the event of a hard outage, eBay has committed to extend all auctions that were scheduled to end during the time the outage occurred. In the case of outages that are 2 hours or longer in duration, eBay will automatically extend the ending time of any affected auctions by 24 hours. In addition, eBay will credit sellers' accounts for any fees that were levied as the auction expired during the outage period. Of course, if you're a seller and satisfied with the bids your auction received prior to the outage, you don't *have to* abide by the automatic ending time extension—you can end your auction on the spot once normal site operations resume.

But, in this online world of ours, things do go wrong and nobody is pleased about it—least of all, the site that was affected by an unforeseen problem.

SOAPBOX Well, I definitely have some opinions about system crashes and the way people respond to them. It's true that a system crash, slowdown, or any other technical difficulty is really inconvenient for everybody. But it's not like it was intentional. Having worked in a technical support position myself, I know how difficult life can be when people are clamoring and complaining about a system problem. In the support person's defense, how about when the system was working fine (usually more than 99 percent of the time)? Nobody seems to call and say, *"Thank you. The system is running great and I'm very happy."* Unexpected system problems are just that—unexpected.

The next point is the way in which people clamor and complain about system problems. In my work, people are pretty professional about their inquiries: *"Do you have an idea about when the system might be back up? Could you contact us when it is? Thank you."* At eBay, unfortunately, you can read the comments from some users on the eBay Q & A Support board who don't have much restraint (or class) when airing their concerns: *"What the @#$% is going on with the !@@#$# system??!! Isn't anyone there at eBay going to lift a @#$!$% finger to fix it?! Come on you #@#@$% support people! We want to bid!!"* That's certainly the sort of message that motivates me to want to help the individual with any and all problems. I don't mean to be crass here, but, really. It's a shame to watch people get into this kind of abusive rant because it really does nothing to speed up a fix to the problem. And the remarks just sit out there, making their perpetrators look like fools, because eBay makes you live with your words. The policy is very clear: "Once you post on the discussion board or in the Feedback Forum, you cannot erase or delete what you have written." So think about it....

When things go wrong, and they will, remember it's not the end of the world or even the end of the auction. It's just a reminder that life is what happens while you're making other plans. eBay is working to continually improve service to its users. Don't be hesitant to use the Q & A board to get some answers to your questions. eBay staff really seem to want to help.

"Well, June, I hope you don't think I was too hard on the Beaver. I just think a smart little person like him should stop and think about his choices and consequences. He'll be fine, you'll see."

chapter 10

E-Motions

OK, people, settle down. It was bound to happen. All that lookin' and biddin' and buyin' and sellin'. It was only a matter of time before someone hollered out.

"I won!"

"I lost!"

"I've always wanted one of those!"

"This auction is great!"

"This auction sucks!"

"My brain hurts!"

There's a lot going on at eBay, and you'll be caught up in it in no time. It happens to most everybody. You find something you want and you casually bid on it. *"Hmm. That was fun."* Then someone outbids you. *"Um, excuse me. I believe I was bidding on that."* You place another bid and reclaim the item. *"Outbid again?! Look, people, I'm bidding on that and I intend to win. Now everybody just back off."*

The e-motions go 'round and 'round, and just about everybody experiences them. The thrill of victory; the agony of defeat. Some users are intense; some are indifferent. They come from all over the world, from all different personal and business backgrounds, and they all have their own particular agendas. Each user brings a unique personal flavor to the auction and it makes for one of the most interesting social forums you'll ever find.

Come with me. I'll introduce you around.

What Are the Other People Like?

This is a great question to ask when you register or consider registering as an eBay user. Unfortunately, there's no real way to find a personality profile on the different eBay users (almost four million of them), so you'll have to just mill about and see who you bump into.

However, you can probably find certain categories of people who share many of the same attributes. These aren't attributes directly related to the individual's personality. Rather, these are some of the characteristics people share based on their experience at eBay.

 SOAPBOX OK, before I start here, I should leave a disclaimer. These are my opinions and my assessments of the different types of folks I've met during my time at eBay. These aren't rigid categorizations nor are they meant to be stereotypes in any way. I offer my view here just to let you know who I've encountered at eBay. Maybe you'll agree. Maybe you won't. But, no slurs or blacklisting here, OK?

The New Users

These people just came from the registration page and, boy, are they happy to be here. They're so wide-eyed and enthusiastic, you can practically hear them giggling as they search through the pages and pages of stuff up for auction. These new users might be a bit overzealous; they might be the kind of folks who contact the seller just seconds after an auction ends, exclaiming they've won and wanting to know what to do next. They're usually pretty even-tempered, cautious types. They don't want to make waves for this new ship they're sailing. They'll have a lot of questions to ask and might make some *rookie* moves. It's OK, though. As long as they're polite and respectful, help them along. They could bring a bunch of money or a bunch of cool stuff of their own to auction. Everybody starts out here. How do you quickly tell who the new users are? They'll have the feedback rating of 10 or less.

The Casual Users

These users have probably been using eBay for a while. They cruise in from time to time, poke through the listings to see what's around, and occasionally drop a bid. They bid quietly, generally without asking too many questions. When you interact with them at the end of a deal, they're typically somewhat curt and concise in communication. Not rude by any means, but not overly excited about the auction. After all, it's just some junk that someone's selling—why give it more credit than it's worth? These users typically have a moderate feedback rating (around 50 or so).

The Professional Users

These users have found eBay to be just what they hoped for: a veritable gold mine of business opportunity. They've seen the eBay population and have carefully evaluated who's buying, who's selling, and what's hot. They might be those professional buyers who seek out and find the goods people are wanting. They hunt up the sleeper auctions and nab 'em while no one else is looking. They sell items like pros. They always seem to come up with that rare or hot piece that everyone is clamoring for. How do they do it? Well, they're probably making a living at this, and they put in a lot of time and effort to buy and sell the things that will keep them comfortably in business. They have a *very* professional style when interacting with others. Customer service and satisfaction are usually very high on their list; if not, they'll start losing business. They're typically not the kind of user you can cut a deal with. They have to maintain a profit margin, but can frequently be good sources for finding the things you're looking for. Their feedback rating is usually quite high (into the hundreds) as proof of their commitment to quality and their customers. These might be self-employed individuals or bona fide businesses that have expanded into the realm of online commerce.

The Elite

These guys are *good.* They're the ones who can bid behind their backs, using a mirror and clicking with their big toe. They've absorbed eBay and assimilated with it to become one perpetual auction organism. They're smooth, clean, and sometimes a bit cocky. They run in cybernetic circles with others of their own stature. They're typically easy to deal with but won't put up with any nonsense or shenanigans. Give these users respect; they've earned it. They usually have an amazingly high feedback rating (yes, often beyond 1,000). They're probably eBay lifers who were around right when the site went live in 1995. They're usually pretty helpful to the other users, and will frequent the chat spaces to drop pearls of wisdom. Their area of interest is probably more focused, and they have become experts at what they buy and sell.

The Not-So-Nice Users

These users aren't as frequently encountered, but they do exist. They're not often outwardly mean (usually), but they can be blunt and a bit cutting. They might be your professional Web rats from the cyber underground. They sometimes bring the Net attitude with them, believing all is fair game in cyberspace. They might not have come to grips with the fact that, even though eBay is in the Internet, it's still a social forum where people should conduct themselves with common sense and restraint. These users might insist your prices are too high if your auction reserve isn't met. They might want to charge you a whole bunch for shipping and handling and then blast you when you ask, *"Why so much?"* They might just be in a bad mood. Maybe they've been burned in some online transaction in the past and (maybe subconsciously) seeking a bit of revenge. Maybe they just weren't brought up with very good manners. Their feedback ratings could include some negative comments. Check their temper ahead of time before you buy or sell with them.

But no matter how much I generalize, there is still a lot of gray area when it comes to the different users you'll meet at eBay. The users' styles are all over the chart, and they're most often a Neapolitan mixture of many of these characteristics. Overall, the really fine users stay for the long haul, and the stinkers tend to get bagged and discarded. The real key to your eBay experience will be how you handle *your* e-motions. Remember the rules of netiquette and use them every time you communicate.

 SOAPBOX Now, having said all that, I would almost guarantee that you'll have excellent experiences with most eBay users. The eBay *community* is real, and it exists thanks to active nurturing from the eBay staff and, most of all, the eBay enthusiasts. The great majority of the community recognizes eBay for what it is and the opportunity it offers. No one with any real integrity wants to poison this pond. The wise members realize that everyone brings something to the party, and the variety of interactions you'll encounter are what make eBay the exciting site it has become.

Competition at Its Finest

It's a battleground in there. Without a doubt, you'll be going mouse to mouse with somebody at some time. You might get in the middle of a bidding war, taking your best shots against others like you who are just as determined to win. You might be barking to hawk your lot of goodies to potential bidders, trying to draw them away from the other seller who might be selling the same thing. It's capitalism. It's an open market. It's fun.

When the competition swings into high gear, e-motion really comes into play, big time. Some people shy away from any kind of confrontation. If they're outbid, they might just go away and look for something else. They don't want any trouble and they prefer not to "battle" for any auction. But some people see opposing bids as a throwing down of the gauntlet and a formal (but friendly) duel. *"Have at you!"*

When you get into a bidding confrontation, you're going to get excited. You can't see your opponents, but they're there and they've just unsheathed their mice. In the beginning, you might feel it as an affront, almost offensive, when someone else bids on something you want. Bidders can repeatedly outbid one another in a tit-for-tat slapfest to see who has the stamina to stay the course. It's not personal. Two people just want the same thing. So, lesson one is to understand that this is not a personal attack. No one is out to *get you*. Most often, they don't even know you.

But you decide you won't back down. Come Hell or high water, you're going to stand triumphant. Now you're on a crusade. This isn't just a bid for some silly item in an auction. This is a bid that represents all the unfortunate ones who were struck down in the battlefield of bids. You will restore honor to their names and dignity to their quest. You shall be victorious! (Getting a little carried away, aren't you?)

You will get impassioned from time to time when you work the auctions. But, when you're in the midst of a bidding frenzy, try to stop and ask yourself, *"Do I really want this item, or do I just want to win?"* Again, this is where the sport of the auction comes in, and the bid-battle is enough to make you bounce in your chair excitedly enjoying the virtual tug-of-war. But what if you win? Well, *Hooray!* Right?

Remember the winner's curse? It can happen to you when you least expect it. You win the auction, and you are the master. You've fought the good fight and to you go the spoils—just as soon as you pay the bill. *"Oh . . . right . . . the bill."* Check your wallet and your ego at the main screen before you jump into the action. Everybody gets overextended at one time or another. Know when to let it rest.

One other thing to watch for when you're in the midst of competition: don't outbid others just because you can. I know it sounds a little stupid, but it has happened. Some users might be very skilled in their bidding, and they might zap an auction just because they saw some excited bidders bidding and decided to go kick their marbles. These would probably be those not-so-nice users, and sometimes they don't even intend to honor their bid. They just wanted to win the auction. *"It's not any kind of agreement you can hold me to. It's just the Internet."* Yeah, right. See ya, Charlie.

OK, but how does this competitive playground affect the moods and attitudes of the folks involved? Good question. Here's what I've seen.

The Euphoric Winner

Hey! Here comes Happy Dan, and he's grinnin' from ear to ear. He just won an auction, and he's ready to tell the whole world about it.

It's fun to win an auction. You see those words, *"You are the high bidder."* It feels good. If the item is something you really want, then you're the one who just grabbed the brass ring. It excites you to the point that you want to go out and win another, and another, and another. Enjoy the happy moment. It's probably what you'll experience most of the time, and it's the reason why eBay is so popular with Net users. I'm happy for you, too.

The Disgruntled Loser

Then there's the user who doesn't win, and he's sometimes not very happy about it and might decide to let you know. This one's a real Poopy Pete. He might be more than disappointed—he might demand restitution. Call him a poor sport or maybe someone who just wasn't ready for the competition.

A story was shared with me about one fellow who was outbid in an auction at the last minute. He was very disappointed and immediately contacted the high bidder to beg for the item; he wanted it that bad. The high bidder, though, wanted the item too and had put up the proper funds to make sure he got it. It was a fair deal by auction rules. Incensed at the winning bidder for not relinquishing his rightful prize, the losing bidder went so far as to post a negative comment in the winner's feedback file. What's up with that?! Obviously, this disgruntled loser was way out of line, and it was necessary to report him to the powers that be at eBay.

In extreme cases, some disgruntled losers had tried to mail-bomb the winner's feedback file, posting line after line of negative feedback. You've heard of *road rage*—this is *auction animosity*. It's not good, and it's best not to get caught up in it. Report this kind of activity to the eBay administrators at once. Old Poopy Pete won't be registered for very long.

 NOTE You won't actually have to deal with this particular ploy from Poopy Pete. eBay has modified the Feedback Forum so that negative feedback can only be posted in reference to an actual auction and can only be posted by the actual seller and high bidder.

When you lose an auction at eBay, just let it slide off like you're wearing a Teflon overcoat. It's going to happen, and you'll move on. Of course, if you *really* want something bad enough, be sure you've put down a maximum bid to cover it. It might cost you a bit more, but maybe you'll avoid the disappointment of defeat.

How Do You Rate?

So what will your auction attitude be? Think about it—your attitude will both follow you and precede you. Part of what makes the eBay community so powerful is the candor community members bring to their interactions. If you're being a creep, they'll let you know. If you're a real jewel, they'll let you know that, too. They give credit where credit is due, and one good turn usually receives another.

Decide, then, what your motivations at eBay will be. Are you just a looky-loo? Fine. Are you going to be a casual user who pops in from time to time? That's fine, too. Are you going to be a die-hard who really wants to make a strong statement and amass a high positive feedback rating? Super cool. You'll need to work for it, though. Whatever your reason for being at eBay, conduct yourself in a way that will ensure the welcome mat is always there to greet you when you return.

Does it really matter? Does anyone really care online? In cyberspace, can anyone hear you scream? Yes, they can. eBay is a big deal to a lot of people. It's a hobby to many, but it's also a way of life to many more. If you've been around the Net long enough, you'll know that people start to develop a sort of *virtual lifestyle.* eBay holds high importance to several million people. They're all working hard to make sure the site doesn't sour. Join them in preserving and improving the way the site works, and you'll see the gains to be had.

part 3

Becoming a
Savvy Bidder

chapter 11

Being an Informed Bidder

If information is power, then you're about to become herculean. You're ready to get in there and take control of how and when you bid. Control in bidding is always in your hands, but here's where you develop and sharpen your shrewdness when you consider those items you will and will not bid on.

You're not just searching for items anymore. Now you're *mining* for more information about what you're bidding on, who's selling it, and who else is bidding against you. This is where you make the change from an average bidder to an informed buyer.

Research the Items You Want

Research, by its name, could conjure up feelings of boring and tedious investigation. When I thought of research, I used to recall all those book reports and term papers I had to write. Sitting for hours in some stuffy old library, hoping to find the information I needed, struggling with the Dewey Decimal System, and being distracted by wondering how that librarian could still find horn-rimmed glasses. Well no more. This is the Internet age.

You'll find you can do an amazing amount of research on the Net at lightning speed. It's fast, it's fun, and it's fairly reliable. A few minutes of looking up information on the Net can often make you an instant expert and can ultimately help you make better bidding decisions on eBay.

For example, assume you're a big *Star Wars* fan and you pride yourself on having one of the most complete collections around—including a rare one-of-a-kind pair of Darth Vader's jockey shorts. Anyway, 1999 is your year because finally the first prequel of the series has been released: *Episode 1: The Phantom Menace.* Fans around the world have been waiting for this cinematic event, and the excitement (and hype) has been at a high pitch.

In late 1998, advance movie posters for the new *Star Wars* prequel started showing up on eBay. Fans went bananas. These posters caught so much attention that high bids were exceeding $100 dollars. Why? Well, they're "rare" and "limited" and "official." Were they? You probably wanted to do some research to be sure.

First stop: your local search engine. Using Yahoo! or Alta Vista or whatever your favorite engine might be, you enter a search for "Star Wars" or "Star Wars Episode 1" or "movie posters." In no time, you're served up a whole bunch of matches that lead you to private and commercial Web sites that cater to your interests. Upon visiting a few pages, you learn that there are some variations to this exciting new poster. You learn about a limited run of 10,000 single-sided posters, some of which have a special watermark on the back only visible under a black light. You also learn about a second print run of the poster that is two-sided. It seems to be more common. Most important, you learn that you can visit the official 20th Century Fox Star Wars home page (**www.starwars.com**) and browse around the official Mos Espa Marketplace (just down the dusty road from the Mos Eisley cantina). Enter the marketplace, and you'll see the featured item for sale is—ready?—the official advance movie poster for *The Phantom Menace.* The price: $12.95 (limit three per customer, please).

Tip Well, since *The Phantom Menace* found its way to theaters, the advance 1-sheet seems to have sold out at Mos Espa. However, don't forget to do some searching at other movie memorabilia sites online. You can bet that a lot of folks have these posters and you can probably still get one for a decent price.

This example shows you that a bit of quick research on your part can make you more informed about the product you want to bid on and buy, and also helps you understand if there are other ways, outside the auction, to get the goods you want. Now, I don't profess total accuracy in my account of the variations of the poster for *The Phantom Menace*—I haven't planned on buying one myself. However, I could hit a few more Web sites very quickly, contact some Web site proprietors, and get the complete skinny on the posters without ever having to leave my home office. If that's not information by convenience, then I don't know what is.

The same can be said about older items you might want to bid on. Internet search engines can usually turn up almost anything you're interested in learning more about. With so many million people on the Net, you're 99 percent assured you'll find someone who has taken the time to document some information about the item or topic that interests you. Just for fun, I did a search on "saratoga trunk" from Yahoo! What's a Saratoga trunk? Well, it's a trunk that was used on stagecoaches in the real olden days; my folks had one in my home when I was a kid (and, no, my folks didn't once *ride* on stagecoaches; they bought the trunk at an antique store). I don't know why I just thought of it, but I did. So something as esoteric as a Saratoga trunk might be difficult to research quickly and easily. The results of my search: I found **www.trunk.com**, a Web site hosted by the Trunk Shop in Portsmouth, New Hampshire, which specializes in antique trunks. Go figure! There I quickly learned about a variety of different trunk styles and the fact that trunks were made within a general time period of about 150 years (1770–1930). The site has FAQs and sells many trunks and also provides an appraisal service for the trunk you may already have. Immediately before writing this paragraph, I had no idea such a place existed or even the period of time that trunks were originally manufactured. I think you see where I'm going with this.

But you don't always have to search the Web high and low looking for information about an item up for auction. In fact, you often don't have to look much further than eBay itself. Much of the information you'll need about a particular auction item is best found on eBay. Look at other listings for the same item (it's common to find many of the same thing up for auction at eBay). Each seller will list the item with differing amounts of descriptive information. You can learn a lot about an item by reading how different sellers have described it. Don't forget to search for completed auctions of that item, too. See what the sellers had to say about their special something, then compare that information to what you're finding in your Web site searches. You might need to go back and hit a few more Web sites or call or e-mail a few people until you're sure you have the facts.

Another thing you can do is contact sellers and buyers from the completed auctions. Although this is not something you'd want to abuse, registered eBay users can get e-mail addresses of other users (the buyers and sellers) and ask them questions about the item they're interested in. Most eBay users are friendly and helpful people. Almost as a rule, collectors in general are pretty excited to help other collectors in their quests. Again, use this privilege responsibly, but don't be afraid to use it. Who knows? Someone might contact you asking about something *you* bid on and bought.

Rare and Hard to Find?

By these terms alone, eyebrows raise and curiosities pique: What do you have that is rare and hard to find? Don't be taken in by cheap imitations, reprints, or other inferior items. This is the *real thing,* and I'm going to make it available to you for this limited time. Uh-oh. You'd better jump at the chance to own such a unique treasure before it's too late. By the way, is it too late?

The terms *rare* and *hard-to-find* can be pretty subjective—what's rare to one person may be not-so-rare to another. Why? A lot of the difference can be a matter of personal taste. You might have a rare autographed photo of Alf (the fuzzy little prime-time alien critter who, even after four years on NBC, never truly caught on). But his autographed photo is probably quite a rare item, considering how few were made before the show was canceled. Anyway, it's rare, and you're ready to sell it. The only problem is that it seems bidders for this item are also rare—you can't find 'em. That Alf autograph might be hard to find, but it could be because no one's looking.

NOTE   By the way, if you're an Alf fan and looking for this photo, just e-mail me. I have one and, boy, is it ever rare.

There is a silver lining here, though. If you like Alf and want to build an Alf collection cheaply and easily, then the odds are in your favor. It's actually quite a pleasant thing when you're looking for some item that means a lot to you and means absolutely nothing to others. You'll probably get what you want without getting soaked.

Next point: if something is so rare, why do you see five up for auction? There are several reasons for this. First, it's possible that the rare item you're looking at is only rare in certain locations. Geography plays a big part in the availability of an item. When Taco Bell's little talking Pablo (the actual name of the shivering Chihuahua) was introduced in the form of a talking stuffed premium, it was only available in certain areas of the United States. This was test marketing because Taco Bell wanted to be sure the little bilingual buddy would have enough consumer appeal. Of course, those of us who've been around see it as more of a controlled shortage to drive consumer demand up just before a widespread availability—which did finally happen. But the point here is that many people couldn't find the little yapping Pablos locally, but could find them on eBay. Heck, I wanted a set to give to my son for Christmas, and I was prepared to pay the average price of $35 for a set of four (they were selling at regional Taco Bell restaurants for $2.99 each). Lucky for me, Pablo made a nationwide appearance in late November 1998, and I got the set for $16. The reality of the situation, though, was that the toys were truly hard to find unless you lived in one of the test market states—where I doubt other eBayers were too inclined to get theirs at the auction. They made some hefty profits, though.

You might ask, when talking about an out-of-production or older item, how multiple copies of those kinds of things can be available on eBay. After all, if they're not being made any more, where is the supply coming from? Did somebody really think to stash away a bunch of something 30 or more years ago, knowing there would be some kind of high demand today? Maybe, but it's probably more likely to go this way: somebody made a *warehouse find*. You might have heard of these; it's when somebody is finally cleaning out that old back room of a store, storage site, or wherever and comes across a box or boxes of something from years ago—filled with nostalgic treasures. Next stop: eBay!

Are warehouse finds a bad thing for bidders? Not at all. Just be aware that an item you haven't seen for years and bid high on might be subject to a radical drop in value when the other 143 just like it show up for auction. If you're buying for investment purposes, your investment value might go south quick when the rest of the stash hits the open market. Again, it's that law of supply and demand. Too much supply; no more demand.

How do you know when you're buying an item that was recently discovered in bulk in a moldy old warehouse? Pretty easily, really. Watch the auctions to see if the same item goes up for auction multiple times. Be especially attentive to the item's condition. If there are several showing in mint (like new) condition, they've probably got a bunch of identical relatives huddled in a box somewhere, waiting to be sprung on the world. If it's an item you've been wanting for a long time (I suspect my Hamburger Hungry ring was from a warehouse find), then you're really in luck because you're getting it in probably the best possible condition. If you see multiple copies of the item you bought, and they're selling for less and less, just look away. You've got yours, and you should be happy about it. If you feel like it, buy another. Many collectors like to buy in quantity when multiples are available and are affordable. That way you have one to stash away and one to use, play with, or whatever.

The final point about *rare* and *hard-to-find* is to watch those terms closely. They can be a real attention-getter for sellers. Whether in the title of the auction listing or within the detailed description, try to read between the lines when you're being sold something that is too good to be true. Many people say, *"If it seems too good to be true, then it probably is."*

You'll need to do your homework—that Net research and so forth—to be sure you can bid with confidence and without getting burned by claims that just aren't true. Sometimes fraud comes into play; some sellers, although a tiny minority, might try to pull the wool over your eyes and pass off some bogus item for a rare original. Be diligent and careful.

Of course, you will find some rare stuff on eBay that's genuine and on the level. When you do, great! There are a lot of terrific and unique items up for auction every day, and they're real treasures when you find them. That's a lot of what makes eBay so much fun.

Investigate the Seller

Should you hire yourself a gumshoe to find out what kind of character this seller is? Is the seller into racketeering? Part of the syndicate or the mob? Somebody who's been run out of three states already? Or maybe it's just a nice guy selling some silly stuff at an auction.

Investigating a seller isn't a covert act or paranoid reaction on your part. It's a good way for you to learn even more about what you're planning to bid on. More important, you'll be better informed before you bid.

What can you learn about an item by doing a little seller investigation? First and foremost, you can learn a lot about the way the seller does business. Check that feedback rating and see what others have to say about the seller. Does the seller ship quickly? How is the quality of the goods the seller sold to other people? How well did the seller package and ship the goods? Is the seller polite and professional? Does the seller have any negative feedback and, if so, who posted it and for what reasons? All of this is easily learned by reviewing the comments other buyers have left for the seller.

Another thing you can find out about an item is, possibly, where the seller got it. Does it matter? Not always, but it could be useful for you to know. If you know what the seller buys, you could see that the item you're buying is something the seller just bought and is now reselling to you—and probably at a profit.

Buying and reselling isn't anything evil or unfair, but try to cut out the middleman whenever you can. Do a search on the seller's eBay ID in the *Bidder Search* box on eBay's search page. What shows up? Check for the same bidder in completed auctions. What has the seller bought at eBay in the last 30 days? Are you bidding on that seller's recent purchase? Again, there's nothing bad about buying and reselling; you'll probably do it yourself from time to time. But every time an item changes hands, it probably costs the next guy a few more dollars.

The other thing that's useful in knowing what a seller buys is whether the shopping list includes something that you already have. Why? Maybe the seller would be interested in doing some trades with you. Maybe the seller has some great *Brady Bunch* stuff for sale that you want. Maybe you find the seller's a real *Hogan's Heroes* fan—and would just love to hear about that *Hogan's Heroes* collection that you want to get rid of. Maybe you two could trade and avoid the whole cost and expense of the auction altogether. You'll probably make a new friend in the process. Just an idea.

Checking Bid History

As you consider bidding on an item, you naturally wonder how much the thing could eventually sell for. How high might people bid for something? Nobody knows because so many factors come into play when an item is being auctioned: how popular the item is, what condition the item's in, how many other bidders might be looking for the same item. You can't predict what will happen, but you *can* look back at what has happened in the past. You can learn a lot from history, even auction history.

The best way to use auction history is for researching final bid prices. Sometimes an item will receive an unusually high bid that would pretty much blow your hair back. *"Why such a high bid,"* you might ask. *"Is that thing really worth that much?"* It's possible that what you want to bid on is a very valuable piece, but it could have been a fluke bid.

When you see an item get a really high bid, check the *Bid history*—that link you'll see immediately to the right of the final number of bids placed on the Item Detail screen (look back at Figure 8-2 to see where the link appears). For many auctions that ended in a high final price, you'll see a list of maybe 10—maybe more—bidders who all contributed to the final price. That's your clue that it was a pretty popular item. But you could also find as few as two bidders listed in the bid history, telling you that what happened was a good old-fashioned auction shootout. Two people *really* wanted the item and they duked it out, probably right up to the end.

An auction shootout—often called a *bidding war*—usually brings on a high final bid, but it's also usually the sign of a fluke price. Since only two, at most three, bidders were involved, the bidding could have been an act of pure competition and might have been one of those heat-of-the-moment things. It's pretty safe to assume the high price realized is not going to be the new benchmark of pricing for the item over the long haul.

In most cases, you can review the final bids for the same item you want to bid on, including the bidding history, to find the average price the item seems to command. That helps you set an expectation in your own mind about how much you might need to bid and be able to spend if you want the same item for yourself.

The bid history also shows you who was bidding and, most important, what their high bids were. You can't see a bidder's maximum bid until after an auction closes. Once the auction's over, all final bids are revealed, showing each maximum bid and how much other people thought the item was worth. If most seem to hover within a few dollars of one another, then that's where the average price can be found.

Tip Be aware that you'll never see the maximum bid used by the high bidder. Rather, the only bid amount you'll see will be whatever increment was required to become the high bidder. The high bidder's maximum bid might have been much higher than what is shown on the bid history page. But that shouldn't be a big deal to you—that bidder now has one of these items and probably won't be bidding against you in future auctions.

Watch for big gaps in the final bid prices, too. Many bidders will bid low on just about everything, hoping to get a great deal. If you see a sizable gap between the lowest bidders and the highest bidders, it might be the sign of some folks looking for a steal. Don't use those bid amounts as your gauge of the item's worth; you might just be fooling yourself.

And, remember, any price history you check can be of help to you, but it still can't assure you what an item will sell for in the end. New users are coming to eBay every day, and they bring their fresh enthusiasm and money with them. Set your own maximum prices and check your own level of determination. But I think you'll be high bidder more times than not.

Check Relistings

When an item is relisted, it's because it didn't sell the first time. Maybe it didn't receive any bids, or maybe it had a reserve price that wasn't met. And, maybe the high bidder backed out of the deal. *(Boo! Hiss!!)* Relistings are your indicator that a deal might be in the works, though.

When a seller relists an item, it's because the original expectations for selling the item weren't met. Maybe the opening bid was too high and it scared bidders away. Maybe the condition of the item wasn't good enough that people would really want to own the thing. Maybe the seller had some negative feedback and other bidders didn't feel confident bidding on the item. Whatever the reason, these are all things you should investigate before you bid.

As I said before, the auction is its own self-correcting marketplace where prices and values come into balance. You can usually find a relisted item easily when you check the completed auctions for a particular seller. If the same item shows up in the completed category but with no bidders, check out the completed item details page (that is, the item number listing when the item was previously up for auction). Check the starting bid of the item and whether a reserve price was set at that time. When the starting bid is lower on the active listing than it was on the completed—and unsuccessful—listing, the seller may be motivated to sell. You might have good luck in this auction this time around.

When you check the item out against its previous listings, be very careful to look at the description and any other conditions of the auction. Maybe the description has changed because it wasn't very clear the previous time. Maybe the title of the item changed; remember that a misspelling can keep an item from showing up as a hit on an item search. Maybe other costs (postage, handling, insurance) have changed since the last listing.

A relisted item also tells you that there might not have been much interest in the item before. Maybe it's a dead item and maybe it's only of interest to you. Again, another good sign that you might be successful in this auction. Do all your research on the item, the past history of the item (in other auctions, not just this seller's), and any pricing indicators. Think about contacting a bidder from the auction the last time the item was listed. Did the seller ever consider negotiating a lower price after the auction ended without an official winner?

Finally, a relisted item may be an open door to negotiate a deal outside of eBay. This is especially true when you find a relisting that includes description text like *"Previous high bidder backed out of the deal."* This really makes a seller sour, and might be the motivation to just get rid of the darned thing. Hello!

A friend told me of a fax machine he was shopping for on eBay. He found one up for auction, and being the fine auction researcher he is, he did some looking into other, similar auctions, past and present, as well as in regard to the seller himself. The fax machine he was bidding on was listed for a reserve price, and the reserve hadn't been met. The machine had been listed a couple of times before. The first time, the reserve wasn't met. The second time, the seller stated he lowered the reserve and found a high bidder. Unfortunately, the high bidder the second time around backed out of his bid. The third time the seller was losing patience. My buddy decided to contact the seller directly (via e-mail) to find out the current reserve price and get a general feeling from the seller. At the same time, my friend thought it would be interesting to go ahead and make an offer for the fax machine outright and see if the seller would be interested.

 ALERT Before we get off on a misunderstanding, be aware that, although the reserve price hadn't been met in the fax auction, my friend was the present high bidder. He wasn't trying to undercut any other high bidder, which would be an unfair and unwelcome tactic.

The seller of the fax machine decided the offer my friend made was fair and, since my friend was the current high bidder, the seller agreed to end the auction early and complete the one-on-one sale. Both my friend and the seller were pleased with the final transaction. Auctions can be ended early, and you'll learn more about that in Chapter 16.

Picture—Perfect?

Many auctions will have pictures included with the description. These are a real benefit—almost a must these days—in helping bidders feel better about the item they'd like to bid on. A good auction listing will include a picture of the item or, better yet, several pictures that give different views of the item (front, back, top, and so on). If there is any damage to an item, it's especially useful to you as the bidder if the seller provides a really good close-up of the damaged area so you can thoroughly inspect it.

While pictures are useful, not all pictures you'll find are very good. Photography is getting easier and easier these days—especially digital photography—but bad pictures still happen. You might find an auction with pictures but they're a bit blurry. Bummer. Maybe the pictures are kind of dark. Too bad. Maybe the pictures have bad coloring or whatever. What can you do to get a better look at the item with the pictures that have been provided? Actually, you can do more than you think with a bad photo.

The real benefit of digital cameras and digital images is that it's getting easier and easier to make adjustments to photos so you can improve the image without taking another picture. If you're a prospective bidder, taking another picture is simply not an option (unless you can convince the seller to do so). But you can grab a copy of the picture in an auction listing, and run it thorough an image editing program to see if you can squeeze a few drops of blood out of the stone.

You can save any picture you can see in an auction listing. Just position your mouse pointer over the image, click the right mouse button, and select *Save image as* from the shortcut menu. Choose a file directory you want to save the image to and, bam, it's yours. Now all you need to do is power up your favorite image editing application and bring in the image you just saved.

For dark pictures, try working with the contrast, saturation, and hue controls. You might find you can quickly get a better look at the item using a relatively bad photo. If the coloring of the image is off, try using the hue or tint controls. Be aware, though, that this method might give you a better look at the item, but you could also deceive yourself into seeing colors you adjusted that no longer match the real colors of the actual item. And if the image is blurry, work with the image sharpening controls. This might help bring out some of the detail you couldn't see before.

TIP Don't forget about those free trial copies of popular software applications you can get right off the Net—including image editing applications. Visit **www.share-ware.com, www.download.com**, or **www.tucows.com**. You'll be glad you did.

If You Have Questions, Just Ask

And that brings up the final topic: if you've got questions, ask. No one is reading your mind out there, but most are willing to help you better understand something you want to bid on. As an informed consumer (that's you), it's your right to ask about an item, and it keeps the sellers honest and committed to being sure they'll properly and truthfully advertise what they're selling.

As a registered eBay user, you can find out the e-mail addresses of other registered users (they can get yours as well, but that's what makes the community a community). If the description of an auction item you're interested in is a little unclear, send an e-mail note to the seller. Remember on the auction details page eBay provides the *Ask seller a question* link, which will automatically pop up an e-mail message creation window. Ask more about the completeness of an item, the color, the markings, the original packaging, the size, whatever it is that will help you feel more confident about bidding. Most sellers are happy to receive e-mail questions because it means someone is seeing the item and is interested enough to want to know more. To the seller, this might mean a nice bid and an eventual sale. You can bet that most sellers will be more than happy to help persuade you (in an honest way) why their item is the one you want to bid on.

When you ask the seller a question, you're also finding out how friendly, responsive, and committed the seller might be. Sellers, pay attention here. If a potential bidder wants to know more about an item, answer the question ASAP. Bidders, you'll quickly find out what kind of business ethics the seller has depending on the tone of the reply you get, how completely your question is answered, and how quickly your question is answered. If you get no reply to your question, that might be a red flag. Would a lack of response suggest a slow seller who might not ship your item quickly? Who knows? But, it's the old saying, "You only get one chance to make a first impression." Bidders, you're going to have to determine for yourself if you would feel comfortable bidding with the seller based upon the way your questions are answered (or left unanswered).

And just a few more things you should be sure you understand *before* you ever place a bid:

■ Make sure you fully understand the shipping method and expected shipping charges. If you only have a P.O. box, understand that UPS won't deliver to it. If you're in a different country from the seller, there are a few options in shipping available. Which one will be used?

■ Make sure you know if carrier insurance is going to be used while your item is in transit to you. Usually the buyer will have to pay for insurance, and a buyer who chooses not to put up the additional dollar or two (cheap) assumes all risk if the item is damaged for any reason.

■ Make sure the seller will pack the item properly for its journey to you. Most sellers do this automatically, and you really shouldn't have to badger them about it. But if you're concerned, ask how the item will be packaged for shipment.

■ Find out if the seller has a return or *satisfaction guaranteed* policy. Many sellers offer a three- to seven-day return period for items. If, after your questions have been answered, you still aren't 100 percent certain about the item, the return privilege will be your best friend.

chapter 12

Understanding the Auction Variations

Variety is the spice of life, and you're going to see some variety among the auctions you run into on eBay. There are only a few basic auction formats that eBay uses, but there is an open end to the creative way in which sellers might work with those formats. eBay is an entrepreneurial venue, and many eBay users are quite clever and creative in the way they work their auctions.

To make you more confident and skillful in your bidding, you'll want to be sure you understand exactly how the bid formats work at eBay. You'll only see the English auction and the Dutch auction in use at eBay. However, these two formats still have some nuances that can be used by sellers. Your task is to quickly understand the seller's approach, the reasoning behind a particular auction format, and how the bidding should take place while an item is on the auction block.

Minimum Bid Auctions

The *minimum bid* auction—also referred to as the *straight auction*—is where bidders start by posting the minimum acceptable bid for an item. That's easy enough. The opening bid has to be the amount the seller establishes as the minimum bid to get the auction started. It could be a low opening bid of $1 or it could be some higher opening bid. It's all up to the seller and the value the seller places on the item that's up for grabs. Once the first bid is cast at the opening bid value, then further bidding follows the traditional *ascending-price* auction rules, where each additional bidder has to offer the appropriate incremental amount in order to have the new bid accepted.

NOTE The incremental bid value for an auction is determined automatically at eBay based on the current high bid on an item. For example, an item that has a current high bid of $5 will only require bidders to raise the bid by 50 cents. If the high bid rises to $25, the new minimum bid increment will be $1. The bid increments are automatically adjusted and applied by eBay as the auction progresses. For quick reference, here's a table explaining the bid increment breakpoints:

Current High Bid	Minimum Bid Increment
$0.01 – $0.99	$0.05
$1.00 – $4.99	$0.25
$5.00 – $24.99	$0.50
$25.00 – $99.99	$1.00
$100.00 – $249.99	$2.50
$250.00 – $499.99	$5.00
$500.00 – $999.99	$10.00
$1000.00 – $2499.99	$25.00
$2500.00 – $4999.99	$50.00
$5000.00 and up	$100.00

You can be relatively successful using only the minimum required bid increment. In fact, many auctions are won at eBay with the simple increment of $1 or less. When you bid, eBay will tell you the minimum increment you must offer. Once you've done that, submit the bid and see what happens.

TIP *"Hey! eBay said I needed to add a 50-cent bid increment, then after I submitted my bid, it said I hadn't bid enough and rejected my bid. What happened?"*

This can sometimes happen when you are entering your bid and someone else places a bid for the same item before yours is submitted and processed. In effect, the minimum bid increment you were about to place was already placed by someone else. Now you need to decide if you want to meet the new minimum bid increment. This can also be a signal to you that bidding might be heating up for the item you're interested in.

Bidding in small increments is the most traditional way of bidding in an auction. Just like you saw on TV or in the movies, bidders keep upping the high bid a little at a time until all but one drop out of the race. Minimum bidding is probably the most time-consuming way to bid—you have to keep adding your next bid if you want to stay in the auction. It's also one of the easiest ways to be beaten in an auction. All it takes is another bidder to add another minimum increment to outbid you and, if the auction's drawing to a close, you might not have enough time to place one more bid.

Proxy Bid Auctions

One of the most dramatic things you might see happen in a live auction (such as in an actual auction parlor) is what's known as placing a *jump bid*. The auctioneer may only be asking for another dollar increment and then, all of a sudden from the back of the room, someone *jumps* up the bid by $100. The other bidders gasp at the boldness of the move. Why would the brazen bidder throw down such a high increment? It's psychology. When a jump bid appears, it's often enough to scare away the small fish who were happily throwing down their nickels and dimes. The jump bid often goes beyond many of the other bidders' maximum bids and helps bring the auction to a quick close.

eBay doesn't have anything quite as dramatic as the jump bid, but it does have a close cousin known as the *proxy bid*. The proxy bid works in a regular English auction on eBay. The proxy bidding system is one that allows bidding to be automatically done on your behalf based on your instructions. Proxy bidding systems are sometimes referred to as *bidding buddies* or, at eBay, as the *eBay elf*. That's cute, but how does it work?

You first saw the proxy bidding system during the discussion in Chapter 8. There, you entered your *maximum bid*, which was the most you would be willing to bid (spend) on an item. Imagine you found an item with a minimum bid of $10. Nobody else has bid; you'll be the first. But, you think, in the event that other bidders come by and want to bid, you might easily be outbid if you only enter the minimum bid amount. You decide the most you would be willing to spend on the item is $35. Enter that as your maximum in the eBay bidding screen. But when you submit your bid and it is processed, the high bid—yours—is only $10. That's how eBay interprets the high bid on the item. You are the only bidder and even though you set a maximum of $35, it only requires a bid of $10 to make you the high bidder.

Then other bidders come by and decide they want to bid on the item. Bidder #2 places the minimum bid of $10.50 (remembering that eBay requires minimum bid increments). Bidder #2 is immediately outbid by you because of the proxy bidding system. You've told eBay you'll bid as high as $35, and since Bidder #2 bid $10.50, eBay bids on your behalf to keep you as the high bidder. The new high bid, still yours, is $11. See how that works? eBay will continue to bid for you until your maximum bid is reached.

So what about the jump bidder? After all, other bidders can enter their maximum bids, too, and not just minimum bids. Along comes Bidder #3, who thinks the item is worth $25 and posts that as a maximum. eBay accepts the $25 bid—and immediately outbids it based on your instructions. The new high bid, again it's still yours, is $26. The proxy bidding system will work the minimum bids back and forth between competing bidders—using the table of calculated bid increments—until one of the bidders' maximum bid amounts is beat. In this case, you're still the high bidder because Bidder #3's maximum of $25 was not high enough to beat your maximum bid of $35. You're still the reigning champ.

Enter Bidder #4—a minor-league Rockefeller who's been looking for this particular item for a long time. Cost is no object for Bidder #4, who plops down a maximum bid of $100. Sorry, tiger. You've just been outbid. The new high bid, which belongs to Bidder #4, is $36—the minimum bid increment required to outbid any other maximum bids. Bidder #4 didn't know it would take $36 to outbid you because eBay didn't reveal your maximum bid. That only emerged after the new bid was processed and it turned out that $35 was the old maximum bid.

Does this mean you're sunk? No. You can get back into the bidding. Remember that if enough time remains before the auction closes (at least 12 to 24 hours), eBay can issue an "outbid" notice to your e-mail account. Or you can periodically check on the auction to see if you're still on top. When you're outbid, you can always place another bid to try to get back in. This time, though, you're at a disadvantage because you don't know what the new high bidder's maximum bid might be. You can only place successive bids or a jump bid (new maximum) of your own to try to get back into the leadership status. In this example, you'll need to bid more than $100 to become the high bidder again.

TIP   What would happen if you put in a new maximum bid of $100 in this auction? You don't know that's what Bidder #4's maximum is, but what happens if two bidders enter the same maximum bid? In eBay auctions, when this happens the bidder who was first to enter the maximum bid amount will continue to reign as high bidder. This is actually interesting when it happens. If you bid a new maximum of $100 and are notified that you have been outbid (by proxy), eBay will report the new high bid is $100. *Ah ha!* Now you know what Bidder #4's maximum bid is, yet you aren't obligated to pay $100 for the item because, by rules of being first, Bidder #4 is still the high bidder. So, back to the minimum bid increment table, are you willing to ante up an additional $2.50 to win this auction? That's up to you to decide. But, to whet your appetite, there is a way you can win this auction at a final bid of $100.01, avoiding the usual minimum bid increment. In Chapter 13, I'll show you how this can be done. In a $2.50 increment auction, you'll find you could quickly shave $2.49 from that minimum increment and still emerge as the high bidder. This strategy is even more effective in high-price auctions where the minimum bid increment has climbed to $10, $25, or beyond. Stay tuned....

The use of the proxy bid system will also answer your question about how you can enter the minimum bid increment in an auction—obviously higher than the current high bid—and then be immediately told you have been outbid. What?! It's almost a slap in the face and a shock the first time it happens. Dumbfounded, you wonder how anyone got in and bid faster than you, or if the whole thing's fixed.

The proxy bidding system issues those immediate outbid messages to other would-be high bidders who haven't beaten the current high bidder's maximum bid. Just as you might get that outbid slap in the face, rest assured that your proxy pal will be doing some face slapping on your behalf as well. Ah, the competitive arena.

Reserve Price Auctions

Just as maximum bids and the proxy system provide some bidding protection to bidders, reserve prices provide protection to sellers. Probably the only thing more disappointing than a bidder being outbid is a seller selling at a loss. What if a seller has an item worth $100, but only gets a final high bid of $25 or $50? That means a loss because for whatever reason, the bids just weren't there. This is a bummer—no one likes to lose money.

The Reserve Price auction helps the seller designate a minimum value for the sale. Maybe a seller doesn't know how much an item is really worth, but does know what it cost. The seller can set the reserve price at the investment value—or any value for that matter—as a way to protect the investment.

 NOTE In many Reserve Price auctions, the sellers might add a line to their description that goes like this: *"Reasonable reserve to protect my investment."* This is a way for the seller to acknowledge that the reserve is there for a reason and not just because the seller is being greedy or something.

Bidding in a Reserve Price auction follows the same rules as straight auctions. The bidders all place their bids on the item and proceed to outbid one another either by way of minimum increments or beating each other's maximum bids. Along the way, bidders are informed they are bidding in a Reserve Price auction immediately when they enter the item details screen. Figure 12-1 shows an auction I bid in that was a reserve price auction.

Just as with other bidders' maximum bids, you won't be able to see the reserve price the seller has specified on this item. How, then, will you know when the reserve price has been met? Oh, you'll know. Let me show you.

First, notice the text link next to the current high bid in Figure 12-1. Clearly, it tells you *reserve not yet met*. The link, if you click on it, will take you to an area of eBay that explains more about Reserve Price auctions. When you place your bid for the item, the bid verification screen (see Figure 12-2) will remind you again that you're in a Reserve Price auction.

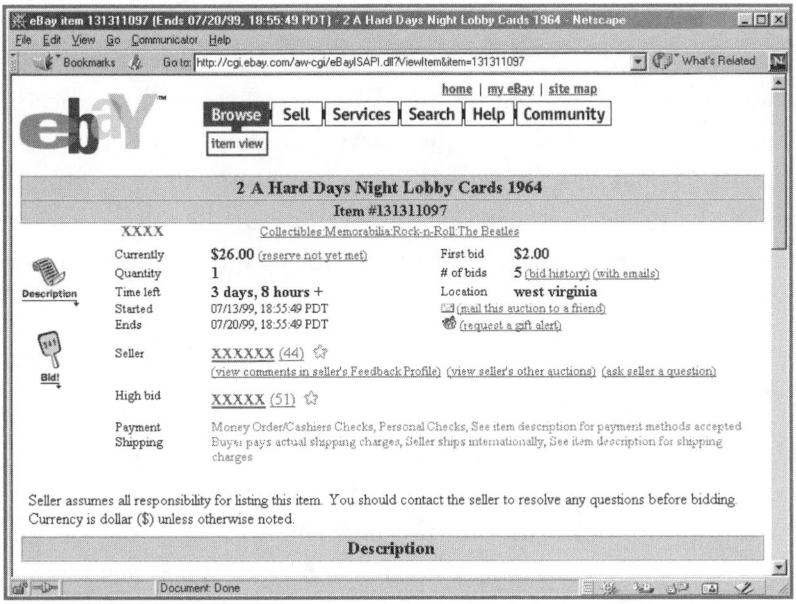

figure 12-1

In the item details screen, you can see the notation next to the current high bid that you are looking at a Reserve Price auction.

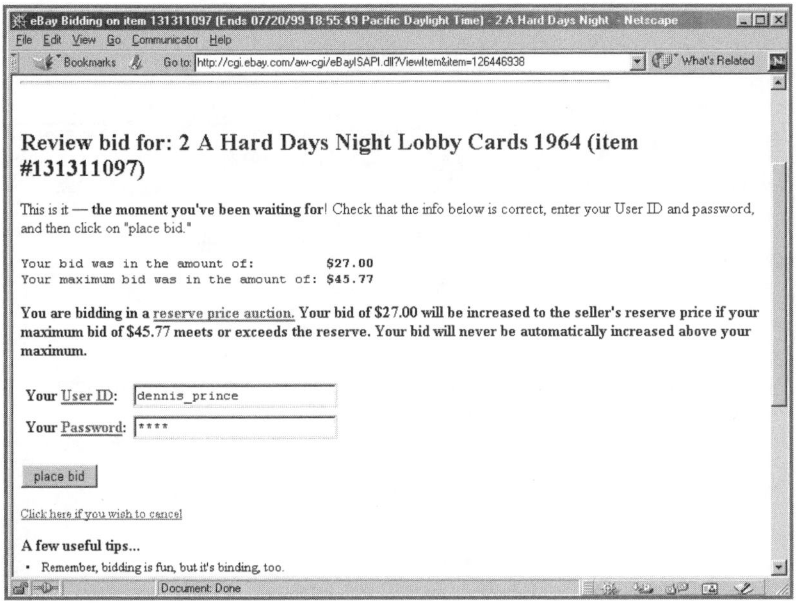

figure 12-2

In the review bid screen, you see the reminder that this is a Reserve Price auction.

In the review bid screen, you get a second reminder that the reserve price hasn't been met. eBay is quickly explaining, before you submit your bid, that the high bid for the item *might* be increased to the seller's reserve price if your maximum bid meets or exceeds the reserve. So, in this case, if your maximum will cover the reserve, the new high bid amount will jump immediately to the reserve price. Bingo! You've just found out the seller's reserve price and, bingo, you've just committed to paying at least that price if you're the winning bidder.

When the reserve price has been met, you'll see a bid confirmation screen like the one shown in Figure 12-3.

When the reserve price is met, it's open bidding from then on with minimum bid increments being all that are required—along with beating the high bidder's maximum bid—to win the auction. On the item details screen, the note next to the new high bid value will read *reserve met*.

But what if the reserve price wasn't met, not even by your maximum bid? If this happens, then the high bid will only increase to the next highest bid increment that would outbid any other bidder's maximum bid, if there were

figure 12-3

Congratulations! You're the high bidder, and the seller's reserve price has been met. You're so lucky!

any. The *reserve not yet met* note would still remain next to the current high bid amount on the item details page. Other bidders would see the same text in the bid confirmation screen that they are bidding in a Reserve Price auction and their bid might be advanced to the reserve price as long as that price doesn't exceed their maximum bid.

Now assume the reserve price is *never* met by the time the auction closes. Then what? In these cases, it can be treated as if the auction never happened. The seller is not required to sell the item to the high bidder if the reserve price was not met. The high bidder is not required to honor any bid if the reserve price was not met. The seller and high bidder can, however, contact one another to determine if a deal might still be reached. Maybe the high bidder would be willing to pay the reserve price after all. Maybe the seller would be willing to accept a little less than the reserve price now that it's turned out the bids just weren't there to meet the original expectations.

The key is that when the reserve price of an auction isn't met, everyone can walk away from the table without any further obligation. The seller might decide to keep the item, work out a deal some other way, or relist the item, possibly at the same reserve price again or maybe at a lower reserve price.

Since you know so much about Reserve Price auctions now, you might have missed the keystone question (or maybe you think I missed it): Why not just make the opening bid the same as the reserve price and avoid the whole reserve price thing altogether? The answer is one with psychological roots: low opening bids will attract more bidders regardless of whether there is a reserve price or not. It's a universal truth and one you'll see proved again and again. You'll learn more about how to best use minimum bid values in conjunction with reserve prices later, in Chapter 16.

 NOTE Just as an aside, it might be interesting for you to know that Reserve Price auctions used to work a bit differently on eBay in days past. Before, the reserve price of an auction was *never* revealed and bidders were *never* informed if the reserve price was ever met. It was like a big secret, and high bidders wouldn't know if they met the reserve price until after the auction when the seller would contact them via e-mail. The eBay community let the folks at eBay know they didn't like this format and asked for some indication whether a reserve price was met *during* the course of the auction.

There's considerable discussion around eBay and its user community as to whether Reserve Price auctions are very friendly to bidders. Some people think a seller might just as well proclaim, *"I'm selling this for this much. Who wants to buy it?"* Some people say they won't even bid in a Reserve Price auction, period. They say it takes all the "auction" out of the auction. My response is that I have no reservations (sorry) about bidding in Reserve Price auctions. I bid in them all the time, and win in them quite a lot. I also auction a lot of items with reserve prices. To me, it goes back to the point that often the auction is a place to have the *opportunity* to bid on an otherwise unobtainable (or truly hard-to-find) item. The reserve just gives the seller some protection, a way to make sure someone doesn't run away with a choice item for a buck. There are a lot of bidders on eBay, but some really good items still can fall into the cracks.

Dutch Auctions

Dutch auctions are a great way for sellers to auction duplicate items quickly in a single listing. They're also great tools for buyers to pick up a more plentiful item at what usually turns out to be a good price.

In a Dutch auction, the seller indicates there are many of the same thing and the whole quantity is available at the same time. The seller lists the auction as a Dutch auction, specifying how many items there are and the minimum opening bid for any bidder to stake a claim on one of the items.

When bidders come to a Dutch auction, they have to bid at least the minimum bid amount as set by the seller, but they can bid on as many items as the seller is auctioning. For instance, say a seller found an old case of Naugas and wants to move the whole box of critters in one fell swoop, with a Dutch auction for all 12 of them. Knowing the rules of a Dutch auction (refer back to Chapter 1 if you've forgotten), you can bid on 1, 2, 5, or however many of the batch that you want to adopt.

When the auction ends, the qualifying bidders are notified and instructed to pay the lowest successful bid for whatever quantity of the item they bid on. Again, make sure, if you're a winning bidder, that you're being asked to pay only the lowest successful bid amount and *not* your particular high bid if it exceeds the lowest successful bid. These Dutch auctions sometimes get

figure 12-4

You don't know what a Nauga is? Well, where do you think Naugahyde comes from?

confused with Yankee auctions. (The ones where you *do* pay your highest bid amount, remember?) You shouldn't encounter a Yankee auction at eBay—it's not one of their supported auction types.

Dutch auctions, by ratio, are much less common on eBay than regular English auctions. Because they're a bit more complex to understand, many bidders will avoid them. Don't let them scare you off, though. They're actually kind of fun, and you can get some great items at great prices. In the next chapter, I'll give you some strategies for bidding successfully in Dutch auctions.

NOTE Because of their format, Dutch auctions cannot be set with reserve prices. That would defeat the whole purpose of the auction because price variation—the main draw of a Dutch auction—would never occur.

Private Auctions

What's a Private auction? Is it an auction where some secret society conducts its own clandestine deals in some virtual back room? No, nothing like that. It's really just a bunch of naughty people bidding on naughty things that they don't want their spouses, clergymen, or mothers to know about.

Now don't get in a huff. I'm only kidding. A Private auction—a very reasonable type of auction to conduct—provides secrecy and anonymity to the bidders in the auction. In a Private auction, eBay suppresses the visible posting of the bidders' user IDs or e-mail addresses. Bidders' identities are revealed only to the seller after the auction has closed and only by way of e-mail. This way, bidders are free to try for certain items that they might not want the general public to know they're bidding on. The seller might recognize that, in some auctions, bidders would prefer some additional privacy and can choose to run a Private auction in acknowledgment of that fact.

Are there benefits to a Private auction? Well, the main benefit is that certain bidders will feel more comfortable placing their bids in a private manner than if the auction had been posted publicly. A bidder whose identity is readily available to the public might not want to bid on that vintage inflatable sheep. The seller loses.

Private auctions, by their nature, are not the most popular of auctions because they are kind of secretive. They usually don't get as much traffic as a regular auction (English or Dutch), but that might be due to the kind of items being auctioned and maybe not directly because of their private status.

chapter 13

Bidding Strategies

OK, people. Step up to the counter, throw down a token and grab a rifle. You're in the shooting gallery. This is where you sharpen your sights, steady your hand, take aim, and hit your target. Bull's-eye!

Bidding at eBay has, to some, become a sport and an art form. Bidding strategies that you can legally and continually apply will make you a more skilled and successful bidder. Placing your bids will be more than just entering numbers and clicking on Web site buttons. You'll develop an intuition—a sixth sense—about when to bid and when not to bid, how to bid and how not to bid. After a while, your bidding will become almost organic—a part or extension of yourself.

If this sounds sort of New Age or something, it's not. Bidding strategies add more flavor to the auction game. They add excitement, make your heart beat faster, and get you more wins than you might think. Try 'em for yourself.

SOAPBOX Let me just start this chapter by saying some eBay users might think the subject matter here is bordering on the obsessive. I guess they're right. These tactics and methods are truly for the *impassioned* bidder; the person who simply *must* have an item and is willing to expend every reasonable and ethical effort to win it. If you're just bidding for novelty and don't care whether you win auctions or not, the information you're about to read might seem a bit over the top. That's OK. But if you've already seen some great stuff for auction at eBay and know you'll be finding even more and better treasures—and you will—then read on. This bid's for you.

Bid. Wise. Er?

When Should You Bid?

This is a point of much debate among eBay community members. Do you bid as soon as you see something, all excited and happy that such an item is up for auction at eBay? Or is that tipping your hand too early, telegraphing your plans? Do you hide in the bushes and wait, wait, wait until the very end of the auction and then spring out and, unannounced, fire off your bid? Or will that risk the auction's ending before your bid has a chance to get in? Do you watch the auction for a period of days, simultaneously checking other new listings to see if something similar (or better) shows up that is more in tune with your wants or needs? Or do you just bid on any old thing, any old time, whenever you feel like it?

All of these scenarios are valid and good ways to bid, but they each have an angle that you can exploit, sometimes interchangeably. The key to knowing when to bid is to also know when others might be bidding or to observe how and when certain people bid. This is especially true when you become known in the community as a bidder of certain kinds of items. (You can be sure that if you bid enough at eBay, you *will* become known.)

So look at the scenario where you might choose to bid the moment you see an item listed. Here's a good example: in 1996, the bizarre film version of *Mars Attacks* hit theater screens. It was a very odd film, based, of all things, on a series of bubble gum cards released in the early '60s. The film's director, Tim Burton (*Batman, Beetlejuice, Nightmare Before Christmas*), served up a twisted view of what might happen if visitors from Mars ended up not being the glowing-fingered lovable imps that we've seen on the silver screen before.

But back to the auction. *Mars Attacks* brought a line of funny little talking action figures that were kind of popular, but not hugely. However, one figure, the *Martian Spy Girl* (see Figure 13-1), was an obsession of collectors because there was only one to be found in each case of figures, and there was also a special nontalking version made only for the K-B Toys stores. Needless to say, when that Spy Girl showed up on eBay, bidders went after her. Almost four years later, this odd little toy continues to pull in consistent bidding activity. The most consistent thing, though, is the price: she typically sells in the range of $30 to $40 (original retail price $5.99).

If I were in the market for a Martian Spy Girl of my own, I'd probably place my maximum bid as soon as I saw one. Why? Simple. Since she continues to pull a consistent price that rarely exceeds $40, then I know the auction *market* typically won't value her much higher. A bidder would just wait for another to come available. So, if I bid my $40 maximum when I see her, then I'm the first one to stake my claim on that auction, and I've locked out other bidders who also won't exceed the $40 price tag. For the most part, I've won because I was the first to throw down $40. Other bidders will probably think, "*Gee, he's already covered that one. I'll go look for another.*" See how that works? Another good reason to bid as soon as you spot the item would be to invoke the eBay early warning system. Actually, that's just something I call it, but when you've placed a bid on an item, you'll be receiving those daily status messages in your e-mail inbox. They're nice little reminders of items you've bid on, and they let you see daily where the bidding stands. If you're outbid within a reasonable amount of time before the auction ends, the outbid notice you receive via e-mail will alert you to take some counter-bid action if you want to win the item. If it's no big deal to you, let the item go.

figure 13-1

The Trendmasters Martian Spy Girl is a favorite among eBay action figure collectors. Must be that hip and happening beehive hairdo disguise.

 SOAPBOX Sometimes I like to bid early to use this automatic eBay reminder system. I bid in so many auctions that I occasionally lose track of them all. I track my important auctions, but others I might be more lax about if they're not crucial to my well-being.

In other auctions, it might be best if you don't bid right away. The variations of the kinds of items is too large for a definitive example, but the principle is universally applied: if you bid too early, you tip your hand to others that you find the item of interest, value, potential, or any other supposed reason that they might want to bid, too. Remember the renowned bidder I told you about in Chapter 1? He liked the silent bidding method because it preserved his anonymity and allowed him to bid without others riding his coattails and driving up the price on the item he wants. Well, waiting until the end of an auction to bid achieves pretty much the same thing. Other bidders don't know you're bidding until the auction's nearly over. By that time, they either won't notice you've bid or they won't have enough time to get in their bids before the auction closes.

 NOTE No, I don't think there are a bunch of leeches out there following other bidders around waiting to pounce after they bid. It's possible, but not too probable. Still, anonymity in bidding can have its benefits in helping you win auctions, as you'll soon see.

So, to some, it's best not to bid on an item until the very end. If you see something you want, make a note of it, research it, ask the seller about it, but for Heaven's sake don't bid on it! Not yet, anyway. In the words of the profound Nigel Tufnel, "*No, don't touch it. Well, don't point at it. Don't even look at it. It can't be played.*"

So what's the big deal anyway? So what if people see me bid on something? Again, it might raise eyebrows that something has value, and they might want to get into the game. Most definitely, HOT! items (those receiving more than 30 bids) clearly raise the visibility of an item for more people to stumble by and see. If you really want something that might draw the attention of others, try to keep it in the back corners of the eBay listings until right before the auction ends. That way, other bidders might be distracted by other popular or HOT! items, allowing you to swoop in and claim your item at a more reasonable high bid and with less challenge. Just remember that other people might be doing the same thing (probably not very many, though).

So when should you bid if you're going to wait until the end? Typically, wait until the last five minutes of the auction to see how the item is currently priced and how many other bidders have stopped by to leave their calling card. Check the bid history and see when the other bidders have placed their bids. That will help you better understand if others have been hanging back in the shadows just as you have. If you've been following the auction for a period of days, try to take note of previous high bidders who were outbid and have come back to reclaim high bidder status. They're probably pretty motivated to win, but also might be bidding in small increments.

If you sense a particular bidder has some sort of true determination to win an auction, perform a search on that user ID under the category of completed auctions using Bidder Search. Maybe this bidder was bidding on the same item in a different auction, maybe this bidder lost that auction, maybe this bidder has clenched teeth about winning this auction. You might want to compete against this bidder, or you might not.

 N**TE** Of course, this kind of impassioned bidding brings a gleeful smile to a seller's face. These people want this thing *bad*. I wonder how much they're willing to pay?

Within the last five minutes of the auction, you're going to find out who else is at the keyboard watching the final seconds tick by. At the end of an auction, there can be a real flurry of activity. If you're really good, you'll be placing your bid within seconds of the auction's ending. A little later in this chapter I'll show you how that's done.

Proxy Bidding Strategies

In Chapter 12 you learned about the proxy bidding system and how it places bids for you. Now you need to understand the best way to use the system to make your maximum bids more successful.

The first question in proxy bidding is, *"How much should you bid?"* I don't know; how much can you afford? That's really what it sometimes boils down to: Who's got the most cashola? But showing your *true maximum*—the real high bid you'd consider placing—early in the bidding might let others see your proverbial slip showing.

Much as when you place an early bid to use as a sort of reminder, you could also place an early bid with a less-than-absolute maximum value to test the waters and see who is out there to outbid you. When bidders start outbidding one another's maximum bids, they'll tend to do so incrementally. That is, they might only have to bid once to beat your maximum, but they also might use a bit of minimum bidding until they finally beat you. Having done so, they might think you're out of the game. Not so. Now you can see who else is in the bidding and see how many total bids have been placed. You can't always be certain how many bids a bidder has placed, but you can do a bit of deductive reasoning to get a close approximation.

Say you were the first bidder on an item. Later, another bidder outbid you. Since there are only two bidders, there should only be two bids, right? Not necessarily. If the number of bids on the item details screen shows maybe four bids, then you know one of the bids was yours, and the other three came from the other bidder—who took three tries to beat your high bid. You're tipped off to the fact that you're up against the kind of bidder who bids in small increments (not a true jump bidder) and whose high bid probably hasn't beaten your previous maximum by much. If the end of the auction nears, and it's still just the two of you, a late bid you enter of maybe $10 could be enough, using the proxy system, to up the high bid and put the other guy away. You become the high bidder because the other guy didn't expect you to come back and place another bid—you had already had your "maximum" beat. Of course, this is all theoretical. Anything could happen in an auction, right?

 SOAPBOX At first read, this might sound kind of mercenary. You're not "putting the guy away" to be mean. You just want the item, and you're willing to use some strategy to get it in the most advantageous—yet fair—way possible. If you think *this* is mercenary, just wait.

Another reason to use a reduced early maximum is pretty much for the same situation just described, but it involves the emotions of the other bidder. Remember how I told you that proxy bidding can deliver the immediate outbid slap in the face to a new bidder? Some bidders won't walk away at the first sign of being outbid. *"OK. Then how about another $5? Outbid again, eh? Then how about $10? Ooh! OK, you wanna play rough? $20!"* I don't know about you, but I picture Curly fighting with a live clam in his soup for possession of a cracker.

Being repeatedly outbid will raise the blood in some bidders, and they'll keep bidding *just so they can experience the eventual high bid euphoria.* If you don't think it's true, wait until you find yourself doing it.

If you place your true maximum bid up front, and you encounter another "determined" bidder, then the item is going to cost you more than you originally intended. You have to decide if you're willing to ante up some more bids to win. Otherwise, you're going to have to let go. Using the early sub-maximum bid works as a decoy and lets you gauge how the bidding might wrap up in the end.

Just remember, for every bidder you're looking to put away, you're just as susceptible yourself. Don't dish it out if you can't take it. Your maximum bid can always be outbid by another bidder, regardless of when you place your final bid. Be ready for that.

The Penny Principle

And how about a way to win an auction with only one penny? Can it be done? Absolutely. But, as a disclaimer, it doesn't mean you'll really only win something for the final cost of a penny. What it does mean, though, is that you can get yourself into the position of high bidder through the use of only one penny.

This is really quite simple, but many people overlook it. Go back to the example where your maximum bid ends up being the same as another bidder's maximum bid. If you both bid $100 as your maximum, whichever of you placed the bid first will still be high bidder—that's just by virtue of being first.

After you find out that the other bidder's maximum is $100, you'll now need to bid at least the minimum bid increment to beat the first bidder. This might not mean much to you since the minimum increment on $100 is $2.50, but it means a lot more if the current high bid is much higher, and so is the minimum bid increment—maybe $10 or $25 or more. With that in mind, what if you had bid $100.01? You win! You win with only an additional penny! Why? Because with a single extra penny, your maximum was still higher than the previous high bidder's maximum. The proxy system only looks to see if one bidder's maximum is higher than another's, regardless of how much higher. Cool, huh?

A lot of bidders like to bid in round numbers—$10, $50, $100, and so on—but eBay doesn't have a rule that says you have to stick to round numbers. Since a lot of bidders bid at the very end of an auction, whoever gets that round number bid in first will be the winner, even though the other bidders bid the same amount. So here come all the $100 bidders at the end of the auction; all except you. You place your bid of $100.01 and are victorious. You immediately strut around your PC in a gloating fashion for all to see—no one else can really see you, but you pretend they can. Good job! You won with a penny.

The penny principle works another way, too. Say you enter your maximum bid early on in the auction. Pretend the maximum you put in is the same $100.01. OK, here comes the $100 gang at the end of the auction. They enter their final bids at the last moment thinking you're gonna be toast. But, lo and behold, you hold on to the high bidder position, if only by your fingernails, with that precious extra penny. Wow! You're good.

Now, your funny little bid doesn't always have to be in a penny increment. Enter a bid of $100.09 or $100.14 or anything that will put you out of the round numbers club and might win you the auction without having to step up to the next logical bid increment. It works.

Dutch Auction Strategy

OK, here are those Dutch auctions again. They're OK; they're just a little different in the way they work. But even though you can be bidding along with other bidders and a lot of you are going to win something, there is a strategy to make sure you'll be among the winners when the auction ends. Even though there are multiple copies of an item available in a Dutch auction, it's still a finite quantity. Most of the time, there will be more bidders than there will be items. You don't want to get bumped out of the running.

Think back to that box of Naugas that one fellow had up for bid in his Dutch auction. There are 12 of them available, but there's probably going to be more demand than Naugas to go around. What to do? Here's what: place a bid that keeps you from getting bumped out of the winning bidders' circle. The circle is the group of bidders left alive after the auction ends. The goal of the strategy is to place a bid that keeps you in the winners' circle but doesn't necessarily mean that you'll have to pay the highest bid that has been cast. Remember that the Dutch auction ends up having the winning bidders pay the lowest successful bid when the auction ends. The strategy is to win, but without increasing that lowest successful bid amount by much, if anything at all.

Bidding in a Dutch auction can take place any time while the auction is active. Again, for the greatest element of surprise, you'll probably want to wait until the very end of the auction to have the best chance at being one of the winners. Let's say the bidding looks like what you see in Table 13-1 just five minutes before the auction ends.

Table 13-1 Dutch Auction Bid Standings for Naugas

Bidder	Quantity Bid On	High Bid
1	1	$25
2	1	$27
3	4	$28
4	2	$28
5	4	$35

In Table 13-1, you can see that all 12 of the available Naugas have been bid on. Does that mean you're too late? No, it just means you're going to have to outbid somebody while still trying to get the lowest possible ending price when the auction is over. But how?

In a Dutch auction, there's something known as the auction *bubble*. When you're *on the bubble*, it means you're at the low end of the bidding range. In Table 13-1, Bidder #1 is "on the bubble" and just looking to have that bubble burst; you're going to be the *pin*-prick that does it. (C'mon, it's a bubble metaphor.)

Again, you'll bid very late to be sure you can get in the winner's circle with less chance of being ousted yourself. You could bid $26, which effectively does away with Bidder #1 and puts you in the circle. Unfortunately, now *you're* on the bubble, and you're Dutch auction fodder. So what you have to do is bid *outside the bubble*. That means you don't need to be the highest bidder in the running, but you need to keep from being the lowest. Look back at Table 13-1 because here's what you're going to do: you're going to bid in the middle of the pack—outside the bubble—to secure your position *right in the middle* of the winner's circle.

If you want to bid outside the bubble using the standings you see in Table 13-1, you'll launch a late bid of $29 or $30. This will keep you from having to commit to a high bid of $35 (or more) while also keeping you $2 or $3 away from being on the bubble. When you bid this amount, you first knock Bidder #1 off the bubble (pop!). But, besides that, you now have Bidders #2, #3, and #4 guarding your flank. They would have to be zapped first before another bidder got to you. You've made your way into the winner's circle and have three other bidders protecting you for only a dollar or two more than they've bid. Now that's insurance.

Say the auction ends, and the result looks like the standings you see in Table 13-2.

Table 13-2 Dutch Auction Bid Standings for Naugas (end of auction)

Bidder	Quantity Bid On	High Bid	
2	1	$27.00	
3	4	$28.00	
4	2	$28.00	
6	1	$29.00	<< you are here
5	4	$35.00	

Well good job, matey. Here's what you've done. First, you got into the winner's circle. Second, you provided yourself with protection by bidding outside the bubble. Third, and most important, you and all the other bidders get your Naugas for the lowest successful bid price of $27. How wonderful!

And you thought you wouldn't be able to understand a Dutch auction.

Sniping

The name alone conjures images of mystery, skill, and pinpoint accuracy. This is the tool of the well-practiced bidder. To some bidders, however, sniping also suggests the less attractive attributes of ambush, deception, and back-handedness. Those bidders have probably been sniped. I've been sniped, and you will be, too. You rarely see it coming, although you know it's out there. Will this be the time you get sniped, or will this be the time you do the sniping?

 NOTE As I write this section, I'm preparing a snipe of my own. There's an hour to go in an auction I'm interested in. Of course, I won't bid yet. There's still plenty of time. Meanwhile, I'll explain my sniping strategy—one that is used by many at eBay—as I wait for the clock to count down.

Sniping is the practice of entering a *very last moment* bid to become the high bidder without allowing *any* time for anyone else to place a counter-bid. What do I mean by "last moment"? How about down to the final *seconds* of an auction? It can be done, but it takes some practice. If you become good at it, the other bidders will never see what whizzed past them—you'll catch those cats napping.

Is sniping a fair practice? Yes, it is. However, you'll find some eBay users— even long-standing community members—who don't think sniping should be allowed. Their reasoning, as I've heard it, is that a last-minute snipe doesn't give the outbid bidder a chance to bid again because there simply won't be time to do so (uh . . . yeah, that's the whole reason *for* sniping). For sellers, sniping could cost them money; if an outbid bidder would have bid again, then the seller could have gotten more for the item. These are good points, and they do have some merit. However, eBay doesn't appear to be moving toward eliminating sniping because so many more eBay users *do* like the advantage it offers.

To the sniping purists, a well-executed snipe is a thing of beauty. It's really fascinating to see how close to the edge some bidders can get in submitting that final deathly bid. It's a game of risk and chance—if you bid too soon, other snipers may we waiting to bump you off while there's still time; if you bid too late, the auction could end, and your last bid might never see daylight. You have to deliver the snipe *just right.*

 SOAPBOX   Obviously, I am a fan of the snipe. I have seen it done and sat dumb-struck as my 30-second bids were wiped away like morning dew on a windshield. It happened to me, but it was so amazing I was more befuddled than annoyed that I had been outbid.

"So tell me already. How is it done?" Glad you asked. Here's how you prepare for and execute a snipe of your own. Ready?

First, understand that eBay runs on a central server clock. It's set to run on Pacific Standard Time (PST) or Pacific Daylight Time (PDT), depending on the season. The eBay clock is always ticking, leading to the final seconds of any and all auctions when their time has expired. The clock never slows down and isn't subject to system hangs or delays or anything. It's perpetual time in motion, and it has no feelings, sympathy, or remorse. You cannot bargain with *the clock.*

What you can do is see how well you can work with the clock. You start by accessing the Internet via your ISP or other connection service. Be especially attentive to the reliability of your connection—it could be lagging a bit; you might have gotten connected at a slower rate of data transfer; your ISP might be having a bad night, dropping your connection again and again. Try to log on at least an hour before the auction you want to bid in is set to end. Then, take extra time to test the connection, fiddle with reconnecting, and check the overall reliability of your connection.

Next, get to eBay's site. How fast is eBay running when you connect to it? Don't just check the home page and general features—get to the search page and into the item details of the item you want to bid on. Item details and bidding take place on a different server at eBay, and it's sometimes slow or occasionally even inaccessible (oh, dread). Work the pages, and be sure you can bounce in and out of the item details quickly and repeatedly. If the server's running slow, take special note of how long it seems to be taking; you'll need to know this to properly buffer your bidding time. Remember, even though the server is ka-chunking to process your bid, the old clock is still ticking.

 ALERT Keep that connection alive! Depending on your Internet service provider, it might be necessary to be actively using your connection to stay connected. Some ISPs (like mine) will disconnect you if a certain period of time expires without your actively browsing around. It's how they keep idle sessions from locking up connection lines that could be made available to other people who are trying to log on. It really depends on the ISP and how many connections it can support at any given time. If in doubt, ask your ISP if you're subject to getting bounced. If you are, keep reloading your browser page or something to keep your connection active. If you're dropped at precisely the wrong moment…aaaargghh! Game over!

 TIP Another thing you might think about is how many different applications you have running on your PC's desktop. Too many might cause a slowdown or even a fatal hang for your PC. Heaven forbid your browser gets stuck and dies.

Now it's just a matter of biding your time. Keep reloading that item details page (clicking on the *Reload* button, pressing Ctrl+R, or whatever) to see how the auction is progressing. If you have more than 45 minutes to go, don't obsess; do something else—just keep that connection alive.

Check back on the item details, reloading frequently to see how the auction's doing. This is when you'll notice other bidders putting in their bids. Some will bid 30 minutes before the auction ends. They might just be *poking* the high bidder—placing little bids to see how tightly the current high bidder is hanging on to the item. If the high bidder is easily outbid, then you're watching someone who either hasn't bid their true maximum or who likes to bid only the minimum increments (or very little more than that).

Watching the other bidding activity as the auction's end draws nearer gives you very important information: how hot the item has become in the final minutes. This is really important because you'll need to make a guess at how lively the final bidding might get. It might cause you to stutter one or two seconds more before you send out your final bid. There could be a bunch of snipers out there. It could also cause you to reconsider bidding; if another early bidder's high bid goes beyond what you're willing to pay, then the game's over. That, of course, is up to you.

Now, when the time remaining gets near five minutes, and assuming you're still planning to bid, it's time to strap on your bidding armor and get ready for the last stand. Keep reloading and watching to see if other bidders pop in some late bids. Within the last five minutes, you might see a lot of action.

Since this is where the action is most exciting, let me show you some time-lapse images of how the snipe is going to go. First, take a look at what I'll be bidding on (see Figure 13-2).

At just under five minutes to go, I can see only one bid has been placed on this item. That's unsettling because, knowing this item, I *know* I am swimming among snipers. And, for the time being, I can also see the current high bid is well within my price range, but I know I'd be dreaming to think I could lock this one down at the current price (yes, it's *that* desirable). Now, I look at the high bidder and see he only has a feedback rating of 5. He's new and may be a bit inexperienced, but with a user name like *jawsquint*, I'm certain this is the sort of item he'll be fighting for. And, then, there are the other snipers. This could be interesting.

SOAPBOX Even within the five-minute window—which is quite a bit of time as far as a snipe is concerned—you'll want to move quickly and efficiently. First, in your current browser window, highlight the URL location of the item details screen (it's in the browser's Location bar), then copy it to your Windows Clipboard (press Ctrl+C; it's the quickest way). Then, to quickly get the second browser window started, use the control key sequence Ctrl+N while the current browser is active. The new window automatically pops up to your designated home page selection. Highlight whatever URL is defaulted in the new browser Location bar, then press Ctrl+V; the URL of the item details screen will be copied in from your Windows Clipboard. Press Enter on your keyboard, and you'll jump right to the item details screen.

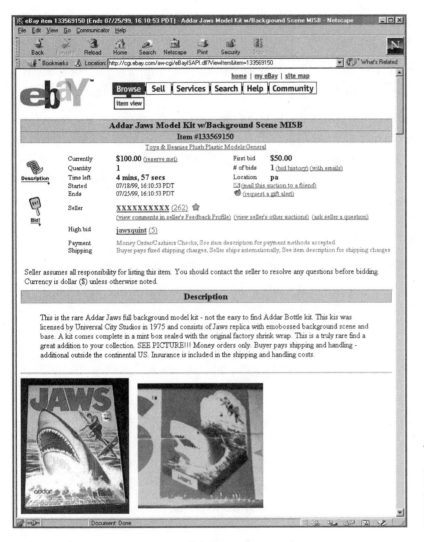

figure 13-2

A rare *Jaws* model kit is my sniping *prey for the day*. This is a highly desirable item among kit collectors and has eluded me for the past ten years.

The time is now T minus 4:57 and counting; time to open up a second browser window. To effectively snipe in an auction, you'll need to use two browser windows. In the new window you're opening, you'll go to the same item details page, but then you'll move on to the bidding screen.

Next, in the new browser window you've opened, move quickly to enter your bid information. In the bidding screen, enter your maximum bid amount. It's truly imperative you enter your real highest maximum bid at this time; there won't be a second chance to go back and bid *what you'd really be willing to spend.*

Once your maximum bid is entered in the bidding screen, click on the *Review bid* button and jump to the *Review bid* screen (see Figure 13-3).

Now, carefully enter your user ID and password. *No typos!*—You won't get a chance to correct any mistakes. So, if your bid information looks good to you, *STOP!* Don't do anything more with this bid. Toggle back to the other browser window you have open (use Alt+Tab for a quick toggle) and continue to reload the item details screen. Be sure to drag the details screen just to the right of your bidding screen so you have clear access to the *Place bid* button (see Figure 13-4).

This is the final countdown. Keep reloading that item details screen. You're approaching the three-minute mark. How is the eBay server responding? If it hiccups a bit or seems a bit slow, consider how that might affect the speed at which your final bid is received. Usually, the speed of a screen reload is about half or one-third the time you can expect for the processing of your bid. Keep reloading the item details screen to get a feel for the response time.

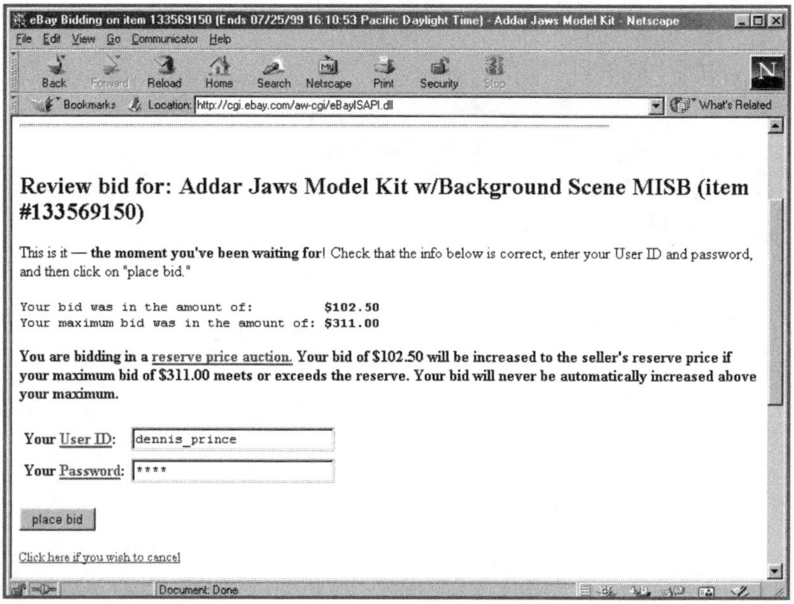

figure 13-3

In the Review bid screen, carefully enter your user ID and password and verify you've entered your true maximum bid amount; you won't get a second chance in this auction.

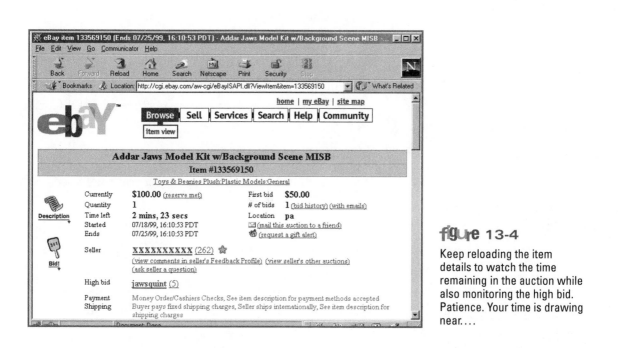

figure 13-4

Keep reloading the item details to watch the time remaining in the auction while also monitoring the high bid. Patience. Your time is drawing near....

Two-minute mark. Steady. Keep reloading. Check the high bid. Has it changed? Check now to be sure that, if it has changed, your maximum hasn't already been exceeded by another last-minute bidder. If it has, but you still want the item, quickly toggle to the bid screen, use the Back arrow, reenter a new maximum bid that you're willing to pay and you think will stand a good chance of bringing home the win. Fast, now; click on the *Review bid* button, enter your user ID and password—*quickly, man, quickly*—and get ready.

One minute!

"Bid now?!"

No, not yet. Wait. Reload that item details screen. There's still time, and you don't want to play your hand too fast. Reload. Reload. Check the response time. Reload. Forty seconds. Reload.

Thirty seconds!

"Bid now, right??!"

Not yet! Hold it together. Almost. Reload every moment you see the clock time redisplayed.

Twenty-five seconds. Twenty seconds. Eighteen seconds! Fifteen seconds! *Twelve seconds??!!*

Quick! Move the mouse pointer to the bidding screen right over the *Place bid* button and . . . hold your breath . . . count one, two, three . . . BID! Click on the button NOW!!

Close your eyes. Make a wish.

You can look now. If your bid made it through in time, you might see the bid result shown in Figure 13-5.

Yes, Figure 13-5 shows that high bidder status was achieved. Fantastic! You see how your maximum bid held up against the previous high bidder's maximum. You see the new high bid amount. You see those triumphant words, *"You are the current high bidder!"* Good job! But was there any time left after that snipe bid? Maybe. It's not over yet. Hold your breath once more.

If you scroll down the screen you saw in Figure 13-5, you'll find out how much time was left after your bid was received and processed. With the snipe this close to the wire, there shouldn't be more than a few seconds left

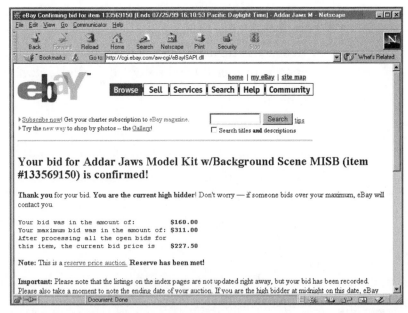

figure 13-5

When your heart stops pounding in your ears, see how your maximum bid held up. Are you the new high bidder?

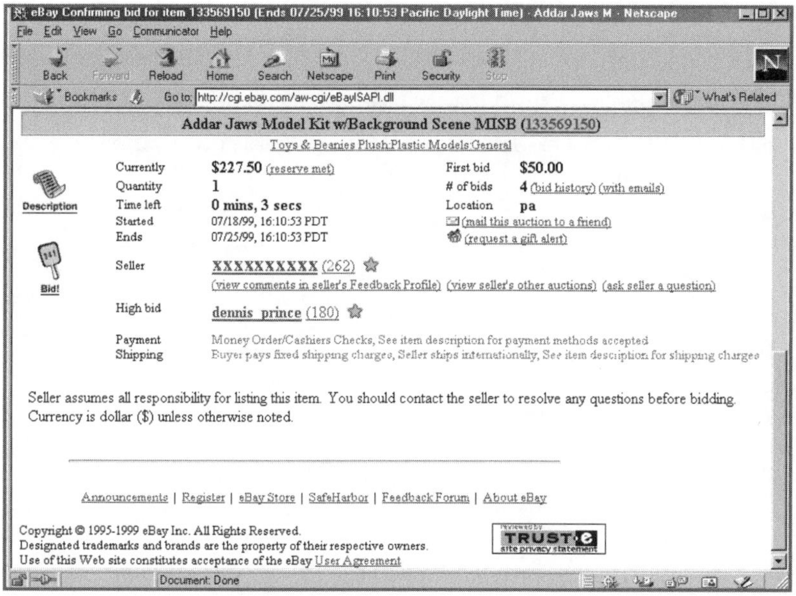

figure 13-6

In the *Jaws* auction, I
delivered a snapping-snipe
that cut all others off within
the last few seconds of the
auction. Chomp!

in the auction. And, for this *Jaws* snipe, that's exactly what I found—look
at Figure 13-6.

Three seconds? That is truly down to the wire. During the *Jaws* snipe, as I
was counting down to placing my bid, two other bidders came sailing in
within the last half-minute to take their shot at the great white grail. Lucky
for me I waited—and also had a perversely high maximum bid to thwart
the other bidders.

But even with three seconds to go, was I absolutely protected from other
snipers? It could take at least three seconds to simply reload an item details
screen. Could anyone else really beat such a last-moment snipe?

Actually, yes. In the world of sniping, three seconds can be plenty of time
for other bids to be processed. If that's so, then it can only be a matter of
who else—if anyone—might be waiting to bid.

So, without further ado, here's the phenomenon you may have heard of.
Many have been told of it, few have experienced it. Ladies and Gentlemen,
Boys and Girls, Bidders and Sellers:

The Amazing Zero-Second Snipe!

File Edit View Go Communicator Help

Back Forward Reload Home Search Netscape Print Security

Bookmarks Location: http://cgi.ebay.com/aw-cgi/eBayISAPI.dll?ViewItem&item=60211079   What's Related

Instant Message Members WebMail Connections BizJournal SmartUpdate Mktplace

Bid confirmed for: Son of Dracula - Ringo Starr, Harry Nilsson (item #60211079)

Your bid was in the amount of: $20.50
Your maximum bid was in the amount of: $42.00
After processing all the open bids for
this item, the current bid price is $22.02

Thank you for your bid! **You** are the current **high bidder** for this item! You will be notified if your maximum bid is exceeded by another bidder.

Please note that the listings on the index pages are not updated right away, but your bid has been recorded.

Important: please take note of the closing date of this auction. At midnight following the close, the seller and the high-bidder will be notified by e-mail, and you have only **three** business days to contact each other before losing your position as high-bidder.

Son of Dracula - Ringo Starr, Harry Nilsson (60211079)
Collectibles:Memorabilia:Movie:Posters, Lobby Cards

	Currently	$22.02	First bid	$20.00	
	Quantity	1	# of bids	2 (bid history) (with emails)	
Description	Time left	0 mins, 0 secs	Location	Lee's Summit, MO	
	Started	01/24/99 20:05:57 PST		(mail this auction to a friend)	
	Ends	01/31/99 20:05:57 PST		(request a gift alert) NEW!	
Leave Feedback (to seller) (to bidder)	Seller	XXXXXX (24)	(view seller's feedback) (view seller's other auctions) (ask seller a question)		
	High bid	dennis_prince (146)			
	Payment	See item description for payment methods accepted			
	Shipping	See item description for shipping charges			
	Relist item	**Seller:** Now that the auction has ended, you can relist this item by clicking here.			

Seller assumes all responsibility for listing this item. You should contact the seller to resolve any questions before bidding. Currency is U.S. dollars (US$) unless otherwise noted.

Document: Done

figure 13-7

I never thought it to be true until it happened to me. It can happen to you, too. A perfect snipe!

Look at Figure 13-7, and you'll see a previous auction in which the perfect snipe was delivered—the eBay clock read *0 mins, 0 secs*!

Is it a trick? Is it a skill? Is it luck? Whatever it is, it's real, and there is no way to beat the zero-second snipe. It's a thing of beauty, and I'm glad it happened for me. I sat back, my jaw agape. Had I really done it? I had never seen the zero-zero counter on the eBay clock. Surely, there is no rival for this snipe. Or is there?

Only two short weeks after levying the zero-second snipe, I delivered another snipe and almost fell out of my chair when I saw the result. At first I thought, "No way! I couldn't have been so lucky as to do it twice." No, I wasn't so lucky—I was mystic. Look at Figure 13-8.

Yeah. Wow. Another zero-second snipe, right? Well, that's what I thought at first, and I was ecstatic. But look again and notice the difference in the eBay clock as compared to Figure 13-7. In this snipe for a *Screaming Skull* lobby card, *there is no clock time to even list*. Within the time it took for eBay to register my snipe, report the result of my bid's effect on the previous high

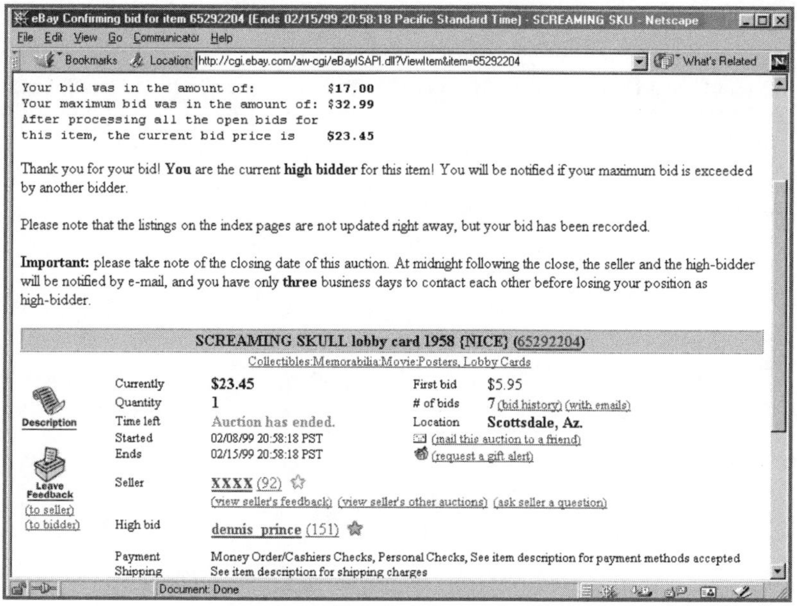

figure 13-8

And there it was. In a bid for a *Screaming Skull* lobby card, the zero-second snipe had somehow been eclipsed.

bid, *then* display the new item details, the auction was officially over. I believe this was actually a *split-second snipe.* This is madness. It's what I call the *Screaming Snipe!*

Whenever you want to review your snipe against the auction closing time, just click on the bid history after the auction closes. You'll be able to compare the time eBay logged your last bid to the time the auction was scheduled to close. Figure 13-9 shows the logging of that screaming snipe.

OK. My whole point here is not to gloat about my snipes or make you feel that you should quiver at my accomplishment. Rather, what I hope I've shown is what I meant about the sport of the snipe; the beauty of a perfectly executed snipe. I can't claim I can repeat the zero-second or screaming snipes at will, and some may think I'm resting on my laurels with two lucky snipes. Fair enough. Take a look at a more recent snipe I delivered (see Figure 13-10).

I've delivered zero- and split-second snipes many times, and you can too. But even if you don't deliver the perfect snipe every time, a well-executed snipe—one placed within the last few seconds of an auction—will still win more auctions as long as your maximum bid holds up. Try it. It's a blast!

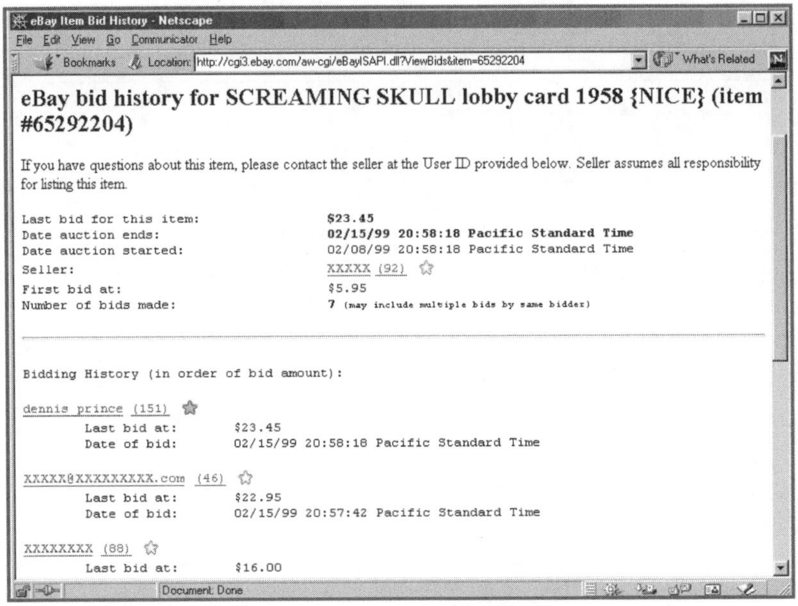

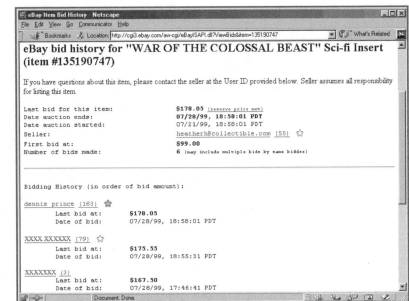

figure 13-9

Check the bid history to see how your bid matched to the closing time of the auction. Hot stuff!

figure 13-10

Nope. It wasn't just a fluke. Here you see another split-second snipe—a *Colossal Snipe*. It *can* be repeated, and you'll probably do it yourself again and again.

ALERT Beware! Sniping presents the risk of not getting your bid processed in time. You should know that, at any time, eBay's server could slow down or hang up, your ISP connection could drop, your PC could lock up. It's definitely a risk to wait until the last seconds before you bid. If you really want something, try bidding about 30 seconds before the auction closes. This will give you a better chance of ensuring your bid is processed. Yes, you're subject to other last-second snipers, but most often you'll arise victorious. Just don't say I didn't warn you.

 SOAPBOX I don't recommend you snipe *all* the time. It's really not necessary. Remember the risk it presents. Save your snipes for those really important or popular auction items.

Put Your Money Where Your Mouse Is

Well, this has all been pretty exciting, hasn't it? So many different ways to bid, so many different ways to win, so many different things to buy. Oh, yeah. I'm *buying* these things. Don't forget about the money.

Your high bids are only as good as the money you have to back them up. Usually, sellers want their money pretty quick—many even state in their item descriptions that payment must be received within 10 days of the auction's close. Will you be prepared for that? Not just the one auction you've won; *all* the auctions you've won.

At this point, I don't intend to counsel you about budgeting your money and setting spending limits (that will come in Chapter 14). Here, I want to let you know that there is actually strategy involved in the amount of money you'll have to bid or, at least, how quickly you can get it. Having funds readily available lets you bid like a pro without the hesitation of wondering how much you can afford.

When you have enough cash funding to support your bids, you can bid higher—obviously—and you can place higher maximum bids that better ensure you won't be outbid. When money is tight, you usually have to play the minimum-increment game. That's an easy game to lose, especially if there are snipers lurking. Just as you learned to snipe in the last passage, remember that you're sniper-bait yourself. The only way to really protect yourself when not sniping is to have a reasonably high maximum that will shield you from lower maximum snipes.

I learned years ago how important it became to have ready cash available. As a collector, I am constantly looking for rare and cool items that will fill the various gaps in my collection. One day a model kit dealer contacted me to tell me of a mint, factory-built store display for the Aurora Products Prehistoric Scenes series. This was a series of kits manufactured in 1971, and the display featured beautifully painted and assembled kits from the series. Factory displays are rare, rare, rare. *This* particular display is one I had first seen in 1971, when I was kid in a store. Since then, I've only seen two available, including the one I'm telling you about here.

I was jubilant that the guy called me to offer it; then he told me how much it would cost. Dread, sorrow, loss, and other such feelings overcame me. How could I ever pay that much? Yes, I want it, but . . . but . . . the mortgage company probably wouldn't share my love for this item, so that was out. My savings account was pretty thin as it was; not an option there. Then I learned about the revolving line of credit.

I'm a member of a credit union, and it offered a line of credit I could draw from at lower interest rates than credit cards. That was the answer. I got an official check cut in the dealer's name and claimed that rare item for my collection.

Don't get me wrong; I'm not an advocate of whimsical spending and going into debt up to your ears. But, managed properly with the discipline to pay down the debt as quickly as possible, a line of credit can give you the edge over other bidders when a desirable item gets pricey. Those with less cash drop out of the running, and that reduces the competition. You will stand a better chance if you have fast access to cash and can repay it within a relatively short period of time.

But I can't stress this point enough: use care and discipline when you borrow funds to win auctions.

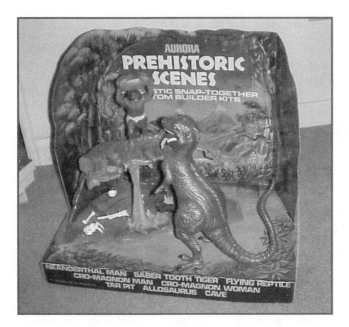

figure 13-11

The ultra-rare Aurora Prehistoric Scenes store display from 1971. Good thing I could get the funds to cover this one.

Knowing When to Walk Away

Is "not bidding" a strategy? Yup, and it's a good one. You can be very effective at the auctions when you *don't* bid at all.

As you watch an auction progress, you'll be seeing how active it is. Watch for how quickly and how much the high bid raises. Most auctions go up in bid value a little at a time. The ones that catch your attention are those that jump suddenly even though there may be several days to go before the auction's over. If one of these auctions catches your eye, take a quick visit to the bidding history on it.

If you see a lot of bidders have bid on an item, then it's obviously popular. No real sign of concern there except it might end up being a costly item when it's all over. Keep a keen eye peeled for a fast-advancing auction that has history of only a couple of bidders. This is a bidding war in the making. If you follow the bidding over the course of days, you might see the high bidders outbidding one another in that old tug-of-war fashion. This means that both are trying to draw their line and stake their claim. When it appears that one bidder has dropped out (maybe a day or two has passed and the other bidder's advance still stands), look out; that bidder might be waiting to snipe.

How does this affect you? Well, if you decide to bid in the middle of a bidding war, you might end up taking on a couple of impassioned bidders, and you'll probably pay a lot for the item. If you think it's an item that might show up again—especially if it's something you've seen before in the completed auctions—let this one go. There's no sense in you getting caught between the Hatfields and the McCoys here. You might find the same thing up for auction later when these two boys have had enough of their feuding.

Now, as a word of caution, remember that one of those bid-happy varmints *didn't* win. The one who didn't might be a little sore about that. What's the aftermath of an auction feud? Obviously, one bidder came out victorious while the other slunk away, vowing to get revenge another day. OK, I'm being dramatic here, but it does mean that the loser is still "at large" and may be actively searching for another one of those items that just got away. That bidder is going to be a fierce competitor at the next go-around. The winner, on the other hand, is probably satisfied and won't be too likely to bid the next time the same item shows up on eBay.

So the point is to avoid those impassioned bid battles if it's possible to get the same item—maybe even in better condition?—during another auction. Just watch for the return of vengeful varmints who might just as soon blow you full of bidder's buckshot rather than go through the agony of losing again.

chapter 14

Managing Your Bidding Activity

Well, you've certainly been a busy bee, haven't you? With all that looking and bidding and sniping and buying, you probably have quite a virtual sack full of stuff. Your simple bid can get you some great things, and it really is quite powerful. But remember that your bid is your word of honor at eBay; it's your commitment to the sellers and to the overall principles of the eBay community. You don't want to throw it around willy-nilly or, worse yet, leave it lying about to be forgotten. It's a big deal; can you feel it?

You have to keep up on where you've been and where you're going, auctionwise. Maybe you don't always snipe but often bid early for some of the reasons you learned in the last chapter. Can you remember everything you've bid on after all that activity? Are you planning on bidding in some auctions over the next few days? Will you be ready for those auctions without forgetting about the auctions you've already won? Is the check really in the mail?

With more than two million active auctions on any given day, most eBay regulars will find plenty of items they'd like to own. Every day you could find at least one new thing you'd like to bid on, but you have to avoid the trap of tunnel vision: *Don't forget today what you bid on yesterday.* That might sound like some phrase out of ancient lore; it isn't. It's something I made up to remind me of how easy it is to let your bidding run away with you. You may have $100 to bid on an item today, but have you already potentially promised some of that money to the auction you bid on yesterday, or the day before that, or the day before that?

Keeping track of your bidding activity is a real key to ensuring you can pay when you win. You'll win a lot; that's good. You might need to pay a lot; that's a different story. However, there is hope, and you don't need to go *cold turkey* on the auction addiction to keep yourself from going into financial withdrawal.

Tracking Your Auctions

Depending upon how complex you want to get, tracking your eBay auctions is really no chore at all. In fact, eBay already has several tools that help you quickly review your bidding behavior.

First, whenever you want to review what current auctions you've bid in and what that high bid might be, turn to the handy-dandy eBay search page. You can always perform a quick search using the Bidder Search box. Enter your eBay user ID there and click on the *Search* button. eBay will list all the auctions you've bid in that are still in progress (see Figure 14-1).

From what you can see in Figure 14-1—which is a view of the current auctions I'm bidding in—you can see that I'm only involved in a few active auctions. What can I say? I know how to practice restraint.

To see only the active auctions I'm bidding in, I chose *not* to see completed auctions in which I've bid; that's the default setting in the eBay Bidder Search box. (Go back and look at Figure 7-6 if you need to remind yourself where the Bidder Search box is.)

With the active auctions search result, you can see if you're still the high bidder in an active auction and what the current high bid is. You won't be able to see the maximum bid you placed here; that was only shown to you in the bid confirmation screen when you first placed your bid. Shortly thereafter, you received the bid confirmation message in your e-mail inbox restating what you eBay Bidder List: dennis_prince - Netscape

File Edit View Go Communicator Help

Bookmarks Location: Pl.dll?MfcISAPICommand=ViewBidItems&userid=dennis_prince&completed=0&all=1&rows=25 What's Related

home | my eBay | site map

Browse | Sell | Services | Search | Help | Community

find items | find members | personal shopper

▶ Subscribe now! Get your charter subscription to eBay magazine.
▶ Try the new way to shop by photos -- the Gallery!

Search tips
☐ Search titles **and** descriptions

Current auctions bid on by dennis_prince (179) ☆

Includes ongoing auctions only. Bold price means at least one bid has been received.

This list includes **all** auctions dennis_prince (179) ☆ has bid on, and in some cases may no longer be the high bidder.

You can click on the **Start Time**, **End Time**, or **Price** links to sort the list.

Items 1 - 3 of 3 total

Item	Start	End	Price	Title	High Bidder
134137817	07/19/99	07/26/99 18:16:36	**$15.00**	1970 Beatles "Let It Be" Lobby Card Set	dennis_prince
132847417	07/16/99	07/26/99 22:49:56	**$11.95**	TV's Creature Features Host "Bob Wilkins"	2 Dutch bids
134090650	07/19/99	07/26/99 17:06:22	**$4.99**	Incredible Melting Man Mexican Lobby Card	dennis_prince

Document: Done

figure 14-1

Now here's a guy with restraint. Only three auctions have his name next to them. This shows good financial planning and excellent self-control.

bid on *and* what your maximum bid was (don't worry; I'll show you another place to find your maximum bid value a bit later in this chapter).

NOTE You'll see if you're still the high bidder in an auction because the search result shows who's in the lead in the column labeled *High Bidder*.

TIP If you only want to see the auctions in which you're the high bidder—not all active auctions in which you've bid—choose the *No, only if high bidder* button in the Bidder Search box.

No sweat, right? So far, I'm only on the hook for $31.95, but I also keep in mind that I have maximum bids out there that amount to $69 for all these items. Still, that's affordable. I might do some more shopping. But is it safe?

Now I'll do another bidder search, but I'll check to see the completed auctions. (That is, I'll check that little *Yes* option button in the area labeled

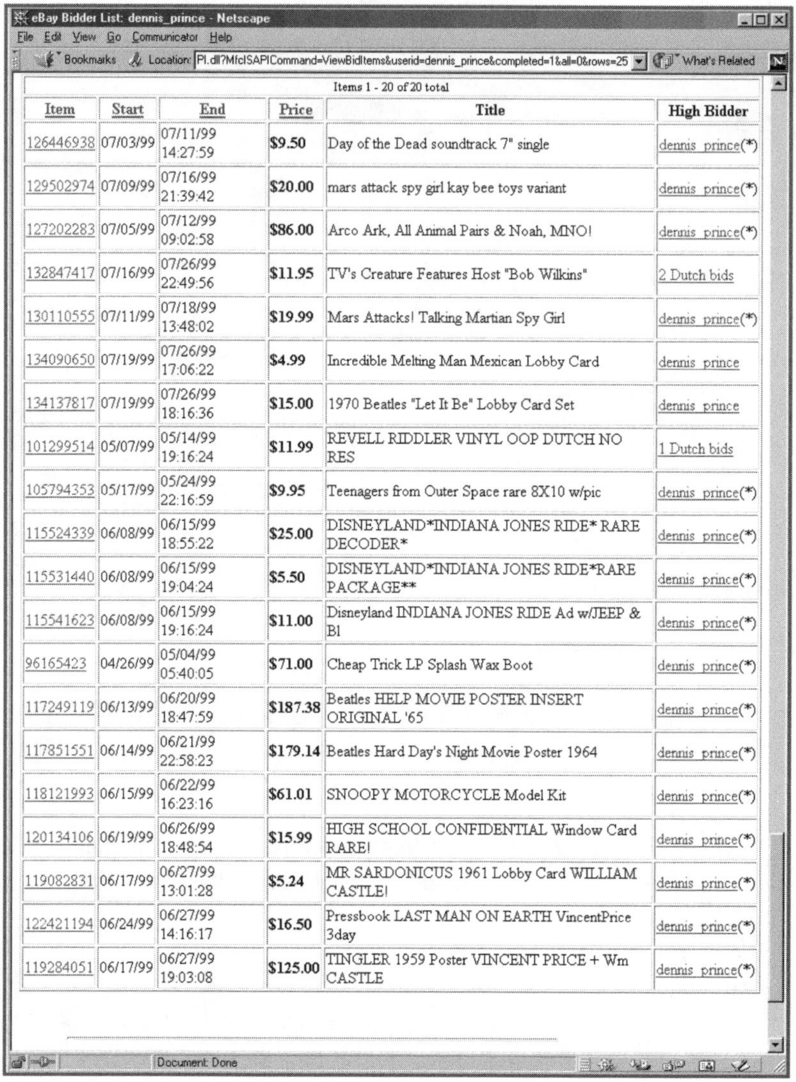

eBay Bidder List: dennis_prince - Netscape

Items 1 - 20 of 20 total

Item	Start	End	Price	Title	High Bidder
126446938	07/03/99	07/11/99 14:27:59	**$9.50**	Day of the Dead soundtrack 7" single	dennis_prince(*)
129502974	07/09/99	07/16/99 21:39:42	**$20.00**	mars attack spy girl kay bee toys variant	dennis_prince(*)
127202283	07/05/99	07/12/99 09:02:58	**$86.00**	Arco Ark, All Animal Pairs & Noah, MNO!	dennis_prince(*)
132847417	07/16/99	07/26/99 22:49:56	**$11.95**	TV's Creature Features Host "Bob Wilkins"	2 Dutch bids
130110555	07/11/99	07/18/99 13:48:02	**$19.99**	Mars Attacks! Talking Martian Spy Girl	dennis_prince(*)
134090650	07/19/99	07/26/99 17:06:22	**$4.99**	Incredible Melting Man Mexican Lobby Card	dennis_prince
134137817	07/19/99	07/26/99 18:16:36	**$15.00**	1970 Beatles "Let It Be" Lobby Card Set	dennis_prince
101299514	05/07/99	05/14/99 19:16:24	**$11.99**	REVELL RIDDLER VINYL OOP DUTCH NO RES	1 Dutch bids
105794353	05/17/99	05/24/99 22:16:59	**$9.95**	Teenagers from Outer Space rare 8X10 w/pic	dennis_prince(*)
115524339	06/08/99	06/15/99 18:55:22	**$25.00**	DISNEYLAND*INDIANA JONES RIDE* RARE DECODER*	dennis_prince(*)
115531440	06/08/99	06/15/99 19:04:24	**$5.50**	DISNEYLAND*INDIANA JONES RIDE*RARE PACKAGE**	dennis_prince(*)
115541623	06/08/99	06/15/99 19:16:24	**$11.00**	Disneyland INDIANA JONES RIDE Ad w/JEEP & Bl	dennis_prince(*)
96165423	04/26/99	05/04/99 05:40:05	**$71.00**	Cheap Trick LP Splash Wax Boot	dennis_prince(*)
117249119	06/13/99	06/20/99 18:47:59	**$187.38**	Beatles HELP MOVIE POSTER INSERT ORIGINAL '65	dennis_prince(*)
117851551	06/14/99	06/21/99 22:58:23	**$179.14**	Beatles Hard Day's Night Movie Poster 1964	dennis_prince(*)
118121993	06/15/99	06/22/99 16:23:16	**$61.01**	SNOOPY MOTORCYCLE Model Kit	dennis_prince(*)
120134106	06/19/99	06/26/99 18:48:54	**$15.99**	HIGH SCHOOL CONFIDENTIAL Window Card RARE!	dennis_prince(*)
119082831	06/17/99	06/27/99 13:01:28	**$5.24**	MR SARDONICUS 1961 Lobby Card WILLIAM CASTLE!	dennis_prince(*)
122421194	06/24/99	06/27/99 14:16:17	**$16.50**	Pressbook LAST MAN ON EARTH VincentPrice 3day	dennis_prince(*)
119284051	06/17/99	06/27/99 19:03:08	**$125.00**	TINGLER 1959 Poster VINCENT PRICE + Wm CASTLE	dennis_prince(*)

figure 14-2

Let the truth be told! This guy's out of control. He must be printing his own money in the back room.

Completed auctions too?) Click on the Search button and see what happens (Figure 14-2 has the sobering details).

Whoa-ho, Nellie! Looks like I've been doing some shopping already. Apparently, I'm quite good at it, too. Once I get my eyeballs back in their sockets, I'll be able to tell you what you're looking at.

First, the format is the same as when you looked at only active auctions. The important detail you see in Figure 14-2 is the little asterisk that appears to the right of the high bidder's name in the last column. That asterisk means the bidder won the auction and that the auction is over. Yes, I've been a little busy, I guess—I like to win, too. Notice the items without asterisks; they're the same active auctions you saw in Figure 14-1. When you choose to see completed auctions too, the list will represent completed *and* current auctions in which you've bid.

NOTE Typically, you'll only see a listing of completed auctions that are no more than 30 days old; eBay's servers would probably burst at the seams if they tried to retain *all* of my auction antics.

So what does this auction listing mean? It means I'd better break out my checkbook and start paying some people for the items I've won. Use the Bidder Search box as a quick way to see where you've been and where you're going as far as high bid obligations. As for me, *"pay to the order of—"*

Another tool that provides even more detailed information about your bidding activity is *My eBay*. No, it's not *mine;* it's the auction management tool called *My eBay* that I first showed you in Chapter 6. My eBay is great at finding and reporting more information about your present and past auction activity.

To access My eBay, click on the aptly named link in the mini navbar at the top of any eBay page. You can also access My eBay using the *Services* selection from the main navigation bar, but the mini navbar way is quickest. As you enter My (your) eBay, you'll see a screen like the one shown in Figure 14-3.

In Figure 14-3, you can see where you'll need to enter your eBay user ID and your password. Then you'll see the *Display Options* column. Use the check boxes to select the information you want to see. In this example, I only wanted to see what I've been doing with all my money, so I just chose the *Bidding items* check box.

Next, there are a some choices to make in the *Seller/Bidder List Options* column. First, enter the number of days you want to review (the maximum, as

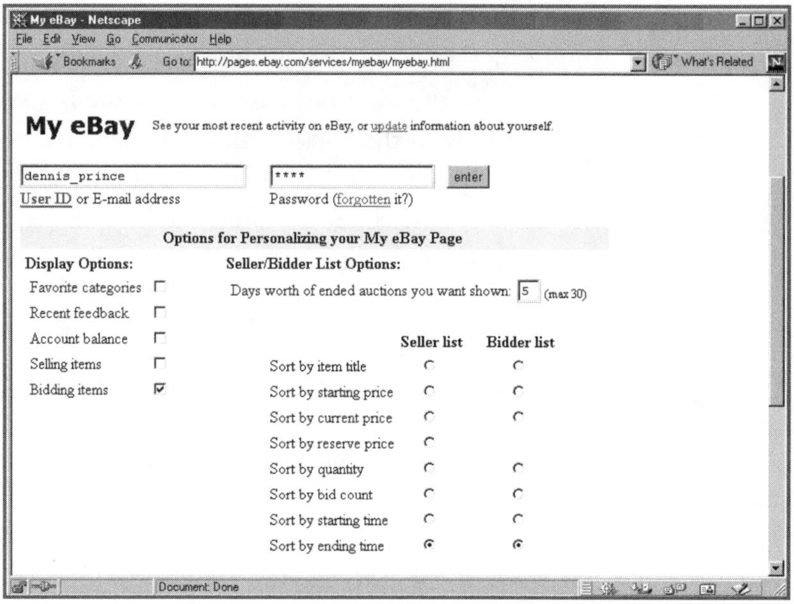

figure 14-3

The My eBay entry screen is where you'll decide what auction data you want to see.

stated on the screen, is 30 days). After that, choose how you want the results sorted. For ease of discussion, I've used eBay's default selection, *Sort by ending time.* You can experiment with other sort possibilities later.

When you've entered your data and made your selections, click on the *Enter* button next to the Password field. eBay crunches through the data and gives you a result that will look something like what you see in Figure 14-4.

A few notes about the My eBay result you'll see; first, each item title is an active link to the original item's detail page. Click on one and off you'll go. Below the item title, you'll see the auction item number, starting bid amount, the current bid value, your maximum bid amount (how handy), the quantity of items being bid on (if it's a Dutch auction, you'll see more than one available), the total number of bids the item has received, the auction start date and end date (including end time), and the time left in the auction. Obviously, if an auction has ended, eBay tells you so. But if an auction is still active, you'll see the remaining time listed in days, hours, and minutes (such as 4d 22h 1m).

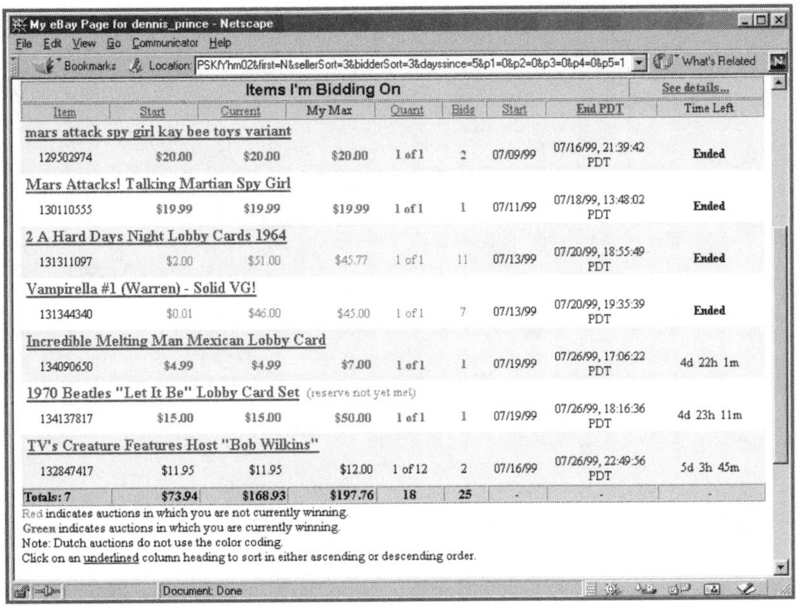

figure 14-4

The results of the My eBay search are much more detailed than what you get from the regular search page.

NOTE If you want to change the sort order on your My eBay screen, just click on one of the underlined (linked) heading titles. The display will be resorted in ascending or descending order for that particular column.

Another thing to notice in the My eBay results: the name or user ID of the high bidder for each item is not shown. But you'll see the auction details where you were the winner displayed in bold green text. When there was an auction you bid in but didn't win, the details will be displayed in thin red text. The red text lets you know that either you were outbid or you were the high bidder but the seller's reserve wasn't met, so it was an action you didn't really win by rules of the Reserve Price auction.

Now there's a cool little addition to this screen you might not notice at first. Look back at Figure 14-4; see in the title bar, *Items I'm Bidding On*, the little link to the right named *See details*. Click on that. When you do, eBay will reformat the results of your original search, but will show the item information in the format of the original item detail listings. You can see an example of the detailed display in Figure 14-5.

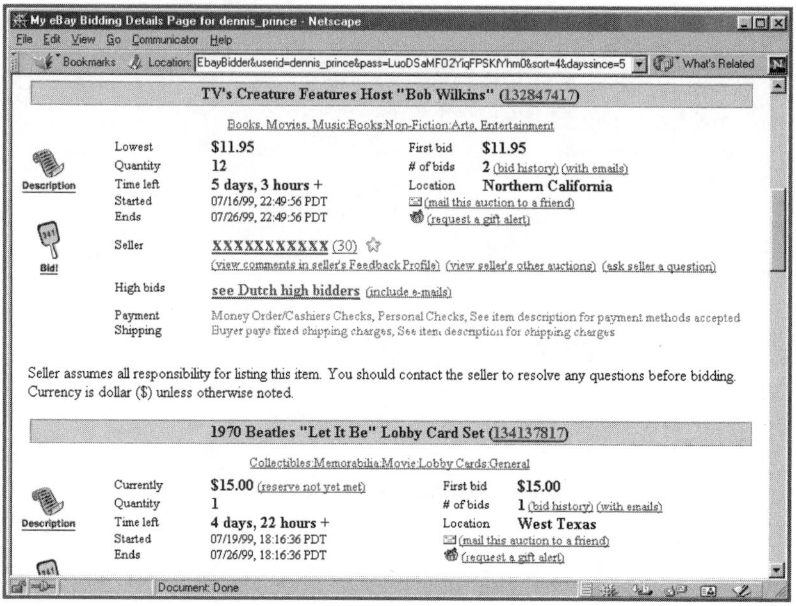

figure 14-5

The detailed view of My eBay
results shows a continuous
display of the item details for
all items you bid on that met
your original search criteria.

Again, what you'll find in My eBay is just a more detailed view of the same information you saw in the eBay search page. It's up to you how deeply you want to review your bidding activity.

If none of these methods of reviewing bidding activity meets your rigorous standards, then you might consider a tracking method of your own. If it's more data you want or it's data that goes back longer than any 30-day period, think about creating a tool that will give you a long-running historical view of your bidding behavior.

If you decide to create a special tracking tool of your own, you can do it easily by creating a simple text document with rows and columns, or by creating a slick little spreadsheet that might do some calculations for you. If you're really anal about the whole thing (and that's not bad), you might want to use a database management application to track all the dotted "i"s and crossed "t"s.

I've been using the spreadsheet method for the past four years. When I started with eBay, My eBay didn't yet exist, and the search page was a pale precursor of what you'll find today. Here are some additional bits of information—beside those readily available in an eBay search—that I have found useful to track:

- Seller's surname

- Seller's e-mail address

- Seller's street address

- Postage paid

- Insurance paid

- Date I was notified by the seller

- Date I sent my payment

- Date seller shipped item (if communicated)

- Date I received the item

- Feedback left (Y/N)?

It might seem like a lot of work to keep all this extra information. Sometimes it is. I like to track these kinds of details, though, because of the number of auctions I bid in. If I tried to remember all these details by way of my memory alone, I'd probably suffer a small hemorrhage. Occasionally, you'll need to follow up on an auction: maybe you say you've never received your item, maybe the seller says your payment never arrived. What information will you have to help support your case?

However you decide to track your bidding activity, it's generally a good idea to get into some regular habit of tracking something. You'll need a good view at what you're bidding on, what you're spending, and if you're following up on your bids in a timely way. If you start to lose track of where your bids are going, you might start missing auction commitments. Sellers don't like that, and you might feel the backlash of negative feedback for your disorganized ways.

I've Changed My Mind, I Don't Want to Bid

Uh-oh. You've changed your mind? Are you kidding?! But you've already bid. *"Um . . . I know . . . but I've . . . um . . . changed my mind."* The kingpin's not gonna like this much. He might have to come over and mess up your cat a bit or spray paint your garbage cans.

For all that I've said about your bid being your word of honor and all that, what happens if you just don't want that item any more? What to do? What to do? Well, you *can* get out of a bid if you change your mind. Actually, you can do just about anything with your bids on eBay if you want to—you just have to be willing to deal with any consequences.

If you bid on an item and then decide it's not what you want, you can *retract* your bid. That's right—you can erase your bid, withdrawing your commitment to pay for the item if you were the high bidder. Although I certainly don't encourage this unless *absolutely necessary*, here's how it's done:

First, choose the *Services* selection from the main navigation bar. Next, choose *Buying & selling* in the submenu. In the *Buying and Selling Tools* screen, select *Retract my bid*. Gosh, are you sure you really want to do this? If you must, click *Retract my bid*. When you do, you'll jump to a screen titled *Bid Retraction Form*.

First, you'll need to read eBay's opinion of retracting bids; it's not going to make you feel all cozy about it. But eBay does realize that sometimes you will have to retract bids for *legitimate* reasons. One good reason for retracting a bid is when the seller changes the description of the item after you've already bid and it no longer seems like the kind of item you were looking for. Or maybe you made a typo when you originally placed your bid, and you're on the line for $1,000 instead of $10. Those are good reasons and would be understood by just about anyone.

Further down in the text on the Bid Retraction Form, you'll read that your bid retraction will be put on public display in the bidding history of the item you're backing out of. All other bidders and the seller will be able to see your bid retraction. It's kind of like being locked up in the stocks in the center of the village. Just hope no one's carrying any rotten tomatoes.

But eBay does give you a chance to plead your case. When you retract your bid, you have the opportunity to tell everyone why you did it. In very reasonable situations, a bid retraction could make sense, and you'll want your day in eBay court.

So scroll down past the finger-wagging text, and you'll see where you'll actually retract your bid (see Figure 14-6).

eBay's bid retraction page clearly states that changing your mind is not a good reason for retracting a bid. But you can do it, and you might escape the seller's wrath if you can show just cause for doing so. Don't make up stories—if you simply changed your mind, then tell the seller that. Auctions are a serious thing, but most people understand that stuff happens, situations change, and even the best-placed bids sometimes go bad. Be honest, straightforward, and to the point.

If you really want to escape retribution for retracting a bid, try to do it well before the auction ends; not the last day and not in the last minutes. That way, the seller's auction has plenty of time to attract more bidders, especially if your retraction lowers the high bid of the item. One thing to be certain

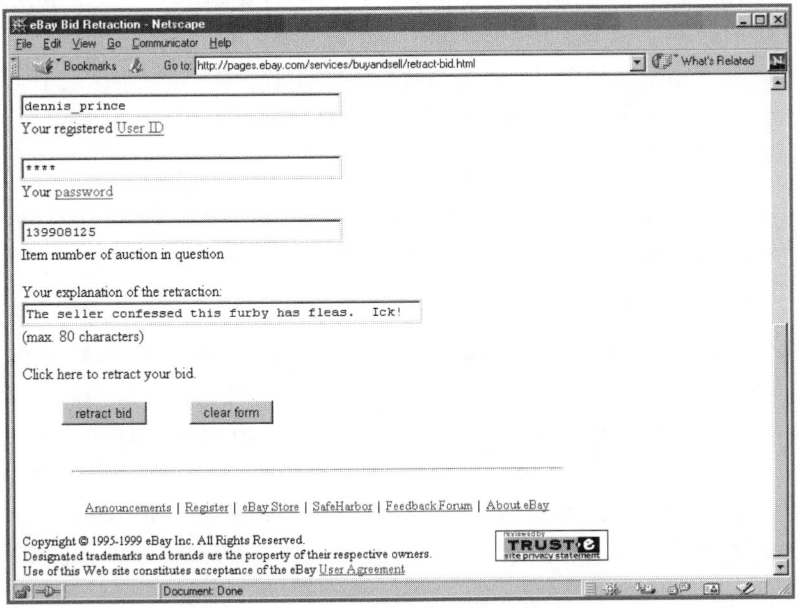

figure 14-6

When you need to retract a bid, you'll need to use the Bid Retraction Form.

to do: contact the seller via e-mail to explain that you are retracting your bid and why. It's better to hear it from you directly than to find out by chance or surprise. If you come forward first, you're more likely to be let off easy.

ALERT Bid retractions are only possible while the auction is still active! If you decide you want out of an auction, you can only post an official bid retraction *before* the auction closes. If you try to retract after that, well . . . you can't. All you can do from that point is back out of your high bid.

Deadbeat bidder! Deadbeat bidder!

Quick—someone give me one of those rotten tomatoes!

SOAPBOX I'm not suggesting you kiss up to the seller when you retract a bid, but you do need to remember that placing your bid is equivalent to signing a contract to buy the item. The seller might get ticked off now that you've changed your mind. This kind of bid retraction makes you look like a real newbie, and even makes you look a little irresponsible. Just warm up a slice of humble pie, tuck in your shirt, and ask for some kindness and understanding.

Although I won't show you an actual bid retraction, I will show you where the retraction will be visible to all. If you enter the bid history for any item, scroll down to the end of the history list. If a retraction were made on an item, eBay would show the bidder who retracted the bid along with the reason for the retraction. Figure 14-7 shows the area where a bid retraction would be displayed.

Yes, you probably saw that other link titled *Cancellation* where the bid retractions would be posted. Cancellations are something only the seller of the item can do. I'll explain more about those in Chapter 19.

By this point you've probably had enough of a tongue-lashing about this topic. I don't mean to make you feel bad or paranoid if ever you need to retract a bid. I think, though, you can see why it's not something you want to get into the habit of doing. Some sellers might not like your reason for retracting a bid and might even leave negative feedback because of it. It's their prerogative to do so, and it's one of the consequences I warned you

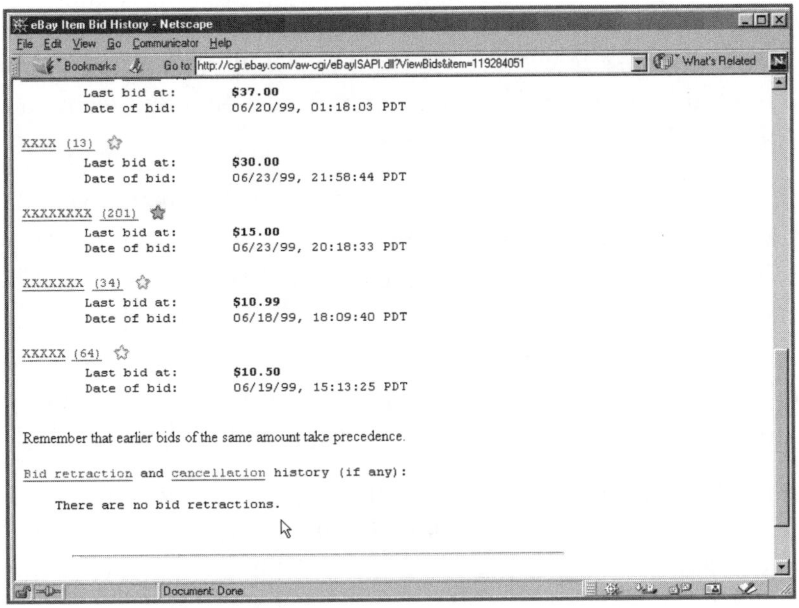

figure 14-7

The public viewing place for bid retractions is at the end of the bidding history page. Let's hope neither you nor I ever enter this Hall of Shame.

about earlier. In more serious situations, if you retract bids too often you might even get suspended from eBay entirely. That would be a consequence I hope you never have to face.

Insufficient Funds

So what happens if your Bonneville breaks, the Olds overheats, or the Pacer pukes? Unexpected things happen, not just with vehicles, but in many areas of your life. Occasionally, something comes up and it costs money you hadn't planned to spend. You can probably scrape together the funds you need to set those unexpected situations right, but what about those pending auctions? Is there money left to pay up on your high bids?

Whether the family truckster blows a gasket, the wind blows a big hole in your roof, or your kid shoots his mouth off and ends up needing some unexpected dental work, you're going to have to get out of those auctions. Here, I'm considering that the auctions you're committed to have already closed, and you're the high bidder. Yay?

Make no bones about it—backing out of the high bid in a closed auction means breaking a purchase agreement. As I said earlier, in many states, your winning bid is a binding agreement. I reiterate this here because I want you to understand the delicate nature of the situation.

OK, first thing you'll need to do is contact that seller, ASAP. Again, be honest, sincere, and apologetic. If you are, I really can't see the seller blowing your hair back for what is clearly an unexpected financial downturn. Maybe, just maybe, the seller will empathize with you and wish you luck (that would be nice). The seller might not be too badly set back; there's always the next highest bidder to check with, and the seller might be able to get pretty much the same value for the item, less the minimum bid increment.

If you back out of a winning bid, definitely offer to pay the seller's listing fee and sales commission fee for that auction. It's the least you can do and, depending on the final value of the item, it shouldn't be something you couldn't afford. It's your way of really *showing* you're sorry about a situation that was out of your control. The seller will admire your gesture and might or might not take you up on your offer.

 SOAPBOX   And for Heaven's sake, don't let yourself get caught bidding on some other item within a day or so of breaking your bid. That will be devastating to your reputation. You might be the recipient of a toasty warm flame-wall if you're ever found doing this.

part 4

You Are the Auctioneer

chapter 15

What Do You Want to Sell Today?

"Will you just look at all this stuff? I can't find nuthin' in here because of all this junk. I should just throw it all out—bunch of junk. Dunno why I've kept it all these years. Look at all these old books, toys, magazines, lunch boxes, records. Well, it's time to call Goodwill. Whatever they won't take goes to the dump. I've had it with this mess."

Do you have a room in your house, apartment, or wherever that seems to bring up this kind of sentiment? If you're like me, stuff seems to find a way of nestling into the far corners of the house—and everyplace else you spend any time—and then staying there for years on end. It's amazing how much you can accumulate without really trying. But is it all junk? It might be clutter, but it might also be treasure.

If you're ready to break out the shop-vac and the leaf blower to rid yourself of some stuff that just won't seem to go away, you're probably ready to become an auctioneer. More than likely, your stuff has value to somebody, and it's time for you to embark on listing your own auctions. It's great fun, it's an adventure, and it's waiting for you.

So open that back room, pull up the garage door, or clamber into your attic. You're going on a treasure hunt and it begins not far from where you're standing.

What Do You Have to Sell?

This is the first question you'll ask— *"What do I have to sell?"* I'd wager you have more than you realize. You don't necessarily have to be a certified collector to have something—anything—that will have value on the auction block. If you've been alive at least 20 years, then you're probably sitting on something that has historic or nostalgic appeal.

NOTE If you've been alive much less than 20 years, then you're not even eligible to be selling or bidding at eBay; according to the site rules, you have to be at least 18 to participate. But even if you aren't as tall as the cutout clown, you can still ride the ride—kind of. Ask Mom or Dad or some other trusted adult to sell your stuff for you. That's not against the rules, and it sure beats mowing lawns.

But anything worth auctioning doesn't necessarily have to be old. As you learned in earlier chapters, even some new items are worthy of auction. Maybe you were one of the lucky ones that happened to be wandering through a store when they opened the case of Furbies. Maybe you found the Mark McGwire trading card that had the misspelling on it. Current items can be just as lucrative as older stuff—sometimes more so.

But if you do have old stuff that seems like worthless trash, don't be too quick to toss it in the ol' ash can. Things as silly as salt and pepper shakers, old photos of people you don't know, bric-a-brac, or almost anything else might fetch some sort of price at eBay. It might not always be a king's ransom, but it's more than what you'll get if you throw the junk away.

When's the best time to find stuff for auction? Spring cleaning, anyone? If ever you find the motivation to do some serious cleaning and decluttering, that's when you'll find all your hidden treasures. Old soda pop bottles, jars, and glassware will usually find some interested bidders. Posters, pictures, and other pop-culture relics of the '60s and '70s are extremely popular. Records, cassettes, and those incredibly nostalgic and obsolete 8-track tapes are avidly sought after. Even clothing and jewelry items will find customers ready to take them off your hands quickly.

So here's the moral—and the phrase you should keep in mind when you're looking to clean out the barn:

"Don't toss that thang. It might be worth sump'n!"

If it isn't worth something, you can always throw it away later without much loss at all. But I think you'll be more successful than you imagine.

 TIP Most any dated printed matter can be of value to someone. Printed matter (magazines, books, newspapers) can have significant historic value to many people. Depending on the subject, bidders might be willing to pay a handsome price for what you have. Remember that *Vampirella* magazine I bid on in Chapter 8? If you missed it, the final outcome of that auction appeared in Chapter 14. Look back at Figure 14-4 and you'll see what that issue finally sold at. Are you sure you don't have something worthless to sell?

Done Any Upgrading Lately?

Here's a real easy one: if you've recently bought something on eBay as a means of upgrading—that is, you already have the item, but the one you just bought is in better condition, more complete, or whatever—then you have something to sell. Sell the one you just upgraded from.

You might wonder if the item you upgraded is really worth anything to anyone else. Well, consider that it was probably worth something to you at one time, right? Maybe it was the first or only one you could find for some time. You might have been tickled to have it even though it wasn't the best possible specimen. Don't you think someone else out there would be just as tickled as you were when you found it? Sure they would. It's like a hand-me-down—only you get paid for it.

Often, you'll find these hand-me-downs flowing through the stream of items, being temporarily owned by many different people. I've already told you that I've seen some of my items change hands on the auction block and elsewhere on the Internet. Just as I was once happy with the item, the next owner was also happy, and so was the one after that and the next one, too.

Know Your Item

You learned about this when you were researching the items you were bidding on. The more you knew about your item, the better informed bidder you became. The same holds true when you're selling. If you have an item, and you're not too clear about all the details of it, do that Internet research.

The more you can tell potential bidders about your item, the more comfortable they will feel bidding on it. You'd be surprised at how thankful bidders are when you can tell them about your item, its origin, and other such details. If they decide to ask you specific questions about the item, your ability to answer them truthfully and completely will let them know you're an expert and you really know your stuff.

Also, the more you know about your item, the better equipped you'll be to assess its true value. Plus you can potentially squeeze some extra bids out of an auction when you can provide those specific little details that might explain the rarity of an item, any reproductions that might exist, or any other specific element that will make your item seem to be the one to own.

Researching the Potential Success of Your Auction

OK. Now assume you've found the treasures you think might be of interest to the bidders at eBay. You've done your item research and know that what you have is a terrific item. Great! That means you've cleared the first hurdle with relative ease. But a little more research will give you a better idea of what you can expect from your auction, and what kind of riches you stand to rake in.

 SOAPBOX Easy there, Rockefeller. I know what you might be thinking. *"I've got a ton of old stuff. I'm gonna rake in a fortune!"* That might be the first thought you have when you decide to comb through your stash to see what you can sell. Immediately, you could be enticed by the notion of making *big money*. Maybe, but maybe not. This is why you're going to do some research first. You need to set some realistic expectations before you get started selling on eBay. If you don't, you're sure to have delusions of grandeur cloud your good judgment. You'll be bummed when bidders end up not throwing bags of money at you.

So your first duty is to do some live market research. Hmmm. Sounds like a drag? It's not. It's easy, and again you don't need to go much further than eBay itself. Sales research on eBay is easy. First, see if what you have to sell is already up for auction. Search for the item you want to sell and find out how many others might be on the block right now. In this part of your research, you're going to be comparing how your item stands up to others already being bid on.

To make this a bit more real, I'll do some research on an item that I'm actually planning to sell. You've probably gotten a taste for the kind of items I like to have around, so I won't let you down here: I'll be selling an original theatrical lobby card (an 11×14 movie photo poster) from 1956's *It Conquered the World*. It's great old drive-in schlock, and it's usually a popular kind of item.

 NOTE   Old movie stuff, if you've got it, is one of those perennial favorites. Almost everyone likes movies, and almost everyone has a favorite movie that they've enjoyed. What's your favorite? I'll bet you can find something from it up for bid on eBay.

To begin, I'll go to eBay's search page and perform a title search for "it conquered." I'll start by looking for active auctions. The results of my search can be seen in Figure 15-1.

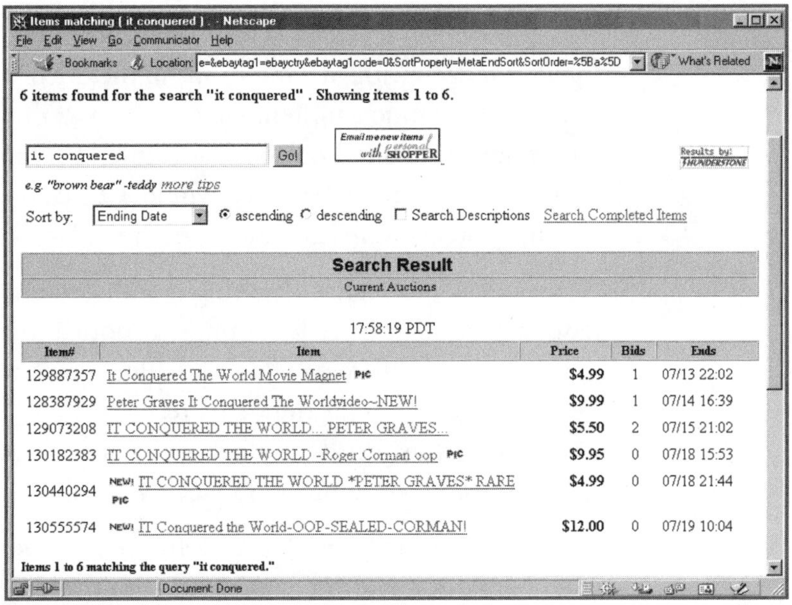

figure 15-1

A search of active auctions shows several items that match the criterion of "it conquered."

Item#	Item	Price	Bids	Ends
129887357	It Conquered The World Movie Magnet **PIC**	$4.99	1	07/13 22:02
128387929	Peter Graves It Conquered The Worldvideo~NEW!	$9.99	1	07/14 16:39
129073208	IT CONQUERED THE WORLD... PETER GRAVES...	$5.50	2	07/15 21:02
130182383	IT CONQUERED THE WORLD -Roger Corman oop **PIC**	$9.95	0	07/18 15:53
130440294	**NEW!** IT CONQUERED THE WORLD *PETER GRAVES* RARE **PIC**	$4.99	0	07/18 21:44
130555574	**NEW!** IT Conquered the World-OOP-SEALED-CORMAN!	$12.00	0	07/19 10:04

6 items found for the search "it conquered" . Showing items 1 to 6.

it conquered   Go!

e.g. "brown bear" -teddy *more tips*

Sort by: Ending Date ▾ ⊙ ascending ○ descending ☐ Search Descriptions   Search Completed Items

Search Result

Current Auctions

17:58:19 PDT

Items 1 to 6 matching the query "it conquered."

TIP Notice that I searched for "it conquered" as opposed to the full title of "it conquered the world." Remembering your good search techniques, a title as long as this one might be shortened or otherwise abbreviated by sellers. Using "it conquered" should be sure to return any *It Conquered the World* items that are up for auction.

You can see that my search brought back six active auction items—not a whopping showing, but indicative there is interest in the film. Items two through five are copies of the out-of-print video. Two of them have bids, so that's encouraging to me. The first item is a magnet of the film's poster artwork. It has a bid, too, and that causes me to believe the film collectors might like this title. As I write this, all these auctions still have a day or more to go before they close. I'll bet they receive some additional bid activity.

NOTE Notice how items #3 through #5 in the listing don't let on they're videos of this drive-in classic. I had to mouse over and review the details of each before I really knew what I was looking at. Many potential bidders won't bother to do that, so I'll teach you how to write better auction item titles in Chapter 16.

So, with only six items returned in my search, and all with very low or no bids, you might not think material from this film would find much of a bidding audience. Well, not so quick.

Your next bit of research is to perform the same search, but this time for all *completed items* with "it conquered" in the title. After all, the only way to really find out how much an item seems to be worth is to find out the end results of previous auctions. Look back at Figure 15-1, and you'll see the *Search Completed Items* link near the search window. Click on it, and you'll see what kinds of similar items were auctioned within the last 30 days (see Figure 15-2).

What you see in Figure 15-2 might grab your attention more than what you saw in Figure 15-1. A few things to notice: first, there seem to be several different types of items from this film that have been auctioned recently; second, all but one of the items received bids, most fetching some reasonably high prices; third, another lobby card from this film recently sold for $24.99 (using the abbreviation *LC#4* – Lobby Card #4).

This information gives you a feeling for the kind of bidding activity that might be out there for your item. From the seven completed auctions, I

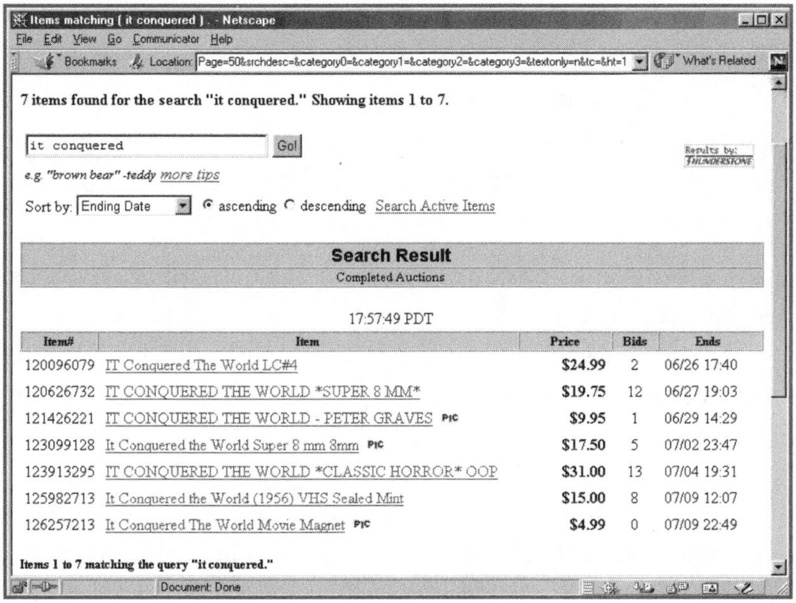
Items matching [it conquered] - Netscape

7 items found for the search "it conquered." Showing items 1 to 7.

it conquered Go!

e.g. "brown bear" -teddy more tips

Sort by: Ending Date ascending descending Search Active Items

Search Result

Completed Auctions

17:57:49 PDT

Item#	Item	Price	Bids	Ends
120096079	IT Conquered The World LC#4	$24.99	2	06/26 17:40
120626732	IT CONQUERED THE WORLD *SUPER 8 MM*	$19.75	12	06/27 19:03
121426221	IT CONQUERED THE WORLD - PETER GRAVES PIC	$9.95	1	06/29 14:29
123099128	It Conquered the World Super 8 mm 8mm PIC	$17.50	5	07/02 23:47
123913295	IT CONQUERED THE WORLD *CLASSIC HORROR* OOP	$31.00	13	07/04 19:31
125982713	It Conquered the World (1956) VHS Sealed Mint	$15.00	8	07/09 12:07
126257213	It Conquered The World Movie Magnet PIC	$4.99	0	07/09 22:49

Items 1 to 7 matching the query "it conquered."

figure 15-2

A search of completed auctions shows several more matches for the criterion of "it conquered." It's the prices that I'm most interested in, though.

would expect that *It Conquered the World* is a relatively popular title, and that I could probably get somewhere around $25 for my lobby card. The lobby card that sold, though, only had two bids. That might mean there aren't too many people looking for these lobby cards. I'll need to keep that in mind when I list mine.

Of course, the next most important research is to look at the description of that other lobby card; it's crucial to understand more about the card and what kind of condition it was in. Whenever you sell something on eBay, be sure your research includes learning more about the tiny details of other similar items. This is what separates the good auctions from the great auctions. Completeness, condition, and authenticity will always be key to getting better prices from your auctions.

I've looked at the other seller's listing and found out his lobby card was in good condition, but it had several border tackholes and a pinhole cluster that extended into the image area. Now, for a paper item from 43 years ago, that's not so bad; the true collector, though, might not want anything less than perfection.

The other important thing to note in the previous auction is that the seller was auctioning lobby card #4 from the set. (Lobby cards came in sets of eight, in case you didn't know.) Why is that important? The lobby card I have to sell is #2 from the set; this might be a card the high bidder—or any other bidder—might need to complete their set. This is good because the auction I want to start won't be for an exact duplicate item.

I also look at the condition of my card. Based on the description given by the other seller, I expect my card is in much better condition. In fact, therefore, that $25 price range seems pretty reasonable. See how quickly you can do market research at eBay? Of course, it really is theoretical; anything can happen at the auction.

 Tip Now, with this sort of information at your fingertips, do you see what other indirect service eBay provides? No? Ever see someone offer to perform appraisals of your collection, keepsakes, or junk? Well, they do. Appraisers charge a sometimes hefty sum of money to evaluate your stuff. Granted, they are trained professionals, but do you really need top-end services for something like this lobby card? Why not just perform some of your own appraisals based on the real market results you find at eBay? It's a global marketplace that is subject to the highs and lows of the economy. Your own appraisals can be based on immediate information about demand and pricing. Just an idea.

But what if during your research you can't find an item like yours? Then what? Well, can you find anything similar to it from around the same time? If not, maybe do some research on the Internet at large. You remember how I found the Saratoga trunk; search for your item in the same way. Maybe there is a Web page devoted to things like your item. Maybe there's a Web page that sells the kind of item you have. Don't hesitate to do some Net research to learn more about what you have and what it's worth.

And if you simply strike out completely, it doesn't mean you shouldn't try to auction your item. If it's not worth much to you, then don't ask for much when you auction it. Let the market guide its value. If you have an investment in the item, then it's OK to look to at least recover that investment. If nobody bids to the level you want, either keep the item or lower the price.

SOAPBOX This is sometimes a difficult area: what if you can't get back what you paid for an item? In this case, it's up to you whether you want to sell the thing or not. If you really have no need for it, sell it for whatever you can get. I believe in a principle I call the *value of past ownership*. By this, I mean that I recoup some value from an item just by owning it for a period of time. Maybe it was something I enjoyed displaying and looking at; maybe it's something I used that served me well but I no longer need. It's kind of like applying depreciation. The thing still has some value, but you've also received a benefit from having it, too. Get whatever price you can out of the item and consider the loss as the price you paid for the personal gain from previous use. If you used it and enjoyed it, well, that was worth something, wasn't it? Selling for less than you paid would still be better than just tossing the thing.

Using Etiquette When Selling Your Item

Are there rules of politeness to observe before you auction an item? Kind of. These aren't rules published by eBay or anyone else, but they're some guidelines that I've developed for myself that seem to have some worth.

First consideration: should you list an item for sale when another seller already has an auction going for the same thing? To me, this isn't the best thing to do. During your research, you'll see if someone else has the same item up for bid. If you list your item while another seller has a matching item up for bid, you might draw away some of those bidders. The other seller might not like that too much. It's nothing you're liable for, but it's really not necessary. The bidders interested in that auction might see your auction and decide to bid there instead. That first seller could lose bids. You might not feel that's your problem ... until it happens to you.

Second, by listing your item at the same time as another current auction, you might make it seem as if the item is pretty easily found. Bidders might not jump, then, when they see the item listed—and that includes *your* listing. You might scare away your own bidders. Bidders *can* be choosers, remember? If they think there's a potential stockpile of something somewhere, they might just wait until they see the best quality item show up.

As a good rule of thumb, if another seller is finding a bunch of bidders for an item and you have one just like it, wait for that auction to close. It could end up in one of those bidding wars I told you about. Remember, at the end of a bidding war, only one bidder is the winner while the other bidders might still be wanting that item. Wait until the day after the other seller's auction finishes and then casually list your item. You might get some great rebound-bidders clamoring to bid up your auction. In the meantime, the other seller wasn't affected by your listing and will have no reason to feel slighted by it.

Second, should you mention another seller's auction when you list yours? Never! Don't even think about it. Let the bidders make the comparisons themselves just as you did when you were shopping for stuff. If you refer to another seller's item, you might come off as knocking those wares or generally bad-mouthing that auction. The seller might not be overly concerned, but in the spirit of community-mindedness, it's best to avoid the potential trouble altogether. If your item is a good one, it will stand on its own merits.

Verifying Your Item Before You List

Here, you should consider again what it is you're selling, how it can be honestly represented to the bidding public, and whether it should be offered up for auction at all.

Use the research you've done to realistically gauge what it is you want to sell. Consider the condition of your item—is it in terrific shape, or does it look like it's been jammed in the back of the garage for years? Is it complete, or are some key pieces missing? Is it broken? Can it be fixed? Are there better ones out there? These are all things that will determine the success of your auction. But, most important, these are considerations that will help you honestly represent your item to the buying masses. Sure, you might get more money if you advertise your item as "mint condition," but just be sure that's the sort of item your high bidder will eventually be receiving. Otherwise, there will probably be trouble.

Then gauge your personal valuation of the item based on facts, not monetary desire. Don't let yourself be fooled into thinking that just because something is old, it must be worth money. Condition becomes a factor here again, but also popularity—both then and now. Some things are doomed to never catch on. If your Ronco Buttoneer never quite did the trick in the '70s, it might not be so hot today, either. Sure, it's almost 30 years old, but that just means it's a 30-year-old piece of junk. Of course, your research will tell.

One thing to definitely consider about your item is whether it's illegal or infringing. Oh yes, eBay management has strict rules on the types of items they *will not* allow on their site. You remember I explained the Legal Buddy system back in Chapter 4—eBay's program to help copyright owners detect bogus and pirated items up for auction. But, added to that, eBay has also laid down some rules about what sorts of things are considered questionable and might be illegal to list on eBay. Briefly, the list of such items currently looks like this:

- Adult-only material
- Animals and animal parts
- Fireworks
- Food
- Human parts and remains
- Police-related items
- Scanners
- Stocks and stock certificates
- Artifacts
- Weapons and knives
- Pirated music, games, videos, software, and so on

It's quite a list—and you can see by the item descriptions how some of these things could be questionable or outright no-no's to list for auction. If you want to learn the specifics about eBay's rules and guidelines for these types of items, go to **http://pages.ebay.com/aw/help/topics-png-items.html**.

Flooding the Market

OK. Assume your item grades fairly well and it isn't on eBay's *most despised* list of nasty notions. As your research continues, you'll want to find out if your item will be one too many on the auction circuit. This is a lot like the point about not wanting to have too many of the same item listed at the same time. If bidders perceive a plentiful supply, they'll probably become a bit indifferent to your item and might let it slide by. Let the other auctions end and allow the bidders to catch their breath.

This also works when you consider that principle of supply and demand. If there are more items than there are people who want them, then you'll be kind of hard-pressed to find some good bidding action. The best thing to do is research the item in closed auctions and see what the bidding was like when auctions were held simultaneously, lightly spread apart, and with gaps of a week or more between listings.

 NOTE Of course, if you had a Furby, Tickle-Me Elmo, or some other craze-creature, it probably wouldn't matter that yours would be listed at the same time as thousands of other similar items. Those instances are a bit rarer, though.

Be Realistic

And this just kind of sums up the setting of your expectations before you decide to list an item for auction: try to base your expectations on what you've learned in your research. Better yet, set your expectations a bit lower, and you'll almost always be pleasantly surprised with the results.

There are the highs and lows of the auction. If you'll remember from my discussion of my first auction (see Chapter 3), I was absolutely taken by surprise when my California Raisins brought me $79—at my very first auction. Sure, I thought there was gold in them thar Webs, and then got a dose of reality as the next couple of auctions were far from being that monetarily successful. Maybe it was a fluke; maybe I just had that one right item at the right time. Whatever, I've found you usually make the best money on an auction when you least expect to. It's when you're really looking for money that the bidders seem not to come. Is it fate, karma, some sort of mischievous auction god? I don't know, and you probably won't either. Just take your best shot with what you have and see what happens. Remember, whatever you get, it will always be more than if you threw the thing away.

chapter 16

Creating a Simple Auction Listing

OK. Grab that gavel—it's your turn to host an auction. It's fun. It's easy. It's what you want to do. Literally thousands upon thousands of people host auctions every day at eBay. If they can do it, so can you.

You know what you want to sell; now you just need to know how to sell it. As you enter the land of auctioneering, you're going to find selling an item can be as easy or complex as you choose to make it. Much has changed at eBay for sellers since the early days; there are many more aids and tools available for sellers to use. But rather than risk overwhelming you with bells and whistles just yet, I'll first show you how to create a simple listing that gets your item up in front of those millions of bidders—and, boy, do they like to bid.

First Things First

Before you get to the point of listing your item, you should have done your research—both about the item and about similar auctions, too. If you haven't done your homework, go back—you'll only be cheating yourself if you don't (see, your teachers were right). If you know your item like the back of your hand, then onward you go.

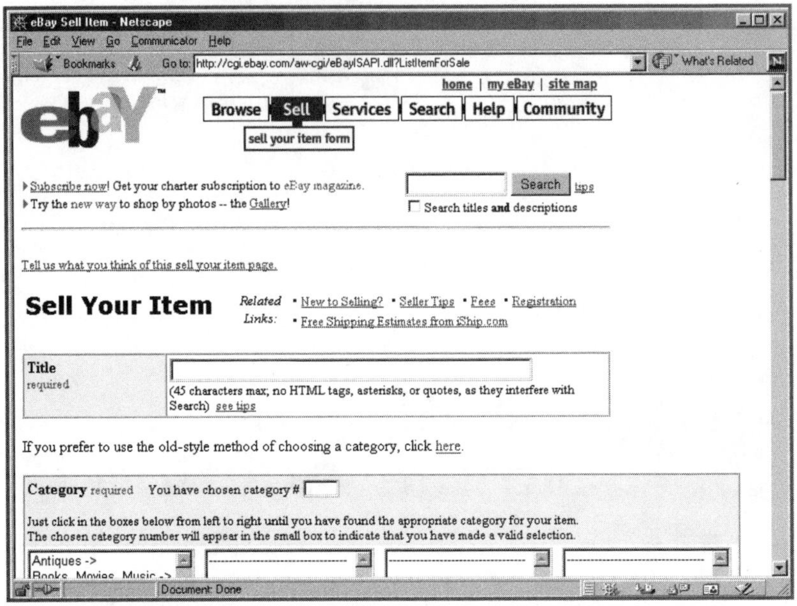

figure 16-1

The Sell Your Item page is where you begin your adventure as the auctioneer. Isn't it exciting?

To make this real, I'll go ahead and walk you through the steps to quickly and easily list the *It Conquered the World* lobby card. I know you want to bid on it yourself, but you're here to learn about selling, so pay attention.

To begin, from the eBay home page, click on the icon that reads *Sell your item* or the main navigation bar selection *Sell*. When you do, you'll jump to the aptly named Sell Your Item page (see Figure 16-1).

Setting Your Item's Title and Category

To begin, you'll need to give your item a title—and it has to be a good one if you want to catch the attention of the most bidders. Looking at Figure 16-2, you can see I've titled this item *IT CONQUERED THE WORLD – 1956 Lobby Card #2*.

You have a maximum of 45 characters to use in your item title, and you need to make the most of them. I chose to capitalize the title because it will have good visual impact in the auction listing screen and in listing searches. Don't worry; using capital letters like this on eBay isn't like you're shouting or anything. Next, I chose to enter the date of the item (1956) so bidders can quickly see that they are looking at an original item and not a recent reproduction. Then I am able to squeeze in that the item is a "Lobby Card"—to catch the attention of the lobby card collectors out there. Finally, I even have room to let the bidders know which lobby card—#2— they'll be bidding on. So, in the space of 43 characters, I've provided the name of the film, the year of the item, the type of item it is, and the specific number of the item. Not bad.

Tip I can't stress enough the importance of a good title for your auction item. You want to be able to catch the bidder's eye quickly while also providing as much information as possible so as to draw people in for a closer look. Most important, you need to put in the specific information that will appear in as many eBay searches as possible. Consider this listing here. This item will come up in searches for "It Conquered the World," "It Conquered," "Conquered," "It 1956," "lobby card," and "lobby." That might seem inconsequential, but bidders—especially those searching for something specific—are prone to enter various searches to quickly find an item. (Recall how I zeroed in on *Vampirella #1* in Chapter 8.) You want to be included in as many search results as possible.

If you had a model kit of the film's creature, you might list the title like this: "IT CONQUERED THE WORLD vinyl model kit." Using this description—especially the words *vinyl, model,* and *kit*—you'll find the bidders searching not only for the subject character, but also those just searching for vinyl models, models, or kits—three other common kinds of collections. There are only 45 characters available and you need to use them with overall readability in mind as well as maximizing search results.

OK. Now you have a great title. The next thing to specify about your item is the category. This is also a very important consideration when you list your item; you want to choose the best category possible so as to attract as many interested bidders as possible. Look back at Figure 16-2 and you'll see that I chose the category Memorabilia: Movie: Lobby Cards: General. How convenient—a category that fits this item perfectly. Actually, there are a whole bunch of categories to choose from, which you saw back when you were searching for items.

There are a couple of ways to choose an item category for your item. The way I did it in Figure 16-2 was by using eBay's progressive category selection tool. Starting from the left, you go from an aggregate category heading,

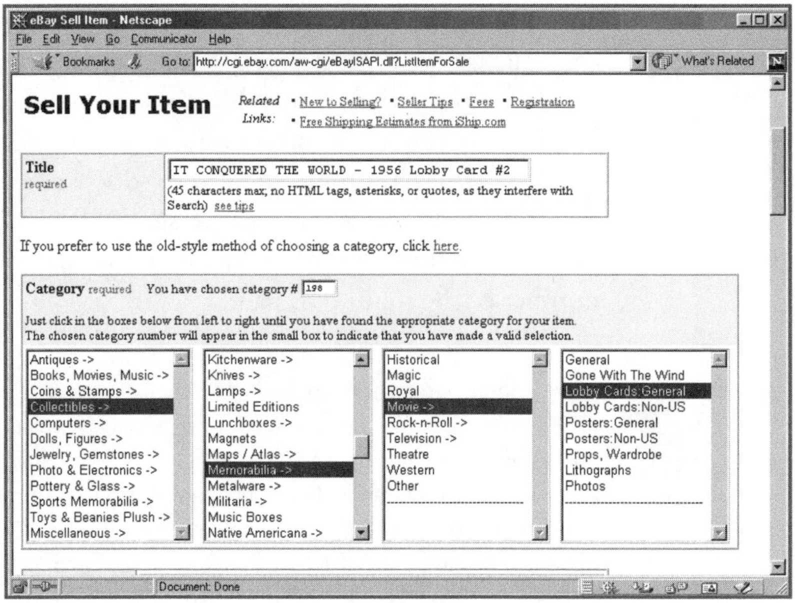

figure 16-2

Every successful auction starts with a great title and the perfect category selection.

drilling down to the most specific category bucket available. If you're not exactly sure how to navigate to the best category for your item, spend some time reviewing the eBay categories as I showed you in Chapter 7.

Before leaving the category selection discussion, notice the link in Figure 16-2: *If you prefer to use the old-style method of choosing a category, click here.* Click the link and you'll be able to use eBay's other category selection tool as shown in Figure 16-3.

Figure 16-3 shows the same major category headings as you saw in Figure 16-2. Just click on the major heading and scroll through a list of subcategories until you find the one you want.

Lastly, you could also select a category for your item while browsing for items. Take a look at Figure 16-4, and you'll see the heading from an eBay listings screen.

The link *Sell your item* lets you immediately go from browsing to listing, selecting the category you're browsing at the same time. The unique thing about selecting your item category in this way is that, while browsing (or

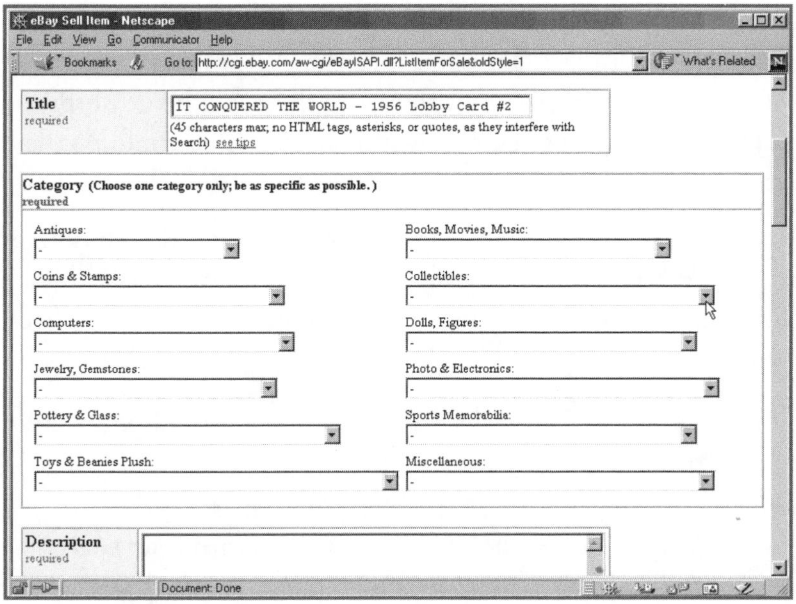

figure 16-3
Want an alternative method to choosing your item's category? Use the *old-style* method if you prefer.

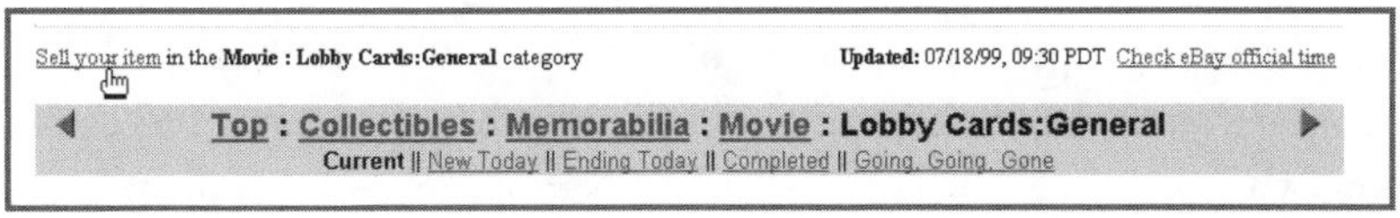

figure 16-4
Use the *Sell your item* link from any category listings page.

researching) other items up for bid, you can easily determine if now is the right time to list your item. Click the link and you'll enter the *Sell Your Item* screen with the category you selected already established.

Entering the Item Description

Once you've grabbed potential bidders' attention with your well-crafted item title, it's time to give them all the necessary details about the item so they're ready to bid. The item description is where you'll be able to provide the details based on your item knowledge (including research) to answer bidders' questions before they're asked. It's also where you'll practice a bit of salesmanship to get the bidders' attention in a way that makes them want to bid on your item.

You definitely don't want to bend the truth here. Provide the most accurate, detailed, and honest description you can, including all information about your item's condition and completeness to ensure there will be no surprises to the eventual buyer (except, perhaps, how much better the item looks than what was described).

In Figure 16-5 you can see the text box where the item description is entered. Don't be alarmed by its relatively small size; you can add as much text as you like, using scroll bars to move up or down and right or left in your description text.

So, pulling out my best verbal palette, here's how I'll paint a picture with words:

> From 1956, here's an original 11 x 14 lobby card from the drive-in classic of alien invasion, "It Conquered the World." This film starred Peter Graves (of Mission: Impossible fame), '50s scream queen Beverly Garland, and tough guy Lee Van Cleef. This is lobby card #2 of the original U.S. set of eight. It features a great color photo of Peter Graves confronting another actor in a street scene of panic and confusion. This card also features excellent border graphics of the alien invader and the film's original logo. The surrounding white border features the standard National Screen Service (NSS) proprietary information. It's printed on the standard heavy pulp paper as were all lobby cards at that time. This lobby card is in excellent condition. Although issued forty-four years ago for the film's original release, this lobby card has fared extremely well. All corners are slightly soft with one showing a tiny bit of paper loss. There is a barely-noticeable quarter inch tear in the left border, but no paper loss there. The white border shows very light handling soiling and is refreshingly free of any pinholes or tape residue. This card is a clean, vivid specimen that's striking to look at and will be a welcome addition to any vintage horror collection. High Bidder will please pre-pay, plus postage. Insurance will be additional upon request. If you have any questions, please feel free to contact me via e-mail. Check my eBay feedback and bid with confidence. Thanks for bidding.

Seem exhaustive? It is, and it's meant to be. Bidders will study this information intently, trying to picture for themselves what this item will look like. You don't want to leave much to the imagination since most bidders will imagine on the high side (picturing the item in the best possible way).

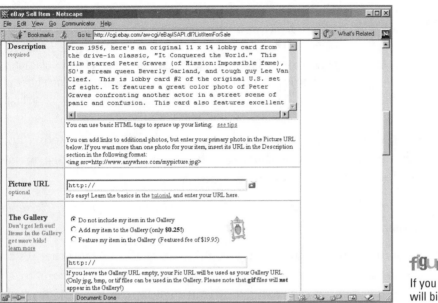

If you describe it (well), they will bid.

Your safest bet is to somewhat undergrade the item, pointing out any and all possible flaws.

Use terms like poor, fair, good, very good, excellent, and mint to give a rating to the item's condition. These are commonly used terms that most people understand. If you like numbers, use a scale of 1 to 10, with 1 being the low end (poor condition) and 10 being the high end (perfect or mint condition). Decide how you would rate the item, then describe it as about a half-grade lower. This helps to keep buyers pleasantly surprised when they actually receive the item.

The whole discussion of rating the condition of your item is a tough one. If you overgrade it, buyers will be disappointed when the actual item doesn't live up to its description. However, if you undergrade it, some bidders may pass on it thinking it's in worse condition than they want to deal with. It's a fine line to walk, and you might try to stress that you are purposefully being strict on your grading policy.

In addition, be aware that these grading policies are quite subjective. What I call "very good" might only be "good" in your book. Be prepared for that and, again, try to grade slightly on the downside and describe any visible faults the item may have.

NOTE In case you're wondering why I don't just get a picture of the item for this listing, it's because I want you to see that you can do quite well just using descriptive text. Not everyone will have a way to get a picture of an item into a listing. If that's going to be your situation, then the following discussion will be of particular interest; you'll see how well-chosen descriptive terms will fill the void when you don't have an image of the item to include. In Chapter 18 you'll see how to use pictures in your listing.

Now read the item description again and watch for the key terms and phrases that honestly describe this item *and* present it in a way that makes it appear as attractive and desirable as possible.

From 1956, here's an original 11 x 14 lobby card from the drive-in classic of alien invasion, "It Conquered the World."

First, you immediately learn the item is old—from 1956—and that it's an original item and not a reproduction of any sort. That's important to all your potential bidders, and it will tell them if they should continue reading.

This film starred Peter Graves (of Mission: Impossible fame), '50's scream queen Beverly Garland, and tough guy Lee Van Cleef.

Next, some quick information about the film, specifically, who appeared in it. This could be important to some bidders who might particularly admire the work of a certain actor or actress.

This is lobby card #2 of the original U.S. set of eight. It features a great color photo of Peter Graves confronting another actor in a street scene of panic and confusion. This card also features excellent border graphics of the alien invader and the film's original logo.

More information about the source of the item—it's lobby card #2 of an original U.S. set of eight (country of origin is really important). Then we get a description of what can be seen on the card—the actual image. This might conjure up memories in a bidder: *"Oh yeah. I remember that part. It really scared me when I was a kid."* This might make the item have a more personal draw to somebody. In addition, it's important to note that there is some great artwork that surrounds the image. That's a real bonus to many collectors.

The surrounding white border features the standard National Screen Service (NSS) proprietary information. It's printed on the standard heavy pulp paper as were all lobby cards at that time.

The next two sentences further authenticate the item by stating it was official property of National Screen Service and it was printed on pulp stock.

This lobby card is in excellent condition. Although issued forty-four years ago for the film's original release, this lobby card has fared extremely well.

Now you'll start to learn of the condition of the item. Using the term "excellent" is pretty promising, but it's applicable in this case; this card is in terrific shape, although I still avoid promising it is in any sort of mint condition. Immediately thereafter is a good nostalgia tug: this item is forty-four years old, having been issued at the time of the film's original release. Wow! That's like film history from the golden era of the '50s. Notice how I also dropped the notion of "drive-in classic" in the first sentence of the description. The bidder might now feel a personal sense of nostalgia for the item.

All corners are slightly soft with one showing a tiny bit of paper loss. There is a barely-noticeable quarter inch tear in the left border, but no paper loss there. The white border shows very light handling soiling and is refreshingly free of any pinholes or tape residue.

Getting to the details, you start to learn about some of the imperfections of the item. Don't omit any facts that might leave the eventual buyer feeling disappointed when the item arrives. Notice the wording that provides reassurance of the item's overall nice-looking appearance ("slightly soft," "barely-noticeable," "refreshingly free"). When you're listing faults of an item, you have to balance that by letting the bidder know you figuratively have the item under the microscope.

This card is a clean, vivid specimen that's striking to look at and will be a welcome addition to any vintage horror collection.

To wrap up the discussion of condition, let the bidders know you took a harsh approach to describing the faults but that the item is still nice to look at. Go on a bit more to assure them that it would be a great piece for a collector to have.

High Bidder will please pre-pay, plus postage. Insurance will be additional upon request.

Now, what are the payment and postage requirements for this auction? Also, if insurance is additional, let the bidders know up front.

Postage and insurance are those evil little twins that tend to tack on a few dollars to an otherwise reasonably priced item. Insurance isn't always necessary; most packages arrive safely without it provided they're packed well. By stating insurance is additional upon request, you let the buyer decide whether to pay for it. Someone who chooses not to pay for insurance is assuming all responsibility for loss or damage while the item is in transit. This is *very* important and should not be overlooked when listing your items. You'll learn all the details of shipping, insurance, and more in Part 5.

If you have any questions, please feel free to contact me via e-mail. Check my eBay feedback and bid with confidence. Thanks for bidding.

Before you close up the description, throw in a glimpse of the good customer satisfaction measures the bidders might expect. Encourage additional questions; you have nothing to hide. Encourage bidders to review your feedback rating (provided it's good); again, nothing to hide. Then, thank them for bidding—maybe they haven't yet, but you're clear that you're glad they dropped by to read your listing. It makes your auction more friendly, inviting, and sincere.

For the sake of this simple listing demonstration, I'll be skipping past the *Picture URL* and *Gallery* portions of the listing form you see in Figure 16-5.

Setting Your Listing Options, Location, and Payment Terms

Once that tantalizing description's in the bag, scroll down to get into the next area of listing details (shown in Figure 16-6).

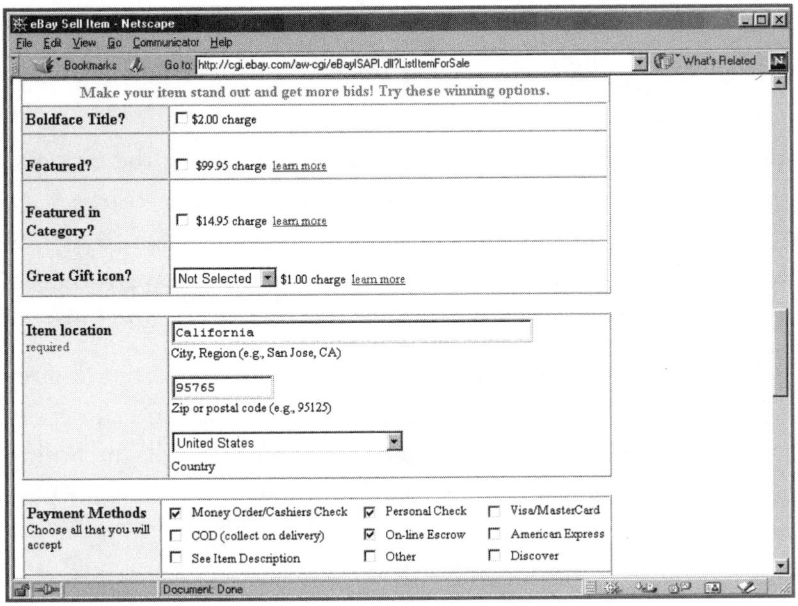

figure 16-6

Scroll down the item listing form to get to the other details of your listing.

First, you can select some special options for your item's appearance in the listing pages:

- **Boldface title**. This is pretty easy to figure out; if you want your item's title to be shown in a bold font, click on this check box. The idea is that a bold title might draw more attention among the tons of other items listed. It costs an extra $2 to get the boldface. It's really up to you. I've never needed this option myself.

- **Featured Auction**. You learned about these in Chapter 7. It costs $99.95 to have your item appear in the site's *Featured Items* category.

- **Featured in Category**. This is something you also learned about in Chapter 7. The cost is significantly less than the site featured option; only $14.95 to get your item featured in a specific category.

- **Great Gift icon**. This is a cute little way to put an extra attention-getting icon next to your item's description. It only costs $1. Maybe Mother's Day is approaching, and you have some combat boots to sell; sounds like an endearing gift item to me.

Next comes the location of your item. Simply specify a city or region, a valid Zip or postal code and a country. No real magic here.

Then comes the terms of payment you wish to accept from your bidders—well, from the eventual high bidder. Here, you will be setting the expectations of all bidders regarding how you want the lucky winner to pay. It's a great way to provide all the nitty-gritty information up front before anyone decides to place a bid. This way, a bidder who doesn't wish to pay in any certain method you've specified can quickly move on out of your auction.

Look at Figure 16-6; there you'll see that I've chosen to accept money orders, cashier's checks, personal checks, and online escrows. You can easily see the other payment terms that are available for you to check, including an option to select See Description if you need to further describe your payment expectations.

Setting Your Shipping Terms

Next on the list is to choose your shipping terms. This isn't where you commit to a specific carrier, but instead you are letting all bidders know if you have any restrictions on where you're willing to ship the item and who is responsible for paying shipping charges. You can see my selections for this item in Figure 16-7.

Besides welcoming international shipments, I've also chosen to tell the bidders actual shipping costs are to be added to the winning bid. You can select from any of the options you see on the screen as you like.

 Tip As a rule, you can expect that the buyer will pay the shipping charges in addition to the high bid amount. It's pretty standard to work it this way in the spirit of that well-known mail order mantra, *"plus shipping and handling."* Here also is where you'll let all bidders know if you intend to ship internationally; I usually do. International money, once converted, is just as good as greenback dollars (or vice versa if you live outside of the United States). However, there's a bit more work involved in international payment and shipping. You'll learn all the details of shipping—domestic and international—in Part 5.

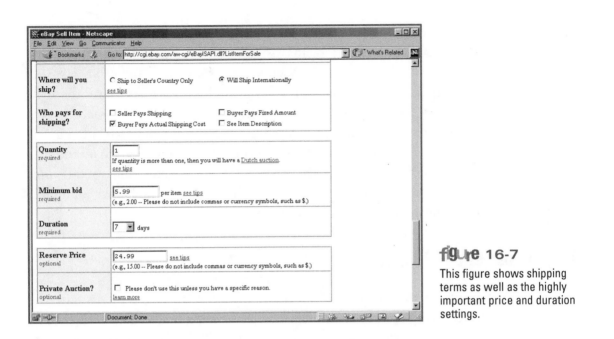

figure 16-7

This figure shows shipping terms as well as the highly important price and duration settings.

Establishing the Minimum (Starting) Bid

Quickly complete the *Quantity* field—it's required and I only have one item—and move along to the *Minimum Bid* field (referring to the middle of Figure 16-6). This is a key field and it makes sense to do some deep thinking here.

This is where you'll be telling the soon-to-be bidders how much is required, minimally, to get your auction rolling. Your minimum bid can be any value you choose, but choose it wisely. The bidders may come or the bidders may go based on what you decide the minimum will be.

Of course, very low minimum bids—like $1—are always a good draw to bidders. People like to think they can grab a good deal and dropping a buck is easier than picking lint out of your pocket. "*Aw, what's a buck. I'll bid on that.*" The bidding might go higher than a dollar (hopefully), but the whole idea is that when it only takes $1 to join in an auction, bidders tend to get involved pretty quickly.

When the minimum starting bid is low, then the subsequent bid increments are low, too. The bid increments, as you now know, are based on the current high bid value of an item. Auctions that start with a bid of $1 will only require an additional 25 cents for following bid increments until the high bid reaches $5. You can bid a lot of quarters before the $5 mark is ever reached. An item with a higher minimum bid value requires larger bid increments from the get-go. That's why sometimes you might need to up the ante by a lot more than a quarter. Bidders often pay attention to this and, depending on the item, might not be willing to pay the higher minimum bid increment and therefore not bid on your item.

Using Reserve Prices

Staying on the discussion of price, suppose you don't want to take the chance that your great item will only get a single bidder who ends up getting your treasure for a single greasy dollar bill. You'd feel like a real dope. Still, you want to grab the attention of those dollar-days shoppers. Is there any way to protect yourself? Of course. Let me introduce you to the reserve price option.

You learned what a reserve price is and how it works on eBay back in Chapter 12. Now, as the seller, you need to know when you should use the reserve price and when you shouldn't. Obviously, the first and best reason to use a reserve price would be to protect the value of your item or the amount of money you have invested in it. If there's a minimum value you could accept for the thing, put a reserve price on it to make sure you don't end up taking it in the shorts. It's your rightful prerogative to list your item using a reserve price and people do it all the time. If you want a reserve price on your item, just enter that price in the field labeled Reserve price. In Figure 16-7, you can see that I've chosen a reserve price of $24.99.

 NOTE eBay's considering levying a small fee for using the Reserve Price option. Notice the link, *see tips*, next to the Reserve Price field; clicking on it will take you to a page at eBay where you can read more about the rules and restrictions of Reserve Price auctions.

SOAPBOX There's a bit of conflict among eBaysians when discussing the use of reserve prices. Some bidders say they don't like reserve prices; to them, they may just as well buy the thing outright. Some bidders dislike reserve prices so much that they won't even bother to bid on an item that has a reserve price, even when it's something they might want. But I take a contrasting stand here (as do many others); the reserve price is a form of protection just in case the item I'm selling doesn't find its *audience*. Maybe I have a lot invested in an item; maybe I paid too much for it. Regardless, that doesn't mean I have to chance practically giving the thing away. Yes, the reserve price can be abused—set a *really high* reserve and it will never be met during the course of the auction. But that just leaves the seller without an official buyer. However, most Reserve Price auctions do just fine.

TIP Some sellers, knowing the potential adverse reaction to auctions with reserve prices, will actually make a point to advertise that their item uses no reserve. You'll often find sellers advertising "no reserve" in their item description. I could use an item description like this:

"IT CONQUERED THE WORLD—lobby card NO RESERVE"

The "NO RESERVE" notation sometimes pulls in bidders from the listing pages or search results. Using this tactic is sometimes good to let bidders know your item is up for grabs on the open market and its price can be as low or as high as the bids take it. Of course, be sure your minimum bid isn't an ambush waiting for the bidders; keep it within a reasonable range to not shoo away the bidders who dropped by to take a look.

If you decide to use a reserve price, set it with care and reasonable expectations. Just because you're thinking, "Man, I'll bet I can get a hundred bucks, easy, for this," doesn't mean you will. Don't let greed get the better of you. If your reserve is too high, it will annoy and alienate serious bidders. Many bidders have a good understanding of what an item should sell for. If they're bidding maximum amounts that should justifiably get them high bidder status, they'll be a bit perturbed when they see the reserve price hasn't yet been met. The really serious bidder might go so far as to bid yet higher. If that still doesn't reach your reserve price, the bidder will get turned off and decide you want too much for your item. As a seller, if you list too many high reserve auctions, you'll develop a reputation for generally wanting more than your items are worth. Potential repeat customers will stop dropping by your auctions.

But assume you're reasonable in what you want in terms of a selling price for your item. You might consider just skipping the whole reserve price thing and setting your starting bid at the minimum that you want for the item. If reserve prices tend to bother some bidders, then why use them?

If setting a reserve price—say for $25—protects the value of your item, you could just skip the whole reserve thing and make the minimum bid $25, right? Sure, but don't forget Dollar Days, my friend; that low starting bid of $1 has a way of psychologically grabbing a bidder even though there may be a reserve price attached.

Psychology? Yes. This is where you learn to become a salesperson and marketing master. Just as you carefully crafted your item description, you'll need to be just as skilled when you put together your item's sales strategy. I know this sounds a bit corporate, and I promise not to subject you to any charts or graphs. However, this market analysis stuff is for real, even in the world of online auctions.

The title of your item was crucial in drawing attention to your auction and the description used terms that would keep potential bidders' attention and further spark their interest, but the pricing strategy is what will make or break your chances of getting bidders to bid.

It works like this: if you think your item, say a book, is worth $25, you could be right. But, psychologically, some people just couldn't think of bidding $25 to get a book auction rolling. It's kind of like why you might balk at paying $20 for something, but when you see a price of $19.99 you think, "OK. That seems reasonable." A price of $20 just doesn't seem right. So, in your auction, set the starting bid at $1 and set a reserve of $25. For some reason, people will bid on your item, and they might even be willing to pay $25, maybe more, but at least your opening bid didn't force them to commit to paying that price from the start. See how it works?

Now assume you need to set a reserve price of $100. If you set a minimum starting bid of $1, is it possible that those dollar-droppers are really going to bid up to your reserve price? Maybe, but maybe not. Somehow, you need to weed out the bargain shoppers, attract the more informed or more serious bidders, but still present a price that is psychologically pleasing. How? Easy.

In your $100 reserve price auction, set the minimum starting bid at $9.99. The $10 price point is very reasonable, it will attract more bidders, but it will also give them the feeling that the reserve price you have set is probably a bit higher than in a $1 auction. In a way, you're silently communicating a hint of what your reserve price might be.

TIP

In Reserve Price auctions, you can generally expect that a thoughtful seller will have a reserve price that equals 5 to 10 times the opening bid. This isn't a hard-and-fast rule by any means, but a seller skilled at telegraphing punches will be letting the savvy bidders know what to expect. Look out if you find a Reserve Price auction with an opening bid of $100!

SOAPBOX

Sometimes, you'll see an auction with a high opening bid *and* a Reserve Price auction indicator. When the opening minimum bid is placed, the reserve is met, too—the reserve price was the same as the opening bid. I know what you're thinking — *"Why would anyone do that?"* Why, indeed, but sometimes it happens. This is really an impractical way to use the Reserve Price auction. My advice: don't do it.

So when shouldn't you set a reserve price? When the value of the item is low enough and you can sell it at that price, don't bother with a reserve. Also, if the item is very popular and possibly scarce, don't set a reserve. In fact, in the case of such items, your setting of a reserve price may make you appear as wanting more than the item easily commands. Just let the bidders do their work; you'll probably get the price you're looking for. And especially when you're looking to rid yourself of clutter, don't set reserve prices. If your reserves aren't met, you'll still have to keep the darned things or trash them for no return at all.

Setting the Duration of Your Auction

The next important decision is how long your item will be up for auction. At eBay, you can choose to have your auction run for 3, 5, 7, or 10 days. Timing of your auction is a topic all its own that goes beyond the discussion of just the duration. You'll learn all about proper timing methods in Chapter 17. For the purposes of getting the item listed, I'll just choose the 7-day option. You can choose the duration by clicking on the little down-arrow next to the *Duration* field and selecting 7 (3, 5, and 10 are the other choices available).

Finishing Up

Just a few more things and you'll be ready to roll. Now look at Figure 16-8 where you'll see the final details you need to address:

- **Private auction**. Just what *are* you selling, anyway? eBay lets you know that you should only use this option if you really have a specific need. Otherwise, don't use it. It tends to tuck your item away in the dark recesses of the listings.

- **UserID/Password**. By this point you're pretty familiar with your eBay identity. Entry of this information on this screen ensures you're a registered user in good standing.

That's it. You've entered the information to list your item. That wasn't so hard, was it? After a few times, you'll be surprised at how fast you can list

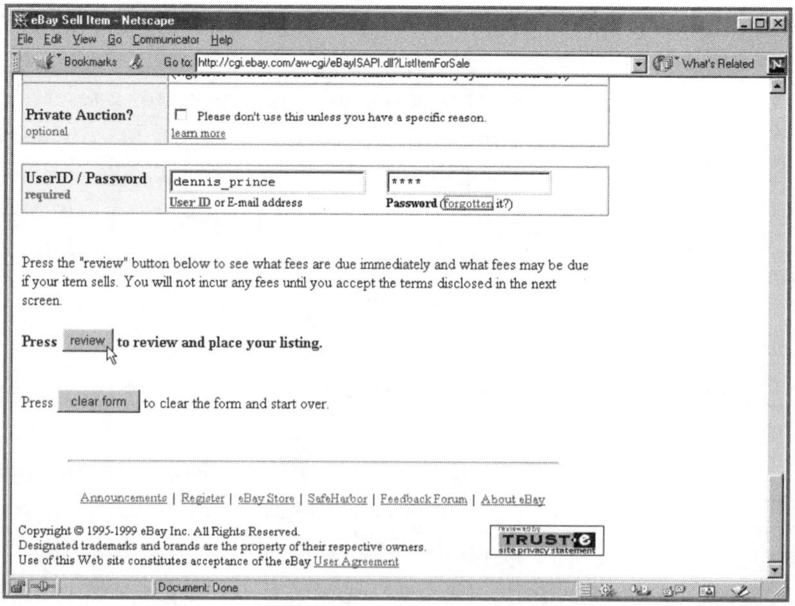

figure 16-8

The final entries and then it's off to review your wonderful listing.

items. Still, before you finish, there are just a few more things for you to consider. . . .

How Much Does It Cost to List an Item?

Ah, the pivotal question. In Figure 16-8, just below the user ID and Password fields, you see some text that hints of listing fees. What are the fees? How much are they? Do they hurt?

You first read about listing fees in Chapter 3, where you learned how eBay turns a profit to maintain and improve the site. The listing fee is the price the seller pays to get an auction started. Don't get bent out of shape; the listing fee is really very small. Besides, where else can you list your item in front of almost six million potential bidders, worldwide? I thought you'd see it my way.

So how much does it cost? Not much. The listing fee is based on the minimum opening bid or the reserve price you set for your item. eBay works on a graduated scale based on the seller's anticipation of the item's final high bid price. Table 16-1 shows you the breakdown of minimum bid and reserve price and the listing fee you'll pay to get your auction started.

Table 16-1 Item Listing Fees

Minimum Starting Bid or Reserve Price	Listing Fee
$1 – $9.99	$0.25
$10 – $24.99	$0.50
$25 – $49.99	$1
$50 and up	$2

•Be sure to check eBay's Reserve Price rules in case usage fees are implemented.

Now, tell me you've been abused when asked to pay $2 to sell an item for $50 or more. I'd do it in a heartbeat just to have the opportunity to make that much on an auction.

 NOTE There will also be a sales commission to pay on your auction based on the final high bid. Again, it's practically tiny compared to how much you might receive from a high bidder. Since commissions aren't applied at the time you list your item, I won't go into those now. You'll learn about commission fees and managing your eBay Seller's Account in Chapter 20.

Any Other Terms or Conditions You Want to Specify?

Is there anything else you want to let your bidders know about the auction conditions? You aren't necessarily confined to the fields you see on the listing form, you know. Consider the following options that you can mention back in your item's description:

- **Prepayment and postage**. If there are any other conditions you want to mention (packaging charges, shipping turnaround times, and so on), you could choose to list those in your item's description.

- **Payment types accepted**. eBay provides check boxes for your accepted payment types (I chose money orders, cashier's checks, or personal checks for this item). If you have further comments about payment types, feel free to add a sentence or two in your description.

- **Response time and payment receipt**. You could choose to add some text like this: *High bidder will be notified within 24 hours after auction has ended. High bidder will need to respond within two days to retain high bid status. Payment must be received within 10 days of auction close.* This sort of text lets bidders know you wish to complete the transaction quickly and efficiently. That's usually OK with bidders because they're apt to be eager to receive the item they've won.

- **Trades welcome**. Many sellers are looking for certain items for their own collections. You might read an item description that offers to trade the auctioned item for something the seller is looking for. Sometimes, sellers will offer to close the auction early if a bidder has the item the seller wants and is agreeable to a trade. If it works for you, why not?

Verifying Your Item Listing

Will this listing process never end? Yes, it will. You're just about there. As you can see, though, there's a lot to consider when you sell an item. The more time you spend thoughtfully preparing your listing, the better chance you have of selling your item—maybe for the big bucks! So if you're satisfied with everything you've had to say about your item, then it's on to verify your good work.

Look back at Figure 16-8, and you'll see the button labeled *review*—it's in the sentence "Press review to review and place your listing." The verification step is where you'll get one more look at your item title, description, and conditions before you set it loose among those millions of eager bidders. They've been waiting to see your item and bid on it with every dollar they have! (OK, maybe a bit over the top, but I want you to be excited; it's fun seeing your items up for auction.) So click on *review*, and you'll see the verification screen as shown in Figure 16-9.

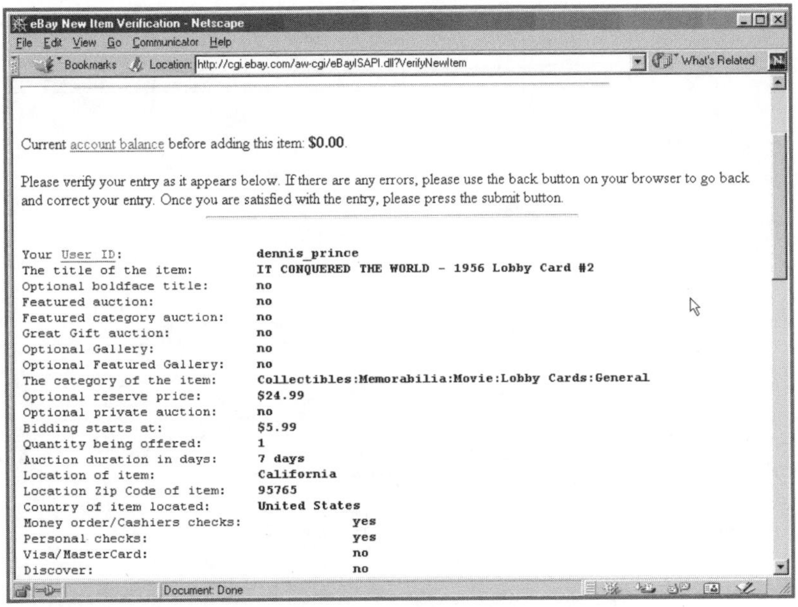

figure 16-9

This is the screen you use to verify the details of your item before you unleash it upon a waiting crowd of bidders.

First, notice the account balance statement appearing below the standard eBay header and navigation bar. You'll learn more about your Seller's Account in Chapter 20. Quickly, though, you can see that I have a balance of –0.00 that I owe to eBay—I'm paid up for any previous listing and final commission fees. When you verify a new auction listing, eBay lets you know what your account status is before you proceed.

Below the account balance statement, eBay will request that you verify the details of your listing before you officially submit it for auction. Verify the details here, then scroll down to continue reviewing additional listing information (see Figure 16-10).

Check more of the listing details after you've scrolled down. Do they look all right? Now, read and reread your item description. This is where you want to spend some time really verifying how you're presenting your item. Make sure you've used complete sentences and proper grammar, and presented an accurate and truthful description of your item; bidders will base their understanding and mental image of your item on this description.

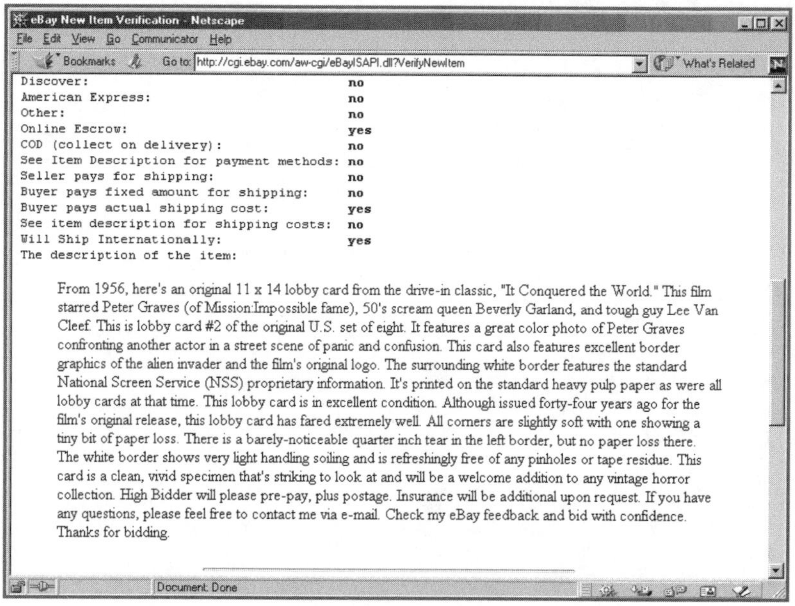

figure 16-10

Scroll down in the listing verification screen to review more item details including the item description.

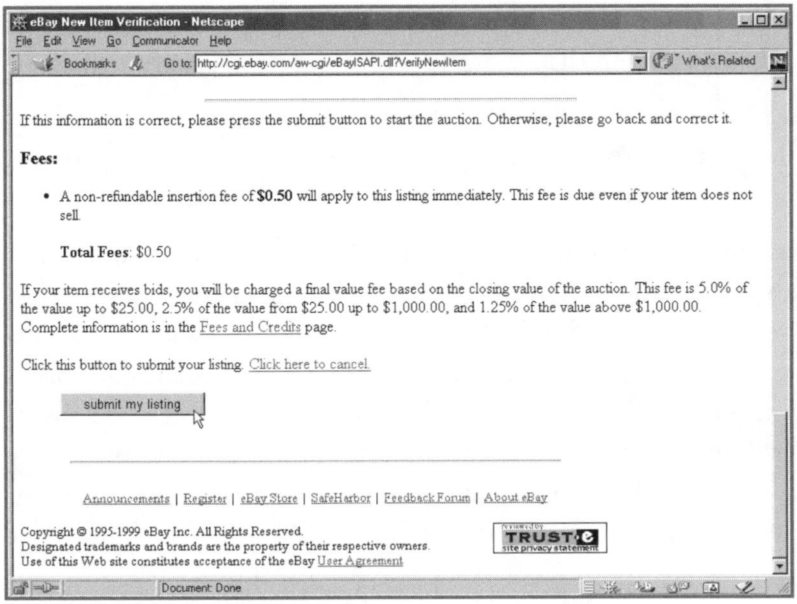

eBay New Item Verification - Netscape

File Edit View Go Communicator Help

Bookmarks Go to: http://cgi.ebay.com/aw-cgi/eBayISAPI.dll?VerifyNewItem What's Related

If this information is correct, please press the submit button to start the auction. Otherwise, please go back and correct it.

Fees:

- A non-refundable insertion fee of **$0.50** will apply to this listing immediately. This fee is due even if your item does not sell.

  Total Fees: $0.50

If your item receives bids, you will be charged a final value fee based on the closing value of the auction. This fee is 5.0% of the value up to $25.00, 2.5% of the value from $25.00 up to $1,000.00, and 1.25% of the value above $1,000.00. Complete information is in the Fees and Credits page.

Click this button to submit your listing. Click here to cancel.

submit my listing

Announcements | Register | eBay Store | SafeHarbor | Feedback Forum | About eBay

Copyright © 1995-1999 eBay Inc. All Rights Reserved.
Designated trademarks and brands are the property of their respective owners.
Use of this Web site constitutes acceptance of the eBay User Agreement

TRUST**e**
site privacy statement

Document: Done

figure 16-11

Before you submit your item for auction, you'll see the listing fee that will be charged to your Seller's Account.

Finally, scroll down one more time to see the fees you'll be charged for listing your item (based on your minimum starting bid or reserve price). Figure 16-11 shows you this final area of the listing form.

 SOAPBOX This is kind of a tip, but I feel so strongly about it that I'll mount the soapbox to deliver it: Spelling counts! Make sure you've done your very best to ensure your spelling is correct. This is your one shot to impress those potential bidders. You've done a great job titling your auction, describing the item, and pricing it to get the most bids. For Heaven's sake, don't blow it with bad spelling. Most bidders forgive some typos but you should really try to do your best here.

And, lest I forget, be sure the spelling in your item title is accurate, too. A misspelled word could mean your item doesn't show up in a search result. Take your time and read it again.

In this example, I'll be charged $0.50 to list this item since I chose a reserve price of $24.99 (remember the reserve price value takes precedence over a lower minimum bid). Since I didn't choose any special fonts, icons, or featured listings, the only fee assessed is the listing fee based on the minimum bid or reserve price. I can live with that.

You'll also see some text that describes the way commissions are assessed at the end of the auction. You can read those as they appear in Figure 16-11, but remember that I'll be going over that in detail in Chapter 20.

If for any reason you feel you want or need to change anything about the listing, now is the time to do it. You can press your browser's Back button to go back one screen to the item listing form. There, you can make any adjustments that you like and proceed to the verification screen again. Do this as many times as you need to until you're satisfied with the listing details. If you've changed your mind entirely and want to completely bail out of the item listing process, click on the *Click here to cancel* link that you see in Figure 16-11. When you do that, you'll jump back to the eBay home page.

But assuming you're ready to start your auction, at the bottom of the listing verification screen, click on the *Submit my listing* button as shown in Figure 16-11. That's it! Your auction has started! Figure 16-12 shows you the auction confirmation screen for your item.

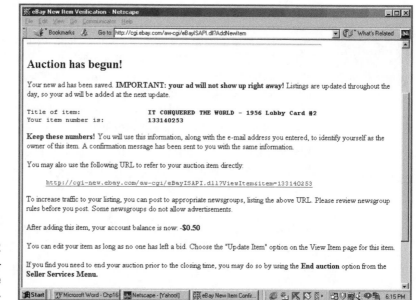

figure 16-12

And there you have it. Your auction has begun, and you're hosting your first sale on eBay.

The auction confirmation screen shows you the title of your item and the all-important item number. The item number is automatically assigned by eBay and will be used to track your auction throughout its duration and beyond.

A few things to note in the confirmation screen: you're immediately informed that your auction ad will not show up right away in the listing pages or in item searches (unless someone searches for auctions by your seller ID). It takes an hour or more before eBay's auction listing update cycle will pick up your new item and include it in the updated auction listings.

Then, notice the URL link in the middle of the page; that's the actual URL of your auction's item details page. Click on the URL right now, and you'll be able to see the finished result of your listing work (see Figures 16-13 and 16-14).

Finally, notice the listing of your account balance. The listing fee has been added to your account balance, and your are given an updated value of what your balance is (in my case, the 50-cent listing fee raised my balance to a whopping –$0.50).

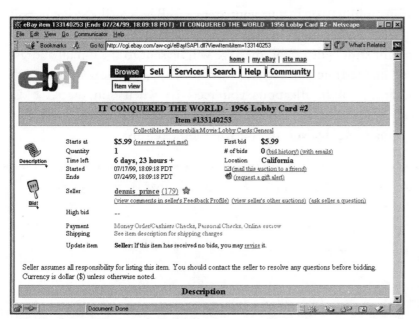

figure 16-13

Here it is; the item details page for your new auction. Looks great!

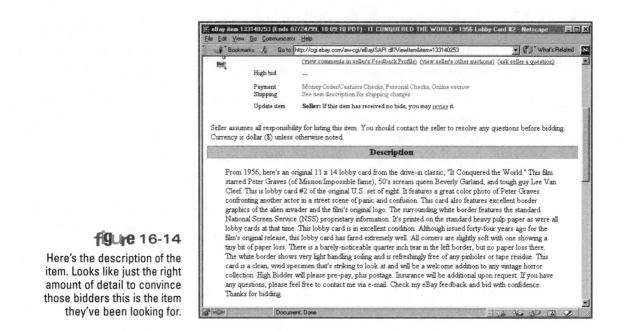

figure 16-14

Here's the description of the item. Looks like just the right amount of detail to convince those bidders this is the item they've been looking for.

E-mail Notification of Your New Listing

Usually within minutes of listing your item at eBay, you'll receive e-mail notification that further confirms the success of your new listing as well as other important stuff. The e-mail message will be sent to the e-mail address you specified at the time you registered with eBay. This works very much like the other e-mail notifications you received when you placed bids, received daily status, outbid notices, or end of auction notices. For a new listing, the e-mail message you receive will look like this:

• •

```
Subject: eBay Listing confirmation—Item 133140253: IT CONQUERED THE
WORLD—1956 LobbyCard #2

From: aw-confirm@ebay.com

To: dlprince@bigfoot.com
```

```
Dear dennis_prince,

Let the trading begin—your item is listed!

http://cgi-new.ebay.com/aw-cgi/eBayISAPI.dll?ViewItem&item=133140253

Title of item: IT CONQUERED THE WORLD—1956 Lobby Card #2

Minimum bid: $5.99

Reserve price (if any): $24.99

Quantity: 1

Auction Ends on: 07/24/99 at 18:09:18 PDT

Your item number is: 133140253

Fees:

Insertion Fee:0.50

*It's important that you make a note of these details, especially
the item number; you will need it in any correspondence with us
about your listing, and in order to make any changes to your
listing.

*You can change your item listing as long as no one has bid on it
yet. Just go to eBay.com, click on your listing, and choose Update
Item. If you can't find your listing, enter its title in the search
window.

*For more tools to help you manage your listing, including adding
information or ending the auction early, check out the services
available in eBay's Buying and Selling Tools section, at
http://pages-new.ebay.com/services/buyandsell/index.html

Best of luck!
```

• •

Near the beginning of the message, you'll see the URL that will take you directly to the item details for your auction. Then you see some details about your auction; they should match what you verified before you submitted the listing. Finally, you'll see a note about how to make modifications to your listing even after the auction has started. Item management is a whole nother topic that you'll learn more about in Chapter 20.

Final Thoughts

To wrap this up, this chapter was titled "Creating a Simple Auction Listing." At this point you may not agree that it looks very simple. Yes, there is a lot of information to enter and even more to consider in terms of your auction tactics and approach. But, rest assured, after you've listed a few items, you'll feel pretty comfortable with it and future listings will only get easier and easier.

In the meantime, start thinking about what you'll list for auction and what approach you want to take to have the most successful auction possible.

chapter 17

Timing Is Everything

It's probably one of the universal truths: timing is everything. You don't want to be too late, too soon, too long, too short, too quick, too slow—you want to be *just right*.

OK, maybe the title of this chapter is a bit exaggerated; timing isn't really *everything*. In the last chapter you found out that there's a lot of consideration to what goes into your auction listings and how you can list your items for best results.

But it is true that your auctions will also do better if you consider the timing involved than if you don't. It follows from the research you've done about the items you'll be listing; you want your item to appear at the best possible time and in the best possible slot to make it (and you) as successful as possible.

Timing Your Auction

So consider the most obvious: is there a best time for your auction? Sure there is. Of course, you'll need to consider the many factors of timing your auction, including the time of day you list your item, the day of the week you list your item, the time of the year you list your item, and how long you let your auction run. Now I'm not off on some tangent here, making a

mountain out of a molehill. These different aspects of how you time your auction will really make a difference. You be the judge.

Time of Day

Is there a best time of day to run your auction? Yes, and here's why. When you list your item for auction, the auction clock starts ticking the moment your auction is confirmed. That means that your auction will end at the precise moment 3, 5, 7, or 10 days from when your auction starts.

In Chapter 16, I chose to run the *It Conquered the World* lobby card auction for seven days. The auction started at precisely 18:09:18 PST on July 17, 1999. So, that means it will end at precisely 18:09:18 PST on July 24, 1999—*exactly* seven days later, to the second. Yeah? So big deal; where's the great mystery in that? It's here: when I listed that auction—and just as you'll list your auctions later—I had to ask myself, *"I wonder how many people will be able to participate in the final minutes of the bidding?"*

Remember that many bidders like to wait until the final minutes of an auction to bid, rebid, or snipe. Your goal as a seller is to time-position your auction so the most people possible can take advantage of last-moment bids. Consider the sort of schedules most people keep—almost everybody works during the regular daytime hours and knocks off in the evening. Therefore, when I sell, I want to take that into consideration when I list my items.

Look at the ending time again: 18:09:18. With the average day's work wrapping up at 5 P.M., I'm allowing 69 minutes for people on the West Coast to leave work, commute to home or wherever, log on to the Net, and bid on my auction. It's not always reasonable for people to bid in auctions during normal work hours; in some workplaces it would probably be frowned upon.

"Johnson? How's that report coming?"

"Hmmm . . . ?" (Auction has 34 seconds to go.)

"Johnson? I asked about that report. How's it coming? You do know I need it before the two o'clock meeting?"

"Hmmmm . . . " (Auction has 28 seconds to go.)

"Johnson? Johnson!"

"Wha . . . ? Ah! Sir. (quickly, switch screen to report) *Yes . . . the report. Uh . . . fine Sir, it's fine. You'll have it in time for your meeting."* (Auction time to go . . . ??)

"You're sure you're focused on it, Johnson? This client is important, and I don't want this botched up."

"No, Sir. You'll have it. I promise." (Auction clock is ticking.)

"Johnson . . . ? You weren't just . . . surfing . . . were you?"

"Oh, um . . . Cowabunga, Sir, no." (Tick-tock, tick-tock.)

"You know that personal use of company equipment is strictly prohibited, don't you, Johnson?"

"Oh, yes Sir. No, not me. Just your report, Sir. I'd better finish." (TICK-TOCK, TICK-TOCK.)

"Very well, then. Carry on, and bring the report to me the moment it's complete."

"Yes, Sir!" (He's leaving. You quickly switch back to auction.)

Auction has ended.

"Damn!!"

(From a distance—) *"Johnson??"*

"No . . . nothing, Sir . . . racken fracken . . . "

The point here is you want to try to take account of the normal work schedule and work around it as best you can. So, six o'clock in the evening should be reasonable for the majority of people who might want to bid.

But, if six o'clock is good, wouldn't eight o'clock or nine o'clock be better? That way everyone would have time to get through the traffic snarls, eat dinner, and *then* log on to bid. That sounds good, but there's a catch: the auction ending times at eBay are Pacific Time (West Coast). What about our friends on the East Coast? For them, add three hours to the clock on the wall. They'd be bidding at 9:09 P.M. where they live to get into the 6:09 P.M. auction. If you decide to end your auction at 9 P.M. by eBay's clock, the folks on the East Coast are staying up until midnight to make a final bid. They might decide their sleep is more important than your auction. The folks in the Central states don't have to wait quite so late, but don't forget them all the same.

 SOAPBOX But what about the international bidders? What time is it where they live? Well, I have to confess that I don't have that cliché row of clocks on my wall telling me what time it is all over the world. Therefore, unfortunately, I'm not able to take world time into consideration when I list my auctions. It's too bad, really, because I've dealt with some great international buyers and sellers. Somehow, it seems to work out for the most part. To them, although I can't always take their time difference into full consideration, I say, *"Great job. Thanks for being involved anyway."*

 TIP Here's something that might increase your international sales: Greenwich Mean Time is equal to Pacific Standard Time plus eight hours. If you want to get serious about reaching bidders on the opposite side of the world (maybe you have something that is all the rage in England), then knowing the time there will help you schedule auctions that will cater to your friends across the globe.

If you're a night owl and you think you'll list your items all night long, that's fine. However, expect that you'll miss a lot of bidders when you do that. I see many auctions that end in the wee hours of the morning. If it's something I might want to snipe, I have to make a decision: bid earlier and hope I'm not outbid, set my alarm so I can get up and bid (a clear sign of auction addiction), or let the thing go and hope I'll find another later. A wee-hours auction isn't destined to fail, but it might miss some bidders who'd rather be dreaming than bidding.

 NOTE Some individuals have been developing special software designed to bid in auctions—snipe, actually—for you while you're away from your PC. I can't personally vouch for any of these programs because I haven't had the opportunity to use them. These aren't commercial products, per se. Rather, these are products that very industrious eBay community members have developed. If you think you'd want to try one, just look for them up for auction. Hint: try looking in the *Computers:Software:General* category.

So you see the impact the time of day can have on your auction's success. Consider this wisely and, if nothing else, ask yourself when the most convenient time would be for you to bid. There are no hard-and-fast rules. Just use your noggin the best you can.

Time of Week

Besides clock time, how about the day of the week? Are some days of the week better than others to start and stop your auctions? Yup. You probably already figured that weekends are pretty good choices for having your auctions end. For the most obvious reason, weekends are a good bet for ending auctions because that's when many people aren't working. They'll probably have more free time to watch for the close of an auction, getting in those last bids. Of course, many people *are* working on the weekend, so don't forget the matter of clock time when ending your auctions, even if they do close on the weekend.

Weekends are also good for starting auctions because you might have a better opportunity to have your auction seen by more people. Since it's not always necessary—sometimes not even wise—to wait until the last minute to browse and bid, many bidders will take the weekend to do very intense searching of the auction listings. With plenty of time on their hands, those browsing bidders might just happen to come across your auction. They'll make a note of the auction, when it's due to end, and how they'll plan their bidding. For you, that's good.

Time of Year

Is there a best time of the year to stage your auctions? Yes, there is. Believe it or not, there are certain months when auctions are more successful than they might otherwise be. It's true, based on what I've seen over the past several years.

I'll start with the beginning of a new year. In January, you can usually expect to see some pretty active bidding, even though Christmas has just passed. Although the rush might not make sense at first glance, January is when many people are shopping because they didn't get what they really wanted for Christmas. I know that sounds kind of spoiled, but it's what I've seen happen and was even what some buyers told me after they won my January auctions. I've even done some active bidding myself right after Christmas; no one close to me seems to be able to find those goofy lobby cards I like so much.

As February and March roll around, auctions are still doing quite well— those are more inclement months; the weather is generally pretty crummy, and there's not a whole lot to do besides surf, surf, surf and bid, bid, bid. Ka-ching, ka-ching, ka-ching.

Near the end of March, though, bidding sometimes tapers off a bit. It's not because of spring; it's because it's tax time in the good ol' U.S. of A. As April 15th approaches, most people are finding out whether they're getting a bonus from Uncle Sam or he's looking for that wad of cash they've been holding back. Since the Internal Revenue Service isn't much interested in what eBaysians want to bid on, the high bids rapidly taper off. If you aren't getting mugged by the IRS, this might be a good time to buy; prices could be low. If you're selling without really needing the cash right now, don't. You'll want to wait.

 TIP Now, if you do have to pay taxes, eBay might be a good place for you to make some money to help offset that unexpected tax payment. You might not get the highest dollars for your items, but you'll probably still get something that helps you with your bill. Think about it.

Through the rest of April and through May, bidding might still be a bit on the light side. People in the United States need time to recover if they've had to pay income taxes. But as June rolls around, so do the bidders. By midyear, people are sometimes ready to treat themselves to some shopping. They've gotten through the winter and the holidays are still a ways off. Annual vacations sometimes cut into bidding, but by and large the bidders are returning to their online love.

Through the rest of the summer, bidding keeps a moderate pace. It's still a good time to find some great buys, so do some value-shopping if you're so inclined. But, as fall approaches, the bidding starts its rise to the higher levels. By mid-September, eBay is a pretty hopping place once again. Of course, this always depends on what you're selling, regardless of the time of year.

When the major U.S. holidays start to hit, you'll see a real spike in bidding; especially for seasonal items. Halloween usually marks some great bidding for all that spooky stuff (a time I tend to bid the most myself). As the calendar turns to November, people are actively considering their Christmas shopping. Even though it might seem that November and December would be times when bidders would be more thrifty—they have to save money for their holiday shopping—I've found exactly the reverse to be true. These days, it seems, people are looking for really unique gifts; everyone has a fruitcake, a back scratcher, and a chia pet. How many places can you still get a pet rock, a *Saturday Night Fever* poster, or a vintage Radio Flyer? You won't find those things in stores; you might find them on eBay, though.

During December 1998, I was watching eBay very closely to see if the bidding would eventually taper off in anticipation of Christmas. Nope. Right up to the day, bidding activity seemed high and bids were flowing faster than spiked eggnog.

 TIP Be aware that during the major holidays, many people are traveling and might not be near their PC to bid. You might want to stage your auctions to end either the week before a major holiday or a week after.

Of course, these observations of calendar dynamics over the past few years can change at any time. As more and more users come to eBay, it's likely that some of those lulls will smooth out and keep the bidding more consistent year in and year out. As a seller, that's great news to you.

Choosing the Length of Your Auction

When you list an item for auction, you choose how long you want your auction to run. In Chapter 16, you learned that auctions can run for 3, 5, 7, or 10 days; those are the only choices available to you at eBay's site. Those choices aren't really an issue—the issue is knowing when to choose one over the other three.

Ten-Day Auctions

I don't like 'em. They're too long. If a buyer is hoping to get a good buy and bids on impulse, there's a great chance they'll be outbid before the auction ends. If a snipe plan is in the works, it's possible the sniper could forget about the auction since it is more than a week away. And a real draw of the auction is getting something cool and unexpected and getting it relatively quickly. As many shoppers are driven by impulse, that thrill could be long gone by the time the auction ends and the final transaction actually occurs. When was the last time you were excited to hear, *"Please allow 4 – 6 weeks for delivery"*?

But, in reasonable defense of the 10-day auction, it's not a bad choice if you'll be auctioning around a holiday; it allows a few extra days for people to be away on a short vacation without entirely missing out on your auction. I still think there are better choices, though.

Seven-Day Auctions

Clearly, the choice most sellers like is the seven-day auction—and it's a good choice. When you let your auction run this long, you have the greatest potential for finding as many bidders as possible without losing their interest in the duration. Remember I cautioned against not too long and not too short? The seven-day auction seems to be just right to capture and hold the interest of the most bidders possible. Plus, if you time your auction properly, the seven days will work to your best advantage.

To properly time a seven-day auction, you'll get the best results by starting your auction early Saturday evening. Your auction will be seen by those bidders searching later that night; they might bid right away, or they might make a note of it and continue to visit it for the reasonable duration. Then your auction is in clear view for all bidders on Sunday, the other weekend day; this way, you've effectively caught the weekend bidders.

When the regular work week begins, your auction will be visible to all the rest of the folks who maybe don't have access to the Net over the weekend— they could be folks who don't own a PC, but might have access to one Monday through Friday (maybe where they work—if it's allowed—or at libraries, college campuses, and so on). Now your auction is visible for the entire five days of the week, and the weekday bidders have seen your item and have bid or made a note to bid on it later.

When day seven—Saturday—rolls around again, you can still catch some of the weekend warriors in plenty of time because your auction won't be ending until the early evening (remembering the West Coast–East Coast timing). Essentially, listing your auction for seven days makes sure everyone possible has seen it for seven full days. Even if bidders only look around one day a week, your auction has been there for them to find.

 TIP There is a rumbling among sellers that Saturday evenings on eBay are much like the five o'clock traffic jam on your favorite interstate highway. It's true—eBay does see peak usage on Saturday evenings and server response time often degrades to a level less than desirable. Hopefully, someone will correct that problem soon. However, as far as optimal visibility for your seven-day auction, Saturday evening is probably still your best bet.

 SOAPBOX The only other downside that I've found with seven-day auctions is that anxious bidders still have to wait awhile for the auction to end. Although to the seller it's best for as many people as possible to see the auction in progress, to antsy bidders it can be agonizing; it means more people have a chance of finding the item and bidding up the price, perhaps even outbidding the anxious high bidder's maximum bid. As a seller, you want more bidders; as a bidder, you want to hurry up and get the thing over with. I've been one of those anxious bidders myself and have just had to wait it out until the auction ended. Heaven help the bouncing bidders when they come across the 10-day torture.

Five-Day Auctions

Five-day auctions don't really have too much advantage one way or the other in regard to your auction strategy. Usually, the five-day auction is just a way to bring closure to your auction a bit more quickly. If you're hoping to make a faster sale or need some extra cash (maybe to offset some bidding of your own) then the five-day auction is a good choice. Bidders, of course, seem to like the five-day auction since it shaves a couple of days from the bidding cycle.

If you think you want to run a five-day auction, again, consider the day of the week that you'll start your auction. Although you can't cover the entire span of a week, you can still reach as many bidders as possible. For five-day auctions, you would probably do best to have them end on Sunday evening. This means you'll need to start them on Tuesday evening. This still works fine for reaching a lot of bidders because you'll cover three days of the regular workweek, plus cover almost the entire weekend.

Three-Day Auctions

The three-day auction is something I call the *eBay Quickie*; it's fast but it can still be effective. If you're looking for a fast sale or the chance to take advantage of a temporary opportunity, then you want the three-day auction.

If you're looking for a fast sale, start your three-day auction on Thursday evening, having it wrap up Sunday evening; that's still the best time to catch the most bidders during the days that they will presumably have the most free time. A lot of sellers will even include a note in their item title stating theirs is a three-day auction, like this:

IT CONQUERED THE WORLD '56 lobby card-3 DAYS!

It's one of those "limited time only" kinds of deals; the three-day auction can appeal to the bidder because it's a quick auction, the bidder can get the item faster, and it helps the bidder believe that chances are better that other bidders might not stumble across it as easily as in a longer auction.

The description of the item should also repeat that the auction is running for only three days; that, along with the modified title, works to build some excitement and a bit of "hurry-up" in the bidders' minds. They won't want to miss this short-lived opportunity—better bid now!

Three-day auctions are great if you have an item that might only have temporary popularity. I like to use the Furby example here. At Christmas time, those Furbies were scooting across the auction block quicker than a poodle across your carpet. Bidders were literally inflamed with the need to get one, and they wanted to get one quick. With the holiday bearing down, time was running out for any bidders who wanted to put a Furby under the Christmas tree. This makes the ideal time to stage a three-day auction. Some Furby auctions had titles like these:

FURBY—in time for Christmas 3 DAYS ONLY!

TUXEDO FURBY—Receive by Xmas 3-DAY AUCTION!

WHITE FURBY—Ships via FedEx 3-DAY AUCTION!

To rabid Furby shoppers, these auctions were a feeding frenzy. These were very popular auctions, especially in the week before Christmas.

With the three-day auction, you will miss a lot of bidders, but you will typically get the hard-core shoppers who are checking eBay daily for some particular item. However, if your item isn't particularly hot or very sought after, choose a longer auction to have a better chance of finding your audience.

A Bad Time Is Downtime

One thing to watch out for when you schedule your auctions is the regularly scheduled downtime that eBay observes for system maintenance. eBay brings the systems down every Thursday night to Friday morning from midnight to 4 A.M. for scheduled maintenance. Even though the systems are down, that perpetual clock keeps ticking.

If you've heeded some of the earlier advice, you realize that having your auction end in the wee hours of any day would not be optimum. But be especially wary of the scheduled downtime.

 N○TE Sometimes the downtime will change, and sometimes eBay will announce additional "scheduled" downtime to respond to other system performance or upgrade issues. To stay informed about the downtime, visit eBay's Announcement Board; get there using the *Site Map* selection from the mini navbar and click on the *Announcements* link under the headings *Community, News.* This is where eBay support personnel post messages about system status, scheduled downtime, and unscheduled downtime.

chapter 18

Spicing Up Your Listing
for Better Results

You're not satisfied, are you? Sure, that listing you created using your wonderful text skills is fine; it will do a good job of drawing bidders—but it's just not enough. You're restless, and you know it's because your listing just doesn't reach out and grab those bidders. You'd better do something about it, then.

If you feel you want to offer more in your auction listing, then more is exactly what you can offer. Maybe you've seen other sellers' listings that really look great—lots of neat text fonts, colors, and really cool pictures. Maybe they have different backgrounds or funny little animated images. If you feel your auctions look second-rate by comparison, then you can quickly fix the problem by adding a bit of spiff and spice to your listings.

Remember, a text listing is fine, and you can do quite well with one if you have the right information in it. Doing fancy listing pages is strictly up to you, but it's going to require some more time and effort on your part. You'll need to roll up your sleeves because now you're going into the realm of Web development. Don't slam the book shut. Even though this means you'll be needing to use the tools of the Web-heads, it doesn't mean you have to be some sort of master programmer to get a look you like.

Most important, always, is the content of your fancy listings. Even if you already know a bit about Web development and feel you can create stylish listings with ease, pay attention anyway. The key to your fanciness is not how many cutie-pie things you can add to your listings, but *how* and *when* and *where* you add them; that's the real secret. Just the right amount of spice at just the right time makes for a stunning recipe; too much too often will make you gag and ruin the result.

Again, developing eye-catching listings is easy, and it's nothing to fear. Trust me.

Knowing the Key Ingredient

OK, the first thing to understand is that you'll be working with the Web development language *HTML* (HyperText Markup Language). It's the native tongue of the Web, and it's what was used to create all your favorite Web sites. From super fancy to super simple, most of what you're seeing on the Internet was created using HTML. Does that overwhelm you (maybe just a bit)? Don't be hesitant. The biggest secret about HTML is this: it's easy—some people just think it's hard.

Millions of Web sites exist on the Net today that have been designed by people just like you and me. Surely this should clue you in that HTML can't be too terribly elusive—not everyone out there with a Web site can have a Ph.D., right? If they can do Web development, so can you.

The great thing, aside from HTML's being so easy, is that eBay can interpret HTML when you include it in the description area of an auction listing. That description box is now your canvas and HTML is your palette. It's a fun kind of artsy thing to do, so get excited.

The HTML I'll show you is very basic, but it can have some great results, which you'll soon see. The bottom line is that HTML is really nothing more than a text document with some funny little markers (known as *tags*) that tell the Web browser what to do with your text. This includes making certain text passages larger than others, in different colors, or in different font styles. You'll see, as this chapter progresses, that using HTML tags is no big deal, and anyone can do it.

Another well-kept secret is that all you really need to create HTML is a text processing application as stripped down as Windows Notepad. That's right! That bare-bones, no-frills little Notepad application is your basic engine to firing up some very cool visual designs. Sure, there are special HTML editors that offer more features, but all you need to start is Notepad. Beauty, eh?

Now, I don't promise to make you an HTML master in this chapter. Far from it. There's really a lot to designing Web pages that goes beyond HTML (things like Java applets, CGI scripts, frames, and so on). Don't worry about that now. The goal here is to get some life into your listings in a way that catches the attention of potential bidders. Remember, the auction is still the main focus here, not Web design. I'll keep it simple.

And sometimes, the simpler the HTML, the *better* your listing will look. An overworked listing will be just that: overworked and obnoxious. It won't pay to make the most complex listing possible. Chances are, if your listing is too complex, it will either take too long for the page to appear (the bidders lose patience quickly and bolt) or it will look so busy that the bidders will lose sight of what it is you're selling (again, they bolt).

If you want to learn more about HTML, souped-up HTML editors, and Web design, see Appendix A at the back of this book; there, you'll find some references that will point you in the direction of becoming a certified Web-head yourself. But for now, just get ready for some simple HTML to make your listings look like something more than simple.

Bait the Bidders and They'll Be Hooked

If you want to use style in your auction listings, you have to use it well. You want to catch the attention of the bidders who decided that clicking on your listing title was worth the journey.

 NOTE Remember, it's the title that has to do the most work. All listing titles look pretty much the same on eBay. For cleanliness, eBay doesn't allow HTML in the title. Therefore, you're still going to have to verbally craft your title in the best possible way. Your title has to have the right information to make your listing enticing and worthy of a closer look.

Since I want to get stylish now, the first thing I need is a *hook*. I want to visually bait and hook the bidders once they've decided to visit my listing. And how is that done? Nope, not salmon eggs—*eye candy*.

Eye candy is anything that has visual appeal, contrast, or somehow grabs the attention of the viewer. In your auction listings, your choice of fonts, colors, and graphics can work to stimulate the bidders' interest, hold their attention, and subtly convince them that yours is the item to bid on. It's the extra effort you put into your listing—without spending hours on it—that will show your care for your auction and your commitment to a high-quality product.

Your goal with a stylish listing—or even a text listing for that matter—is to grab the bidders, give them enthusiasm (dare I say lust?) for your item, and get them to bid. Once they've placed their bids, they're in. You've engaged them, and they'll be more likely to follow the auction, watching how their maximum is holding up against other bidders, and possibly fighting for the item if a bidding war gets going. If you've given them something good to look at that presents your item well, it might be easier for them to decide to place that bid that keeps them hooked.

TIP Be careful or your hook will tend to gouge the bidders. You want to *hook* the bidders with tantalizing visuals, not *impale* them with outlandish, gaudy, and cluttered eye-junk. Avoid the temptation to overdo it, showing off how much you know about creating fancy pages. Less is more.

SOAPBOX Think it would be cool if your listing had *music*, too? Well, think real hard about that one. Many people will tell you it's easy and great to have a theme playing along with your listing. Easy? Yes. Great? I'm not so sure. A sound file is easy enough to add, but remember that it, too, takes time to load. The bidder might be waiting for the browser to finish loading, but not be able to see *what's* loading. Then, all of a sudden and out of nowhere, the Hamster Dance blares from the PC's speakers.

Some sound files, depending on what they are, can be startling when they finally kick in. In an office environment, they're a dead giveaway that you're surfing where you shouldn't be. I tend to believe sound files fit quite well in Web pages and, when used properly, are quite effective in creating an atmosphere. In an auction listing, though, I don't think they add much. You be the judge.

Using Easy HTML for Killer Listings

So, at this point, I've decided to cancel the text listing for the *It Conquered the World* lobby card. Instead, I want to use some HTML and other goodies to dress it up and really make it the best I can.

 NO**T**E In Chapter 19, I'll show you the steps to cancel or modify an active auction listing. For this chapter, let's just pretend the previous listing never happened, OK?

The first task for a stylish listing is to give the bidder something to look at. It can start as simply as using an interesting or evocative font, or typeface for the text. You've probably seen all kinds of different typefaces as you've surfed the Web. Each style of type seems to add character and feel to the information being presented; it also says something about the Web page owner—if only the desire to show a little personality. The item you're planning to auction has personality; the text that describes it should have personality, too. It's a snap to do it.

How about a real quick demonstration? I've already decided I don't like the typeface for the *It Conquered the World* lobby card; I want something more interesting—maybe something that suggests a bit of campy dread. In my original text listing, here's what part of the description looked like using a simple Times New Roman font:

> From 1956, here's an original 11 × 14 lobby card from the drive-in classic of alien invasion, "It Conquered the World." This film starred Peter Graves (of Mission: Impossible fame), '50s scream queen Beverly Garland, and tough guy Lee Van Cleef. This is lobby card #2 of the original U.S. set of eight. It features a great color photo of Peter Graves confronting another actor in a street scene of panic and confusion. This card also features excellent border graphics of the alien invader and the film's original logo.

It's great text, but it just doesn't capture the foreboding mood of what I'm selling. How about a different typeface? Using HTML, you can change the text to look like this:

From 1956, here's an original 11 x 14 lobby card from the drive-in classic of alien invasion, "It Conquered the World." This film starred Peter Graves (of Mission: Impossible fame) 50's scream queen Beverly Garland, and tough guy Lee Van Cleef. This is lobby card #2 of the original U.S. set of eight It features a great color photo of Peter Graves confronting another actor in a street scene of panic and confusion This card also features excellent border graphics of the alien invader and the film's original logo

Ooh. Now I'm in the mood. This example gives the text a sort of off-balance, other-worldly look that makes me feel more like bidding on this eerie lobby card. How hard was this to do with HTML? Well, that's the part that's not intimidating. All it took was a couple of simple tags before and after the text:

```
<HTML><BODY>

<FONT SIZE=5 COLOR=RED FACE="STYLUS">

From 1956, here's an original 11 x 14 lobby card from the
drive-in classic of alien invasion, "It Conquered the
World." This film starred Peter Graves (of Mission:
Impossible fame), '50s scream queen Beverly Garland, and
tough guy Lee Van Cleef. This is lobby card #2 of the
original U.S. set of eight. It features a great color photo
of Peter Graves confronting another actor in a street scene
of panic and confusion. This card also features excellent
border graphics of the alien invader and the film's original
logo.

</FONT></BODY></HTML>
```

That's all there is to it. The " < >" symbols are the HTML tag indicators that will specify the characteristics you want applied to your text. In HTML, there are *start tags* (like "<FONT>") and *end tags* (like "</FONT>"). The text that you enter between the tags will be interpreted as HTML code and visually altered according to the function of the tags you choose. So what it all boils down to is creating a simple text document and adding the HTML tags that will make the text look however you'd like. You could do that. The effort is minimal; the result is terrific. In my example above, by using these tags (sometimes called tag *pairs*—the start tag and the end tag), I've told the Web browser to show my text in a different font. With this simple adjustment, I've just improved my listing's effectiveness twofold. When you use HTML tags with your text, you're actually creating an *HTML document*. See, now you're a "coder."

Be careful with typefaces. It's possible that some fonts you have available on your PC won't be available on someone else's. That means the font you choose might not show up on another PC the way you intended. In the new PCs being manufactured and marketed today, most come with a common set of standard fonts. Stay with those, and you'll usually be OK.

Oh. One more thing: choose a font that's legible. Some fonts just don't hold up too well when used in paragraphs of text. Either change the size of the font (make it bigger to be more readable) or use the font selectively for special title lines or something like that. You'll see more of this as you continue on in this chapter.

Now, based on those two tips you've just read, maybe you want to add some variety to your text. You can experiment with different text sizes, fonts, and colors all within the same HTML document. Good variation will break up the monotony, so long as you don't overdo it.

In Figure 18-1 you'll see a very simple example from a previous auction of mine where I used text size and color in my HTML code to make a certain point about the item I was auctioning.

If you look at the text in Figure 18-1, you'll see I gave special treatment to the word "COLOR"; I wanted to really accentuate that the lobby cards in that

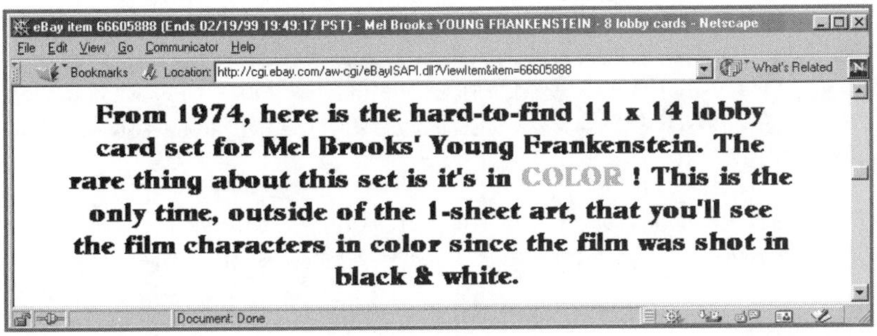

eBay item 66605888 (Ends 02/19/99 19:49:17 PST) - Mel Brooks YOUNG FRANKENSTEIN - 8 lobby cards - Netscape
File Edit View Go Communicator Help
Bookmarks / Location: http://cgi.ebay.com/aw-cgi/eBayISAPI.dll?ViewItem&item=66605888 What's Related

From 1974, here is the hard-to-find 11 x 14 lobby card set for Mel Brooks' Young Frankenstein. The rare thing about this set is it's in COLOR ! This is the only time, outside of the 1-sheet art, that you'll see the film characters in color since the film was shot in black & white.

Document: Done

figure 18-1

Using a different text size and color really brings the bidder's attention to the fact that there's something unique about the item being auctioned.

auction were in color, whereas the film itself was shown in black and white. For this item, that's a key detail, and I want to be sure the bidders know it.

What were the tags to make this text font size and color change? Here's all it took:

```
<HTML><BODY>

<FONT SIZE=5 COLOR=black FACE="old century"><STRONG>

From 1974, here is the hard-to-find 11 x 14 lobby card set
for Mel Brooks' "Young Frankenstein." The rare thing about
this set is it's in

<FONT SIZE=5 COLOR=green> COLOR </FONT>!

This is the only time, outside of the 1-sheet art, that
you'll see the film characters in color since the film was
shot in black & white.

</FONT></BODY></HTML>
```

You can see that I chose an overall font size, color, and style ("face") at the beginning of the HTML document. Then, I made a font size and color change right before I displayed the word *COLOR* by adding a new FONT tag. Right after the word, I returned the font size and color to what they were before by using the "</FONT>" end tag. The visible result is that only the word *COLOR* stands out, drawing more attention in my listing than it otherwise might.

In addition to font size and color, you want your listing text to have some good readability built in. That means things as simple as paragraph breaks. That's easy to do. Rather than have a big block of sentences all run together, you can easily separate the points of your description—as in this mock-up text for the *It Conquered the World* lobby card:

From 1956, here's an original 11 x 14 lobby card from the drive-in classic of alien invasion, "It Conquered the World." This film starred Peter Graves (of Mission: Impossible fame) 50's scream queen Beverly Garland, and tough guy Lee Van Cleef.

This is lobby card #2 of the original U.S set of eight It features a great color photo of Peter Graves confronting another actor in a street scene of panic and confusion.

This card also features excellent border graphics of the alien invader and the film's original logo

The paragraph breaks are done using the "<P>" tag. For this example, the text and HTML tags now look like this:

```
<HTML><BODY>

<FONT SIZE=5 COLOR=RED FACE="STYLUS">

From 1956, here's an original 11 x 14 lobby card from the
drive-in classic of alien invasion, "It Conquered the
World." This film starred Peter Graves (of Mission:
Impossible fame), '50's scream queen Beverly Garland, and
tough guy Lee Van Cleef.

<P>

This is lobby card #2 of the original U.S. set of eight. It
features a great color photo of Peter Graves confronting
another actor in a street scene of panic and confusion.

<P>

This card also features excellent border graphics of the
alien invader and the film's original logo.

</FONT></BODY></HTML>
```

NOTE No, I didn't forget anything in that HTML code. The "<P>" tag is quite forgiving, and does not require you to use the "</P>" end tag. In HTML, the "</P>" end tag is *implied*; it's not absolutely needed to get the HTML results you want. Beware, though, because some older versions of your favorite Web browser might not display HTML documents the way you want if the end "</P>" tag is missing. This should really be the exception; most newer versions of Web browsers understand the implied end tag and will display your HTML document just fine.

Still looks pretty easy, huh? That's what I was telling you; HTML really isn't that difficult, but the results are terrific.

So you can see that it's real easy to add some character to your auction just by working with some very simple HTML tags that will make your item's description take on a personality that's more flattering to the item up for bid.

TIP Now, do yourself a favor and copy the HTML code you find in this chapter. It's the makings of an HTML template that you can use over and over again. Most of the tags you'll see in this chapter are pretty standard, and you'll need to use them in your own HTML code. All you'll really need to change is the text between the tags, and you're off to the auction. It's easy to use Windows Notepad to create an HTML document template. Just save it, then open it again whenever you need to create new HTML-enhanced auction listings. Then, when the HTML document you'll use for your listing is complete, all you have to do is select it all, copy it to your Windows Clipboard (using Ctrl+C), and paste it (using Ctrl+V) right into the description box of the auction listing form. Gad, this is easy, isn't it?

A Picture's Worth a Thousand Bucks

I've been yakking about this *It Conquered the World* lobby card for some time now, but you still haven't seen it, have you? OK, so take a look at it in Figure 18-2.

Now you've had a chance to see the item I'm auctioning. What do you think? Go back to Chapter 16 and reread the text description; is this what you pictured in your mind? Does it look better than I described it? Do you want to bid on it even more now that you've actually seen it? Are you sorry that you've seen it at all?

figure 18-2

So this is what all the panic is about? I'm not sure what's more frightening: that goofy looking creature or the fact that Peter Graves believes that silly thing could conquer the human race.

Whatever your reaction, now you have a more concrete vision of what the item is and what it looks like. You might say, after seeing the image, *"Oh, that's a lobby card. I remember those. I just didn't know that's what they were called. I want it."* Or you might say, *"How stupid! Who'd want that piece of cinema slop?"* OK. But either way, the bidders now know exactly what they are (or aren't) bidding on.

Besides giving clear representation of the item, pictures in auction listings work to further entice a potential bidder. Maybe you saw this movie but didn't particularly care for it. The text listing describes it well, but, even so, it's nothing you care to have. However, after seeing the image, maybe it reminds you of your past or a period of time you're particularly fond of. Maybe you think the artwork and overall layout is kind of cool. Whatever, seeing the item might inspire someone to bid when the text alone wasn't enough to do the job. The picture works to further attach that hook to the bidder.

Most important, the image shows the bidder what to expect as far as completeness and condition of an item. When I talked about the tiny imperfections in the lobby card, I did my best to tell the bidder what to expect. Now, with a picture, I can *show* what those imperfections look like in the overall presentation of the item. Reading about the problems with this card might have been a turn-off; seeing what they really look like—or in this case, how insignificant they are—will lessen the negative impact while still presenting the most honest description I can muster.

I can almost guarantee that you'll get more bidders if you can show pictures of your items. Some bidders just don't want to take a chance on buying something sight unseen. They need proof before they'll bid. But once you show them the item, all cards are on the table and the bidder can make a more confident bid. The great thing about those pictures is they can be looked at again and again. A bidder who gets outbid can double-check on why that first bid was a good idea. For a bidder who's properly hooked, that picture is going to call out for another bid to reclaim the item. And for a bidder who hasn't yet jumped in—still dithering after several looks—that picture will act as a lure to jump in and place a bid.

How to Get a Picture of Your Item

If you decide you want to include a picture of your item in your listing (and I hope you will), you've got some advance work to do. First, you have to get the image itself. You can do this using a digital camera or scanner. These are the most common methods to get those all-important images for your listing. Remember that the camera is great when you have a three-dimensional item; maybe shoot it from various angles to give an all-around presentation of the thing. If you're going to sell a two-dimensional item, use a scanner for the best results. The camera will still work fine, but the scanner can give you a really sharp image that shows all the intricate details.

Well, that's just fine, but what if you don't have a camera or scanner. Are you left out? Are you going to have to settle for text listings all the time? Maybe, but there are still other ways to get those images.

If you don't have a camera or scanner, don't give up just yet. Do you have a friend who has the hardware? Maybe you can borrow it. Maybe your friend will agree to scan your items or photograph them for you.

You can also use the now old-fashioned method of photographing your item with a film camera. When you have your film developed, many developers will develop to a digital image. Bingo! You're in business. Take a bunch of photos of several items and get them all digitally developed at once. Or feed the photographic prints into a scanner.

Altering Pictures

Once you get a picture of your item, you might need to clean it up a bit. Maybe there's some stuff around the item that doesn't need to be in the picture. Maybe the exposure is a little off, and you'd like to correct it to get a more accurate representation of your item. Whatever, you might need to make a few alterations to your picture before you take it to the auction.

Image editing is getting easier and easier with some of the newer editing software. As you learned in Chapter 5, many of these editors are either free or can be used on a free trial basis. They all work a little differently, but they can all make the adjustments you need so that your pictures are the best they can be.

If you need to do some simple cropping of an image, then do so. Anything in the picture that possibly detracts from what you're really selling is just eye-junk. Clean it up.

If your image is a bit out of focus, use your editor's *sharpen* feature to bring some crispness to the picture. Don't overdo it, though. Too much sharpness and your picture will take on an overly grainy or blocky look.

If there's any potential controversy about image editing, it probably comes in the area of changing brightness, contrast, or hue. With these areas of editing, you can drastically change the appearance of your image to the point that it no longer truthfully represents your item. Using brightness, contrast, and hue, you can quickly turn a dingy, dirty item into a striking thing of beauty that looks practically new. Is that how your item really looks? If it isn't, then be very careful not to skew the appearance in a way that will skew the bidders' perception and eventual satisfaction.

 ALERT There was one time I made a contrast and hue modification to an item's image to bring it back to reality. The picture I took made the item look better than it really was. The item was a little faded, but the picture had a color saturation that made it look bright and fresh. Fearing I might mislead my bidders, I dialed back the color and contrast a bit to restore a somewhat faded appearance. This is something you'll need to watch when you take pictures of items; sometimes the pictures are better than real life. But that high bidder's gonna get the real thing, and you don't want any misleading photos to cause a real upset.

Storing and Queuing Up Your Pictures

Once you have your picture, you need to get it someplace where it can be used for your auction listing. This is a real key, folks: just because you have a picture of your item, that doesn't mean you can hang it on eBay with the text of the listing and go on your merry way while the bids roll in. You have to store it somewhere on the Web so eBay can retrieve it and display it along with your item description. Whenever you see images and text and whatever else on a Web site, all that content is stored on some server that is always running to be sure your content can be seen at any time, day or night. You'll need to make sure your item pictures are available in the same way. Sound like a snag? It's really not, but it does require a bit more work on your part.

What you need here is a place to *host* your images—eBay doesn't volunteer to do that; its servers are crammed already. That means you'll need a Web site somewhere that can store your images, make them easily accessible for eBay to retrieve, and are sure to be available 24 hours a day, seven days a week. Sounds like you need your own Web site, huh? Maybe, and maybe not.

If you have your own Web space—something you often pay for when you hook up with an ISP or other Internet access service—then you can store your pictures there. The place you store your pictures will have a URL just like anywhere else on the Web. The biggest difference is that the URL associated with your image will contain only that—your image! It's not like a whole Web page; it's just your item's picture.

TIP Check out your ISP. Many offer free Web space as part of the regular monthly connection fee. You can usually get a reasonable amount of Web space that can host your active auction images. Ask the support people at your ISP.

Now, if you don't currently pay for Web space with an ISP or your ISP doesn't offer free space, you can still find a place to put your images for use in your auction listings. The great thing is that it can be done for free.

There are several commercial sites on the Internet that will give users around 10MB of Web space free. You can create a Web page with that space or just store a bunch of pictures. These are known as *free Web hosting sites*, and there are several to choose from. You may wonder what the catch is—*if my ISP won't give me free Web space, why would some Web hosting site do that, especially when I don't pay them anything?* Advertising. That's why. The catch is you'll need to sift through a whole array of advertising banners, boxes, and buttons as you navigate through these free sites. Still, it's no big deal when you consider that you'll soon have a free home for your auction images.

NOTE You get what you pay for. Some of the free sites can be a little quirky at times. They could be cumbersome, they could be slow, they could be subject to occasional interruptions. Still, my experience is that they're usually online and reliable—otherwise they'd lose all their advertisers.

Of the free Web hosting sites, these are the most frequently used by eBaysians:

- XOOM (**www.xoom.com**)

- Tripod (**www.tripod.com**)

- Angelfire (**www.angelfire.com**)

- Yahoo!Geocities (**geocities.yahoo.com/home/**)

These sites all provide free Web space to create a Web page of your very own; that's their whole purpose. So build a Web page; it's fun—and it's often required for you to continue to use the free services. In fact, these sites also offer a bunch of good tutorials about Web development and HTML coding. And if you're a good member of the free Web site community, you'll have a place to store those images of your auction items.

NOTE If you only use these free hosting sites to store pictures, you'll probably get yanked. The site administrators see that as an abuse of the free service. All they ask is you create and maintain a Web page—as simple or complex as you like. Also, be sure to read the site's rules; these typically restrict users from creating commercial Web pages for the sole purpose of generating income. Their operators also don't want to see any nudity, sex, or pornography on their site. One bare bum, and you'll get shut down quick.

Once you register at a free hosting site, you can navigate around to learn how to make use of your new Web space. Each site has a file manager of some sort where you can upload images of your files quickly and easily. Your picture now has a home on the Web.

NOTE Because these free hosting sites have a file manager area with file uploading utilities, you shouldn't have to bother with things like FTP (File Transfer Protocol) utilities on your PC. That's another bonus for the free hosting sites.

Now, before I leave the topic of uploading images to the Web, I should tell you there are several sites that provide image hosting mainly to serve online auction-goers. They don't require you to have a Web page to host your images. Some image hosting sites provide the space for free and some charge a *per image* fee. Each image hosting site offers different services, so you'll need to check them out and judge for yourself. Here are just a couple of the sites you could check into:

- AuctionWatch (**www.auctionwatch.com**)
- Auction Pix (**www.auctionpix.com**)
- Classy Pix Image Hosting (**www.classypix.com**)

Adding an Image to Your Auction Listing

So now it's time to add the picture to your listing. Finally, huh? Sure, it took a little while to get here, but you can see there was some stuff you needed to do first. But now the time has come to combine your photo with your text and see what you get.

There are two ways to add pictures to your auction listings. First, eBay provides a special place where your image can be easily added. The eBay item listing form has a field labeled *Picture URL* (refer back to Figure 16-5); it's the quickest and easiest way to add a picture to your listing and doesn't require any additional HTML. Since this field isn't part of the description content, the picture will appear outside your descriptive text. To illustrate, I'll go ahead and use the Picture URL field to show you how to use it and what the result will look like.

First, what *is* the picture URL, anyway? Well, that's the actual Web address where your picture can be found. Remember, eBay will need to know the location of your item's picture so it can go get it when someone looks at your item detail page. I'm going to make an assumption here: I'll assume you're going to use one of the free Web hosting sites for storing your item images (after all, you seem like you know a good bargain when you see one).

Personally, I like to use Yahoo!Geocities for my Web and image hosting; I've been using that service for almost four years now, and I'm pretty satisfied.

Whatever hosting site you use, you'll access that site's file manager and will actually be able to display your image by clicking on the file name or something.

NOTE How you access your images will depend on the file management utilities your hosting site uses. There's sure to be plenty of help and instruction available at the site you choose; make use of it to become fluent in using the site's services.

As an example, I've uploaded the *It Conquered the World* lobby card image to my Yahoo!Geocities file manager. When I search through my files there, I can click on the file name (it's a hyperlink), and the image will be displayed for me (see Figure 18-3).

So what's the URL for my image? Well, it's in the Location bar at the top of the browser window. *That's* all I need to put in the eBay Picture URL field? Save yourself the headache of trying to retype that address, though. Just drag your mouse pointer over the text and copy it to your operating system's Clipboard. One typo and the image will never be found.

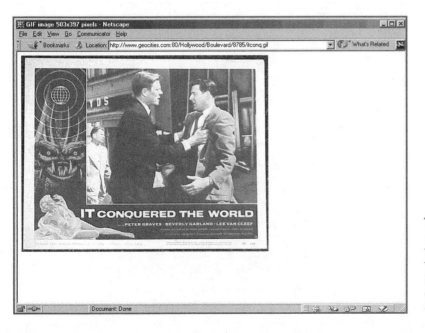

figure 18-3

Here's my image in my Yahoo!Geocities file manager. The URL for the image is found in the Location bar at the top of the Web browser window. See it?

Go back to the eBay listing form and paste the image URL from the Clipboard. That's it! You've just added an image to your listing. What will it look like? Well, first you'll be asked to confirm that eBay is finding it properly when you verify your auction. Look at Figure 18-4, and you'll see the point where you verify that your image is showing up correctly.

If you can see the image properly, then go for it; click on the *Submit my listing* button and get your new and improved auction going. Click on the URL that eBay displays when your auction confirmation is posted, and you'll get your first look at what the image looks like using the Picture URL field (see Figure 18-5).

When you look at your item listing, you'll see that the text modifications you added using HTML show up great. Scroll past the description, and you'll see the image itself. Looks great!

A real benefit to using the eBay Picture URL field is that when you do, you'll get the 📺 icon to appear with your item title in the item listings pages (see Figure 7-3 for an example) or the **PIC** icon that appears with your item title in search results (see Figure 15-1 for an example). Both are

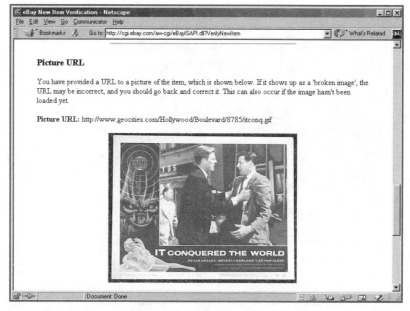

figure 18-4

Before you go live with your enhanced auction listing, be sure your image can be seen.

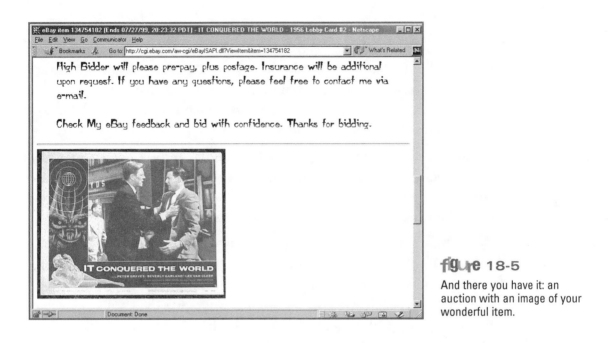

big-time upgrades for your listing. They immediately tell bidders that they can see an image of your item. Remember, some bidders won't bid on items if there isn't an accompanying picture. The picture icons quickly communicate that bidders won't be let down. They'll be your auction title's best friends.

Mixing Images and Text in Your Item Description

But something's still wrong? You're just not satisfied, are you? You want more dazzle? No problem. Kick it up another notch. Some listings look better still when you can intermingle pictures and text within the description area. That makes your listing look like a full-fledged advertisement for your item, and it will really be a treat for bidders to see.

OK, now we're getting fancy, but it's still very easy to do. You'll just need to break out a few more HTML tags. No problem. Put on your marketing hat 'cause you're gonna really sell this thing.

I'll go back to that lobby card again. (I've gotta sell that thing soon before I wear it out.) Now, I've decided on the Comic Sans font; it looks kind of informal, like a quick and friendly note. But I also really like the border art in the card; it would look great all by itself within the listing to further set the mood and promote the piece. For that, I'll go back and edit the image of the card, cutting out a portion of the artwork to use in the description.

Remember, you want to hook the bidders and grab their attention quickly so they won't stray away. You can do that by showing them something interesting right away, and not necessarily the item they'll be bidding on. So, with a bit of extra work and some fast and easy HTML, I'll change the item listing so it looks like what you see in Figure 18-6.

So, what's going on in this listing now? A lot, really. The first thing the potential bidder reads in the description is the film's original tag line, *"Every man its prisoner . . . every woman its slave!"* So it's not the lovable, glowing-fingered space traveler you were hoping for, but it's an original part of the film's advertising, and it catches the bidder's attention right away. Whether

figure 18-6

I've rolled out the red carpet for you, you fiendish thing from another world. This listing is quite an upgrade from that no-frills text listing in Chapter 16.

you use a catchy phrase or some quick image (I actually put the film's logo right under the tagline), you want the bidder to read or see something interesting from the get-go.

Next, you'll see I took another picture of the lobby card and cut out just the side artwork. I've used that in a way so it will jump out at the bidder; it really catches the eye. I've then wrapped the enhanced text description to the right of the artwork to begin describing the item.

Later in the listing, you'll see a small image of the entire lobby card. The bidder has a chance to see exactly what there is to bid on. Although I'm showing the item, I've decided to keep all of the descriptive text—just in case my hosting site should become temporarily unavailable and the images can't be seen.

The next paragraph goes on to describe the condition of the card. I don't skimp here, even though there is a picture of the item. The picture can't truly reveal the minor imperfections with this item. Upon visual inspection, the buyer will see the faults; I want to be sure all bidders are fully informed about this item's condition.

Hopefully you'll agree that this listing is far superior to the text-only listing. The only real difference is what you'll enter in the *Description* box on the listing form—that's where your super-duper, interstellar HTML magic will go. And you might also use the *Picture URL* field to add a picture if you choose not to include pictures within the body of the item's description.

So, without further ado, here's the final HTML code I used in the description box to make the listing you see in Figure 18-6:

```
<HTML><BODY>

<FONT SIZE=4 COLOR=BLACK FACE="ARIAL">

<P ALIGN="CENTER">

Every man its prisoner . . .

<FONT COLOR=RED><STRONG><I>

every woman its slave!
```

```
</I></STRONG></FONT>

<IMG ALIGN="CENTER" SRC="http://www.geocities.com:80/
Hollywood/Boulevard/8785/itconqlog.gif">

<P ALIGN="LEFT">

<IMG ALIGN="LEFT" SRC="http://www.geocities.com:80/
Hollywood/Boulevard/8785/itconqart.gif">

<FONT SIZE=3 COLOR=RED FACE="COMIC SANS MS">

From 1956, here's an original 11 x 14 lobby card from the
drive-in classic,

<FONT COLOR=RED>

"It Conquered the World."

</FONT>

<P>

This film starred Peter Graves (of Mission: Impossible
fame), '50s scream queen Beverly

Garland, and tough guy Lee Van Cleef.

                    <P>

This is lobby card #2 of the original U.S. set of eight. It
features a great color photo of Peter Graves confronting
another actor in a street scene of panic and confusion. This
card also features excellent border graphics of the alien
invader and the film's original logo. The surrounding white
border features the standard National Screen Service (NSS)
proprietary information. It's printed on the standard heavy
pulp paper as were all lobby cards at that time.

<P>

<A HREF="http://www.geocities.com:80/Hollywood/
Boulevard/8785/itconq.gif">

<IMG ALIGN="RIGHT"
SRC="http://www.geocities.com/Hollywood/Boulevard/8785/itconq
2.gif"

ALT="It Conquered Lobby Card">

</A>
```

This lobby card is in excellent condition. Although issued forty-four years ago for the film's original release, this lobby card has fared extremely well. All corners are slightly soft with one showing a tiny bit of paper loss. There is a barely-noticeable quarter inch tear in the left border, but no paper loss there. The white border shows very light handling soiling and is refreshingly free of any pinholes or tape residue. This card is a clean, vivid specimen that's striking to look at and will be a welcome addition to any vintage horror collection. Click on the image here to see a larger view.

<P>

High Bidder will please pre-pay, plus postage. Insurance will be additional upon request.

If you have any questions, please feel free to contact me via e-mail.

<P>

Check My eBay

<A HREF="http://cgi.ebay.com/aw-cgi/eBayISAPI.dll?View Feedback&userid=dennis_prince">

feedback

</A>

and bid with confidence. Thanks for bidding.

</STRONG></FONT></BODY></HTML>

 NOTE One great feature about eBay and HTML: the listing verification screen is perfect for looking at the results of your HTML creativity. Just as you learned in Chapter 16, you can verify your item and use the *Go back* function to return to the listing form and make further tweaks. When using HTML, this is a real benefit because you can make little adjustments to your HTML, move forward to check it, go back and tweak, go forward to check. Go back. Go forward. Go back. Forward. Back. I'm getting dizzy. But use the verification until your listing looks just right.

TIP   OK, *big tip* here: don't forget to make a Notepad copy of your finished HTML listing document before you start your auction. That finalized code is still retrievable from the description box on the listing form. Before you submit your auction, grab that good code and make a copy for future use. Then, when you list other items, all you'll need to do is call up the template and make some adjustments to it for the specific item you'll be auctioning. You might want to include more tags than I have for this auction; that's fine. Whatever you come up with, make a template of it (even copy the one I have here); you'll save a lot of time for each successive item you list.

A Few Subtle Tricks

"Nothing up my sleeve . . . presto!"

"Wrong hat?"

"I take a seven-and-a-half."

"Now here's something we hope you'll really like."

If you've looked closely at that HTML code, I'm sure you've seen a couple of little dillies I threw in for good measure. These are little bonus features that add just a bit more convenience to my listing. The more convenient my listing is, the better the bidders might like it.

First, I'll show you the rest of the listing page by scrolling down in the browser window (see Figure 18-7).

The first convenience to the bidder is the small image of the lobby card—it's actually a hyperlink that, when clicked, will take the bidder to the larger image of the item. I tell the bidder about it in the description where it reads, "click on the image here to see a larger view." Although you might not be able to readily tell, there is a thin colored border around the lobby card image and, if you pass your mouse pointer over the image, the tell-tale pointing hand will appear along with the link's descriptive text box. It's a hyperlink, and you can click on it! I offer this as a service to my bidders—they can choose to take a closer look at the item before placing their bids.

Hey. Why not just include the large picture in the listing? Well, the larger the image, the longer it takes to load (appear) in the listing page. Some bidders might not wait long enough. Using a smaller image (often referred to

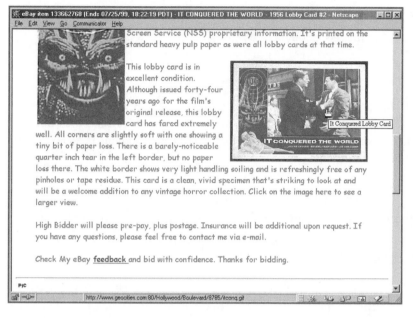

figure 18-7

Here's the rest of the item listing. See anything slightly peculiar (besides the conquering carrot creature)?

as a *thumbnail*), I can load and show the picture to bidders quickly before the impatient ones decide to leave.

NOTE In some Internet studies, it has been reported that a Web developer has only three seconds to catch a visitor's attention before their finger hits the mouse button and they split. For that reason, you have to be sure your images load quickly. It's just a part of this fidgety, mouse-clicking, microwave-watching society everybody's caught up in.

I created the image link using the HTML *anchor* tag; it allows you to specify any certain text or image as a hyperlink anchor that can refer to some address on the Net. In this case, the anchor points to my Yahoo!Geocities page where the full-sized image is stored. The special anchor tag and specifications, as extracted from the complete HTML code, is as follows:

```
<A HREF="http://www.geocities.com:80/Hollywood/
Boulevard/8785/itconq.gif">

<IMG ALIGN="RIGHT"
SRC="http://www.geocities.com/Hollywood/Boulevard/8785/itconq
```

```
2.gif"
ALT="It Conquered Lobby Card">
</A>
```

ALERT HTML anchor tags will only work for an image that you include within the description of your auction item. Images that are added using the eBay Picture URL field cannot be used as anchors. The Picture URL field doesn't allow lengthy HTML code to be entered.

Quickly, you can see that the anchor begins with the "<A" tag, then followed by the reference tag "HREF," and then followed by the image source tag "SRC" that contains the URL address of where I want the anchor to take whoever clicks on it.

The next line of HTML is what puts the actual image into my listing. It looks a lot like the anchor code, but notice the anchor takes the viewer to the page that has just the image file *itconq.gif*, whereas the image displayed in the listing is the smaller *itconq2.gif*.

NOTE I could have just as easily left out the anchor tag and just displayed the small *itconq2.gif* image. It would look the same, but the link to the larger image wouldn't be available to the viewer. I thought it was important to let the viewer see a large picture, so that's why I included the anchor.

One more thing about the anchor and displayed image: notice the *ALT = "It Conquered Lobby Card"* in the code. It's a good idea to use the "ALT" tag every time you include images in a Web page. Some people choose not to automatically load images when they view Web content so they can get to the information more quickly, without waiting for any included images to load and appear. The "ALT" tag lets you enter alternate text that will show up if the viewer doesn't have automatic image loading turned on—it's what you see as descriptive text in Figure 18-7. In this way, the viewer will at least see some descriptive text of what the image is without actually seeing the image. If it's intriguing enough, the viewer might click on the text to view the image. If there's no text associated with the image, the viewer might just skip over it. Rats! Another one got away.

The last tag is the "</A>" end tag, which marks the close of the anchor. Back to the listing now: notice how the word *feedback* is also a hyperlink; it's in a different color and it's underlined. Here, I pointed to my eBay feedback page. Everyone who registers at eBay will get their own feedback page where other users post the good (and the not-so-good) comments about users. I'm pretty proud of my feedback, and I want to make it easy for bidders to quickly see what other eBay users have said about me. Rather than make the bidder go off and hunt down my feedback, I'll just add another anchor that points to my feedback page. At the click of the mouse, the viewer can go off and review my feedback, and then just as easily return to the listing page, hopefully having decided to bid. Here's the part of the HTML that included the feedback anchor:

```
Check my eBay

<A HREF="http://cgi.ebay.com/aw-cgi/eBayISAPI.dll?
ViewFeedback&userid=dennis_prince">

feedback

</A>

and bid with confidence. Thanks for bidding.

</HTML>
```

It's another anchor just like the one I already described. This one's actually easier because I'm only making the word *feedback* act as the link; I don't have to include the long "IMG SRC=" tag that pointed to an image URL for the big image of the lobby card.

OK, one last little trick, and this one's pretty clever. You'll remember that I said using eBay's Picture URL field will give your item title the little picture icons on the listing and search result pages. Now, if you have images within the HTML of your description, you won't need the Picture URL field. That's right, but then you miss out on the all-important picture icons. Don't fret; there's a simple way around this.

Wherever you see one of those picture icons on an eBay page, you can right-click on them and save them to your PC (they're images in their own right, after all). Then upload the tiny little image to your image host. Once that's done, you can specify the URL of that tiny image in the eBay Picture URL field. Any image, no matter how small, that is entered in that field will gain you the picture icons that will appear with your item's title. If you'll look once more at Figure 18-7, you'll see one of the little picture icons appearing after the end of the item description. Isn't that cute?

The reason I mention using the picture icon instead of another actual image is because another image will take more time to load. Once the pictures in your item description are loaded, don't make the bidder's browser continue to crunch for a duplicate picture that's already been shown.

Add Inter-Listing Hyperlinks

Something else to think about: just as I showed you how to use anchors to link to larger images or your eBay feedback page, you can also choose to link to a Web page of your own. Maybe you have other items just like the one you're auctioning for sale on your personal Web site. If you want to potentially draw thousands of customers (or *millions* of customers, or *billions*, or . . .'scuse me, got all frothy) to your site, just add a link to your Web site; many people will take the trip if they like what you're selling at eBay—they may want to see what else you have.

Advertising Your Auction Listings

One last thing to leave you with: don't forget to advertise your auctions. It's easy, and it sometimes makes a difference.

The first way to advertise is on a Web site that you might own and operate. Many sellers on eBay have their own Web sites or online businesses. You'll often see a link on their Web sites that leads directly to their current auction listings page on eBay. Likewise, they'll use the link I mentioned earlier that leads back to their Web business right from their item listing.

Another way to advertise your auctions is on USENET; that's where you'll find all the different newsgroups devoted to various topics. A lot of people use the newsgroups to chat, share information, and sell things. There are a lot of groups devoted to collectibles, computers, or anything else you might want to buy. If you're auctioning an item on eBay that might be appropriate to one of the newsgroups, post a message that tells about your item and includes the URL link to your auction listing page. eBay doesn't mind at all; in fact, it's great advertising for the site anyway. Remember, it was USENET that first made me aware of eBay. I don't think I've ever been the same since.

Wrapping Up

I know this was quite a bit to cover, and I covered it quickly. Don't get hung up on the HTML; it's really quite easy. If you've never worked with HTML before, don't worry. It just takes a bit of getting used to. However, after you've seen it a few times the tags will get real familiar. It's a very repetitive coding structure—you'll reuse those tags over and over again, and you'll get some great results when you do.

If you want to see some more ways to create a fancy listing for your auctions, check Appendix B in the back of this book; I've put a few more variations on how an item can be listed using even more HTML tags. The code I used to create the listings is included, too. Feel free to copy it. I don't mind.

Remember, if you want to learn more about HTML, check in Appendix A for some great resources that will help you along. You can also find a handy reference page for common HTML tags from eBay's Help, Basics page. If you're already familiar with HTML, then go to the head of the class—and on to the next chapter.

chapter 19

Managing Your Auctions

Well, listing your items is certainly fun, and it's even more fun to watch the high bids go up and up. You've got great stuff out there, people want it, and you're now fully engaged in the fun of selling on eBay. But even though your auction is in full swing, you might still need to do some maintenance. It's nothing too hard or overwhelming, but if you want to be successful, there are a few things you'll want to think about and watch out for while your auction is running.

Just as you put a lot of thought and effort into presenting your item for auction, now you'll want to keep an eye on it, dust it off, or add little touches that will make it even more desirable to those hungry bidders. So roll up your sleeves again. It's time to tend your shop.

Just whistle while you work.

Answering Bidders' Questions

Well, as with any buy-and-sell scenario, people who are interested in your stuff are going to want to ask questions. When you were bidding, you learned that asking questions was what helped you understand what you intended to bid on and how the seller approached the auction business. If you didn't like either—the item or the seller—you probably decided to move on to another auction. This time you're the seller, and you're in the spotlight; it's now up to you to convince the soon-to-be bidders that yours is the item they'll want to bid on.

Whether you used a simple text listing or a fancier HTML advertisement, bidders will still want to ask questions. Maybe they want more information about the item's date or origin. Maybe they want to know more about its condition. Maybe they just want to check you out a bit to see if you're the vendor who will provide the best and most trustworthy service. Whatever their need, be ready for their questions.

NOTE If you're new to eBay and have a very low feedback rating, expect that you'll be tested a bit just to be sure you're a good Joe or Jane. Don't be offended; it's all part of being new on the block. Take the opportunity to wow them all, letting them know that the best seller ever to hit eBay has just arrived. (Pssst . . . that's you.)

When a question comes your way, be glad—it means that someone is interested enough in your item to bother with the extra effort of contacting you, and that's the sign of a true potential bidder. Reply to any question as soon as you possibly can and in the most direct and polite way you know how—it's that Golden Rule again, so polish it up.

Without being overly pushy, go ahead and add a bit of sales pitch in your reply. That person asking the question is curious about your item and might be teetering on the edge of deciding to bid or not. Answer the question, and maybe add some additional tidbit of information that further entices them to bid. This is especially important when your item may have already received some bids and the current bid is quite high; that potential bidder asking the question is trying to determine if you and your item are really worth the big bucks.

As an example, here's an e-mail dialog I had with a potential bidder regarding an item I was auctioning (this is the exact e-mail exchange that took place—without the potential bidder's address, of course).

First, the bidder's question:

• •

```
Subject: young Frankenstein lobby set

Date: Thu, 18 Feb 1999 20:02:55 -0500

From: "Joe"

To: <dlprince@bigfoot.com>

is each card individually numbered,?( example(25/50) meaning
twenty-fifth of fifty.) on the bottom? if so what numbers are they,
if all different please list by photo description , THANKS!!
```

• •

SOAPBOX Now here's a little pointer for you whether you're a buyer or seller. Look at Joe's original message: he didn't use very good grammar or writing style when he asked his questions. It's no big deal, though—it seems to be the way of quick electronic communication these days. However, I like to take a more professional approach when I create my messages. It lets others know I'm paying attention to detail—and that translates to a better feeling overall that you're a safe bet as buyer or seller.

Next, my reply:

• •

```
Subject: Re: young Frankenstein lobby set

Date: Fri, 19 Feb 1999 07:18:32 -0500

From: <dlprince@bigfoot.com>

To: "Joe"

Hi Joe,

Thanks for your interest in the lobby card set. Yes, this is an
original lobby card set as distributed by National Screen Service
(NSS) in 1974. Each card bears the standard numbering format: for
this set, "74/249" appears in the lower right-hand corner in the
title strip. In very small print is also the standard NSS propri-
etary info. Each card in the set is numbered sequentially 1, 2, 3,
and so on. I arranged them in order in the auction listing.

What I especially like about this set is that we finally get to see
the monster in color!
```

I hope this answers your questions about their authenticity. Please
let me know if you have any other questions.

Best,

Dennis

● ●

And, his response:

● ●

Subject: young Frankenstein lobby set

Date: Fri, 19 Feb 1999 09:51:23 -0500

From: "Joe"

To: <dlprince@bigfoot.com>

THANKS! I will be in the bidding, JOE

● ●

Now, from that exchange, I helped "Joe" understand what he needed to feel
comfortable bidding on my item—and turned him into a bidder. In my
images of the item for bid, the fine printing on each card wasn't very visible,
although someone familiar with this kind of item probably would have
enough knowledge not to have to ask the question. Joe might be new to collecting lobby cards, or might not have even seen a lobby card before. Maybe
he heard to watch out for unofficial (bogus) movie material or something.
Whatever the reason, I wanted to provide enough information so he'd know
I was on the level and he could feel safe bidding on my auction. Those
details I gave him were enough to ease his concern.

I answered quickly because the auction was scheduled to end in less than 14
hours—if I dragged my feet getting back to him, he probably wouldn't have
had time to bid. Even though he waited until late in the auction to ask his
question, you can see from his response that my quick effort to reply was
well worth it; Joe decided to bid based on what I told him.

The other reason I was quick to reply was to give Joe the confidence that I
monitor my auctions and e-mail closely. That will translate into a feeling that
I'll probably honor the commitment quickly if Joe bids and wins and takes that
big leap of faith—that is, sends me his money in the expectation that I'll send

him the goods. It's just good business to do everything possible to reassure a potential buyer about my reliability; nervous bidders don't risk those big bucks.

I suppose that I could have let Joe's question go unanswered. I already had bidders, and he did ask his question kind of late in the game. His message wasn't worded the best, and it might have led me to believe he was a bit disorganized. Just as Joe's checking me and my item out, I'm checking him out, too. OK, maybe he's not an English scholar, but he seems friendly and he did make the effort to contact me. I checked his feedback rating, too—from the comments I saw there, Joe seemed to be OK as far as some of the other users are concerned.

NOTE I'm not trying to pick on Joe at all, but notice how easy it is to develop an opinion about someone based on their communications? Be sure to keep that in mind when *you* communicate.

OK, so what if I don't get back to Joe very quickly? After all, I'm a busy guy—working multiple auctions, holding down a full-time job, writing books. I've got a lot to do, and Joe's just one guy surfing eBay. Here's why I don't give Joe the old heave-ho: *he just might turn into my high bidder!* Of course, I can never be sure, but I can't afford to take that chance. Based on what I told Joe, possibly including *how* I told him, he bid near the auction's close and upped the previous high bidder by $20.

Joe could have also been a previous high bidder; maybe he was outbid by someone else before the auction ended. Maybe Joe wants this item pretty bad, but just isn't 100 percent sure that my auction is the one he should fight for. Remember, when that bidder bids, he gets involved and might become hooked. When he gets outbid, he might need a gentle tug to keep him hooked and keep him in the game. Your presale interaction with the bidder can often be the making of a great final bid. You're providing good customer service, and that sometimes makes all the difference whether you get that final bid or not. Alas, poor Joe got outbid right at the end, but he put up a good fight. He probably made me some money, even though he didn't get a chance to pay me himself. I like Joe.

Bottom line: Good Customer Service = Good Bids (usually).

Revising, Improving, or Abandoning Your Listing

When you created your auction listing, whether using simple text or the fancier HTML approach, you put your best foot forward and gave it all you had. You're proud of that listing for the way it attracts bidders, the way it provides a good, accurate description of your item, and maybe for the way the pictures or layout make it a fun listing to look at. But, for all your good intentions, you just might find out that you've left something out or made a mistake, or maybe the whole thing just bellied-up and you didn't catch it. Oh crud. Now what? Well, don't fret. There are a few remedies available to cure your auction ailments.

Revising Items

First, suppose your listing is pretty good, but you noticed the title isn't quite right or (gulp) there's a misspelling. It's OK. Maybe you didn't notice when you first listed it, but you're not sunk yet. If no one has bid yet, you have the option of revising your listing. Listing revisions are allowed to let you make quick fixes or modifications before anyone has bid. This way, if your title's not quite right or the description lacks a certain detail or one of the selling conditions isn't what you really had in mind, you can make the change quickly and painlessly. To do this, just go into your auction's details screen and click on the *Revise* link just above the item description (where the finger is pointing in Figure 19-1). You can click on the *Revise* link and jump to a verification screen that looks like what you see in Figure 19-2.

What can you revise on your listing if you haven't yet received bids? You can make changes to the title of your item, change the category, add information to the description (including making HTML changes), change or add images, or change the payment and shipping options. It's always possible you could make a mistake or leave something out when you first add your item; eBay gives you a chance to make the changes you need before anyone bids.

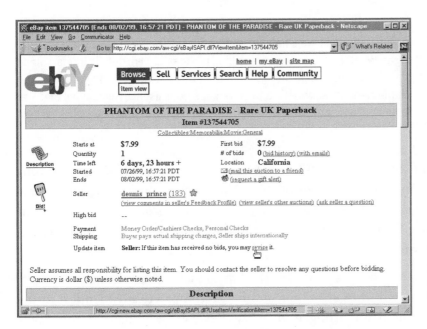

figure 19-1

Don't bail out; use the Revise option to make quick fixes to your listing before anyone has bid.

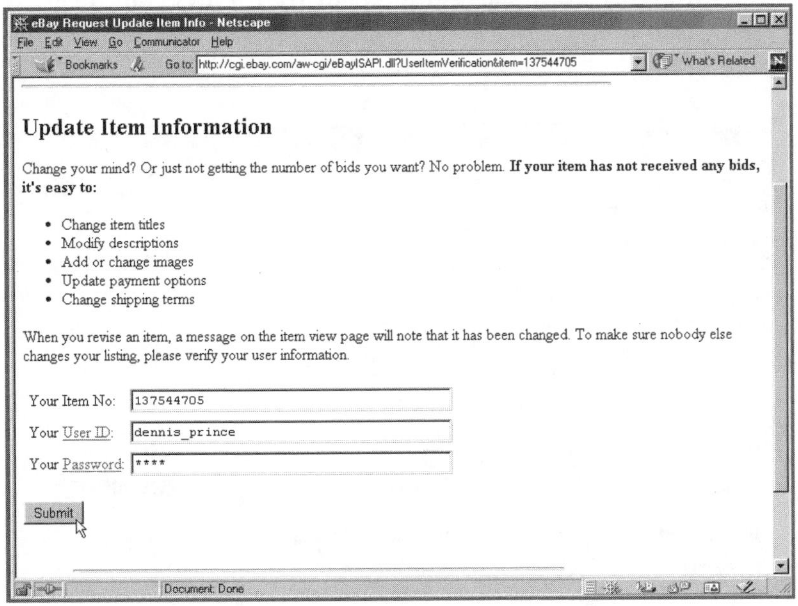

figure 19-2

The Update Item Information form is where you'll start the process of revising your listing.

Tip No matter how closely you review your listing during the new item verification step, you should also make a habit of reviewing your item just after you list it; that way, you get to see what the bidders will be seeing in the final item details format. Since there is a lag time before your item shows up in the eBay listings, you have the chance to make any changes necessary before anyone sees your listing. Remember that you can only revise an item if no one has bid yet. If a bid has come in, the *Revise* link will not be available.

As you can see in Figure 19-2, you'll need to enter your item number, your user ID, and your password (this ensures that only *you* can update your item; nobody else). Click on the *Submit* button, and you'll see an item update form that is very similar to the new item listing form (see Figures 19-3 and 19-4).

Make whatever changes you need or want to make, then click on the *Verify* button. eBay will then show you another screen practically identical to the verification used for listing new items. Review the updated information carefully and, at the bottom of the screen, click on the *Update* button. Now, eBay will crunch through your updates and reload your item details page. If you look at Figure 19-5, you'll see a new notation now exists next to the

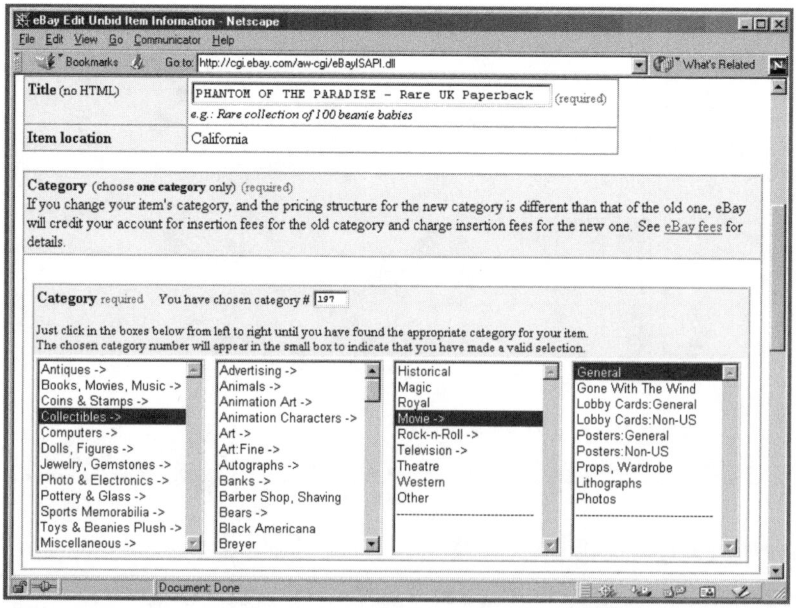

figure 19-3

In the first part of the item update form, you can modify your item's title and category.

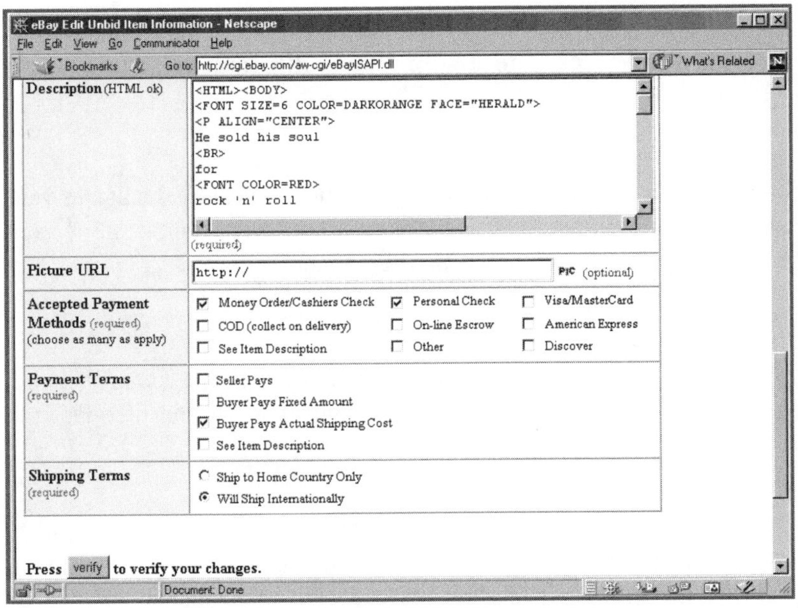

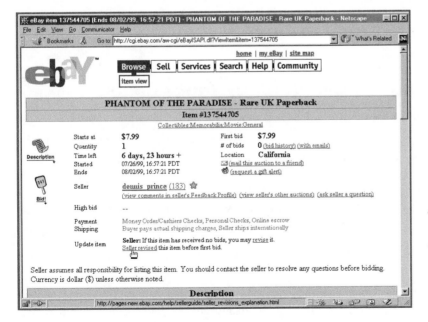

figure 19-4

Scroll down further in the update item form to make changes to the description, payment methods, payment terms, and shipping terms.

figure 19-5

Once you've made a revision to your listing (before receiving any bids), eBay will report that a revision has been made. Just FYI to those bidders out there.

Update item heading: *Seller revised this item before first bid.* This lets all bidders know that you made a change to some item information; that's just a benefit to the bidders to know about the revision.

 NOTE The words *Seller revised* are actually a link when they appear in your revised Item Details screen. If you click on it, you'll jump another eBay page that explains what seller revisions are and what they mean.

 NOTE eBay doesn't report *what* changed about the item, just that it was changed. It's another way that eBay is working to promote honesty and information to all bidders.

 NOTE Notice that you can't change *everything* about an item. You can't change the item number, location, minimum bid, reserve price, auction duration, or any special listing features you might have originally chosen. Item updates are just for the smaller details. If you really need to change some of the elements I've just mentioned, you'll need to end your auction early and start again. You'll learn how that's done a little later in this chapter.

Changing the Category for Your Auction

Here's a useful option: if ever you want to change the category of your auction listing, you can, even while the auction's running and getting bids. In fact, you can change the auction category as many times as you like.

Typically, you wouldn't change the category more than once or twice—you might have chosen the wrong category when you first listed or thought to use a better one once the auction was under way. No matter. Changing the category of your auction is fast and simple.

 NOTE In the discussion about revising an item, you saw that was one way to change an item's category *before* any bids had been placed.

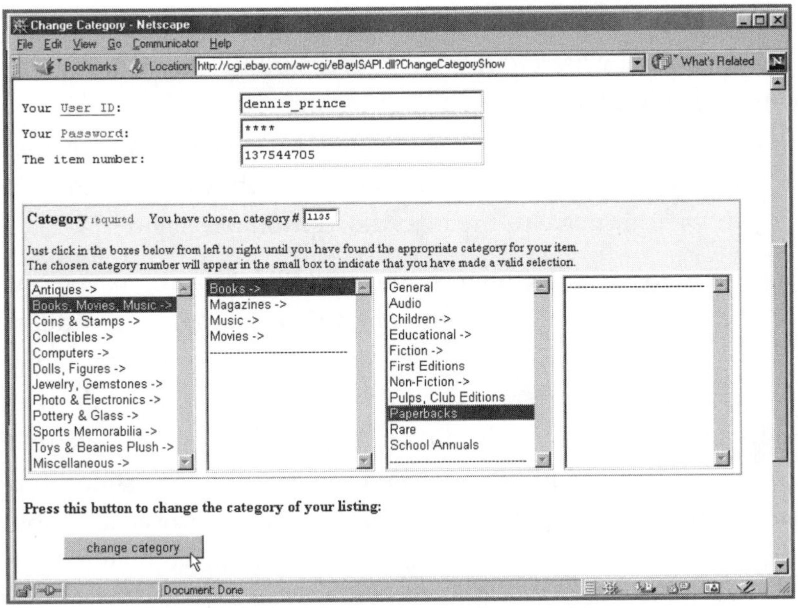

figure 19-6

Change the category of your
auction item using this simple
form.

First, click on *Services* from the eBay main navigation bar, then choose the
submenu selection *Buying & selling*. Once in the *Buying and Selling Tools*
page, find the link labeled *Change the category of your item* and click on it.
When you do, you'll find a screen like the one shown in Figure 19-6.

Just enter your user ID, your password, the item number, and then choose
from the categories just as you did when first listing your item. When you've
selected the category you want, click on the *Change category* button shown
at the bottom of Figure 19-6. That's it. Easy, huh?

Adding to Your Item

Once you've received even one bid on your item, you no longer have the
option of revising your listing. But what if you need to add some information
or maybe tack on an additional image? Well, you're not sunk yet. eBay comes
to the rescue again by giving sellers a way to add to their item descriptions.

To add to your item's description (it's all you can really add at this point since the other item details are what bidders based their bid decisions on), go to the eBay main navigation bar and select *Services* and then *Buying & selling*. Find the link labeled *Add to your item's description*. By clicking on that link, you'll find yourself in a new screen where you can verify who you are and what changes you want to make to the item description (see Figure 19-7).

Why might you need to add something to your item? Well, again, maybe you left out an important detail that you want all current and potential bidders to know about. Maybe another user pointed out some little fact you didn't know about your item or you weren't originally clear about; now you want everyone else to know it, too. Maybe you decided to add a new picture that better represents your item. Most often, you'll think about making additions to your auction when you keep getting the same questions over and over again from potential bidders. If enough people are e-mailing you and asking the same question, it's time to make an addition to your auction listing.

Whatever the reason for the addition, you can enter any text, HTML, or image pointers you want in the box labeled *The text to add to your description*.

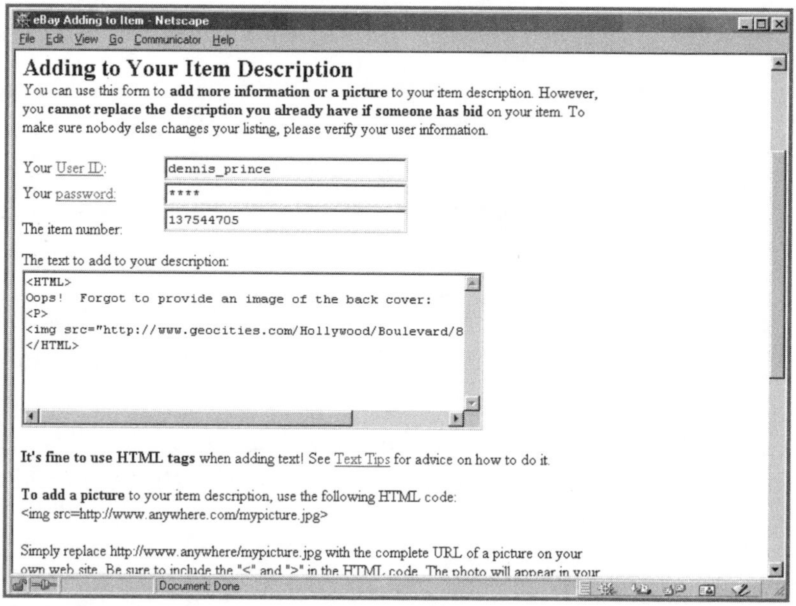

figure 19-7

Let eBay know who you are and what item number you want to add something to. It's that easy.

Once your information is added, scroll down a bit further in the screen and click on the *Review* button. When you do, you'll get to review your additions just like you reviewed the listing when you first started your auction (see Figure 19-8).

In Figure 19-8, you can see the effect of the addition I made. Since my addition was an image, I wanted to be sure eBay could find and display the image properly. When I was satisfied the addition was going to work, I just clicked on the *Add To Description* button. In standard eBay fashion, I got another confirmation screen that told me the addition was recorded successfully. Figure 19-9 confirms my addition went off without a hitch.

And, just to bring this to a close, look at the item description again, this time in the revised item details page, and you'll see how eBay recorded and displayed the addition (see Figure 19-10).

Looking at Figure 19-10, you're seeing the bottom of my item's description (I scrolled down so you could see the addition). See how eBay notes the date and time the addition was made? This is so bidders will know exactly when you added something to your auction's description. This might be especially

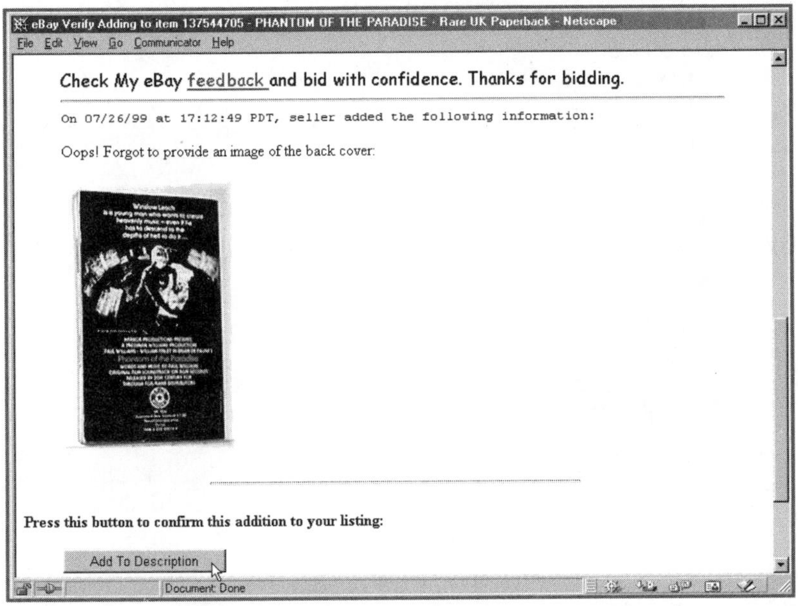

figure 19-8

Dang! I forgot to add an image of the backside of the item I'm auctioning. No matter—I can still add it relatively painlessly.

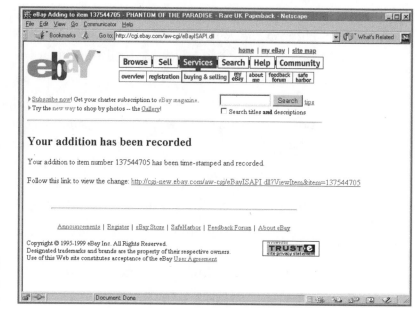

figure 19-9

As easy as pie, you can add to your auction's description.

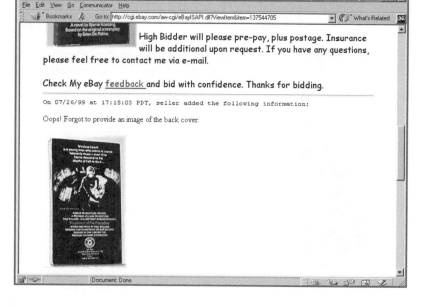

figure 19-10

When you add something, eBay displays the new information with a date and time stamp to show when the addition was made.

important to someone who has already bid—people always want to know if you're making additions after they've bid. Again, this is all in the interest of being as up-front and informative as possible about any changes made to live auction listings.

 ALERT Think those additions through, carefully! When you add to your active listing, you give bidders a valid reason to retract their bids. If any addition you make can be interpreted as changing the overall identification or presentation of the item, a bidder can rightfully bail out.

Cross-Listing Your Auctions

Here's a neat thing to do to enhance your active auction listings and possibly increase your bids. When you have more than one auction running simultaneously, try cross-listing them.

A cross-listing is basically a pointer to other auctions you have running on eBay. First, recall that on every auction detail page, there's a link titled *View seller's other auctions*. When anyone clicks on that link in one of your listings, they'll be able to see what else you might be auctioning. That works fine, but it's not real catchy to the eye; the link is kind of small and the result is simply a title listing of the seller's other auctions.

A flashier way to get bidders to visit your other auctions is to use those great images you have, combined with the HTML anchor tag; just like I anchored the lobby card image in my *It Conquered the World* listing, you can show thumbnail images of your other auction items across all your listings. Figure 19-11 shows one way I used a cross-listing.

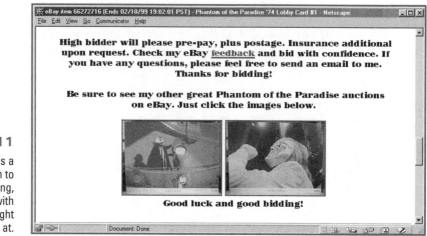

figure 19-11

Using image anchors is a great way to bring attention to other auctions you're running, advertising them along with the item a bidder might presently be looking at.

In a previous auction (shown in Figure 19-11), I actually had three lobby cards from the same film up for auction at the same time. Through cross-posting, I included the images of the other two cards in each item details page. This way, a bidder who might be interested in the film could see that I had other, similar items that might be tempting. To avoid being obnoxious about the cross-listing and to avoid detracting from the item the bidder was currently looking at, I put the cross-listed image anchors at the end of the item description.

Now, the trick about doing cross-listings is that you'll need the eBay item details page URL to anchor to. Remember, that's the URL that eBay provides onscreen when you successfully list your auction (refer back to Figure 16-12) and again in the e-mail confirmation of your auction; it's the official Web address of your auction listing. The URL is something you'll get only *after* you've started the auctions you're planning to cross-list. If you guessed you'll need to use either the item revision or item addition function to do your cross-listing, you guessed right.

Because I planned to do the cross-listing from the outset, I added the three lobby card listings, got the URLs, then made the HTML code changes to my item descriptions using the *Revise* option before I received any bids on the items. (I used that lag time between when I list an item and eBay grabs it to tuck in the updated item listings information.) Here's the HTML I added to the item description you see in Figure 19-11:

```
Be sure to see my other great Phantom of the Paradise
auctions on eBay. Just click the images below.

<P>

<A HREF="http://cgi.ebay.com/aw-cgi/eBayISAPI.
dll?ViewItem&item=58888495">

<IMG HEIGHT=150 WIDTH=200 SRC="http://www.geocities.com/
Hollywood/Boulevard/8785/potp5.jpg" ALT="Lobby Card #5"></A>

<A HREF="http://cgi.ebay.com/aw-
cgi/eBayISAPI.dll?ViewItem&item=58889743">

<IMG HEIGHT=150 WIDTH=200 SRC="http://www.geocities.com/
Hollywood/Boulevard/8785/potp6.jpg" ALT="Lobby Card #6"></A>

<BR>

Good luck and good bidding!
```

You can see in the HTML code I added, I used the actual eBay auction listing URLs as the anchors and then applied those to thumbnail images (using the HEIGHT and WIDTH tags to resize the images) that a bidder could easily click on. In my days of retail sales, this was called "suggestive selling." You know, kind of like when the guys at the local electronics store ask if you want a stereo or computer to go with that pack of batteries you're buying. Well, maybe not that ambitious, but you get the idea. In my auction listings, the cross-listings are there to say, *"If you like this film, you might be interested in these other lobby cards I have for auction, too."*

Canceling Your Auction

And now the cloud of dread moves overhead. What if you're looking at your auction listing and thinking, *"Well, crap. This is a complete mess and it's beyond hope. I've completely screwed up and everyone's going to see it. Now what?"* You're not alone; it's happened to me, too. Sometimes the listing of your dreams turns out to be a nightmare instead. It's important that the listing properly represents the item you're auctioning. Sometimes it all goes hooey regardless of your efforts to salvage it. So, if it doesn't fit, you must . . . uh . . . quit.

If you were in a bit of a hurry when you listed your item and overlooked something important like the duration or minimum bid amount (meaning what's specified isn't what you want after all), then a revision or addition is clearly out. There's only one thing to do: eject!

If no one's bid on your auction, you can just cancel it without any further fanfare. When you cancel your auction, you'll just stop it dead in its tracks, and it will all be over. To do this, just go back to the handy-dandy *Buying and Selling Tools* page and select the link labeled *End your auction early*—that's really what you're doing; ending it before the scheduled end date.

NOTE What about your listing fees? Remember, those are nonrefundable at the time you list. However, if your auction ends or you cancel it before bids have been received, you can relist. If the item sells the second time around, eBay will refund the insertion fee (but not special option fees, such as *Featured* status, a bold title, and so on). See the section titled "Relisting Your Item" later in this chapter.

As an example, I'll show you how I ended the first listing of the *It Conquered the World* lobby card. After I clicked on the *End your auction early* link, I was taken to a page titled *Ending your auction* (see Figure 19-12).

So, again you need to verify that you're *you* before you can end the auction. Enter your user ID, password, and the item number of the auction that you're going to end. After that, click on the *End auction* button. Zap! It's gone, right? Well, not yet; eBay's going to give you a bit of auction management counseling first. Look at Figure 19-13.

Figure 19-13 shows you another of the familiar verification screens. eBay reminds you to consider your action if you have a high bidder on your auction or if you're just impatient about getting bids (and reminds you about those Johnny-bid-lately snipers). You don't want to jump the gun. But for now, just assume no one's bid and you really want to cancel the auction; that's the case in this example. Click on the *End auction* button and you'll jump to one more screen, shown in Figure 19-14.

And with that last button click, eBay confirms that your auction is over. A premature burial to say the least, but it's your option if you need to use it. You can now move on to create the auction listing you really wanted.

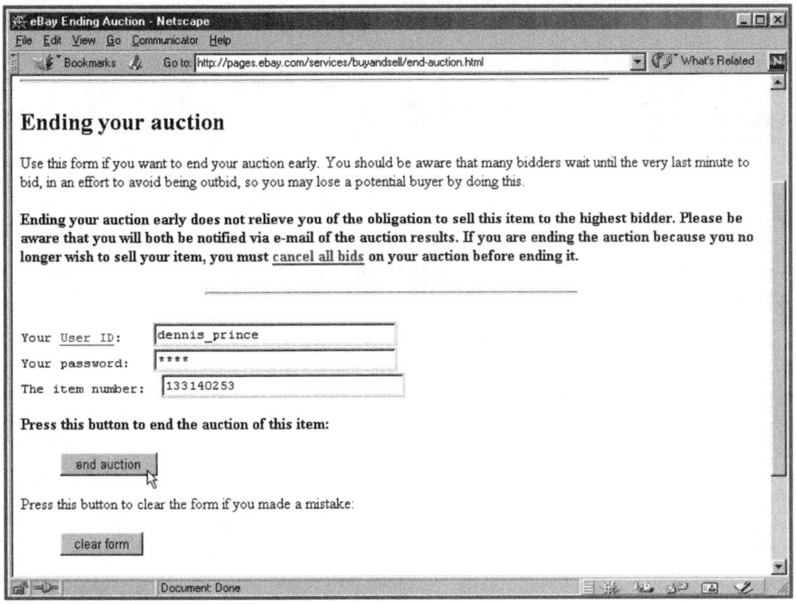

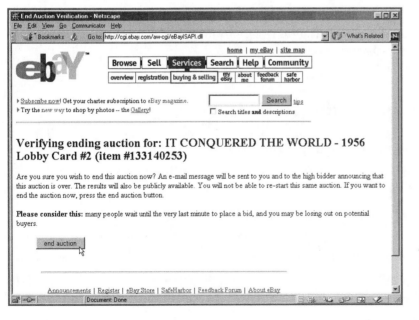

figure 19-12

Sorry, but that text version of the *It Conquered the World* lobby card just didn't look like it would scare up enough bidders.

figure 19-13

eBay just wants you to be sure you know what you're doing. Are you sure?

figure 19-14

That's it. You've gone and done it. Your auction has ended early. Congratulations?

NOTE After you end an auction early, if you intend to relist the item, you'll find an eBay feature that makes it real easy to do. You'll read about relisting an item a bit later in this chapter.

It's the Last Day and Still No Bids

Assuming again that your listing really looks great, it has all the right information, and it really promotes your item well, you might find yourself wondering, "*Well, how come nobody's bidding?*"

Is it the last day of your auction, and you're still waiting for someone to place the minimum starting bid? Welcome to the club. Sometimes your auction is an immediate draw, and other times it tends to just draw out. How come? Who knows? One thing's for sure: often, a watched auction gathers no bids. I think Aesop said that (or was it eSop?).

Well, if the auction's not yet over, then just let it ride. You never know; someone might be watching your auction and waiting to snipe at the last moment (kind of an honor, really; your auction being worthy of a snipe). Remember the discussion in Chapter 13 about bidding strategies? Maybe there are several bidders-to-be who just aren't looking at your auction—at least that's what they want everyone else to think. Wait it out. Snipers hate it when they case an auction for days and the seller winds up closing the thing down early. D'oh!

While you're waiting for the auction to end, review the way you worded your item description, the category you put it in, the minimum bid, or anything else that might render your auction isolated, passed over, or generally avoided. Maybe some revisions or additions are needed before the auction ends.

When Bidding Activity Stalls

But how about when your auction went live and was met with several quick and well-priced bids? Great! You're a hit. It's always fun to see some quick reaction to your listing. It's encouraging and kind of exciting. You'll hope it never stops.

Then, it does stop. All of a sudden, no more bids. Your auction seems stagnant. It just sits there looking for another excited bidder like the ones who came by a few days ago. Hey, where did everybody go?

In many auctions, you might see some active bidding when the listing first shows up on the listing pages and search results. It's new goods on the auction block. It has the "new" icon in the listing pages, and it catches people's eye. After your item's been around a couple of days, though, it can kind of get lost among all the other items that have aged out of the new status. Don't worry, though; your item's not destined for the Island of Misfit Toys.

Actually, the mid-auction lull is common. Thinking of applied bidding strategy, the early bids could have been those folks looking to stake their claim on your item. They wanted to bid the perceived market value first and some may have fought it out a bit in the beginning. Then they wait. It's the old game of cat and mouse: who's going to be lurking around to place that last-minute snipe? Who's been hanging back since the auction began, keeping their identity secret? The action could very well pick up again on the final day (remember the *Jaws* snipe from Chapter 13—the high bid more than *doubled* within the last thirty seconds).

Also, if your auction received a bunch of bids right away and the high bid value increased very quickly, it might have already found its market price. Once someone has reached or eclipsed the perceived value of the item, the auction's pretty much over for all intents and purposes. Still, wait it out until the end. You might see more bids before it's all over.

Reasons to End an Auction Early

Now I want to take you back to the reasons why you would end an auction early. You learned how to do this when your auction listing turned out to be a disaster. But, assuming the listing was fine, you can still choose to end your auction early whenever you like. However, there are some consequences you might run into if you decide to cut your auction short.

First, the other reasons you might decide to close your auction early—other than if it's just messed up. Again, maybe no one's bidding on your item or the bidding has stalled. It's a bit of a disappointment, and you might want to throw in the towel. Don't. Remember that snipers might be lurking in the pixels out there, waiting to pounce at the last moment; give them that opportunity. You might still make a sale or get one more high bid before it's all over. If you just don't want to stick it out, then end your auction and be done with it. If there are no bidders, there's no problem; if there are bidders, you'll just sell to the high bidder of the moment.

Next, you could decide to end the auction early because someone asked you to. Really? Why would someone *ask* me to end an auction early? Am I being *gonged*? Don't they like my auction? Actually, they might like it a lot, and that's why they want you to end it.

You might get an e-mail message from a potential buyer who wants to make an outright offer for your item, asking you to close the auction early and sell the item right now. Is this bad? Maybe not. The person contacting you might want the item but is just too impatient to wait for the auction to naturally expire. Or maybe this person doesn't want to chance other bidders' possibly outbidding or upping the high bid as the auction progresses. This is where you'll need to make a choice: do you accept this offer (which is a sure deal for a set amount), or wait it out until the end? If you wait, the bidder might decide to retract the offer. (Of course, if this bidder has the current high bid, then *that* bid will have to be honored if it wins). But, maybe the immediate offer is higher than the current high bid. If the offer is retracted, you might lose that extra profit. Hmmm . . . decisions, decisions.

TIP If you ever decide, as buyer, to see if a seller will end an auction early, be sure your immediate offer is higher than the current high bid. If you're the current high bidder, you need to give the seller some extra incentive to cut off other bidders that might come along. Don't insult the seller by offering only what your current bid is. If you're not the current high bidder, you'll need to bid in the auction until you are. This, of course, might or might not work to your plan, depending upon how much it will cost to make you high bidder.

SOAPBOX I was once asked by a bidder to end two auctions I had running. The guy asking was the high bidder on both, but he didn't want the potential competition the auctions might bring. He made a nice offer for the items—higher than his high bids at the time—but I thought the items would do real well and decided not to end my auctions early. He stuck it out with me, and ended up still being the high bidder but at a lower price than his early-close offer. In a way, I lost. In a way, he won. In a word, *damn*. At least he was kind enough not to rub my nose in it.

ALERT If you're sitting there curling your toes at my nonchalant discussion of offers to end auctions early, rest assured that I *know* eBay frowns on this sort of activity, considering it an unfair practice in the general rules of the auction. However, as eBay is a venue and, so long as a buyer and seller are in agreement and are not unfairly cutting off or scamming another user, I contend the matter is up to you. But if you go asking for eBay's advice, don't expect much gleeful assistance.

Back to other reasons why you might end your auction early, consider what might happen if your item meets some terrible fate. I'm thinking about if it gets busted, broken, torn, trashed, lost, messed up, jacked up, or blown away. If *anything* happens to an item you're auctioning that makes it less than what you described—by completeness or condition—then it's time to yank that auction quickly.

If you have kids, for Heaven's sake, get those auction items out of reach. Kids love to handle, fondle, fold, spindle, and mutilate neat items that people might be bidding on. Save yourself the heartache; if you're auctioning it, store it away in a safe place. Please?

OK, now you have a bunch of reasons for ending your auction early. What, then, do you do if your auction has a high bid but the high bidder hasn't asked or isn't aware that an early closure is looming? What will that bidder think? Do? Whatever it is, it'll probably be loud. You'd better contact that bidder first.

If your auction has a reserve price and it hasn't been met, you can end your auction without much trouble at all. Just end it. Out of courtesy, you'll probably want to send an e-mail notification to the high bidder to announce that you've stopped the auction. That message might inspire a final offer; entertain the proposal unless you just don't want to or can't sell the item anymore.

If your auction has a legitimate high bidder, then by eBay policy you are beholden to that bidder to sell your item at that high bid price. (Of course, it works the same way when you *do* want to sell your item; the high bidder is obligated to honor the bid.) So what do you say to your high bidder if your item is no longer going to be available? Hmmm. How are you at tap dancing? This might not set too well with that bidder. Still, if it must be done, do your best to be sincere in explaining why your auction is closing and why you'll not be able to offer the item, regardless of the current high bid. Maybe you'll get off easy and the bidder will understand. Maybe the bidder won't be so happy and will possibly leave negative feedback for you—that's the bidder's right in a situation like this. Ending your auction early and refusing to sell is a lot like retracting a bid: it's frowned upon and makes you look like a novice. Do what you have to do, but be more careful next time. It's OK; the community will give you a second chance.

Canceling Bids on Your Auction

Well, that doesn't sound like a very friendly thing to do! Why on Earth would you want to cancel bids that have been placed on your item? Actually, eBay doesn't want to see anyone cancel bids because it means something's not going well for either a seller or a bidder. Therefore, so sellers won't fall into canceling bids willy-nilly, eBay cautions that bid cancellations should only be performed by sellers for good reasons:

■ **A bidder contacts the seller and wishes to back out of a bid**. This is an alternative to the bidder performing a bid retraction; the seller could consider performing the cancellation from that side. This isn't always a bad thing—maybe the bidder goofed and wants to get rid of the bad bid and bid again. It's up to the seller on this one.

■ **The seller can't properly identify or contact a certain bidder**. This is a case where maybe a bidder has negative feedback, and the seller wishes to contact that bidder to make sure this is a serious bid. If the seller is unable to establish two-way communication with a bidder, the seller is free to cancel that bidder's bid.

■ **The seller has decided not to sell the item after all**. Did I mention you can end your auction early if you just don't want to sell the item anymore? You can. Maybe you listed it in an act of whimsy or loss of good judgment. Maybe you were listing the item for a friend who later decided to keep the thing after all. Who knows. If you've changed your mind and don't want to sell after all, you can end your auction—but you'll need to cancel all bids first.

Canceling bids is easy. Again, visit that *Buying and Selling Tools* page and find the link titled *Cancel bids on my item*. Using that link will take you to a bid cancellation screen as shown in Figure 19-15.

As you can see in the bid cancellation screen, you'll need to enter your user ID and password, the item number, the user ID of the bidder whose bid you're canceling, and an explanation for canceling the bid.

When you cancel a bid in one of your auctions, the result will be a note in the *Bid history* page for the item (refer back to Figure 14-7; bid cancellations appear in the same place as bid retractions). As you know, the bid history is public access information; be sure you have good reason for a cancellation. If you feel right, then do it.

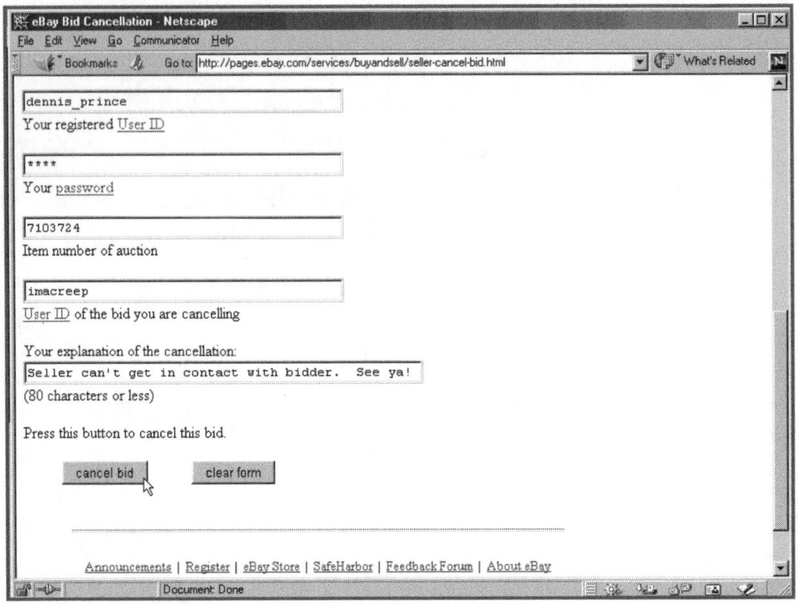

figure 19-15

There's a special place on eBay to cancel bids in your auction. Use it judiciously, though.

Keeping Track of Your Auctions

Managing auctions is even more important when you're the seller than when you're the buyer. It's not too difficult to do, but you'll be glad you put in the effort to monitor what you're selling, when you're selling it, and to whom you'll be selling it.

The discussion in Chapter 14 introduced the many tools eBay provides that help you track your auctions. You can use the eBay Search page, using the Seller Search function (for both current and completed auctions). That's probably the most straightforward tool to use when you want to regularly monitor activity right up to the closing of your auctions (it's hard not to get in the habit of counting those proverbial chickens).

You can also use the My eBay tool to perform a more detailed search and listing of your auctions. You used that before to get the details of the auctions you were bidding in; you can also use it to get the details of the auctions you're hosting. The detail is the same except that, instead of My eBay reporting what your maximum bid was (when you're buying), it will report what your reserve price is (when you're selling). Figure 19-16 shows you what the My eBay detail looks like for the auctions you are hosting.

Remember, the eBay Search page and My eBay will only provide details of auction activity (buying or selling) from the past 30 days. If you're anything like me, you're going to want some more durable records that can provide a longer-running history of your auctions; they also come in handy if you run into any disputes or difficulties long after an auction has ended. Since these two eBay tools are limited in their time horizon, you might want to create some sort of tracking tool of your own.

 NOTE Disputes and difficulties? Like what? Well, what if a buyer claims to have sent the payment and not received the item? Do you have some record that you did or didn't get the money?

What if a buyer says the item never arrived long after you said it was on the way? Do you have a record of when and how you shipped it?

These are just a couple of details that eBay can't track for you. They bear some careful consideration, though.

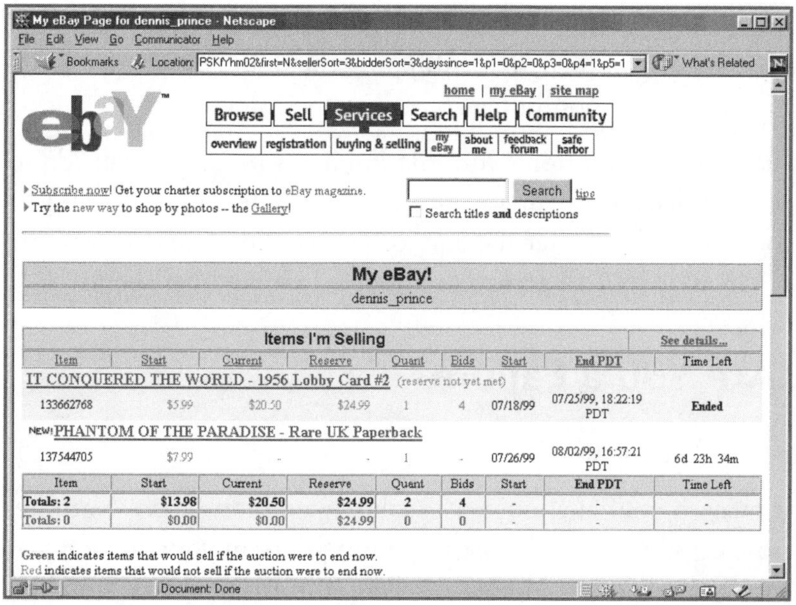

![My eBay Page for dennis_prince - Netscape screenshot showing the My eBay page with Items I'm Selling table]

Item	Start	Current	Reserve	Quant	Bids	Start	End PDT	Time Left
IT CONQUERED THE WORLD - 1956 Lobby Card #2 (reserve not yet met)								
133662768	$5.99	$20.50	$24.99	1	4	07/18/99	07/25/99, 18:22:19 PDT	Ended
NEW! PHANTOM OF THE PARADISE - Rare UK Paperback								
137544705	$7.99	-	-	1	-	07/26/99	08/02/99, 16:57:21 PDT	6d 23h 34m

Item	Start	Current	Reserve	Quant	Bids	Start	End PDT	Time Left
Totals: 2	$13.98	$20.50	$24.99	2	4	-	-	-
Totals: 0	$0.00	$0.00	$24.99	0	0	-	-	-

Green indicates items that would sell if the auction were to end now.
Red indicates items that would not sell if the auction were to end now.

figure 19-16

My eBay is back! This time, it's your helper to track the details of the auctions you're hosting.

In Chapter 14 I explained some of the details about your bidding activity that you might want to track in a spreadsheet of some sort. You can extend that spreadsheet—or create an entirely new one—to track the auctions you'll host. This is what I do. I'll keep all of the information eBay offers me (high bidder ID, high bid value, number of bids, auction dates, and so on) but I also like to keep some additional bits of information for the longer haul:

- High bidder's surname
- High bidder's mailing address (snail mail)
- Date bidder was notified about payment
- Date bidder responded that payment is being sent
- Date payment was received
- Method of payment (money order, personal check, or whatever)
- Insurance requested?
- Date item shipped
- Shipping method and tracking number (if any)

This is all information that might come in handy as you complete your auction, receive payment, and prepare for shipping the item. You'll learn more about how to close the auction in Part 5 of this book.

I know that tracking the additional information in a spreadsheet will add to your auction workload, but it might save a lot of time and headaches. If something goes wrong long after the auction has closed, would you rather have those key facts at your fingertips or struggle to remember them?

If It Doesn't Sell, Are You a Failure?

"They're all gonna laugh at you."

What does it mean if your auction gets absolutely no bids? Zilch. Nothing. Nada. Big goose eggs. Really, it doesn't mean much except your auction just got passed over. Nobody cares. After all, you are competing with 2.5 million other listings. Of course, it's good to take a moment to reflect on what might have caused your auction to go untouched.

Go back to research mode. See if other auctions similar or identical to yours were taking place at the same time. If so, did those auctions get bids? If they did, check the other sellers' pricing strategies, descriptions, or anything else that looks different from your listing. Maybe you need to make a few adjustments and have another go-round.

When you're performing this post-auction research, be especially keen to see if the auction market was flooded with items like yours. If so, you'll probably want to wait for another time when there are fewer of the item to choose from, giving your auction more of the spotlight.

While you're at it, research the larger market, too. Go outside of eBay and check the Internet for any information about what you're selling. Maybe there was some sort of breaking news about your kind of item.

The bottom line is that practically everyone has auctions that don't get bid on. The thing to keep in mind, outside of possibly being overoptimistic in your bidding expectations, is that you probably just haven't found the right bidder and that bidder hasn't found your item. Many items can sit in the listings without a single bid, be listed again, and get all kinds of bids. I can't say I know why this happens, but it does. You'll just need to be patient as you wait to find your bidder.

 N0TE If your item doesn't receive any bids, you won't be charged any further eBay fees (commissions). Your original listing fee, however, is gone and you won't be able to reclaim that. It's just part of the small cost to get your item in front of those 5.6 million bidders.

Relisting Your Item

So, what about relisting an item that doesn't sell? That's fine. You're always free to list something for auction as many times as you like (provided it's not offensive or illegal or something). Relisting is just another of those helpful features you'll find on eBay.

Relisting an item is actually easier than listing it the first time. If your auction has ended—either by natural causes or by premeditated termination—and there were no winning bids, just revisit the item details screen. Your closed auction would look something like the one you see in Figure 19-17.

In Figure 19-17, you can see the link *Relist this item,* where the pointer is pointing. See, not only will it be easy to relist, but there's a potential refund awaiting you, too. So, click on that *relist* link, and you'll whisk away to the item relisting screen shown in Figure 19-18.

As you can see in Figure 19-18, relisting your item will really be a breeze; it has almost all the original information still in the listing form. Just enter your password, make any title, category, or payment and shipment changes that you'd like, and move on to review the item description. If you used HTML in your description, it will all still be there.

TIP   If you used images in your listing, be sure those images are still stored where your IMG SRC= tags are pointing. If your images have been moved or deleted, you'll need to get them to a place where eBay can access them again.

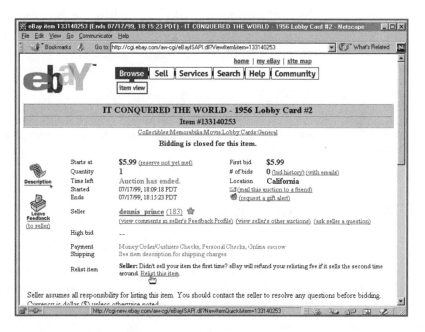

figure 19-17

When the auction's over, you might still be able to breathe life back into it if the item didn't sell the first time around.

The screenshot shows a Netscape browser window titled "eBay Sell Item - Netscape" with the following form fields:

UserID / Password	dennis_prince
	User ID or E-mail address Password (forgotten it?)
Title (no HTML)	IT CONQUERED THE WORLD - 1956 Lobby Card #2 (required)
	e.g.: Rare collection of 100 beanie babies
Item location	California (required)
	e.g.: San Jose, California
Item location zip code	95765 (required for items in USA)
	e.g.: 95125
Country where the item is located	United States (required)

Category (choose **one category** only) (required)
Fees for items within Vehicles and Real Estate categories were changed on April 24, 1999. These changes will limit the total fees charged to sellers for items listed in these categories, regardless of the selling price of the item. Many sellers will find that this new pricing structure provides lower total fees for items sold in these categories.
See eBay fees for details.

Antiques: -
Coins & Stamps: -
Computers: -
Books, Movies, Music: -
Collectibles: Memorabilia: Movie: Lobby Cards: General
Dolls, Figures: -

figure 19-18
The Relist Your Item screen uses the same form as when you listed the first time.

Move on to verify the pricing and duration of your relisting. Choose any special appearance features and, when you're satisfied, move on to verify your listing by clicking on the *Review* button. The review process is the same and, when you're ready, click on the *Submit my listing* button. That's it. You'll get the same verification and e-mail confirmation of your relisted item just as you did when you listed it the first time. Isn't that easy?

Don't forget, you'll be able to receive a refund on the insertion fee you're charged by eBay when you relist your item. You will be charged a fee for inserting (listing) your item even though this is a relisting. If your auction didn't receive any bids the first time around or you had a reserve price that wasn't met, and then the item sells the second time around, the insertion fee you were charged during the relisting will be refunded to your eBay account.

 The cost of special listing options like *Featured* status, a bold title, Gallery, and others are not refundable on relistings.

There are a few minor conditions to getting the relisting insertion fee refund:

- You have to relist your item within 30 days of the first listing's closing.

- Your first auction can't have received any bids if it was a straight auction. If it was a Reserve Price auction, it can't have had the reserve price met.

- You have to relist the original item; you can't use the relisting feature to list an entirely different item.

The conditions shouldn't be hard to meet when you're relisting your item. Given how easy it is to relist, the rebate you can receive is a great incentive to give your auction another chance.

part 5

After the Auction

chapter 20

Closing the Auction and Making Contact

Whether you're bidder or seller, the day comes when an auction ends on eBay. Maybe there was a last-minute flurry of activity: perhaps an auction of yours was nabbed by a last-minute sniper; perhaps you were a last-minute sniper yourself in an auction you wanted to win. Whatever your role, that item details page will soon display those words, *"Bidding is closed for this item."* All right, but now what happens?

When you bid in auctions or hold auctions of your own on eBay, it sometimes takes on a kind of surreal sense. After all, this is just a Web site on the Net. It's like entertainment where people play an auction game, wondering who's got the skill, knowledge, and determination to be the high bidder. And when the virtual gavel has dropped, you sit there and think, *"Well, that was fun."* Yes, it was fun, and now it's time to enjoy the benefits of that game: collecting your prize or collecting your money.

You're going back into the physical world where real people exist, and it's time to engage in a real-world exchange. Some people think this is where the hard work begins. To a degree, they're right, but this *is* the whole point of eBay: getting people together to trade their wares.

Last Bids

Potentially the most exciting time in an auction is just before it closes. The adrenaline is rushing both for those who intend to snipe and those who are hanging on, hoping their maximum bid will thwart the last-second attacks. The apathetic clock just ticks along while you and I and any other interested parties out there race to reach the finish line and snatch the title of "High Bidder."

If you're bidding, know the item you're bidding on and use the right strategy that will make you victorious. If you're selling, just sit back and see what happens. Soon enough, it will all be over, and you'll be ready to move on to the next stage of the auction excitement.

Assessing Your eBay Commission and Account Status

Well, if you're a seller, this is the time you'll pay the cyber-piper. It's time for the commission to be calculated for the item you've just auctioned based on the final high bid. The commission, you'll recall, is the percentage you pay to eBay for the opportunity to use the site for auctioning your item.

Here's how the commission is calculated:

- First you pay 5 percent of the amount of the high bid (at the auction close) up to a high bid value of $25.

- Then you pay an additional 2.5 percent fee on any amount of the high bid that is within the price range of $25.01 to $1,000.

- And last, you pay 1.25 percent of the remaining high bid amount that exceeds $1,000. If you're real lucky, you'll be paying this percentage.

So, for example, here's what the commission would be for an item that sells for a high bid of $1,200:

- 5 percent of the first $25 = $1.25.

- 2.5 percent of the amount between $25.01 and $1,000 ($974.99) = $24.37.

- 1.25 percent of the amount above $1,000 ($200) = $2.50.

In the end, for the item that found a $1,200 high bid, the commission the seller would need to pay would equal $28.12. Now, depending on what kind of opening bid or reserve price the seller chose, the listing fee charged would cost, at the highest, $2. Assuming that to be the case, the final cost to the seller for this auction would be $30.12. The seller clears a final profit of $1169.88. I'd gladly pay $30.12 to see that kind of return on my item.

NOTE A few notes here: First, in the case of a Dutch auction, the eBay commission will be based on the lowest successful bid price multiplied by the total quantity of items sold.

Then remember that choosing any of the special fonts, icons, or featured auction status for your item, will add to the cost of your original listing fee.

And, if you're a bidder, remember there is no charge from eBay for that. You'll just need to pay for the item if you're the high bidder.

The eBay charges (listing fees and commission) are captured in the seller's active eBay account. Your eBay account will track the fees you owe to eBay, and you can review your account status any time you like.

If you want to see how your account is looking, use the eBay main navigation bar, selecting *Services*. Then choose the submenu selection labeled *Buying & selling*. You'll find a link labeled *Check my seller account status* on the *Buying and Selling Tools* page. Click it and you'll see an Account Status entry screen as shown in Figure 20-1.

You can see from Figure 20-1 that there are some options available regarding how much of your account information you want to see; you can choose from a variety of selection criteria that will report just the amount of account activity you're interested in. You can even choose to see *all* of your account activity since the day you first registered at eBay. (It'll take a while, though; better go get something to eat while you're waiting.)

TIP Your eBay account information isn't subject to 30-day aging like the auction listings. It's *all* there for you to see.

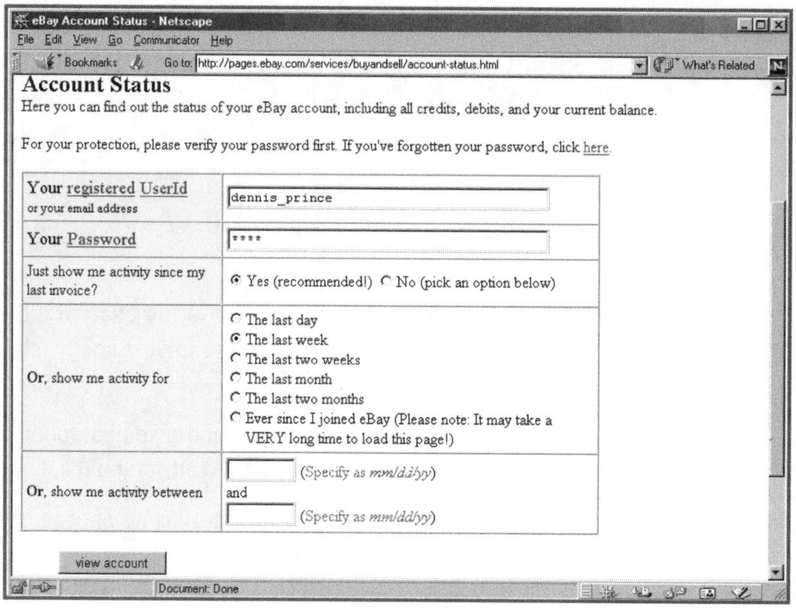

figure 20-1

If you want to check out your current account status, enter your registered user information and select the account information you want to see.

As an example, I chose to view my recent account status changes. To see the results, I just clicked on the *View account* button (lower left in Figure 20-1). The result is shown in Figure 20-2.

The account status page is self-explanatory; you'll see the list of charges (or credits) that have been assessed to your eBay account. Remember, if you're only bidding at eBay, you won't have any of these sorts of charges applied to your account.

At the top of the page, you can see quite plainly the current balance in your account; for me, it's a balance of $1.50 that I owe eBay for past auctions I've held. Below that, you can see some information about you and how your personal eBay account is identified.

As for the rest, here's what you're seeing in the detailed activity table on the account status page:

- **Ref #.** eBay's own reference number for the account activity the site is recording for you.

- **Date.** This is the date of the activity.

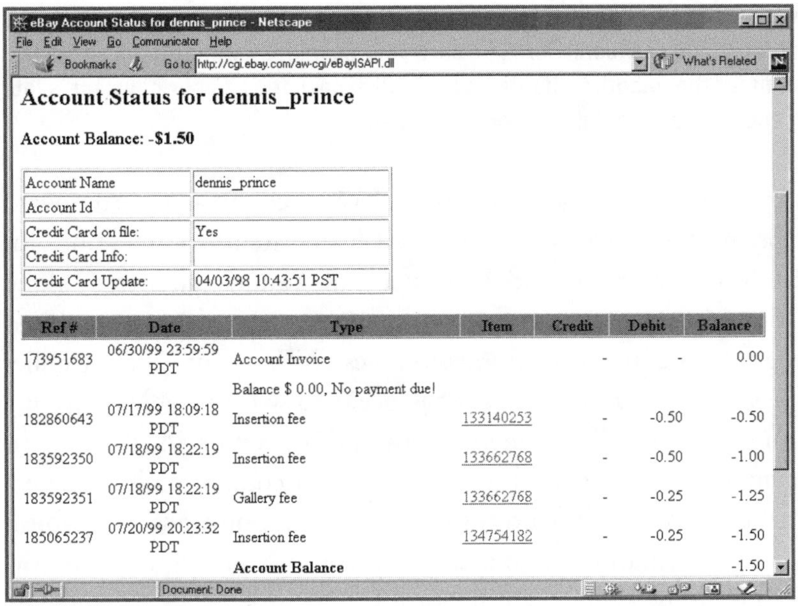

figure 20-2
The account status page shows the activity and charges for the items you've auctioned.

- **Type**. The kind of activity that prompted the entry against your account. You might see auction insertion (listing) fees, commission fees, invoicing records, and maybe even a relisting credit.

- **Item**. This is the auction item number that the fee or credit is associated with.

- **Credit and Debit**. Quite simply, whether eBay's refunding money to you (credit) or billing you (debit).

- **Balance**. You'll see the cumulative balance of your account in this column.

eBay collects account fees on the first of every month for the auctions you've held during the previous month. If you have provided your credit card information to eBay, your eBay account will be automatically paid every month against your credit card. If you have not provided eBay with a credit card, you'll need to pay using a payment coupon—eBay's online payment form that you can print and use when mailing account payments. Find it from the main navigation bar (use *Services, buying & selling*, then click on *Make payments toward my account*).

NOTE When paying eBay with a payment coupon (you can use a check, money order, VISA, or MasterCard), be sure your payment reaches them by the last day of the month for that month's charges. eBay will assess fees if your payment is late and may suspend your account if you don't pay at all.

When you first register, eBay sets you up with a $10 credit—applied toward your future listing fees—which lets you start listing items for auction right away. The credit is not a freebie; it's kind of a loan. You just go merrily along your way listing items *until* you use up your $10 credit, through a combination of listing fees and auction commission fees. When your account tallies up to (maybe slightly over) a $10 debit balance, you won't be able to list any more items until you provide payment. At this point, you decide if you want to send a payment via snail mail (using the payment coupon plus a personal check, money order, or credit card information) or if you want to establish your credit card information in your seller's account, allowing all fees, now and in the future, to be charged automatically.

SOAPBOX I gave eBay my credit card information for automatic billing the moment my initial $10 credit limit was due and payable. I wanted to list more items, but I couldn't until eBay got paid that $10 loan. I didn't want to wait for my payment to crawl through the post office, so I keyed in my credit card number, and I've been a happy camper ever since. I have *never* run into any trouble as a result of giving eBay my credit card number; I just hold a lot of auctions and get the monthly bill. For me, it's better than the headache of remembering to send a payment.

If you don't want to let eBay automatically bill your credit card, then you'll need to send those payment coupons, along with your payment, to eBay's offices in Dallas, Texas.

How you pay your fees is entirely up to you; you should consider both options—credit card or payment coupons—based on your personal preferences. Since I want to get back to the discussion about the item you just won or sold, I'll simply direct you to eBay's information page about fees and billing: use the main navigation bar, select *Help*, select *Seller guide* from the submenu, then click on the link labeled *Fees*. You'll find all you need to know about how eBay assesses those fees and how they'll help you handle your account.

NOTE It's not necessary to wait for official billing from eBay before you close the auction with your high bidder. In fact, you wouldn't want to wait for eBay billing since that only occurs on the first day of each month.

eBay Notification

OK, assume the bills have all been paid, and it's back to the auction. Now that the auction has closed, you can expect to see some notification from eBay. Naturally, the first notification of an auction closing will be on the item details page.

Take a look at Figure 20-3; it's a closed auction where I was the high bidder—yippee. Take a look at the figure and notice the changes in the page now that the auction is closed.

Of course, you'll see just below the item title the words *"Bidding is closed for this item."* Big clue there. The amount shown to the right of *Currently* is the final high bid. Then, notice that to the right of *Time left* are the words *"Auction has ended"*—there is no time left. Over on the left-hand side of the

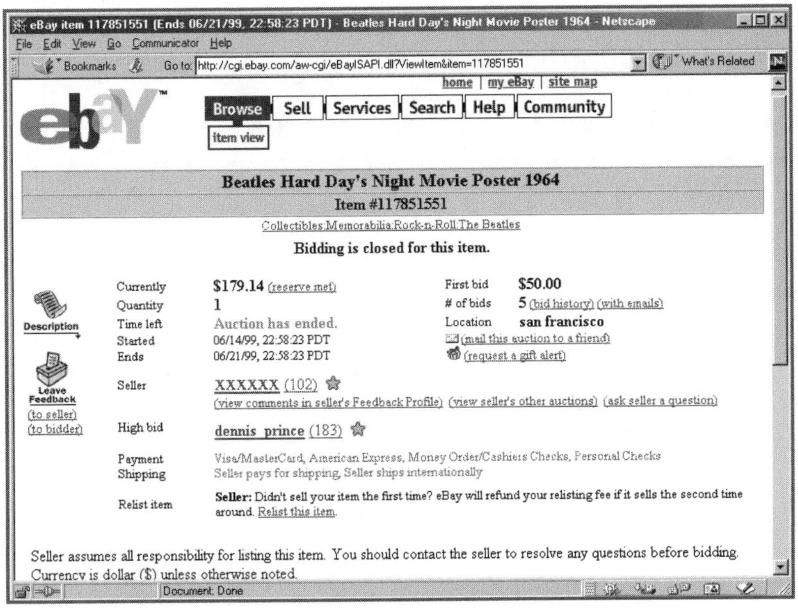

figure 20-3

When the auction's over, some of the elements of the item details page will change.

page, you'll see the *Leave Feedback* icon; this is where the bidder's paddle icon was once displayed while the auction was still active. And the last difference you'll see is the appearance of the relisting link near the bottom of the screen: *"Seller: Didn't sell your item the first time? eBay will refund your relisting fee if it sells the second time around. Relist this item."* (This is an eBay standard and shows up whether or not there was a successful high bid. You won't use it unless things didn't work out, of course.)

When an auction ends, that item will fall off the item listing pages and will no longer show up in the search results for active auctions. Since it is a completed auction, you'd need to look for it using the Completed Auctions search.

 NOTE Other good ways to find completed auctions are to use the Seller Search, selecting to see completed auctions, the Bidder Search, again with the completed auctions selection, or the actual URL of the auction's item details page. Remember that completed auctions are only displayable for 30 days after the auction has ended.

Besides the changes you'll see on eBay regarding a closed auction, both the high bidder and the seller will receive an e-mail message that tells of the completed auction: the *eBay End of Auction* notice. You'll see it arrive in your e-mail inbox and it looks like this:

• •

Subject: eBay End of Auction—Item # 117851551 (Beatles Hard Day's Night Movie Poster 1964)

From: aw-confirm@ebay.com

To: seller@someplace.net

CC: dlprince@bigfoot.com

Dear seller and dennis_prince,

DO NOT REPLY TO THIS MESSAGE. PLEASE ADDRESS YOUR MAIL DIRECTLY TO BUYER OR SELLER.

This message is to notify you that the following auction has ended:

Beatles Hard Day's Night Movie Poster 1964 (Item #117851551)

Final price: $179.14

Auction ended at: 06/21/99 22:58:23 PDT

Total number of bids: 5

Seller User ID: seller

Seller E-mail: seller@someplace.net

High-bidder User ID: dennis_prince

High-bidder E-mail: dlprince@bigfoot.com

Seller and high bidder should now contact each other to complete the sale.

IMPORTANT: buyer and seller should contact each other within three business days, or risk losing their right to complete this transaction.

The official results of this auction (including e-mail addresses of all bidders) can be found for 30 days after the auction closes at:

http://cgi3.ebay.com/aw-cgi/eBayISAPI.dll?ViewItem&item=117851551

If you won an auction in which the seller has at least a positive feedback rating of 10, you can send a gift alert. This is a great feature if you're buying gifts or if you're a little late on your gift-giving. To use this feature, see:

http://cgi3.ebay.com/aw-cgi/eBayISAPI.dll?ViewGiftAlert&item=65292204&userid=dennis_prince

If you have trouble contacting each other via e-mail:

http://pages.ebay.com/aw/user-query.html

Please leave feedback about your transaction:

http://cgi2.ebay.com/aw-cgi/eBayISAPI.dll?LeaveFeedbackShow&item=117851551

For other valuable "after the auction" needs:

http://pages.ebay.com/aw/postauction.html

• •

eBay has a new mailing address for sellers who mail checks and
money orders:

eBay, Inc.

P.O. Box 200945

Dallas, TX 75320-0945

This address is for check and money order payments only! All other
correspondence should still be mailed to:

eBay, Inc.

2005 Hamilton Avenue, Ste 350

San Jose, CA 95125

• •

Thank you for using eBay! If you have not already done so today,
it wouldn't hurt to mention eBay to a few of your friends!

http://www.ebay.com

Item Description:

This is the 14x22 window card version of the 1964 movie release,
full color and similar to one sheet, but smaller. Near mint
condition.

• •

Wow. Lots of information in that message. Most important, and this will set
the tone of how closing a auction will work, you'll read the first line in the
message, *"DO NOT REPLY TO THIS MESSAGE. PLEASE ADDRESS
YOUR MAIL DIRECTLY TO BUYER OR SELLER."* What does that mean?

These first two sentences are the epitome of what eBay is all about: it is a
venue for buyers and sellers to meet, and that's all. eBay doesn't get involved
in the actual transaction. Once the auction's over, the two people
involved—that's the high bidder and the seller—work between themselves
to bring closure to the deal. eBay provides some fringe benefits to the users
after their auctions are complete, but the physical deal is nothing that eBay
can get involved in.

SOAPBOX OK, this a prime opportunity for me to throw in my two cents. eBay's stance that it is not involved in the transaction or verifying the merchandise that changes hands can be a point of question for some users and many onlookers (you know, the busybodies who are casting stones but haven't tried the auction for themselves). However, with four years of online transactions under my belt, I really find this is the only way to fly. More often than not—99.9 percent of the time in my experience—the actual transaction has gone off without a hitch. I've met some great people through eBay, some of whom I occasionally keep in touch with.

It might be argued that eBay should also work in the completion of the transaction, but I believe that would only create more rules for buyers and sellers to abide by and would almost certainly require eBay to charge additional fees.

When the auction is over, don't get hung up about having to forge ahead on your own. If you're buying, you're probably really anxious to get that cool thing you just won. If you're selling, you probably want to collect the proceeds of your auction. Both of these motivations practically always ensure that the final transaction will go well and that the two people involved will be quite competent to finish the business just fine on their own. Still, there are ways you can provide additional protection to help the transaction along. You'll learn about those points in the following chapters.

OK, with that being said, take a look at the information in that End of Auction notice:

- **Buyers Please Remit Payment to Seller**. This sentence appears just before the details of the auction. It's the point of the auction's close—it's time to pay. No problem.

- **Final price**. Here's what the bidder is required to honor and what the seller is expecting to collect (plus shipping, insurance, or whatever.)

- **Auction ended at**. Quite simply, the date and time the auction was officially closed.

- **Total number of bids**. Just kind of an FYI for both the buyer and seller. This information doesn't really have any effect on anything at this point.

- **Seller User ID**. This is the ID of the seller who had posted the auction.

- **Seller E-mail**. OK, real important information here: this is the registered e-mail address for the seller of the item. This address was confirmed as valid by eBay at the time the seller registered. This is the address the high bidder can use to contact the seller.

- **High-bidder User ID**. This is the ID of the high bidder for the item; if you were the high bidder, this will be your ID.

- **High-bidder E-Mail**. Another key piece of information. This lets the seller know the verified e-mail address that can be used to contact the high bidder.

NOTE Remember, as a registered eBay user, you can find the e-mail addresses of bidders and sellers by clicking on a user ID (you'll need to verify you're registered before eBay provides the other person's e-mail address). You can also access the main navigation bar selection *Search* and the submenu selection *Find members*. This is one I haven't shown you yet—the Find Members page lets you see other registered members' *About Me* pages, their feedback profile (yes, another way to find it), their *Email Address and User ID History* and their *Personal Contact Information* (street address, home phone number, and so on).

ALERT Whenever full contact information about another eBay user is requested, eBay will e-mail the full contact information for *both* users. The user who made the request will get the information requested; the user whose information was requested will receive the same bits of information about the requesting user. This way, both individuals are aware of the request and of each other, so no shenanigans.

Now, take special notice of the next two sentences that appear just after the auction details in the End of Auction notice:

- Seller and high bidder should now contact each other to complete the sale.

- IMPORTANT: buyer and seller should contact each other within three business days, or risk losing their right to complete this transaction.

Wait a minute. You said eBay doesn't get involved in the actual transaction. Doesn't this imply that they *are* getting involved?

Not at all. These two sentences—especially the second one—are just statements to further impress that the buyer and seller are now on their own, but they should both try to get in contact with one another and complete the transaction as quickly as possible. These two sentences just apply a bit of hurry-up to the two people involved, hoping to encourage the completion of the deal so each person can move along to other auctions.

The three-day statement you read above isn't a hard-and-fast, strictly enforced rule. The lag time of the transaction is solely up to the buyer and seller. However, the three-day statement does give one or both parties an indicator of what is acceptable in closing the deal. If either the buyer or seller is not responding, the other person could actually invoke the power of this statement to get out of their obligation in the auction.

The rest of what you read in the End of Auction notice gives you background info on the different pages on eBay's site that you could visit if you want some tips or general guidance in closing the deal.

Communicate!

So the time comes to reach out and make contact with that other person. The key here is to start communications right away. It's not even necessary to wait for the arrival of the eBay End of Auction notice. You can get the other person's e-mail address from within eBay, so do it and get cracking.

Quick communications will signal that both buyer and seller are committed to completing the auction in good faith and in a timely manner. A quick start shows that both intend to stand behind their auction obligations, and it helps to promote trust and security as the actual transfer begins to take place.

If you're the buyer, you probably want that item you just won. You'll be eager to communicate with the seller to say you want to send payment quickly so you can get your coveted item quickly. However, the eBay culture tends to suggest the seller should be given the chance to make first contact. Be patient. Besides, since the seller will be collecting money, it shouldn't take long at all before you get the word that it's time to pay.

If you're the seller, you want to let the buyer know the auction is over, and it's time to pay. You're establishing your expectation that you intend to close this auction quickly, requiring payment in a reasonably short time. In return, you'll let the buyer know that you'll send the item with the same attention to quick turnaround. Since you're expected to make first contact, you'll set a good example by doing so within 24 hours after the auction closes. Remember, the buyer is eagerly waiting to hear from you.

As you might expect, this is the time when the buyer and seller go into "business mode"—there's a transaction to complete, and it has to take place between two complete strangers (unless you've dealt with one another before). It's like a job interview: you'll meet, shake hands, start talking business right away, and assess your confidence in each other rather quickly. Sure, an auction doesn't have the impact that a job interview does, but it still should be handled promptly and professionally.

Last, the initial communications are what will be setting the expectations for the buyer and the seller. This, again, is where both parties will get a feeling for how reliable the other person is. You want to look and sound as trustworthy as possible. Remember, you're probably strangers; the bidder wants to know if it's safe to send money and the seller wants to know if it's safe to send the item.

Clean and Clear Communication

Back in Chapter 19, I stressed the importance of good communication using good grammar and style. Again, good writing isn't just for writers anymore. More than ever, the world uses writing as the most common form of communication. E-mail is practically the preferred way to speak to others, so you want to be sure your e-mail messages can convey who you are without portraying who you aren't.

When you contact the person on the other side of the auction, be sure to look your best. In most instances, this will be the first time you ever contact that person. You only have one chance to make a first impression; make it a good one.

Use complete sentences in your messages, punctuate to the best of your ability, and—most of all—be polite and friendly. Get to the point and be clear about why you're writing.

First Contact

OK, since you're dealing with real people again, it's time to pull out the bag of manners. By and large, this goes back to a lot of the discussion from Chapter 4 about netiquette. This time it's a bit different, though, because you'll be closer to making actual contact than when you just dash about in Web pages.

If you're the high bidder in an auction, it's perfectly understandable that you'll be excited, especially if you fought to the end. Although it's great that you've bid on and won somebody's auction, don't be overanxious about following up. Remember, *give the seller a chance to contact you first*; after all, it was the seller's auction. Most people will contact the high bidder well before eBay distributes the End of Auction notice.

Time was, in the earlier days of eBay, that sellers would wait to receive the official End of Auction notice from eBay and forward that along when they contacted the high bidder. Using the notice was more official looking. However, it seems this isn't as much a custom anymore; sellers are contacting bidders using their own custom End of Auction notices. This isn't a problem since all the information regarding the end of the auction is available on the closed auction item details page. In just a moment, I'll show you the notice I use when I contact the high bidder in my auctions.

Some sellers are just as excited at the end of the auction as the high bidders are. I've had sellers send notification of payment due just minutes after an auction I won had ended. And that's OK, because it shows the seller is eager to close the deal and get the item in my hands. However, notification can occur any time within 24 hours after the auction has closed without creating a presumption that the seller is dawdling.

Nonetheless, as a seller, you want to send a message to your high bidder very soon after the auction has closed. By all means, do everything possible to contact the bidder at least within the recommended three-day window of the auction's close. Otherwise, the bidder will start to wonder if you really have the item that you advertised, and you'll look sloppy or disorganized or worse.

As I said earlier, it's not necessary to wait for eBay's official End of Auction notice before you contact your high bidder. Here's the note format I generally use:

• •

```
Subject: end of auction: Phantom of the Paradise Lobby Card #1

Date: Sat, 8 Apr 1999 07:33:21 -0800

From: Dennis <dlprince@bigfoot.com>

To: highbidder@bidnet.com

CC: Dennis <dlprince@bigfoot.com>

Congratulations!

You were the high bidder in this auction. Please send your payment
of $9.70 ($6.50 + $3.20 Priority Mail) to:

Dennis Prince

1234 Main Street

Anytown, CA 12345

If you wish to have your item insured, please include an additional
$0.75.

Please reply to this message so I'll know I was successful in
reaching you. Please also provide your mailing address so I can get
your item packed and ready to ship.

Thanks for bidding!

Dennis

dlprince@bigfoot.com
```

• •

It's a pretty straightforward message. I first want to congratulate the high bidder on winning. Then I want to immediately state the total cost for the item—this will be the high bid price plus postage costs. I then provide my snail mail address where the payment should be sent, and give the buyer the option to have the item insured for the appropriate additional fee. Don't be concerned about calculating postage and insurance fees during this chapter's discussion; I'll cover all that in Chapter 22.

Next, I ask for a response to my e-mail message so I'll know the e-mail address provided for this bidder via eBay was valid. I also ask for the bidder's snail mail address to begin the packaging and addressing of the item—it's another way to verify that my high bidder is real.

And, finally, I thank the bidder for bidding. That goes back to the friendly customer service that I want to provide. I always want people to be glad they chose to bid on one of my auctions.

The real essence of the way I've done the letter is to make first contact, let it be known I'm ready to collect, and verify I'm able to reach the high bidder. With all that done, I want to finish with a "feel good" kind of thought that acts as my virtual handshake of good faith.

 NOTE You'll see that I also carbon-copy (CC:) myself on all my messages. This way I'll be getting a copy of the e-mail I send, which will help me keep track of my communications with other bidders or sellers. I've created a separate folder called "Auction Correspondence" to keep these copies so they don't get lost when I clean out my inbox. Alternatively, since most e-mail applications have a *Messages Sent* or *Outbox* folder, you could just drag a copy of your sent message from the Sent folder into an "Auction Correspondence" folder for long-term archival.

OK, that's great, but what if you're the buyer? Suppose you haven't yet heard from the seller even though the auction has closed? For me, if it's day three after the auction closed and I haven't heard from the seller, here's the kind of message I'll usually send:

• •

```
Subject: end of auction: Teenagers From Outer Space Lobby Card

Date: Sun, 16 May 1999 10:18:14 -0800

From: Dennis <dlprince@bigfoot.com>

To: seller@sellnet.com

CC: Dennis <dlprince@bigfoot.com>

Hi,

It looks like I was the high bidder for this lobby card. Please let
me know how much I should include for postage as well as your mail-
ing address, and I'll send payment right away.
```

```
Thanks for making this item available on eBay.

Best,

Dennis

dlprince@bigfoot.com

eBay User ID: dennis_prince
```

• •

The goal of this message is to be short, pleasant, and to the point. If I haven't heard from the seller, I'll go ahead and make first contact in a very polite and anticipatory way. I'm making it clear that I have the money, and I just want to know where to send it. At the same time, this is my way of finding out if this seller can really be reached. I'll even go the extra step to thank the seller for auctioning this item. Again, this is that initial virtual handshake again. I'll just hope the seller is out there to return the handshake very soon.

 TIP If a high bidder is really anxious and jumps in first to make contact right after the auction is over, you can be fairly relaxed about answering—though there's much to be said for responding promptly, and you do, of course, really need to reply before the three days are up. However, if there has been a lag of two or three days without the seller making contact, then the high bidder's effort to make contact should be treated with immediate response from the seller and even a bit of apology. If you're the seller and you haven't contacted that high bidder for days—be swift and apologetic in your response. Already you're behind the eight ball because the high bidder isn't too sure if you exist or whether you're very reliable in following up on transactions. How comfortable will that bidder feel about sending money to you, wondering how long it might take you to send the item? Do all you can to quickly reverse those apprehensions if you left matters so long that even a patient high bidder felt it was necessary to make the first contact.

Reserve Price Not Met?

Here's an interesting situation: what if the auction ends but the reserve price wasn't met? Is it necessary for any communication to go on here, or does everyone just walk away without so much as a murmur about it?

By eBay's auction rules, an auction whose reserve price has not been met is basically a dead auction. The seller isn't required to sell, the high bidder isn't required to buy. Everyone gets off scot-free. But a little conversation is still in order. After all, the seller *was* hoping to sell that item, and the high bidder *was* interested enough to bid on it. There might still be some potential here.

As a seller, I like to contact the high bidder in my reserve auctions even if the reserve price wasn't met. I'll let them know what the reserve price was and see if they'd still be interested in doing a deal.

 Tip Hey, consider quickly lowering your reserve price here if you think you might have been a little overoptimistic in the beginning. When you contact the high bidder, mention your reserve price, but leave an opening for a bit of negotiating. Chances are you won't get your full reserve price—a bidder willing to go that far would have bid it while the auction was running—but you might get something close to it.

So, when my reserve price isn't met, here's generally what I'll say to my high bidder:

• •

Subject: end of auction: Star Wars original '77 8x10 color lobby set

Date: Sun, 25 Apr 1999 18:43:02 -0800

From: Dennis <dlprince@bigfoot.com>

To: highbidder@bidnet.com

CC: Dennis <dlprince@bigfoot.com>

Hi,

Thanks for bidding in this auction. Unfortunately, my reserve price wasn't met. I had placed a reasonable reserve of $65 on this set of color lobbies (you were only $15 away). If you like, I can offer this set to you for my reserve price, plus postage, before I relist it.

Let me know if you would like them. If not, thanks for bidding all the same.

Best,

Dennis

dlprince@bigfoot.com

• •

This message works to see if I can salvage a deal. My high bidder isn't required to work with me any further at this point, but might still have some motivation to own the item; I want to work with that motivation while it's still alive.

I'll begin by thanking the high bidder, of course, for bidding at all, then I'll mention what the reserve price was. At this point, if the highest recorded bid was pretty close to my reserve, I'll say that in my message.

TIP Actually, this is a key point since you, as the seller, don't know what the bidder's maximum bid was; maybe in this case the bidder stated a maximum of $60—just $5 away from my reserve price. Will it look reasonable to kick in a measly five bucks more to get this great item? Could be.

So, if the high bidder might be interested, I'll offer a chance to own the item *before I relist it.* That last phrase is kind of the sales push; you're letting the bidder know you're not destitute or desperate to sell the item right now at a real low cost—you'll just relist it if it doesn't sell this time. Now the ball's in the bidder's court to decide (quickly) whether to get the item or not. This just encourages a bit of hurry-up on the bidder's part to decide so you can get on with your business.

Now, if you're the high bidder in a Reserve Price auction where the reserve wasn't met, here's what you can do if you haven't heard from the seller. Send a message to the seller to say you're still interested in the item. Try something like this:

• •

```
Subject: end of auction: Star Wars original '77 8x10 color lobby
set

Date: Sun, 25 Apr 1999 18:43:02 -0800

From: Dennis <dlprince@bigfoot.com>

To: seller@sellnet.com

CC: Dennis <dlprince@bigfoot.com>
```

```
Hi,

I was the high bidder in your auction, but I see the reserve price
wasn't met. Could you let me know if you'd still like to sell the
item? Maybe we can work out a deal?

Thanks,

Dennis

dlprince@bigfoot.com

eBay User ID: dennis_prince
```

• •

Here, I'm trying to find out how motivated that seller is to get some cash in hand. First and foremost, by contacting the seller, I'm making it clear I'm a serious buyer, and I would be a sure bet to follow up on sending whatever the negotiated price of the item might work out to be. As buyer, I'm trying to see if the seller was a bit overoptimistic about setting the reserve price. I won't directly ask what the reserve price was because that might work against me in that it could immediately set the price on the seller's terms. Rather, I'll ask if the seller still wants to work out some sort of deal, leaving an open door to a bit of mutual negotiation.

In either of these cases—seller contacting high bidder or high bidder contacting seller—there are no guarantees that a deal can be reached. The high bidder might decide to walk away from the item if the motivation to own it has died (and it can die quickly); the seller might decide not to sell the item at anything less than the reserve price, which ends the story if the bidder doesn't want to go that far.

Sometimes, if there is interest on either side of the auction, but a little give-and-take is required, use postage costs as the negotiating chip. If you're the seller, offer to sell at your reserve price, which will also include postage and insurance charges. If you're the buyer, offer to pay the reserve price as long as it includes postage and insurance charges. It's not a big amount of money either way, but it makes for a good way to break a deadlock in the negotiation.

And, if no deal is reached, agree to disagree. Sometimes the seller and high bidder have different motivations in regard to the auction. If you can't arrive at a win-win situation, just let it go. Be polite, thank one another, and move on. No fuss. No muss. If you're the seller, relist the item; maybe somebody desperate to own it just missed the first auction. If you're the bidder, keep an eye open for the relisting; maybe the seller will decide to drop that reserve price a bit after all.

The bottom line of this whole discussion is that, even though a reserve price might not have been met during the course of an auction, it's still good business to make contact to close the deal. Whether or not an eventual sale takes place between the two parties, it's much better than just dropping the whole auction cold without any communication at all.

TIP If you're responding to a reserve auction message, still use politeness. Don't reply to the seller saying something like, *"That price is ridiculous. No thanks."* Equally, if you're the seller, don't reply to a buyer saying, *"Take it or leave it."* These are real turn-offs, but you'd be surprised how often I've been on the receiving end of this kind of communication.

NOTE Don't be surprised if, as a seller, you get messages from other eBay users asking about your unmet reserve price even though they hadn't bid during the auction. This usually happens for one of two reasons: either the person contacting you missed out on the auction but would really like the item and might offer up your reserve price right off the bat, or the person contacting you is looking to get your item cheap, and wondering how motivated you are to make a sale.

SOAPBOX I'm on a roll here with parenthetical thoughts, so here's an opinion for you: if you're going to contact a seller and make an offer for an unmet reserve price auction, be reasonable in what you offer. I had someone offer me $10 for an item that, although the reserve wasn't met, did draw a high bid of $53. I'm sorry, but this offer was downright offensive. Needless to say, that message wasn't even deserving of a reply.

Keeping Track of Your Communications

Just a quick bit of bookkeeping here. It's often a good idea to keep track of your communications after an auction has ended. Whether you keep all your e-mail messages in your e-mail account or track when messages were sent and received in your auction tracking spreadsheet, you might find it pays to have that information readily available.

If a bidder claims not to have heard from you after an auction, you'll want to be able to provide the facts—one way or the other. The same goes if you're the seller and you're waiting to hear back from your high bidder; you'll want to be able to follow up, citing when you sent a first or second message to let the bidder know it was time to pay.

I actually use both approaches: I log when my communications are sent out (and responses received) in my auction spreadsheet. To back up that information, I also store the actual e-mail messages in a file folder in my e-mail account. This way, I quickly have the dates that communications were sent (from my spreadsheet) but I also have the details of what was written in each message (from what's stored in my file folder). To keep my e-mail account from getting out of hand, I'll delete all messages that pertain to any particular auction after 30 days—that is, 30 days after I've shipped the item or after I've received the item. Any issue that arises beyond 30 days would be rare, and I would still have the date of the communication recorded on my auction spreadsheet.

Following Up

Two or three days go by and you haven't heard from the other person? Hmmm. Got a deadbeat out there? Maybe. Maybe not. But it might be time to do a little following up.

The first thing to remember when you're waiting to hear back from other people regarding an auction is that they probably have real jobs and real lives. To the majority of users, eBay is only a hobby or pastime. That won't excuse any irresponsibility on either party's side—the auction still has to be honored—but everybody needs to remember that people get busy, and "stuff" happens.

When you don't hear back from the person you're trying to contact, send a follow-up message. If you're a seller, it might look like this:

• •

Subject: Reminder: end of auction—Young Frankenstein lobby set on eBay

Date: Tues, 27 Apr 1999 20:19:37 -0800

From: Dennis <dlprince@bigfoot.com>

To: highbidder@bidnet.com

CC: Dennis <dlprince@bigfoot.com>

Hi,

I was just following up on this auction in which you were the high bidder. I haven't heard back from you since I sent the message telling you the final cost and address to send your payment.

Please let me know if you received my first message. If so, please let me know that you still want this item and when you will be sending your payment. If you didn't receive my first message, here is the information again:

Total cost: $68.20 ($65.00 + $3.20 Priority Mail)

* please add $1.00 additional for insurance if you like.

Send your payment to:

Dennis Prince

1234 Main Street

Anytown, CA 12345

Again, thank you for bidding on my auction. I'll look forward to your quick reply.

Best,

Dennis

dlprince@bigfoot.com

• •

This message is a polite reminder to the high bidder to make good on the bid. For that reason, I use the word *reminder* in the subject line of my message; it's a gentle wake-up call. I won't attack the bidder, though, because maybe my first message never got through. If so, the bidder and I can deal with that. The fact is, I won't know if it arrived or not, but I'll give the bidder the open door to make good by providing all the necessary information of how much final payment will be and where the payment should be mailed. I'll close the message by thanking the bidder for bidding (keeping it friendly still), but also making it clear I'll be expecting a quick reply.

If you're the high bidder and haven't heard from the seller, you have the right to send a reminder that you're waiting to close the deal. Remember that by offering the item for auction on eBay, the seller made a contract to sell the item at the successful high bid price as long as the pricing conditions were met. So if you're still waiting to hear back from the seller, try a follow-up message something like this:

• •

Subject: 2nd Message: Teenagers From Outer Space Lobby Card on eBay

Date: Wed, 19 May 1999 21:43:29 -0800

From: Dennis <dlprince@bigfoot.com>

To: seller@sellnet.com

CC: Dennis <dlprince@bigfoot.com>

Hi,

I haven't heard back from you regarding this auction I won. Please let me know what the postage cost will be and where I can send my payment. I'd like to complete this transaction as soon as possible.

Thanks,

Dennis

dlprince@bigfoot.com

eBay User ID: dennis_prince

• •

Now, if you're the one who's lagging in the reply, then hop to it and get back to that bidder or seller. You'll build yourself a real crummy reputation with others faster than you can say, *"Yeah, but if you'll just let me explain—"* If you've been understandably tied up (out of town or something), then just be honest when you reply and then follow up with exceptional communications thereafter. People understand that life goes on outside eBay.

No Reply

And what if you just never hear back from that no-good so-and-so? What then? Well, you should first give it one more shot with a third e-mail note. It could look something like this:

• •

Subject: FINAL NOTICE: end of auction—Young Frankenstein lobby set on eBay

Date: Mon, 3 May 1999 10:03:09 -0800

From: Dennis <dlprince@bigfoot.com>

To: highbidder@bidnet.com

CC: Dennis <dlprince@bigfoot.com>

Hello,

This is a final notice to you regarding your high bid in my auction on eBay (item #66605888). I have twice tried to contact you regarding honoring your high bid and sending your payment. I have not heard back from you.

Please reply immediately and tell me whether you intend to honor your bid. If you choose not to, I will offer the item to the next highest bidder or relist the item; your bid will be negated. I will also have to leave a negative message about you in the Feedback Forum.

If there has been any reasonable delay, please let me know. I would still be interested in closing this deal with you.

Sincerely,

Dennis Prince

dlprince@bigfoot.com

• •

You can see that I'm taking a heavier-handed approach on this one. I'm frustrated because the bidder isn't following up (incidentally, this is a fictitious example). So, I'm laying out the facts: you haven't replied; I expect you to honor your bid; if you don't honor your bid, you lose the item; I'll be leaving a negative feedback note on eBay; there's still time to redeem yourself, so act quickly.

ALERT Slow down there, Trigger. Before leaving negative feedback for a user, please read the discussion of the Feedback Forum in Chapter 23.

The reason the message is so curt is that I have better things to do than chase down deadbeat bidders. Also, I'm documenting my attempts to make contact. This message, as well as the others I've sent and saved, will be my trail in case the bidder comes back later saying I never released the item. Remember, I've been copying myself on all messages I send. I *have* the facts.

And if after this third message I still don't hear back from my high bidder, I cut the deal off. I'll make my offer to the next bidder to see if I can place the item there—the second-place bidder's maximum bid is probably very close to the winner's. If that bidder no longer wants the item, I can contact other bidders, or I can just decide to relist the item again. Of course, I might visit the deadbeat high bidder's feedback page and leave a negative note something like this:

Contacted high bidder three times. No reply. No payment. Beware.

That's really all I need to say to get my point across while letting other eBay users know something about this bidder in case their paths cross. It's not necessary to go into a verbal assault with all sorts of colorful language. This simple statement says it all.

NOTE Again, I'll show you how, when, and why to use the eBay Feedback Forum in Chapter 23.

Once you've cut the deadbeat bidder off, just move on. No need to dwell on the situation or continue to try finding the person. Here's what you can do, though: go get your money back. What?! From whom? From eBay.

Yes, one more surprise awaits you at eBay. If you're a seller and one of your auction deals goes sour, eBay will offer to reimburse the commission they charged you against the final high bid price (referred to as the *Final Value Fee* in these instances). As a seller, you can request that eBay refund the Final Value Fee of your closed auction if one of the following happens during the course of closing the deal:

- The high bidder never responds to your End of Auction requests (provided you allow *at least* the customary three days after the auction's end).

- The high bidder backs out of the deal and refuses to pay.

- The high bidder's payment is not good (say, the check bounces or there's a stop payment on it).

- The high bidder returns the item after the deal and requires a refund (I'll talk about refunds more in Chapter 22).

- The high bidder can't honor the bid due to an unexpected personal emergency.

- The high bidder claims the final transaction terms are unacceptable.

Then, as if this wasn't great enough news, eBay also promises to return partial credit of the Final Value Fee if one of the following situations arises:

- The final sale price was actually lower than the final bid price (maybe due to an item's condition or something), and the seller and high bidder mutually agree on a lower selling price.

- The high bidder backed out, but the seller was able to sell the item, at a lower price to a lower bidder.

- One or more bidders in a Dutch auction back out of their deals.

Like I said, this is fantastic news to sellers whose sales go down the drain. There are just a few things to know and rules to adhere to when making this Final Value Fee refund request:

- Sellers *must* allow the high bidder at least three days to respond to a notification to pay their high bid.

- Sellers have to make the refund request within 60 days of the auction's end.

- eBay will apply the refund in the form of credit to the seller's eBay account.

- eBay will identify the *deadbeat bidder* in the transaction and might take disciplinary action.

- A false claim for refund will result in the *seller* being immediately suspended from eBay.

This form of seller protection is just another of the registered user features that eBay offers to keep the site as successful as possible. I've never had to use it, but it's great to know it's there.

Now, if you were the high bidder and the seller hasn't responded to you, then you should take a little action. Feel free to send a final e-mail message of your own. It might look like this:

• •

Subject: Last try: Teenagers From Outer Space Lobby Card on eBay

Date: Mon, 24 May 1999 11:59:09-0800

From: Dennis <dlprince@bigfoot.com>

To: seller@sellnet.com

CC: Dennis <dlprince@bigfoot.com>

Hello,

I've tried to get in touch with you twice before about this auction I have won. You haven't replied, and I assume you either don't have

```
this item or you've decided not to sell it. Whichever, I'd appreci-
ate if you'd let me know why you haven't responded. If I don't hear
back from you within the next two days, I'll consider the auction
void, and I will not be obligated to honor the high bid I placed.

If you have this item and wish to honor your obligation to sell it
to me at my winning high bid, please contact me immediately. Other-
wise, I will consider leaving a negative note about you in the eBay
Feedback Forum.

Sincerely,

Dennis Prince

dlprince@bigfoot.com

eBay User ID: dennis_prince
```

Again, there's no bones about it in this message; I'm a frustrated high bidder, and this seller isn't standing by the bargain. So, I'll make the final
attempt to get through and, if I get no reply, then I'm relieved of my high
bid obligation. Again, I've been copying myself on all of these messages, so
I'll have the document trail if the seller ever comes back to accuse me of
being a deadbeat bidder. As a bidder, if a sale falls through, you're really out
nothing, so don't expect to see the same kind of remuneration as sellers get
when their deal goes sour.

SOAPBOX Just to wrap this chapter up, I should tell you that I've very rarely
been in the situation where I'm not getting replies to my messages.
Usually, both people in the auction are eager to close the deal. But if you do run into
some trouble, the examples I've given in this chapter can help you decide how and when
to react. The messages you see are my actual templates. (I change the details about the
item, of course.) Using templates, especially when there's a problem, helps keep me
from expressing myself or reacting in a way that would be overly negative or generally
in poor judgment. I just let the template do my talking.

chapter 21

Payment

And now, the money. If anything is going to make you nervous about an online auction, it'll be the thought of dealing with the money. Money does strange things to people, and people do strange things about it. But the whole issue of payment at the close of an auction doesn't have to be a big hassle; you just need to understand the written and unwritten rules of that end of the game.

Who Goes First?

A good question, but if you were noticing, I tipped my hand about this one back in Chapter 16 and then again in Chapter 20; the *buyer* will usually need to pay first.

In my auction listings, you'll always read this line:

High Bidder will please pre-pay, plus postage.

Then, after the auction, my e-mail to the high bidder includes this:

You were the high bidder in this auction. Please send your payment of $9.70 ($6.50 + $3.20 Priority Mail) to:

Traditionally, the burden is on the buyer to send payment up front before any item is shipped. It goes back to the rules of mail order in general: you send your money, and you get your item shortly thereafter. To avoid any surprises, I let all bidders know that I will be expecting payment in advance right in the body of my auction listing's description. Anybody who has any question or concern about that can immediately choose not to bid or can contact me for an explanation.

Then, when the auction has ended, I state in my end-of-auction notice that payment should be sent promptly now that the auction has closed. The bidder should know that prepayment is a condition of the auction and shouldn't be caught off guard by it.

This leads to the whole discussion of trustworthiness: can the bidder trust the seller with the money? Well, as you've been reading this book, you'll know that I've been continually emphasizing the need to be responsive, courteous, sincere, and honest. All this model behavior sets the stage to make each party willing to trust the other when it comes to the point of sending money.

Likewise, if you're the high bidder in an auction, then you'll know prepayment is the usual modus operandi. So hopefully you fully checked out the seller of the item you were bidding on, either through the eBay feedback rating or by asking direct questions about the item. Maybe you even did some searches to check out the seller's other auctions—and bid activity, too. Through your investigations, you will have decided if you had enough faith in the seller to want to bid on the item, which further establishes how trusting you'll be when it comes time for you to pay.

But, no doubt about it, sending payment in advance is a bit of a leap of faith. Trust your instincts and trust the comments of others (via eBay's Feedback Forum) to guide you in how you place your trust. Don't let this part of the deal hang you up, though. This is done on a daily basis, and it's a relatively rare occurrence when someone gets stiffed after they've paid.

Methods of Payment

The good thing about paying for an item you've won on eBay is that there are several different ways to pay. As a seller, this is great because you can be flexible in how you'll accept payment. In the end, the availability of different forms of payment will help ensure both buyer and seller can find a payment method that's mutually agreeable.

Popular Ways to Pay

First, look at the most widely used forms of payment.

Money Orders

These are as good as cash because they require cash (or a debit card) to purchase. Buyers can't write checks for money orders, so there's no way a money order can ever bounce. To a seller, the money order is the easiest and most reliable form of payment outside of actual cash. In fact, most sellers will provide an incentive to buyers to use money orders: items paid for with a money order will be shipped within 24 hours of receipt of payment. To the buyer, a money order gets the item on its way quickly, which is good, but it also provides a method of tracing the payment: each money order issued has a tracking number and has two parts. The main part of the money order is the actual check that will be sent to the seller; the other part is a stub or receipt that bears the same identification number as the check and can be used to trace or replace the money order.

Cashier's Checks

Also known as *teller's checks,* these are official checks issued by banks, credit unions, or other financial institutions where customers might maintain an active account. Cashier's checks are just as welcome as money orders because the check is official, and it can't be issued unless the buyer has the funds to cover the amount of the check. Once the check is issued, that amount is immediately deducted from the buyer's account; it's as good as the money that was used to draft it. Although some sellers believe a cashier's check can be canceled (stopping payment), this is typically untrue. In most cases, cashier's checks can only be canceled if the original check is returned to the institution that issued it.

Personal Checks

Personal checks are one of the most widely used forms of exchanging funds. Personal checks are fine for payment on auction items, but most sellers will (or should) state that personal checks need to clear the seller's bank before the item paid for will be shipped. Hey, checks sometimes bounce. If a buyer has an overdrawn checking account, that check sent to the seller might not have enough funds behind it. If you're a buyer and you send a personal check, first expect the delay for your check to clear, but by all means be sure it won't bounce. The seller's bank will almost always slap on a *returned check charge* when a check bounces, so the seller will usually come back to the buyer and not only demand an explanation but also demand payment of the returned check charge. But, most often, personal checks will clear just fine, and the transaction can be completed without much trouble.

Credit Card Payment

Since many businesses and qualified merchants deal on eBay, you might have the option of using a credit card to pay for an item. If you can pay by credit card, ask for a phone number to call to make payment rather than writing your credit card number and expiration date in an e-mail message. The phone call will usually verify that you're dealing with a true business or merchant. If you're a seller, you should know that some statistics report people are willing to spend up to 250 percent more using credit cards than they would otherwise. It's the whole phenomenon of "buy now, pay later." If you're going to get deep into selling on eBay, you can investigate establishing your own merchant account so you can accept credit card payment from your high bidders. For more information, visit

- www.1stAmericanCardService.com
- www.ezmerchantaccounts.com
- www.merchantacount.com

These are just a few online sites you can visit to learn more about setting up a merchant account. Perform an Internet search using the keywords "merchant account." I haven't used any of these services myself, but they might be worth checking out.

> For the buyer, using a credit card might be the most desirable way to pay—credit card charges can be disputed in case a problem arises. If you're a buyer and aren't receiving what you paid for, contact your credit card issuer to dispute the charge. Most often, the issuer will work on your behalf to help you get what you bought—or get your money back. Also, some credit cards provide Buyer Protection programs that offer additional purchase protection, warranty extension, and item replacement guarantees. Now that's peace of mind.

Cash

Sure, cash still works these days. Many sellers will accept cash, but most discourage it. Cash can be lost in the mail or received by dishonest sellers who claim they never got it. You can't trace cash, so it's not preferable to use it. Yes, it's sometimes convenient, but you bear the risk when you send it.

> If you're in the United States and an international bidder wins your auction, you might receive cash. It's often easier for international buyers to get U.S. dollars from their banks than to get international money orders. To both seller and bidder: be very careful, communicate when the cash was sent and received, and move that transaction through quickly. More on international payment a little further on.

Other Ways to Pay

Then, of course, there are a few less conventional but still effective ways to make payment.

Escrow

Remember the escrow service *i-Escrow* that I first told you about in Chapter 4? This is the escrow service eBay endorses, and it is uniquely suited for online auction purchases. Typically, escrow services would be used when the final sale price of an item is high; the escrow service adds an extra layer of

security during the final transaction, but it's not free—you can expect to pay around 5 percent of the item's final cost to the escrow site. Escrow services are useful, though, if you have any concern about a buyer or seller following through on a sale.

I've used i-Escrow myself and would cheerfully do so again, if I was selling or buying something that cost enough to make the price and the extra effort worthwhile. (They were offering escrow transactions free of commission for a limited time when I experimented with the service.) In a somewhat unorthodox move, I asked a seller if he'd mind testing the escrow process for an item I had won. He graciously agreed. The process was very straightforward and nicely controlled. eBay offers a hyperlink to buyers and sellers that takes them directly to i-Escrow after an auction. An escrow transaction for the item is opened and both buyer and seller have the opportunity to establish the conditions of the transaction to their mutual agreement before any movement of money or merchandise takes place. As the buyer, I elected to use my credit card to place the funds in the escrow account. i-Escrow then notified the seller to ship the item. When I received the item (insured and registered), I was allotted a two-day inspection period before being required to either accept the item—and release funds—or to reject the item and return it to the seller. This transaction went off without a hitch.

In the end, both the seller and I agreed the process was very secure and offered additional assurance to both of us that no shenanigans could take place. i-Escrow paid the seller very promptly after I verified satisfaction with the item. However, expect to do a bit more cooperative work when choosing this path (accessing the Web site to perform next steps) and also expect about a week to two weeks before the whole transaction is complete. However, for high dollar items, this might be a good payment alternative to consider. As I said earlier, I wouldn't be averse to doing it again.

TIP A neat by-product of using escrow services is they allow for payment by credit card—that's how I paid. As a seller, you could easily inform prospective bidders that you can accept credit card payment, provided an escrow transaction is arranged. It's a great way to give the buyer one more alternative for payment without having to open a full-fledged merchant account of your own.

COD

Although most of those TV ads told you *"No CODs allowed,"* you can choose this option if you're buying or selling. Essentially, the seller will register the item with the carrier as COD (cash on delivery); the buyer receives the item and pays the carrier the item price plus the COD charges; the carrier service then pays the seller the value of the item. This works pretty well, but it does cost extra—and the buyer and seller will need to work out who will be responsible for paying for the COD charges.

Trades

And some buyers and sellers will even entertain the idea of exchanging goods for goods rather than cash for goods. Hey, once the auction's over, the buyer and seller are free to agree to anything that's mutually beneficial.

International Exchanges

Remember that eBay spans the globe, allowing buyers and sellers to meet from opposite sides of the Earth. That's pretty cool, but what about when it's time to pay? How do I send the right kind of payment to another country, or how do I collect my payment from someone who's using a different monetary system than I do?

In these cases, you're best off using an *International Money Order*. If you're the buyer, you can get this kind of money order from your local post office. They sometimes cost a little more than a regular money order (about $3 to $8), but they let you use your local currency to send funds that the seller can easily cash and convert into their local currency, whatever it may be.

There's a lot of international buying and selling going on at eBay, and it all seems to work out pretty well. In fact, the second auction I ever held ended up with a high bidder who was in Switzerland. It felt pretty bizarre to think of my item traveling across the globe to a home in the middle of Europe. But, through the use of an International Money Order, the exchange went off without any problems.

NO**TE** Remember, if you don't want to ship your items internationally, you have the option of announcing in your listing that you'll ship only in your own country. Of course, international money seems to spend just as well as local money, so why limit your potential to reach bidders? All the same auction rules and restrictions apply no matter where somebody lives.

The Check Is in the Mail

Now—back to those good communication practices of yours. More than ever, you're going to want to be communicating as the actual exchange of money starts to take place. It's pretty unsettling for a buyer to send money and not hear if it's been received or not. Equally, it doesn't sit too well when a seller is expecting payment, but doesn't hear from the high bidder that payment is on the way. Communicate; that's all there is to it.

When you're buying, you'll want to send your payment as soon as you get confirmation from the seller regarding the final price. As soon as you have the information you need, get that payment in the mail. However, don't just send a check or money order in an otherwise empty envelope. Believe it or not, some buyers will just send a check for an amount of money with no indication of what they're buying. It's usually a good bet that they're the high bidder on one of your auctions, but rarely can you match up a real name with an eBay user ID or registered e-mail address.

In one case, I received a check all by its little lonesome, and I needed to scan through my auction spreadsheet to try to match up who it might be from. Remember, if you're buying, you're most likely dealing with a seller who is managing multiple auctions. If for no other reason, provide some message about what you're sending money for just so you get your item quicker; the seller won't have to try to track you down or figure out what to send you. You might open the box and find a vintage inflatable sheep instead of that vintage Nauga you were expecting. Now you've got some explaining to do.

One of the best ways to identify yourself with the item you're paying for is to include a copy of the message the seller sent you after the auction ended. Be sure you include your full mailing address with your payment; don't expect the seller to pull that from your check or the return address on your envelope. When I send payment, I print my mailing address clearly on a blank piece of paper in the envelope; many times, sellers have used that as the address label when sending the item to me. Other buyers will include a preprinted address label. And if your handwriting is a bit scrawly, provide something the seller can easily read and decipher. Otherwise, who knows where your item will end up?

After you've mailed your payment, let the seller know right away that the money's on the way. Send a quick e-mail message like this one:

• •

Subject: Payment on the way: Teenagers From Outer Space lobby card

Date: Wed, 19 May 1999 07:33:21 -0800

From: Dennis <dlprince@bigfoot.com>

To: seller@sellnet.com

CC: Dennis <dlprince@bigfoot.com>

Hi,

I just wanted to let you know my money order in the amount of $24.50 is on the way for the Teenagers From Outer Space lobby card I won on eBay. Please let me know when my payment arrives and when you will be shipping the card.

My address is:

Dennis Prince

1234 Main Street

Anytown, CA 12345

Thanks. I'll look forward to hearing back from you and receiving this lobby card.

Best,

Dennis

dlprince@bigfoot.com

eBay User ID: dennis_prince

• •

You'd have to try pretty hard to overcommunicate when you're closing an auction deal. Keep in touch with the seller and repeat your commitment to the deal. Notice that I included my mailing address in this message. That's just in case my writing was a bit illegible in the note I sent along with my payment.

Now, if you're the seller, acknowledge the buyer's message that payment is on the way. You're working to forge a trusting (though temporary) business relationship. Things will flow a lot smoother for both of you if you keep the communication working in two directions:

• •

```
Subject: Re: Payment on the way: Teenagers From Outer Space lobby
card

Date: Thurs, 20 May 1999 17:05:21 -0800

From: seller@sellnet.com

To: Dennis <dlprince@bigfoot.com>

CC: seller@sellnet.com

Hi Dennis,

Thanks for your message. I'll let you know just as soon as your
payment arrives. Since you're sending a money order, I'll be ship-
ping your package within 24 hours of its arrival.

Since you provided your mailing address, I'll get the lobby card
packaged up and ready to ship. I'll e-mail you when it goes out.

Best,

Mr. Sellers

seller@sellnet.com
```

• •

So far, so good. When the payment arrives, send another message to let the buyer know it reached you safely. This is actually a time of a little anxiety for the buyer. Remember, sending payment in advance is scary—the buyer is sitting there hoping it's going to be received and replied to by an honest seller. So, back to the e-mail:

• •

Subject: Payment received: Teenagers From Outer Space lobby card

Date: Mon, 24 May 1999 20:09:42 -0500

From: seller@sellnet.com

To: Dennis <dlprince@bigfoot.com>

CC: seller@sellnet.com

Hi Dennis,

Your payment arrived today. Thanks! The card is all set to ship,
although the post office was already closed by the time I got your
payment (I wanted to get the card out to you today). It will go out
in tomorrow's mail for sure, traveling via USPS.

Thanks for such a quick payment. I'll be sure to leave a positive
note for you on eBay. If you're satisfied with the card when you
receive it, I hope you'll consider leaving a positive note for me
as well.

Best,

Mr. Sellers

seller@sellnet.com

• •

In this message, good ol' Mr. Sellers was excellent about letting me know my payment arrived safe and sound and that he was prepared to ship the item I won. Notice that he also let me know *how* the item was traveling—via the United States Postal Service (USPS). It's a good idea to let the buyer know that a U.S. mail carrier will be bringing the item, and not another carrier such as UPS.

Now, Mr. Sellers is a real good eBaysian because he's already letting me know he'll be leaving a positive note in my Feedback Forum file. That's great; it rewards me for being such a prompt payer, and it increases my feedback rating so others will know I'm a good guy. I'll get into the Feedback Forum more in Chapter 23.

By the way, if I had chosen to pay with a personal check, even though I might have been quick about it, here's the kind of message that Mr. Sellers might have sent to me:

• •

```
Subject: Payment received: Teenagers From Outer Space lobby card

Date: Mon, 24 May 1999 20:09:42 -0500

From: seller@sellnet.com

To: Dennis <dlprince@bigfoot.com>

CC: seller@sellnet.com

Hi Dennis,

Your payment arrived today. Thanks! I've deposited the personal
check you sent and expect it should clear within the next seven
days. The card is all set to ship, and I'll get it into the mail
just as soon as my bank clears your check. I'll send another e-mail
to you to confirm shipment.

Thanks for such a quick payment. I'll be sure to leave a positive
note for you on eBay. If you're satisfied with the card when you
receive it, I hope you'll consider leaving a positive note for me
as well.

Best,

Mr. Sellers

seller@sellnet.com
```

• •

Another great message from Mr. Sellers. He's confirmed that my payment arrived and that it's been deposited in his bank account. Of course, I'm certain that I have the funds to cover it; if I'm not 100 percent sure, though, I'll be balancing my checkbook and making any necessary transfers real quick!

Bad Checks

And what if the funds just aren't there? Is it a call for a meltdown? Is the auction a sham? Maybe you should give it up since every other transaction will probably go the same way.

Not! Don't throw in the towel so quickly and don't let loose the hounds in haste. If a buyer's payment—often made using a personal check—springs back from your account and lands on the teller's counter, you'll want to calmly see what happened.

First of all, contact the buyer immediately if ever a check is returned (bounces). I would expect that any well-intentioned buyer would be quite embarrassed that this happened and will probably work pretty hard to make things right. The least you can expect is that the buyer will reimburse you for the returned check charge your bank laid on you—the buyer should offer this, but don't be shy about asking for it.

Next, give the buyer a chance to explain what happened. Maybe the old checkbook was just a little out of whack. Maybe an unexpected bill temporarily goofed up the financial picture. Whatever the reason, give the buyer a chance to plead the case and make it right. Kicking somebody who's down won't do much good. In fact, I believe giving people a chance to make things right will usually cause them to excel in correcting any problems that may have sprung up.

But what if the buyer isn't doing anything to make things right? What if all you're hearing are complaints that the check was good and that the bank will have to unsnarl things, and in the meantime, you should go ahead and ship the item out? Anyone smell rotten eggs? In situations like this, the burden is back on the buyer, who has to get things squared away quickly in order to regain your confidence and maintain the position of high bidder in good standing. If someone starts rambling on and on about *"It's not my fault. You cashed my check too soon,"* or anything else like that, you've probably got a stinker on your hands. The safest thing for you to do is politely let that bidder off the hook and rid yourself of this transaction quickly:

• •

Subject: Regarding your returned check

Date: Mon, 8 Mar 1999 20:09:42 -0500

From: Dennis <dlprince@bigfoot.com>

To: bounsen@rubberchecks.com

CC: dlprince@bigfoot.com

Dear Mr. Bounsen,

It seems you and I aren't able to resolve this situation about your check that did not process through my bank. At this time, it doesn't make sense to continue with this transaction. Please send me a check for $10 to cover the charge my bank levied against me due to your check being returned as unpayable. I will not hold you accountable for your high bid in my auction.

I ask you send the $10 reimbursement within 5 working days. I will not leave a negative note for you on eBay if you can clear this slight matter up quickly.

I'm sorry we couldn't complete this deal; maybe another time.

Sincerely,

Dennis Prince

dlprince@bigfoot.com

• •

Don't hold your breath that Mr. Bounsen will come through with that reimbursement for the returned check. If he couldn't reach a resolution to the check in the first place, he's probably not going to care about the charge your bank put on you. If he never comes through, just let it go and call it a small loss. To continue to dog him would not be in your best interest. If it makes you feel better, though, feel justified in considering leaving a negative note in his feedback file. Maybe you'll spare other sellers from the same encounter, or maybe Mr. Bounsen will get his act together.

NOTE Don't forget to see Chapter 23 for more details and advice about posting negative comments in the Feedback Forum.

In the meantime, you've effectively cut Mr. Bounsen off, and you can go on to sell the item to the next highest bidder or relist it.

NOTE Don't forget your right to request a Final Value Fee refund from eBay. This is one case where it would apply. Look back to Chapter 20 for the discussion, if you need.

Hello? I Sent My Payment Two Weeks Ago

If this happens to you, it's a bummer. It's rare, but some users have reported that they've sent payment for an item and never heard back from the seller. Terrific. Now what?

Well, ever since David Horowitz went off the air and Judge Wapner retired, everybody's been at a loss for what to do in these kinds of situations. But, if you believe you've been ripped off by an unsavory seller, there are some steps to take to build your case.

NOTE The instructions for handling things when your item doesn't show up as expected will probably change slightly when the eBay Insurance program is in full swing. Until then, the bulleted list in this section is your best bet for this sort of sad situation.

Here's what to do:

- Gather up all correspondence you've traded with the seller up to this point; you'll need a detailed document trail.

- Follow up with your bank or the institution that issued the check to see if it has been cashed.

- Send e-mail to the seller asking for status of your payment's receipt; make it clear you suspect there is a problem and you want assurance your item will be shipped promptly. DO NOT get into any verbal assault or angry exchanges. Threats are a definite no-no here; they can come back to haunt you.

- If you're getting no response, log on to eBay and request the seller's registered information; pick up the telephone and call directly if you have to.

- If things aren't resolved, file a formal complaint with the U.S. Postal Service or Attorney General. Hey, this is considered mail fraud and it's serious stuff. Visit the National Fraud Information Center online at **www.fraud.org** for more information about dealing with mail fraud.

- Send a copy of your formal complaint to eBay at

> Attn: Fraud
> eBay, Inc.
> 2005 Hamilton Avenue, Ste. 350
> San Jose, CA 95125

eBay won't get in the middle of the situation and won't act as an arbiter in these cases. However, someone there will probably look into the seller's history to see if there is a recurring problem that might require the seller be suspended from all future use of eBay.

- Let the seller know you have filed formal complaints. The rat should realize that failing to deliver is an offense subject to prosecution.

- Consider posting negative feedback for the seller; there's no reason others should have to endure this kind of mess, too.

Hopefully this will just be FYI for you; it would never be fun to have to go through all this if a deal goes bad. In my eBay history, I've never had to travel down this rocky path. Still, it's nice to know that you do have some recourse and remember that eBay takes fraud *very* seriously. Most important, you'll find the other good users at eBay will support you if you have truly been scammed. They're just as pleased as you to have all the crooks and creeps out of eBay.

chapter 22

Shipping and Handling

So you're moving right along now. The payment's in, and the check has cleared. By this time, the seller (that's you) has the money, and the high bidder can't wait to get the goods. So far, things are going well in the physical world. Now it's only a matter of getting that well-auctioned item into the new owner's hands. But you'll have to get it there safely.

You're a distribution center now. You're entering the world of mail order packaging and shipping. Although I know I've said every step up to this point was key to success, this is truly a critical stage: that item you described so well in your auction now has to make a little journey—maybe across town or maybe across the world. You need to make sure what the buyer receives will still match that glowing description that got all the bid action going a couple of weeks ago.

So whether you need to box it, bag it, seal it, or tag it, the time has come to swaddle that item in a cozy brown wrapper and bid it a fond farewell as it makes its trek from Point A to Point B.

What Do You Have to Ship?

The first thing to deal with when you're shipping an item is the item itself. What is it you're shipping? How big is it? How fragile is it? Can you get it out the door? Can you get it in the car?

Hopefully, you've been thinking about how you'll ship your item long before the auction actually ended and definitely before you told the high bidder how much to send you to cover shipping. Now is not the time to be realizing, *"Gawrsh. How am I gonna mail that thang?"*

Most items can be easily boxed or bagged or something. For the purposes of this chapter, I'll assume what you're sending is of manageable size and shape. If it's not—maybe you sold a boat, a car, or a battleship—then you probably won't be able to deal with the shipping preparation yourself; you'll need to call in a moving company or something. If your item is particularly odd-shaped or requires some sort of very special handling, take it to a professional packing service (you'll find them in the yellow pages of your phone book). But, again, assume you're dealing with something that you can manage yourself, OK?

Tip Remember—if you're going to need outside help to ship something, find out what it'll cost before you advise the high bidder what to pay. That extra $3.20 for Priority Mail won't go very far toward getting your old walk-in ceramic kiln to its new home....

Where Can You Get Shipping Supplies?

So, start by finding the stuff you'll use to ship your items. This is actually easier than you think, and it doesn't necessarily require you to visit one of those office supplies stores or "box-it" places. (They're fine, but you don't need to go to one just yet.) Use your cost-conscious noggin, and you'll be surprised what you can find for free.

If you don't mind doing a bit of foraging for packing supplies, start at the place where you work. If you work in some kind of office building, you're bound to trip over some excellent packing materials on a daily basis. Office supplies and office equipment are usually well packaged—sometimes over-packaged—and the plain brown leftovers are just what you'll need. Look for sturdy corrugated boxes with top flaps that can be sealed securely with tape. Be on the lookout for boxes that still have packing peanuts inside (you know, the little Styrofoam pieces that often look like Christmas ribbon candy or Quisp cereal). When you find boxes like this, they've probably just been unpacked, and they make a great instant-shipping solution for you.

 TIP Hey, if you want to be friendly to the environment, be on the lookout for Eco-Foam filler. It's an all-natural shipping product made from specially processed corn starch and can easily replace Styrofoam. It's biodegradable, and it smells and tastes like Puffed Wheat.

Also keep an eye open for bubble-pack sheets: the larger bubble sheets are excellent filler; the smaller bubble sheets are great for wrapping around the item you'll ship. Also look for different types of packing foam or large Styrofoam or Eco-Foam sheets; these are great for lining the insides of boxes to create a sturdy cocoon for the item you'll be shipping. Just about all this stuff can be found lying around business offices. If it's going to be trashed, pitch in and save yourself a buck while you're at it.

 NOTE If you think this kind of scavenging is lowly or reprehensible, think again— and look around. You'll be surprised how many times you see people walking the hallways looking for boxes for the exact same reason as you.

Of course, before you take any of this free stuff you find lying around, be sure it's OK with the office personnel, and be doubly sure the security guards know you're only taking out empties. You don't want to find yourself in Officer Fife's security office, having to explain that yours is only a corrugated crime.

But what if you don't work in an office building? No matter. Even if you don't regularly roam the carpeted corporate halls, you can probably still find free shipping supplies wherever you work. But if you can't, go check out some of the retail stores in your area and let them know what you're looking for: trash. Well, let them know you're looking for boxes and such; they might let you know the days they stock their shelves, and they might have some empties to pass along for free.

By now you've probably noticed that you're recycling. That's cool. So many packing supplies these days are made to be reused. Then, while you're looking for the stuff you'll need, sometimes you won't have to look past your own front door; why not reuse the supplies that others have used to ship stuff to you?

If you're buying stuff from other sellers on eBay, they'll be shipping your items in (hopefully) good quality boxes and such. Reuse those. The real key with reusing any packing supplies is to be sure they're still sound, sturdy, and good protection for the things you need to ship. While packing peanuts and bubble-pack hold up well, some boxes tend to weaken after they've been used a few times. If you sense a box is showing excessive creasing, bumps, tears, or just beginning to feel generally flimsy, it might be best to trash that one and look for something a bit sturdier. Just ask yourself if you'd want something you bought to be shipped in that particular box.

Now, if you've struck out on all those ways to find free supplies, don't forget you can go to most of the major mail carriers for supplies as well; most of those are also free. Most carriers will provide free boxes, bags, and envelopes to help you ship your items. Since this stuff is free, don't expect to find a huge range of sizes available. However, you'll probably find a box or envelope that will suit your item just fine. I like to use the United States Postal Service (USPS) for most of my shipping, and they have a good variety of free packing supplies. You can either take your item to the post office and have it packed and shipped on the spot, or you can order packing supplies right off their Web site (**www.usps.gov**) for delivery right to your door. Then you can pack the item whenever you need in the privacy of your own home. Remember, it's free!

 NOTE The free stuff from USPS is only for *Priority Mail*, *Express Mail*, and *Global Delivery Services* shipping. Your free packaging will bear the applicable service branding and will require you pay the postage costs applicable to the packaging you use. Since I almost exclusively use Priority Mail, I'm not complaining.

Don't stop there. If you like the idea of being able to order packing supplies online from the USPS, you'll be surprised at the number of other packing supply companies that deal on the Web. Go to any Internet search engine and start a search using the key words "packing and shipping supplies." You'll be amazed at how many companies want to help with all your packing and shipping needs. Most of these places charge for the supplies you want, but the assortment of stuff is incredible.

Since it is sometimes necessary to *buy* packing supplies, you can always go to retail office stores to buy padded envelopes, mailing tubes, and specially sized boxes to best protect what you'll ship. Most often, these packing and shipping supplies are reasonably priced, especially at the larger office supply stores or one of those big membership warehouse stores—they'll probably have the best prices. If it's filler material you need, visit one of those *box-it* kind of stores; you can find bags of packing peanuts big enough to jump in.

 NOTE Recycling supplies is great and will work for you 95 percent of the time. Sometimes, though, it's necessary to buy exactly the box or bag or filler that will ensure your item makes it to the buyer safely. Don't get cheap if it means the item will be at risk.

Boxes, pouches, and mailing tubes will come and go in your revolving inventory of shipping supplies, but here are a few things you'll always want to keep on hand as your core set of packing tools and supplies:

- Clear shipping tape (have lots of rolls of this stuff around—it's the *duct tape* of the shipping world); a self-cutting dispenser is a real bonus.

- Filler and bubble pack (it can be fun to play with, too).

- Various sized pieces of corrugated cardboard (you can scrounge for these, too).

- A sharp (but safe) utility knife.

- A box of 9"×12" (or larger) manila envelopes.

- A box of standard legal-sized envelopes.

- Sharpie permanent marking pens or other good medium line markers for addressing packages.

- Blank white paper (like 8.5"×11" printer paper) for writing thank-you notes to buyers or even to use as box labels.

■ Blank self-adhesive address labels (these are really icing; I use the blank white paper for this and just tape it down to the package).

These will be your weapons of choice that you'll reach for all the time. It's better to have this stuff readily on hand whenever you need it rather than having to run to the store when you're up to your elbows in packing peanuts. *("Shoot, man! The mail carrier's due any minute, too!")*

Packaging Techniques

You have all your boxes, bags, fillers, and accessories; now you need to get the item packed up safely and securely before you send it off to its new home. Sometimes, good packing can be an art. Many people have tried-and-true methods that always ensure the items they ship arrive safe and sound. You, too, will find methods that work for you and that you can just repeat again and again. Your driving goal is to make the items you ship come out of the box looking the same as when they first went into the box (or bag or envelope or whatever).

Before you begin your packing, you need to develop a mental image of what your package is about to experience in the world of mass-mail handling. Understand that the different package carriers out there handle thousands and thousands of packages every day. They've got a lot to move, and they're moving it quickly. Expect that your package will be dropped, dragged, pushed, poked, thrown, thrust, and every other action verb that might conjure up images of fast and furious moving things. Most carriers use machines to scoot packages along. Machines can't read words like "fragile" and "handle with care," and they don't have feelings. These machines just belch out packages all day and all night. They're loud, dirty, and they have lots of funny things that hang down and stick out all over the place. Unless your package has eyes, it probably won't be able to dodge some of these mechanical appendages. So, between the hands that toss and the machines that churn, your package will be wading through a battlefield of modern mail handling.

With that in mind, following are some tips for packaging up different kinds of items to make them battle ready.

Photos and Other Flat Items

It's amazing, but many photos and small posters I've received through the mail have made it safely in nothing more than a plain manila envelope. Flat envelopes usually do well in transit, but be sure you use cardboard inserts or a sturdy (nonflexing) cardboard envelope to mail flat items. For the best security, place the item between two pieces of oversized cardboard and tape the pieces together. Then slip the cardboard pieces into a medium-to-heavy thickness manila envelope. Be sure to use clear shipping tape on the flap. You may think that tasty strip of tongue-activated adhesive will protect the envelope's contents; think again—and then seal it well with a quick strip of tape. Another great way to mail flat items is to use one of the USPS Priority Mail shipping boxes, except keep it flat and seal the ends. These tend to stand up to any mail sorting room barrage. And, since the package is sturdy and oversized, it can't be forcibly crammed into that little 5"×5" metal mail crypt where the rest of your mail winds up every day.

Sturdy shipping tubes also work well for these sorts of items, but they will add curl to the item. For a poster or print, this is typically OK. Photographs tend to be a bit less forgiving when they're rolled. Although the photo will eventually flatten out, some buyers might not like receiving a picture that looks more like a scroll.

Glassware, Pottery, and Other Things That Go Bump

Whenever you're shipping anything that's really fragile, you'll need to take a lot of care to be sure the one item you send will still be one item when the buyer receives it. For fragile items like this, it's best to use the double-box method; you'll be putting a box within another box. Start by wrapping the item with bubble pack and placing it in a suitably sized box filled with more bubble pack or packing peanuts. Seal that box up, and then place it in a slightly larger outer box. It's best if the outer box is big enough to allow you to put an insulating barrier of bubble pack or packing peanuts around the inner box (if you can get them, Styrofoam or Eco-Foam sheets about 1" to 2" thick work as an excellent inner barrier). Make sure there's enough space at the top to add a layer of insulation between the top of the inner box and the top of the outer box. It's OK if you slightly overpack the outer box at the top; that will make sure the inner box stays snugly in place during its trip—just don't overdo it so much that closing the outer box begins to crush the inner box. Tape up the outer box securely. You can write "fragile" on the outer box; this might get the package some special handling, though I tend to believe it only eggs on bored package handlers.

Small Items

Small items are usually a breeze to pack, but you still need to take into account how fragile the item might be. If you're shipping jewelry or small crafts or something breakable, use a box that is small and stout, but still leaves room for padding around the item inside. When a pair of Red Wing boots start tap dancing on the top of your package, you'll be glad there's some extra buffering around the item inside (and the recipient will be, too). I've read of other folks who like to slip the item in a Ziploc bag before they put it in the shipping box; apparently excessive moisture can be a problem. That's probably not a bad thing to keep in mind. When you're sure the item is nicely bagged and padded, seal up that box and bid your neat little package bon voyage.

Framed Items

If you're shipping artwork, lithographs, or anything else that's been framed, you'll need to take some real care. First, if the item is behind glass, it might be best to disassemble the framed item, glass, and frame before you pack it up. This way, every element can be individually wrapped in bubble pack or slipped between stiff pieces of cardboard. Depending on the size of the item, you might need to buy a special box designed specifically for shipping artwork. Lots of bubble pack or foam sheets will be especially crucial to be sure your item makes it to its destination safely. Be warned, though: properly packed and shipped artwork can tally up some hefty shipping costs.

With anything you pack, you want to be sure you secure it well inside the box. When you've finished your packing, give the box a good shaking. During this test, silence is truly golden. If you hear anything moving, there's a good chance more things will be moving when the package finally gets to its intended destination. If you hear something moving, you might want to open the package and beef up the inner packing. If the item is pretty sturdy or is made of paper and you don't think a little movement will cause any problems, then use your good judgment in determining if it's carrier worthy.

Being Cost-Conscious When You Pack

First and foremost, you want to be sure you choose the packing materials that will ensure the safest journey for your item. But there are times you can overdo it and end up with a ghastly heavy package that's going to cost an arm and a leg to ship.

These days, you see a lot of Styrofoam, Eco-Foam, and air-filled packing supplies being used. Why? It's because these materials are extremely light in weight while still providing excellent protection for the item being shipped. If you think cardboard is great for stiffening but maybe pressboard would be even better, you'd be right, but that pressboard is going to add a few extra pounds that will translate into higher shipping costs. The cardboard will probably do just fine.

Wadded up newspaper works pretty well for internal filler, but too much of it does tend to get heavy. That's why your Sunday paper hits the driveway with such a *smack*. You can use wadded newspaper for smaller packages without adding too much extra weight, but large boxes will get heavy quick. Use bubble pack or packing peanuts instead.

The best of all worlds that you should be striving for is a fine balance between good protection and light weight. It's achievable if you try.

Bullet-Proof Isn't Necessary

Although I told you to prepare your package for the barrage it will endure during its journey, be sure you still make it penetrable to the dear recipient at the end of the line. It's kind of like your Grandma who insists on taping every edge of your Christmas present; by the time you get into the gift, your fingers have so many paper, tape, and box cuts that you hope she got you a tin of Curads this year.

Remember that the buyer has to be able to get to that precious new possession without destroying it in the process. If you use lots of packing tape—which isn't bad since you want to keep the package closed during its travels—be sure to leave some space inside the package for a knife of some sort to be used to open the package up without slicing the item inside to ribbons.

TIP
If you're the buyer, always use extreme care when cutting through packing tape on a package you receive. Any damage you inflict will most likely end up being your fault. Put the machete away and go get a little hobby or utility knife.

If you've packaged an item in a special way to protect it and it needs special attention when it's opened, tell the recipient. *This end up*, *Open with care*, or *Use no hooks* (*??!*) are all things you can write on the outside of a box to tip the buyer off that it might be wise to take some extra time when extracting the treasure. If there are special measures to be taken when actually removing the item from its internal packing, include an explanatory note inside that can be easily seen when the package is first opened.

Choosing the Best Carrier

Well, this is largely a matter of personal opinion and preference. Most of us have some horror story to tell about the guy who must have stomped a package because his boot print is there to prove it. Other stories abound about the friendliness (or lack thereof) that greets you when you step up to the customer service counter. Do wild gunfights really break out in the back room?

All carriers work hard to provide good, quick service, but that comes with a cost: the people at the front counter might have already used up their supply of smiles and "thank yous" by the time you step forward, and your package (one of thousands for the day) will not always be handled gingerly, dusted off, and coddled with joy as it comes down the conveyor belt. You might like the services or transit times that one carrier provides over the others. In most cases, choosing a carrier will be a matter of preference based on past experience. However, there are some things to consider that might force your decision a bit.

First, think about cost. For most general packages, I still find USPS to be the most reasonably priced for the quick service they offer. I can pay USPS $3.20 to get an item to its domestic destination in two or three days (that's the *Priority Mail* service). It might cost me $5 to get that same item to the same place using UPS, and it will take a few extra days to get there. Superfast and overnight carriers and couriers like DHL and Federal Express—FedEx to its friends—will give you faster delivery, but they'll take your money fast too.

Next you'll need to consider the services the carrier provides. Most often, this will be a matter of package insurance, tracking services, speed of delivery, and proof of delivery. For some carriers, you'll pay extra for these services, but the base shipping rate is low. With other carriers, the extra services are already included, but the base shipping rate will probably be higher; you're not getting extra services for free because you've already paid for them. You'll need to decide how valuable and how fragile your item is before you can decide which carrier will give you the service you need at the best possible price. That's how you'll decide on the right carrier.

But cost and services aren't all that matter when you're choosing a carrier. Sometimes, you'll need to consider your buyer's particular situation. Some buyers might not be able to receive packages delivered by some carriers. For instance, if your buyer wants the package delivered to a post office box, then clearly the USPS is the only choice. Commercial carriers and couriers (UPS, FedEx, and the rest) can only deliver to street addresses (homes, apartments, or businesses).

Also, some carriers might require the recipient to sign for the package. If that's not convenient for the buyer, you'll both need to agree to use a different carrier—or maybe a different delivery address. Check with your buyer to find out if there are any special considerations that need to be thought of when you choose the carrier.

Finally, you'll need to consider the size of the item you're shipping. Some carriers—like USPS—don't handle *really big* packages too well. You might need to use UPS or another carrier if your item is particularly large.

Determining Postage Costs

This can sometimes be a real trick. Postage costs are often difficult to pinpoint accurately until the time you're at the carrier's office actually shipping the item. But you have to tell your buyer how much extra to include with the payment to cover postage costs *before* you actually ship the item.

The weight of the package will vary until the item is completely wrapped up and ready to ship. Believe it or not, silly things like packing tape and address labels will all add to the weight of the item. Postage costs are calculated to the ounce, so any little addition to the package—necessary or otherwise—is going to cost more.

If you're a real die-hard about shipping stuff, you'll probably have one of those cool postage scales (not one of the little ones but the larger kind that pediatricians use to weigh babies when they're not shipping stuff). These are designed to calculate weight and postage costs for items shipped through the U.S. Postal Service. The scales are available at most office supply stores, but they can be kind of expensive. However, if you plan to ship a lot of packages that could weigh quite a bit, it might be worth the investment; it'll help you calculate postage costs before you get to the post office. When the scale shows the weight of the package, it also shows the corresponding U.S. postage costs.

 NOTE Some of the newer scales can even print the postal meter tag that will be affixed to the package. These hook up in your home or place of business via a phone line and will debit your special postage account every time you weigh and meter a package. You're like your own little post office; all you need is a starched blue shirt and little wool shorts. Oxford walking shoes are optional.

If you only plan to ship flat items that can fit in manila envelopes, then one of the little scales will do just fine. Most of these are really reasonably priced and can usually weigh items up to two pounds. Just like their bigger brothers, these little jobbies will also provide the corresponding postage costs.

Of course, international shipping is a different story. Calculating postage costs for shipping items abroad is usually something you'll need to let the pros do for you. A lot of the cost depends on the kind of package, the actual size (dimensions) of it, and of course where it's going.

One of the coolest things to come along in a while in regard to shipping packages and determining postage costs are the various online rate calculators. That's right, for the major package carriers, you can log on to that carrier's Web site and find a special rate calculator that helps you determine a pretty accurate cost of postage, domestic or international. All you need is the weight (or a very close approximation) to help you decide how much your package will cost to ship. These online solutions are great to use when quoting postage costs to your buyer. There might be a slight difference when you actually ship the item, but if you've put the item in the packaging you intend to use and weigh it, the cost you quote will be very close to the final fee.

Use Good Judgment When Billing for Shipping

I would hope this would be a point that doesn't have to be stressed too emphatically, but unfortunately some folks tend to overcharge a bit much for "shipping and handling." The section is for those tempted to put their thumb on the scale.

First rule of keeping your customers happy and coming back: don't bump up the postage costs *at all*. If U.S. Priority Mail costs $3.20, then don't ask for $4 or $5. Buyers remember how much they were charged for postage, and most of them will be reading that little postal meter tag on their package when it arrives. If your item went too cheaply in the auction and you think you can squeeze an extra buck or two in postage charges, think again. This strikes a real flat note with just about everyone. Be a straight shooter, and your buyers won't feel the need to shoot back.

TIP If you really want to please your buyers, provide a refund if you accidentally overcharge them for postage. That's a real pleasant surprise to most everyone, and it's a sign of your unfailing honesty. Of course, don't spend 33 cents to mail back a quarter, but if you accidentally overstated postage by more than a dollar or so, send it back. This kind of stuff really blows away the competition and probably earns you more positive feedback points.

Then there's the whole notion of charging the buyer for "time and handling." Sorry, people, but I blow a raspberry on this one. Most buyers don't appreciate being told how valuable your time was when you packaged up the item they paid $50 for and in which you had invested only $5. Sure your time is valuable, but so was theirs as they worked to earn that $50 they sent to you. They're not asking for a deduction for the time they spent earning the money in the first place; you shouldn't ask for a special premium for the time you spend earning it from them.

And should you charge a buyer for packaging materials? If you're curious about my opinion: No. With all I've said about how free packaging material can be, why charge a customer for it? It will make you look like you're trying to squeeze a few extra drops of blood from the stone. In the majority of instances, packaging shouldn't cost you much, if anything at all.

SOAPBOX I know these topics can be real bones of contention, and I might have raised a few hackles—maybe yours—just stating my opinions about them here. In fact, that's why I decided to quickly jump up on my soapbox so you'd know this is an opinion of mine, but one I stand behind. I believe there is something known as the "cost of doing business." Whether you use the auctions as your sole source of income or for some extra activity on the side, there's going to be a cost of time and materials if you want to be successful at it. If you overcharge buyers for postage, materials, or handling time, they'll probably not be too quick to bid on any auctions of yours in the future. If you charge a flat rate for postage regardless of the item (some people do), then you'll miss a lot of good bids on lower-priced items. Nobody wants to win an item for $5 and then have to pay some flat rate of $6 for "shipping and handling." If the item truly bears the cost, that's fine; if it's just a "policy" of yours, I'd reconsider that policy before bidders begin to reconsider you.

Registering and Insuring Packages

Somewhere along the line, you'll need to consider a little protection. Protection for those packages will help you feel more secure as they journey from your safe hamlet to their eventual new homes. Even though you've packaged your items well and given them every chance to arrive in tip-top shape, you might want to add one or two extra measures to be sure both you and your buyer will not be surprised with potential bad news.

First is insurance. You can insure a package you ship for just about any value you like. Some carriers provide insurance as part of the basic shipping costs (UPS provides automatic insurance for your package up to $100 when you pay for basic surface-rate delivery); other carriers will charge for insurance and will *not* provide it unless you specify and pay for it. All the carriers will eventually charge you something for insurance as the value of your packages rises higher and higher.

 Be sure to see the different carriers' Web sites for more information on the specific schedule of insurance coverage and associated costs.

The cost of insurance is pretty low compared to the protection it provides. If your poor package ends up on the wrong side of a boot or disappears somewhere in the Bermuda Triangle, you'll be glad you insured it.

Consider what happens if a package is damaged or lost: As the seller, it's the unwritten law that you're responsible for the package's safety until it reaches its destination. Are you willing to take a chance that the package will make it there intact or at all? Are you prepared to provide a speedy refund to the disappointed buyer? If you're not, you'll want to discuss insurance.

Insurance is another of those cost add-ons that will increase the final cost of shipping a package. Insurance can cost as little as 75 cents and go up from there depending on the value you want to insure. Since insurance costs extra, and since it is considered part of shipping expenses, my remedy is to let the buyer be the judge. If you'll recall from the listing examples I showed to you in Chapters 16 and 18, my item description clearly stated, *"Insurance additional upon request."*

Tip Insurance is something I learned about the hard way. I never asked about insuring packages, assuming any buyer who wanted insurance would make a specific request for it. One time I sent a package to a buyer who soon contacted me stating the package was damaged in transit—and so was the item inside. The buyer was now requesting authorization to return the item for a full refund. Now I was in a pickle: I wanted to keep the customer satisfied, but neither of us had talked about insuring the package. The item, upon return to me, would be of less value than before. Again, I didn't want the buyer dissatisfied, but I didn't want to take the entire loss. So, since neither of us ever talked about the option of insurance, I believed we needed to share the burden. In the end, I let the buyer keep the damaged item but also refunded half of the price. I ended up keeping what amounted to the original investment I had in the item, and the buyer was satisfied that we found a compromise that served us both.

With that last tip I just shared, you can understand why I've decided to let the buyer choose to pay for insurance or take a chance on doing without. Recall in my end-of-auction e-mail messages that I again ask the buyer to include additional money for insurance if it's wanted (see Chapter 20). In this way, I've put the burden back on the buyer, but I've also given the buyer the option not to spend the extra money. I always pack my items as securely as possible, and all but maybe two have made it safely (out of literally hundreds). If, however, something happens to a package in transit and the buyer chose not to pay for insurance, well, that's the breaks.

Sometimes, though, even I break my own rules. Occasionally I'll go ahead and insure a package even though I haven't been paid or asked to do so. If an item received a really high bid but the buyer chose not to insure it, I might throw down a couple of dollars myself just for peace of mind. If the item ended up being expensive and something bad happened to it, that buyer wouldn't be happy. I can stand on the point that the buyer didn't elect to pay for insurance, but it could still be a messy situation to sort out and settle. Sometimes, I just think it's easier for me to insure the item myself while still walking away with a tidy profit.

To insure a package, all you really have to do is fill out a little form, tell the clerk how much you want to insure the package for, and pay the fee. The clerk will put a neat little sticker or stamp on the package marking that it's insured. When an item is insured, the buyer will have to sign for it before the carrier will release it; that way, no recipient can claim it was never received—there's that signature on file. And when you insure a package, you (the seller and shipper) will get a receipt; by all means keep it in a safe place until you hear the buyer has received the package in good health.

TIP   Whatever carrier you like to use—even if you like to use several—grab a handful of their insurance forms and take them home with you. When you're packaging up your items, you can fill out the forms ahead of time and lightly tape them to the package so you won't forget to pay for the insurance. If the buyer paid for insurance and you forget to request it at the carrier's counter, you better start writing an apology, preparing to refund what the buyer paid you for insurance, and hoping the buyer's item makes it safely.

And what happens if an item is lost or damaged in transit? Who's responsible for picking up the pieces, so to speak? The answer is that it depends on the carrier and its methods of processing claims. Generally, though, carriers will require a reasonable delivery period to pass before someone can make a claim of nondelivery. *("It's lost! It's lost!")* If the item is damaged, either the sender or receiver will need to file a claim with the carrier.

Since filing a claim might work differently across the different carriers, the first thing to do if an item is lost or damaged is for the buyer to contact the seller immediately. The carriers have "windows of opportunity" in which claims for damaged or lost goods need to be filed before that window closes and someone's out of luck. If you've received an item that was insured and is damaged, or don't receive it all, contact the seller right away and, working with the carrier's claim process, begin to set the wheels of restitution in motion.

SOAPBOX   If you're the buyer and receive a damaged item or the item never shows up, don't demand the seller immediately refund your money. Understand that the mishap is an equal surprise to both of you, and the refund would not make sense until the two of you—with the carrier's help—can sort out what happened. It's really rare for something to be lost or destroyed in transit (at least in my 20 years of mail-order experience). Be patient, work together, and take it all in stride. Hopefully it will never happen to you.

Tip
Now, sellers, just because you insured a package, don't think you're free from having to do a good job of packing the item. Some carriers will reject insurance claims if the packaging of a damaged item looks like it was lousy to start with. Use good judgment here.

So what about registering packages? What will that do, and what will it cost? Quite simply, registering packages ensures that the recipient on the other end provides a signature at the time the package is delivered. It's the best way to track the actual delivery of the package, heading off any dispute—real or fabricated—about the package's never reaching its destination. If the recipient's signature is on file, there's not much to dispute except maybe sloppy penmanship.

When you insure a package, it is virtually registered; it will be tracked to ensure it makes its trip safely. If you do not insure a package, you might need to request having it registered. For example, the USPS provides package registration, certified mail status, or return receipt—all of which provide proof of delivery—for a nominal fee of about $1 to $3.

Some carriers like UPS and FedEx will provide automatic registering and tracking services for packages you ship with them, although they might not always require signatures at the time the package is dropped off. (Ever play doorbell ditch with the UPS guy? You hear the doorbell ring, you go to the door—nobody's there. Did the package standing on your doorstep somehow ring the bell itself?) This is fine, I suppose, but it doesn't prevent some passer-by from nabbing that interesting little box on your porch while you're at work. Most packages would be fine sitting around waiting for you to get home, but if the item's expensive, it's best to have a signature required before the carrier drops it off.

The fun thing about registered and tracked packages is that you can easily log on to many carriers' Web sites and track your package's world tour by entering the official tracking number. On specially designed package tracking pages, people like you and me can see the various stops our packages have made and how close they're getting to their destination. It's kind of fun to watch the process work in front of your very eyes.

chapter 23

Satisfaction Guaranteed!

Now comes the gingerbread. It's time to add the spice to the batter, the icing to the cookie. This is where you put your personal stamp on what you do. You'll serve up what you promised, then add an extra touch or two that will be met with unexpected delight.

As I trust you've learned through reading this book and actually using eBay, the more you put into the auction experience, the more you'll get out of it. After the auction, when it comes time to work in the physical world, you can see that prompt, pleasant, and timely communications serve as the ingredients of a good virtual relationship between a buyer and a seller. It's the basic principle behind why people return to a product, a place, or a person: if it is a good experience, it will make people want to repeat it. Real trust is developing between two people, and that's the most valuable return on investment anyone could hope to gain.

Mediocrity just doesn't cut it, though. Anyone can meet the usual expectations that have become a part of the eBay community ethic. You can send your payment in a reasonable amount of time; you can ship your item in a way that gets it to its destination safely. Meeting expectations is certainly the way to go and not to be underrated—but *exceeding* expectations is really where it's at.

Make that extra effort to let the other person know you're glad to be dealing with them. Do something special to that item you're shipping so the buyer will smile with delight; make them gladder than glad that they chose *your* auction. Give that extra little push in what you do, and you'll tap into the heart of what's making eBay such a great place to buy and sell cool stuff and meet some great people while you do it.

Follow Up as Buyer and Seller

Always keep that communication flowing. You've been so good about it this far—there's no reason to slack off now. Here are a few extra tips that will help both buyers and sellers do a bit more for the other person and make the auction and transaction flow smoother.

Buyers

Remember to keep that seller informed about when you sent your payment. If you say, *"I'll mail payment right away!"* then be sure you do just that. If you can't mail your payment for a couple of days, let the seller know; they'll appreciate the "heads up" of knowing it might be an extra day or two before your payment arrives. It's better to be honest and up front if there's going to be a slight delay than to drag your feet and keep the seller wondering. Sellers understand that some delays happen. If you're honest and conscientious about fulfilling your bid obligation, the seller will know you can be counted on to come through as quickly as possible.

Regarding the payment itself, if you can, send money orders or cashier's checks instead of personal checks. To a seller, these are as good as cash, and they show that you want the seller to know immediately you can be trusted (no bouncy checks to worry about). The seller can pack up and ship your item quickly with the confidence of knowing the money is truly in the bank; besides, it also means you'll get your item sooner. Sellers often appreciate money orders and cashier's checks because the sooner they can ship your item the sooner they can check it off their to-do list.

If you want to pay using a personal check, understand that the seller will most likely need that check to clear their bank before shipping your item. It's not a slam, and the seller isn't insinuating you're some check-bouncing boob. The seller has the right to be paid in full—and if you're the seller, you should expect to exercise this right, too. Be patient while your check is processed by the seller's bank. It could take a week or two, but that's what you agree to when you use a personal check.

Then exercise a little patience once you've been notified that your item is on the way. Give that package a reasonable amount of time to arrive. Don't badger the seller—nobody wants to hear, *"I haven't gotten it yet. When did you ship it? Are you sure you shipped it?"* Find out what service the seller used to ship your item, and give it a little time. Of course, during peak mailing months (like November and December), understand that it will probably take a couple of extra days for your package to arrive. For all other times of the year, give your item at least a week to ten days to arrive before you call out the bloodhounds. Keep in mind the distance between you and the seller—if you're shipping across continents, definitely expect a longer transit time. And, if there truly does seem to be some sort of delay, send a polite and appropriately inquisitive e-mail note asking if the seller will provide some details about the shipping of the item. Don't jump down the seller's throat and start slinging nastiness because your package is delayed; it might not be the seller's fault.

When the package does arrive, send a quick e-mail message to the seller to say the package made it safely. The seller wants to be sure you got your item as expected. Sure, no news is good news, but it really helps the seller bring closure to the deal when there's been a confirmation that the eagle has landed with all feathers still attached.

Sellers

The sellers are the ones who really need to communicate at this stage, and they have the best opportunities to exceed the expectations of the buyer. Sellers, like buyers, also need to use some patience and can easily exemplify that to the buyers' delight.

The first thing a seller needs to do is wait for the payment to arrive. The buyer might encounter a slight delay that keeps that payment from getting into the mail as quickly as it should. Give a buyer who warns of a slight delay the chance to make good. Letting you know when a slowdown has occurred is admirable, and you can return that gesture with your vote of confidence that the payment will come through in reasonable time. If the payment doesn't seem to be arriving soon enough, it's OK to politely ask if the payment has been sent. Let the buyer know you haven't received it; maybe it's been misrouted in the mail. If a payment is late in arriving, it might be as much a surprise to the buyer as it is to you; together, you can work to figure out what happened.

When the payment does arrive, send an e-mail note to say you've received it. The buyer is really the one taking a risk here—putting good money on the line and hoping it doesn't just vanish without a trace. Let that buyer know the payment is now in your hands; the info will provide the double reassurance of knowing that the money made it and that you're truly honest in your intentions.

More important, let the buyer know when you'll be shipping the item. Then be sure that you actually ship the item when you say you will. If you announce that you'll ship within 24 hours of payment when someone pays using a money order, you'd better live up to that. A buyer might go a bit out of the way to get a money order to you just to get this fast service; it would be a waste of effort and good faith if you delayed shipment.

If the buyer chooses to pay with a personal check, that's fine too. Let the buyer know when you receive and deposit the check. When the check clears your bank, let the buyer know all is well and the item is on the way. Waiting for a check to clear is an anxiety for the buyer: Will it clear fast? Will you forget to ship the package when it does clear? Will you disappear entirely after you've gotten the money? Even though somebody chooses to use a personal check as payment, be sensitive to the buyer's natural excitement and impatience about receiving the item—the extra wait, though perfectly justifiable, is a drag for the buyer to endure.

A really pleasing gesture here is to ship immediately to a buyer who pays with a personal check *if* you've dealt successfully with that buyer in the past. That buyer will be genuinely impressed and flattered to be regarded as a trusted customer whose check is as good as gold. Real classy touch.

When you notify the buyer that the item is on the way, say what carrier you've used (if you hadn't already made special agreed-upon shipping arrangements). If the item is being shipped using a tracking number (like UPS or USPS Express Mail), include the tracking number in the note so the buyer will be able to follow the package's progress right on the Web. That's kind of exciting for the buyer.

Without going overboard, always thank the buyer for having bid on your item. After all, nobody *has* to bid on your auction, and you want to treat your high bidder like a true customer. Let them know their business has been valuable to you. After all, a happy buyer just might visit your next auction.

The real key to great—not just good—communication is when both parties have a clear understanding of what's going on and what their expectations should be every step of the way. Nobody likes it when they begin to believe they'd *"better follow up on that deal because I haven't heard anything"* or *"better check in with that other person to see what the delay is."* You'll quickly find that timely and sincere communication will be important in keeping the deal on an "up" note, heading off potential problems and defusing any troublesome situations before they arise or get out of hand.

Expect that, at one time or another, there will be a wrinkle in a deal, and it might not run as smoothly as you would like. Take it from the perspective that everybody's human and that life happens while you're busy making other plans. Most people have regular jobs, families, and other obligations. That's certainly no excuse to be slack in fulfilling auction commitments, but it's not the end of the world when you encounter a hiccup. Keep cool, smile, and work through the situation. You'll be happier in the end.

 NOTE I once contacted a buyer to let him know I hadn't received his payment, asking if he'd been able to send it yet. (It had been about seven days since he e-mailed me saying his payment was in the mail.) When he received my message, he responded immediately stating the payment was sent the day he sent the e-mail confirmation. Hmmm. We both wondered what the delay was. The buyer asked if I'd wait a couple more days to see if his letter would show up. He seemed sincere, so I didn't mind. As I was about to contact him again to let him know his payment still hadn't arrived, he sent me a message saying his letter had just showed up in his own mailbox. It seems he got my zip code wrong, and the post office was unable to deliver the letter to me. I was actually happy to hear this—at least his letter (and the money order inside it)—wasn't lost. Three days later the money order was in my hands. The next day I sent out his item.

The point is that because the buyer and I kept in close and cooperative communication, we avoided any doubt or suspicion toward one another. Despite the unintentional delay, it ended up being a great transaction for both of us. We've since posted positive feedback for each other in eBay's Feedback Forum.

The Cover Letter

I really like this one. Perhaps the easiest way to add a touch of extra care for your customer is to include a friendly letter inside their package. The cover letter is really kind of a thank you note, and it lets you pretty much introduce the buyer to their new item and repeat your thanks for their winning bid. In my cover letters, I usually write something like this:

• •

Hi Steve,

Here are your *Young Frankenstein* lobby cards. I hope they'll meet or exceed your expectations.

Thanks for bidding!

Best,

Dennis

• •

This is a simple note, but it really says a lot. First, it gets the buyer ready to inspect the new item and builds a bit of anticipation when you say *"here it is."* Old Steve might be thinking *"Cool! I've been dying to see this."* He's getting excited already. Then, before he actually lays eyes on the item, the next line of the letter lets him know you hope he'll be satisfied with his purchase and maybe even exceedingly delighted; you're showing your honest concern that he'll be pleased. Finally, when you thank him for bidding and wish him your best, you're letting him know his business was important to you, and you're glad the two of you could work this transaction together. It's a "feel good" kind of thing, and I've seen it make a positive impact on most of my customers.

Besides working as the prelude to unpacking the item, the cover letter also brings a clean closure to the physical part of the auction. The cover letter adds a personal touch to the final exchange; it's as if you were able to reach out, shake the buyer's hand, and say *"Thank you. I've enjoyed this."*

SOAPBOX   To me, there's something strangely cold about receiving an item without a note of any kind accompanying it. It's like the person on the other end never really existed in the physical world. You pull out the item, look at it, then look inside the package to see if there's anything else: a note, a slip of paper, a receipt? Nothing. OK ... I guess this is it. Thanks ... whoever you are.

It would be like taking a date out for a great night of fun and returning her to her home, at which point she gets out of your car without saying a word, walks up the front path, and goes inside the house. The door closes behind her. The porch light goes out. You're left listening to the chirp of crickets and a dog barking in the distance. Brrrr.

If you really want to make a connection with your buyer, be sure the cover letter is handwritten as implied in the example. When you take the two minutes to actually *write* the letter, you show that you are a real person on the other end of the deal. A typewritten, printed letter tends to be a bit mechanical and has that distant, mass-production feel.

Dress Up the Item

Show you care even more and give that item you're shipping a little shine. It's fine to pack an item for safe shipping, but can you pack it in a way that shows extra care for it during its journey and even make it look better than when it appeared in your auction listing?

Although I fully covered the ins and outs of packing and shipping in Chapter 22, you'd be surprised at how excited and appreciative buyers are when they can plainly see how much care you took to get their cherished prize to them safely. If you're shipping multiple items to somebody, pack them so they truly cannot cause mutual damage. Add cardboard separators inside a box in addition to the wrapping you put around each item. If the journey ends up being a bit rough and the outside of the package shows it, the buyer will be nervous—then delighted—when it turns out the inside of the package was built to withstand whatever the carriers could dish out.

And how 'bout the item itself? How does it look? Is it clean? Without altering the appearance or condition of the item in a negative way, maybe you could give it a quick wiping down or dusting off. If you send a dirty, dusty item to your buyer, it'll make it look like you didn't care enough to make the item presentable. Whatever you do, though, don't scrub an item to the point that you damage it—but a light sprucing up is usually harmless and will most often be more pleasing to the buyer.

ALERT Look out! Some collectors are real sticklers about the "historical aging" of an item. I've talked to some collectors who regard even the lightest sprucing up as a form of fraudulent representation. They contend that removing the acquired soiling on an item also wipes away its true history and makes it look newer and less authentic than it really is. Uhh…yeah. I don't happen to agree with this sentiment. If I'm going to get a collectible, I don't want it to be some grimy, cruddy, gooky thing. I'll want to clean it up and display it proudly. But I have to respect the purist collectors and their personal convictions.

If you sense you're dealing with a "purist," maybe leave the item as is or, at least, mention in your correspondence that the item is a bit dirty and ask if they would be opposed to it being lightly cleaned off. You'll find out real quick the kind of collector you're dealing with.

Then, once the item is looking all dapper, there's an easy way to make it look even better on first sight: slip it into a protective sleeve or wrap it in a clear poly bag. You'll give the item a newer, more collectible look. This is especially true for books, comics, magazines, and lobby cards (love those). Protective sleeves add a sheen to the item and will generally result in a better first impression. The protective sleeve you provide will actually save the new owner from having to get one for the item. It won't cost you much of anything for the extra protection, and the buyer will love it.

Posting Feedback on eBay

Well, this is the big payoff for the excellent service and conscientiousness you showed when you completed your deal. eBay's Feedback Forum is where buyers and sellers post their comments about one another for all to see. If you recall from earlier chapters, the Feedback Forum is how you'll build that feedback rating number that appears next to your eBay user ID. But how do you use it? Simple.

First, get acquainted with the rules and philosophy of the forum. Using the main navigation bar, select *Services*. In the submenu, choose *Feedback forum*. As quick as that, you're at the eBay Feedback Forum introduction page (see Figure 23-1).

Review the information presented on the introduction page—you'll discover the Feedback Forum is a public bulletin board where eBay users learn more about each other based on the comments that have been posted. Comments, you'll see, can come in three flavors:

- **Positive**. This is a note of praise and will be posted by a user who has good news to share about you and the transaction you have just completed. Each positive note will add +1 to your eBay feedback rating.

- **Neutral**. Hmmm. Well . . . not a bad thing, but not necessarily a good thing either. A neutral comment might be left if a user wants to share something about their interaction with you that wasn't up to

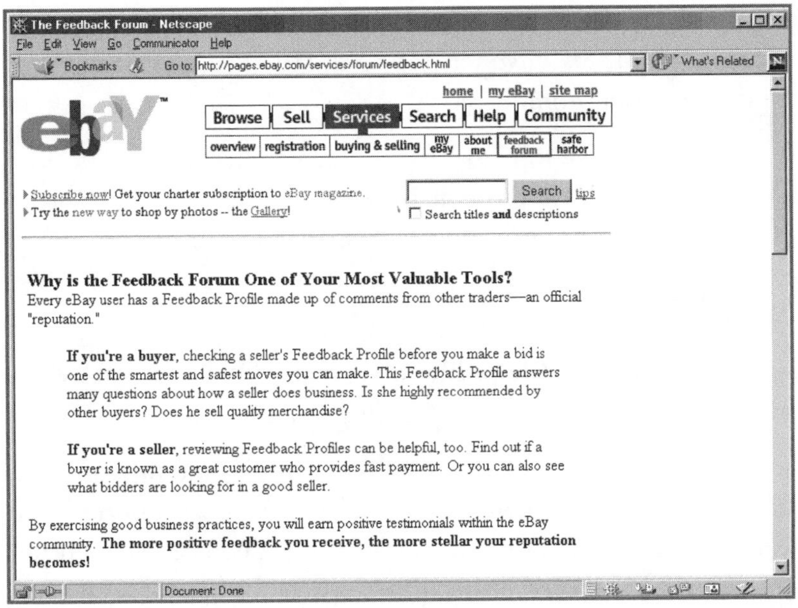

figure 23-1

Take the time to review what you'll see at the eBay Feedback Forum introduction page. This is the heart of the eBay community.

their reasonable expectations, but doesn't feel strongly enough to post negative feedback. A neutral note has no effect on your overall eBay feedback rating, but it's still not as desirable as a positive feedback. Be aware that you can earn neutral notes from other users who have lost their registered status; any positive note from these folks will be converted to neutral.

■ **Negative**. Uh-oh. Someone's real unhappy with you and one of your auctions, and they've just let the rest of the community know about it. This is a drag because whatever happened, it left a negative impact on that other person, and you're going to feel their wrath. Every negative comment you receive on eBay will apply a –1 to your overall feedback rating.

Within the Feedback Forum, you'll find you can do several feedback-related things:

■ **See feedback about another user**. Probably the most-used feature of the forum, though you also know you can review the feedback by clicking on a user's feedback profile number.

■ **Leave feedback for another user**. I'll show you this one in just a moment.

■ **Review feedback others have left for you**. *Definitely* something you'll be interested in monitoring.

■ **Review feedback you've left for others**. Are you keeping up on the feedback you need to leave for your buyers and sellers? You'll want to for many of the reasons I've already expressed in this chapter. This feature helps you keep track of the feedback you've left and the feedback that you still need to post.

■ **Make your feedback profile public or private**. Odd, yes, but available for you to change. I'll go into this in just a bit, too.

As you can see, there's a lot to this whole feedback thing—and for good reason. Feedback matters and the core eBay community has supported and relied on it since the early days of the site's operation. The Feedback Forum was the first form of customer protection devised for use at eBay just months after eBay first went live. However, some users have felt it isn't effective enough—that it doesn't really do a thing to head off or ward off bad business. I disagree. When you consider getting into a potential transaction with another eBay user you don't know, you'll probably first visit their Feedback Profile to see what others have said about that particular individual. If someone has a truly bad experience, it serves the community when those facts are made public. In the positive vein, it's just as beneficial to the other eBay users when there is feedback to review, helping us all make better decisions regarding who we will deal with.

So the key to interpreting another user's feedback rating is not just to look at their feedback rating number but to actually read the comments others have left. The rating number may reflect a mix of positive, neutral, and negative comments. You need to assess for yourself whether you believe the person you're about to deal with is a good Sam or a bad apple.

 SOAPBOX This is a tricky situation for me because it makes me deal with the whole issue of forgiveness. When I see a user with a reasonably high feedback rating, but two or more negative comments have been posted, it's hard for me not to become a bit hesitant. If there's more good than bad, that says something. However, what was it someone could have done to earn a negative note? Was it a mistake? An irate customer on the other end? A disregard for a previous deal? Or what? My point is that negative comments can sometimes make a larger impact than the simple −1 deduction they cause.

But the Feedback Forum is truly effective because it's a reward system that I believe really works. With more and more users joining eBay daily, the only thing that quickly separates the wheat from the chaff is a user's feedback rating. Just about everyone I've dealt with has worked hard to make the transaction quick and pleasant, knowing the reward will be a positive comment in their feedback profile. New users are motivated to do good business and begin building their own eBay reputation—one of which they can be proud. The comments are actual customer testimony and recommendation, and they really make a difference.

So how do you leave a comment in the Feedback Forum for another user? Several ways, actually. First, if you're at the Feedback Forum introduction

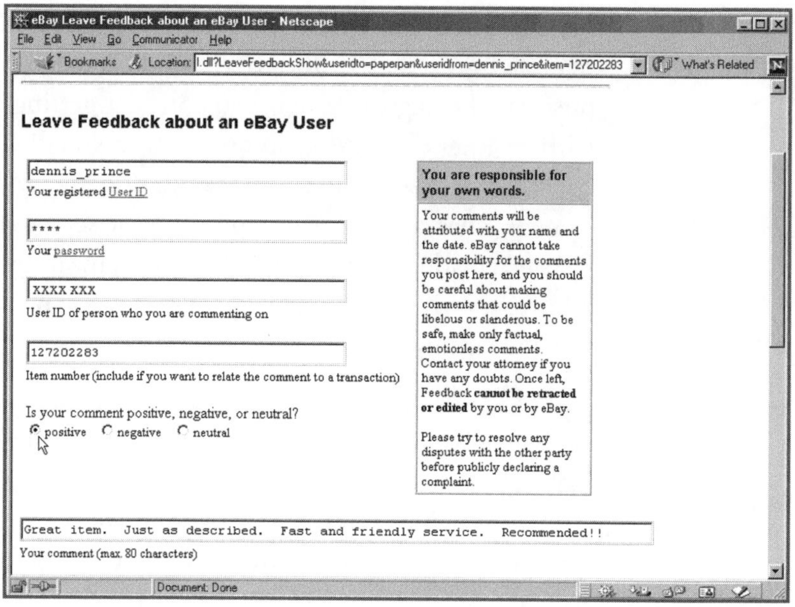

figure 23-2

Leaving feedback for another eBay user is as easy as using a simple fill-in form.

page, find the link titled *Leave Feedback about an eBay user.* Click it and you'll jump to a similarly titled screen (see Figure 23-2).

Now, before I discuss using this screen, you should know there are other ways to get to the feedback form. You could easily click on a user's feedback rating number whenever it's displayed and make your way to the feedback posting page. However, the *best* way to leave feedback is directly from the item details page of a closed auction—one in which you were either high bidder or seller. When the auction is over, the bidder's paddle icon on the details page is replaced with the *Leave Feedback* icon (refer back to Figure 20-3); there you can click on links to leave feedback about either the seller or the bidder. Why is this the best way? Well, first, using the item details entry point automatically fills in your user ID, the other party's user ID, and the item number of the auction you're responding to. That saves some work for you. More important, though, feedback is really most effective when it can be directly referenced to an actual transaction. Think about it: If you're reviewing someone's feedback, wouldn't you want to hear from other users who have actually dealt with this person during a real transaction situation? It's just like any product testimony—you wouldn't be inclined to believe someone who *assumes* a product would *probably* be the best on the market, though they've never actually tried it personally (*". . . these are not paid actors"*). Yeah, right.

SOAPBOX OK, so you're realizing that it's not absolutely *required* to specify an auction number when leaving feedback. If transaction testimony based on real auction transactions is the best, why would eBay allow feedback posting *without* specifying an actual auction? Well, the belief is that the community members often work among themselves, helping each other, answering questions or providing general guidance. Some users believe that sort of help is valuable and would like to publicly acknowledge users for their efforts, even though their interaction wasn't related to an actual auction. With all I've spouted about the power of the community, I'd have to agree.

So, regardless how you get there, when it's time to leave feedback, here's all you do. Referring back to Figure 23-2, be sure to enter your registered user ID, your password, and the ID of the user for whom you want to post a comment.

ALERT Leaving negative feedback requires that you specify the item number! Yes, that item number has been an optional entry *until* you believe it's time to post a negative note. All negative postings must be related to an auction that went bad. No "general" bad comments are allowed.

The real key on the *Leave Feedback* page, though, is how you'll categorize your feedback comment: the little option buttons that let you choose whether to leave a positive, negative, or neutral comment. Just below the option buttons, you'll see the text field where you actually enter your comment. You have only 80 characters to express yourself. Use short little statements that quickly get your feelings across.

When you're satisfied with your comment, scroll down a bit further (see Figure 23-3). You'll see some text that explains the impact of the feedback you're leaving—once you've said what's on your mind, it's there for good. Take care in what you write because this is a public forum: the Libel and Slander brothers could pay you a visit if you get reckless in the things you say. But for this example it's a good transaction and I'm ready to post. Just click on the *Leave comment* button you see near the bottom of the screen. After you do, you'll see a confirmation screen like the one shown in Figure 23-4.

figure 23-3

Be sure you understand the
impact of your comments, then
post them for all to see.

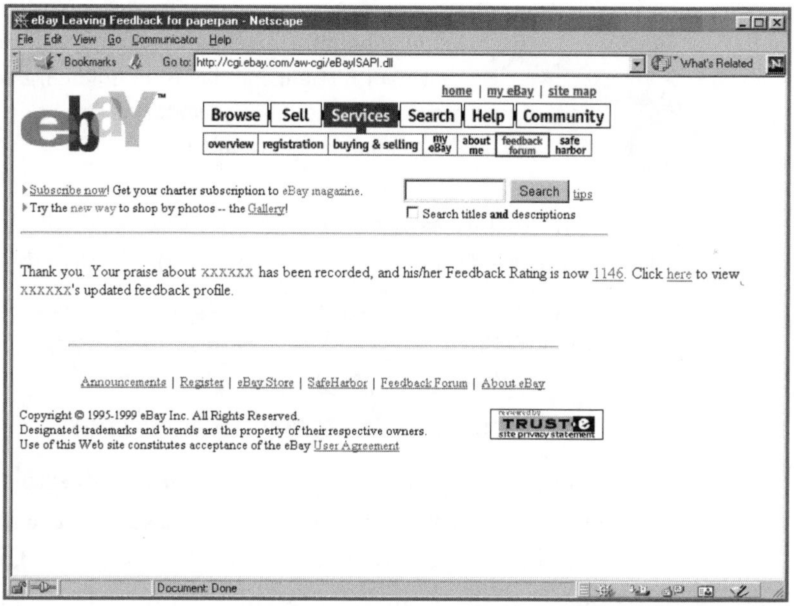

figure 23-4

When you've posted your
comment about another user,
eBay will show you the
effect—positive, negative, or
neutral—of that comment to
the user's overall feedback
rating.

Believe it or not, it actually feels good to see another user's feedback rating increase as a result of your posting. It's even more exciting to see *yours* increase, and then read what others have actually said.

Real quickly, then, take a look at some of the comments other users have posted to my Feedback Profile (see Figure 23-5).

Right away, eBay shows my *Overall profile makeup;* it's a composite view of how many comments of different types I've received since I first began with eBay as well as a glance at what's been happening to my feedback rating within the last six months. This is where you'll distill how someone ended up with the feedback rating number tied to their user ID.

I'm kind of pleased with my rating these days. 187 positive comments; that's great! Why, though, do only 183 count toward my feedback rating? eBay put in a little safeguard some time ago to prevent the same user from artificially stoking up a feedback rating number by posting multiple positive notes for anyone. Therefore, your positive rating will only increase with the number of unique eBay users you deal with. It's just like politics: if you want high approval ratings, you need to shake a lot of hands.

NOTE The same applies to negative feedback. A single user cannot post multiple negative notes with each one taking a toll on your feedback rating. That was a problem in the past, but eBay jumped into action to head off any more of those spitting contests among its users.

---

eBay View User Feedback for dennis_prince - Netscape

File Edit View Go Communicator Help

Bookmarks   Go to: http://cgi.ebay.com/aw-cgi/eBayISAPI.dll?ViewFeedback&userid=dennis_prince   What's Related

Overall profile makeup

187 positives. **183** are from unique users and count toward the final rating.

4 neutrals. **3** are from users no longer registered.

0 negatives. **0** are from unique users and count toward the final rating.

eb **ID card**   dennis_prince (183)

Summary of Most Recent Comments

	Past 7 days	Past month	Past 6 mo.
Positive	0	3	36
Neutral	0	0	1
Negative	0	0	0
Total	**0**	**3**	**37**

Auctions by dennis_prince

Note: There are 3 comments that were converted to neutral because the commenting users are no longer registered.

You can leave feedback for this user. Visit the Feedback Forum for more info on feedback profiles.

If you are dennis_prince (183) , you can respond to comments in this Feedback Profile.

Document: Done

figure 23-5

By clicking on the feedback rating number associated with my user ID, I can see my overall standings in the "Good User" club.

You can see that I have four neutral comments. Hmmm. What's up with that? Well three were previously positive comments, but the users who posted them have since left eBay. Remember, whenever people drop out of eBay registered status, any positive comments they've left will be converted to neutral—those comments will have no effect on your overall rating. The fourth neutral was from a user who apparently clicked the wrong feedback type—it was a glowing comment, but posted as a neutral. Oh well.

Of course, you want to see what the other users actually had to say about you, right? Scroll down in the Feedback Profile screen, and you'll see the different comments that have been posted (see Figure 23-6).

In the listing of actual comments posted, you'll see the registered user ID of each person who posted a comment, *their* current feedback rating, when they posted the comment, and the comment itself. If they chose to comment in regard to a specific auction item number, that will be shown as well.

figure 23-6

So what did they have to say?
I hope only good things!

NOTE When an auction number is shown next to a posted comment, it's often an active link to that closed auction's item details page. Remember, closed auctions can be viewed for up to 30 days after the auction has ended. When you see an item number next to a feedback comment, but it's no longer an active link, it means that item has aged off the closed items listings. The number will always be there, but it won't always be an active link.

"So what's with the little stars next to a user's feedback rating?!"

Those stars are the ones I introduced in Chapter 4—extra points of recognition given to users when they achieve certain milestones of positive feedback. Take a look at the eBay Star chart in Figure 23-7 and you'll see what each star means and when it's awarded.

Just because we're big people doesn't mean we don't each still find a certain thrill from getting a star of recognition. They're fun, and they feel good.

Now go back to Figure 23-5; there, you'll see a link at the bottom of the screen titled *Respond to comments*. This is a feature that lets a user respond to a comment that was left by another user. Maybe there was a ruffling of feathers, and a negative comment was posted. Maybe the two users worked

figure 23-7

What will other eBay users see in your stars?

out their differences since then. The response feature lets the user who received the negative comment respond to it; everyone else will be able to see the original comment and the response.

NOTE Feedback responses will not alter the user's overall Feedback Rating.

Comment response is done using a special variation on the feedback profile page. For simplicity's sake, assume you click on the *Respond to comments* link you see in Figure 23-5. You'll jump to a new screen as shown in Figure 23-8.

Once you've identified yourself, click on the *View feedback* button, and you'll jump to the screen shown in Figure 23-9.

You're now in a Review and Respond screen. Here, you'll see all the same user comments you saw before, but there's a little return envelope icon attached to each comment that has been posted; that's where you click to post a response to any comment you've received. Most often, this would be used if you had a negative or neutral comment and wanted to tell your side of the story.

figure 23-8

The entry screen into the Feedback Forum where you can respond to other users' comments requires you to verify your registered status.

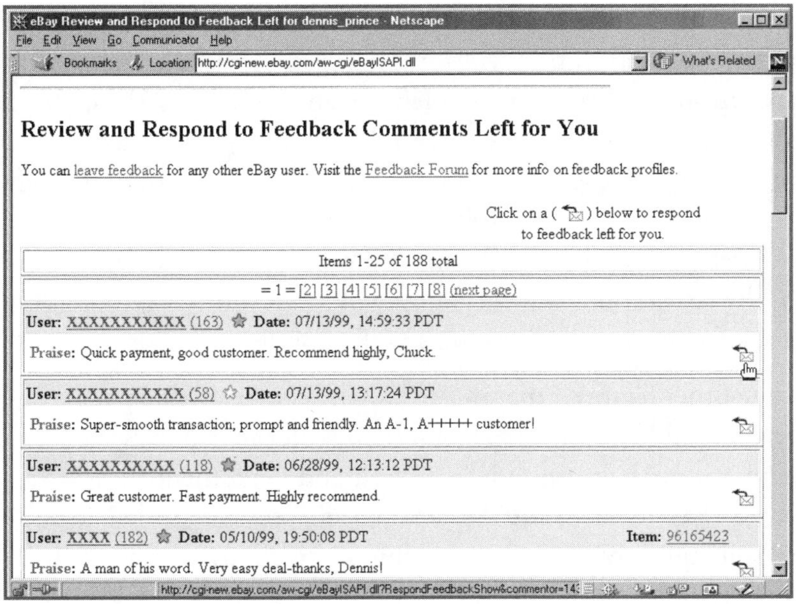

figure 23-9

Notice anything different about this feedback comment screen? What are those little return envelope icons?

The feedback response function was another one of the ways that eBay took its community's concerns to heart. Users reported that they wanted a way to respond to certain comments that had been left in their feedback profile—and, nicely enough, eBay listened.

Additional Features of the Feedback Forum

Remember, there are a few Feedback Forum features I hinted at earlier in this chapter. First, besides reviewing the feedback in your feedback profile, you can also view the feedback that you have left for other eBay users. One way to do this is to go back to the Feedback Forum introduction screen and click on the link titled *Review feedback you have left about others.* You'll need to again verify your user ID and password, and then you can progress forward to view the comments you've left about other users (it will look the same as the feedback response screen). Don't forget, this is a great tool to help you keep track of who you've left feedback about and who you might have missed.

In the *Review feedback you have left about others* screen, you might encounter the same envelope icons as in the *Respond to comments* screen. The envelope icon will show up for comments you've left for another user and for those comments to which that user has responded. If you like, you can also post a *follow-up* comment to the user's response. It's done the same way as an original comment or response, but the follow-up fosters better communication between eBay users, greatly helping to smooth out any problems or misunderstandings (the last section of this chapter will show you an example). Of course, feedback follow-up will not have an effect on feedback ratings.

And, there's one other feature I mentioned earlier: you can make your feedback profile either public or private. That's right, you can suppress the feedback comments people have posted about you and keep them from being viewed by other eBay users. Naturally, your profile defaults to being public—visible to all registered eBay users—unless you choose to change it.

If you want to change your profile to private, go back to the Feedback Forum introduction screen and click on the link titled *Make feedback changes public or private*. When you do, you'll see a screen like the one shown in Figure 23-10.

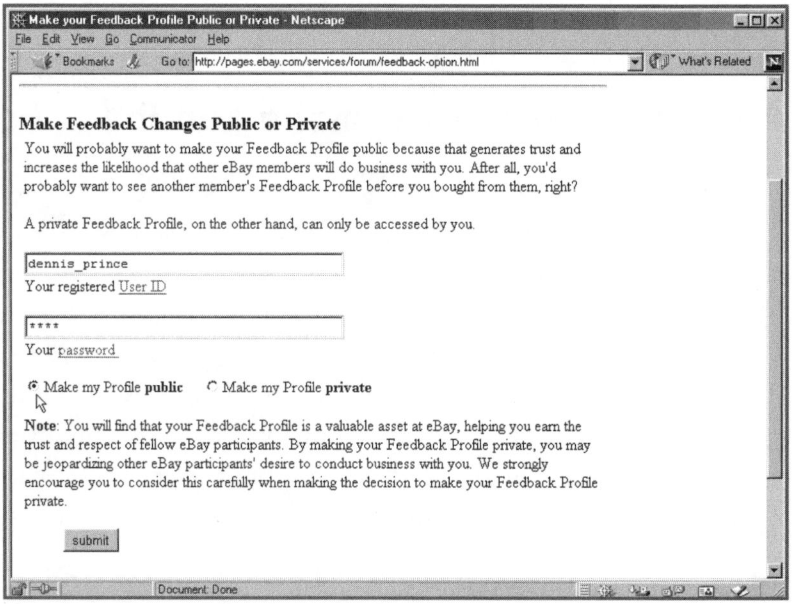

figure 23-10

It's up to you if you'd like to have your feedback publicly visible or privately viewable only to you.

Feedback comments are extremely valuable in helping other users determine what kind of user you are and how you have behaved with other users. eBay even cautions that making your feedback profile private will potentially alienate other users. More bluntly, it's a downright turn-off. If you make your feedback private, others will be curious about what you're hiding. Some sellers even state in their auction descriptions that that they will not accept bids from users with negative or hidden (private) feedback. It's a choice that's up to you to make, but consider it carefully.

A Few Guidelines When Leaving Feedback

The first thing to consider is the timing of your feedback. When the feedback is positive, leave it as soon as you can. Other users want to see their positive rating increase as quickly as possible. If you've just completed a good transaction, leave feedback right away. That way, you won't forget about it, and you'll also encourage other users to leave a similar note about you.

 N○TE Many eBay users—including me—actually prompt each other for positive feedback. Providing the deal is going well, it's OK to say, *"I'll post positive feedback for you; I hope you'll consider doing the same for me."* It's not looking for a handout, it's just acknowledging the value of the Feedback Forum.

Don't feel pressured to leave a note too soon, though. If you're a buyer and have a received a positive comment for making a fast payment, it's still OK to wait until you actually receive the item you bought and are certain you're satisfied before you consider leaving a positive note for the seller.

What about those negative comments, though—when should you leave those? Well, that's a stickier situation. First, if you believe you're having a problem with another user, do your best to work the problem out one-on-one before resorting to leaving negative comments. Use e-mail communications or even telephone the other person (remember, you can get registered user info from eBay if you're registered too). Do everything you can to work the problem out between the two of you before you consider airing the dirty laundry at the Feedback Forum.

Still, if things aren't working out even after your best efforts, then feel justi-fied in leaving a negative note. Again, make sure your comment pertains to the problem with the transaction, is not libelous, and is not threatening in any way. (Be especially sure about that last point!) It's really too bad when the time comes to post a negative note; expect that you might receive one in retaliation as a measure of the other user's displeasure. If things really get out of hand, contact eBay directly using the *Help* selection from the main navigation bar, then *Community standards* from the submenu, then the link, *Complaints about other eBay users.*

NOTE In case you're wondering, I've *never* left a negative comment about another eBay user. I'm pleased and fortunate to say that all my dealings over the years have been great. I've run across a few minor bumps along the way—you proba-bly will too—but it's never been anything that wasn't resolved with a little effort from me and the other user.

The real key to dealing with problem situations you might encounter is to wait a day before you react. You might be a little overemotional at the time something sets you off. Give it a day, consider your alternatives (maybe a neutral comment will make your point without inciting a knee-jerk reaction from the other user), and then decide if you still want to leave that negative note.

ALERT Choose your battles wisely! Give it some serious thought before leaving negative notes. I've already mentioned that posting a negative comment could earn you one in return. Whether that retaliation is justified or not, it can still hap-pen. You've also made a potential enemy on the site for the rest of your eBay days. If you feel it's right to leave the negative comment, then do so. Just be ready for the recoil.

If a negative feedback volley occurs, it doesn't necessarily mean there is no room for reconciliation. If, somehow, you and the other user have found a way to come to terms with one another, you can bury the hatchet using the Feedback Forum. You can *both* post responses and follow-ups to the nega-tive comments, and then go on to post positive comments on each other to effectively erase the −1 effect of the negative comment on your feedback ratings. A negative comment will still be in each of your profiles, but the responses, follow-ups, and offsetting comments will help other eBay users see you both worked out the situation. It could look like this:

- **Complaint**: I sent my money more than a week ago; no response; I've been robbed! A crook!

- **Response**: I was called out of town unexpectedly. Buyer now has item. Sorry for the delay.

- **Follow-up**: Everything's fine now. Item is great. Thanks for clearing this up.

- **Praise**: A fine and honest seller. The complaint posted on 7/28 was peacefully resolved.

The seller would provide the same follow-up and offsetting comment as the buyer did in the previous example. It's refreshing to see when users work out their differences, and it's a testimony that you are both committed to working through even the most difficult of situations.

 SOAPBOX One final thought about working things out: going the extra yard to settle a difference might keep you from being perceived as a risky deal. Think about it—if you consistently leave negative feedback, others might wonder if the problem is yours and not the other guy's.

I know someone who says he's been rear-ended 12 times on the freeway, though he swears it had never been his fault—but that doesn't make me at all eager to take a ride with him. Get my point?

chapter 24

Going Offline for Other Deals

With so many different items up for auction at eBay in so many different categories, what else could you possibly want? Well, with so many people listing items on eBay, just think about the mountains of stuff they probably have that hasn't been listed yet. It's just like when you go to a collectors' show, flea market, or garage sale:

"Hey, you wouldn't happen to have a . . . ?"

"Do you have any more of these somewhere?"

"This is great, but I'm also looking for. . . . "

When you host an auction or win an auction, you're making contact with someone who may well have an interest in the same sort of stuff you do. Don't be surprised if one item that sells turns into the opportunity to sell or buy a few more things without much more effort.

Meeting People Who Share Your Interests

This is actually one of the nice by-products of eBay: you'll come in contact with a whole bunch of people who probably share some of your affinities for certain stuff. I've met a lot of people through the auctions and have maintained good contact with them even though our first encounter was more than a couple of years ago. Again, this is what a community does: it meets, interacts, and remains in touch.

Often, the people I meet introduce me to others who also share those same interests. Pretty soon, you're networking with people in a nice two-way, three-way, or many-way kind of interaction that is great fun and can be of great value, too.

If you're a collector of just about anything, the more people you meet, the better your chances are of finding those things you really want. Remember that at eBay, you'll come into contact with people from all over the world; that really increases your odds of meeting great people and finding more of what you want.

 TIP Don't forget to visit the eBay Virtual Bulletin Boards. You'll meet lots of users there who are having fun discussions about the things they like most. Grab a cup o' joe, hit the Site Map, and go to the various chat links under the *Community* heading; the links to good company are right there.

What Else Do You Have?

So, as you're wrapping up that high bid purchase of yours, ask the seller if there's anything else around similar to what you've just won. Maybe that one item listed—the one you won—was only a test to see if the auction market might have interest in that kind of item. Maybe the seller has more of the same or something even rarer.

When you follow up on your pending deal, ask if the seller has something else you're looking for. More often than not, you'll find a bunch more where that one came from. Sellers often don't mind when you ask; in fact, when I'm selling, I welcome it.

When you're buying, and especially when you're treasure hunting, you need to turn over every rock you find to increase your odds of coming across that thing you simply must have. So don't be bashful; just ask. A seller who doesn't have what you're looking for could be the one to refer you to someone else who might. If that doesn't work, most sellers who deal in particular kinds of items might offer to keep a record of your name and what you're looking for. (Actually, if they followed my earlier advice, they have a nice little spreadsheet with the buyer's information already on it; that spreadsheet can work double-duty as a want list, too.)

But if the seller does have what you want, you might be able to strike a deal right there on the spot without having to bid on it in a future auction. A direct sale might be appealing to the seller, too. However, be prepared that the seller might want to list the other item—the one you want—to maximize potential profits. That's the seller's prerogative, and you shouldn't begrudge them if they go that route. Still, maybe you'll get a quick heads-up when that certain something does hit the block so you can be sure not to miss out on the bidding.

 Tip As a buyer, you might suggest a "package deal" when you pay for the item you won while also wanting to buy another item the seller has. Offer a reasonable price for both items; maybe the seller, seeing the potential to quickly and painlessly increase immediate income, will take you up on your offer.

Suggestive Selling

This one works for the seller. I first told you about suggestive selling in Chapter 18 when I showed you how to cross-list your auctions. As the transaction begins to wrap up, let the buyer know if you have more of the same type of item on hand. You might get a polite *"No thanks"*—but maybe it'll be, *"You do?! Cool! I want that too!"* OK, maybe the bidder won't be that excited, but might still be interested in buying another item or two that you haven't yet listed in the auctions.

Don't force your other items; just mention what you have and let the buyer decide whether they're interested. If you deal in a certain collectible or something, maybe you have a Web site or physical store; let your buyers know about that. Also, if you have a printed catalog of other items for sale, include that in the package when you ship an item that someone has won.

The great thing about suggestive selling is that you can do it with customers you've already dealt with and with whom you'd welcome future business. If your buyer has done a great job fulfilling an auction obligation, then you already know that's a customer you can trust. But if that buyer was a bit of a pain to deal with, you'll now know to avoid them in the future. In a way, you're screening your future customers without being dishonest or underhanded about it.

Just as I mentioned earlier, if a buyer asks for something that you don't happen to have, offer to keep an eye open for it. Make a note in your auction spreadsheet about what that buyer is looking for; it's practically a guaranteed sale if you find the item and price it reasonably. What could be easier?

This boils down to the way of collectors: they are each other's *cronies*. By that I mean that they form a vast network of roaming eyes, always on the lookout for something either for themselves or for someone else. When I come across an item I know someone else wants, I know they'll be thrilled that I've found it—and think how thrilled you'll be when one of your cronies finds something *you* want. It's a real *one-hand-washes-the-other* arrangement, and it's been going on for years. eBay just helps you find more hands to wash and more hands that will wash yours, too.

The USENET

Don't forget the USENET and all those great newsgroups. That's how I first learned about eBay, and I haven't been the same since. But there's a lot of buying and selling that goes on right in those newsgroups; don't ignore that. Increase your sales potential by posting items for sale in a newsgroup that will reach the right kinds of customers. And if something bombs out on eBay, try selling it direct—or vice versa.

TIP Be careful if you choose to use more than one sales venue to advertise and sell your items. Before you realize what's happening, you could have a bunch of customers—that's good—but more than you can serve in a timely and satisfactory fashion—that's bad. Just don't overextend yourself. Believe me, it's easy to do.

Helping the Less Fortunate Ones

"Poor little guy. He never saw that sniper coming. Look how sad he is now. He really wanted that thing. Poor little guy."

Well, in practically every auction, there's a winner and a loser (maybe more than one loser). What if you see an auction that got some spirited bidding, and you have an item just like it? I see a window of opportunity, don't you?

Of course, you can always list your item after that other auction ends and see if the losing bidders will flock to your listing, or you could think about the direct method. You have to be real careful when and how you do this, but you can send a short e-mail message to the loser in an auction to say you have a similar item that you'll sell directly. Start by offering it at that bidder's maximum bid; the forlorn bidder just might jump at your offer. If you want to increase your chances of making a quick sale, offer your item at a price 10 percent to 20 percent lower than that bidder's maximum bid—provided you won't be taking a loss yourself.

ALERT Do not—never, ever—contact bidders in an auction that's still in progress in an effort to direct sell to them the same kind of item they're presently bidding on! If you do, then you're engaging in an unfair practice known as *bid siphoning*—stealing bidders away from an active auction. If you are ever caught doing it, you'll probably be suspended from eBay.

Finding these opportunities for direct sales is pretty simple because, if you're doing your market research, you'll be finding other auctions that have just ended in which items like yours have just sold (or not). Then it's really up to you if you want to list your item for auction, or if you want to try the direct approach.

TIP Don't sell yourself short. If an auction that just closed saw some furious bidding, you might stand to make even more by going through the auction process rather than doing a direct sale. Remember, those bidders who lost out might be even more determined than ever to win if they could just get another chance. Ka-ching!

chapter 24

Now, if you're determined to do the direct sale approach, what will you do if there are multiple losers in a completed auction? Easy. Send an e-mail note to however many of the losing bidders you choose, telling them that you have the same item for sale, how much you are asking for it, and then state that you'll sell it to the first person to reply. That's kind of exciting, isn't it?

So, how should you word your message to these less-than-fortunate but still financially sound would-be bidders? Try something like this:

• •

```
Subject: Widget for sale

Date: Sat, 13 Mar 1999 07:33:21 -0800

From: Dennis <dlprince@bigfoot.com>

To: losingbidder@bummer.com

Hi,

I noticed you had bid in an auction for a purple widget on eBay. I
have one of these to sell myself and thought I would contact you to
see if you'd like to purchase mine directly before I list it for
auction. I'm asking $25 for it, and it's in excellent unused
condition.

If you think you'd be interested or would like more information
about my widget, please reply to this message. If this message is
unwelcome to you, please disregard it; I won't contact you again.

Sincerely,

Dennis

dlprince@bigfoot.com
```

• •

This message works fine when you're contacting a single bidder. Notice the extra politeness in my approach. This is definitely by design because this person probably doesn't know me, and I'm asserting myself by contacting them unsolicited. Like I said, this kind of selling, if you choose to attempt it, is often a very sensitive subject. In your message, provide an immediate escape if the recipient doesn't want to be solicited in this way. Assure them you will not contact them again. Of course, it could work out that the potential buyer is glad to hear from you and might contact you to see about arranging a deal. Great!

ALERT No spam! I'm approaching this whole matter of contacting losing bidders carefully because it can be misconstrued as "spam"—unwanted messages that appear as junk mail and annoyances to the recipients. Some people might get uptight that I even suggest this method of direct sales. Some might think this is a way of taking advantage of someone after they've lost an auction. Some might live by the adage, *"Don't call me; I'll call you."* I agree wholeheartedly, but if you didn't know I have what you're really looking for, how would you ever know to contact me?

Again, this is why the e-mail message you send should be very polite and to the point. Don't add images or anything else that would make the message larger to download (that costs some online users money for every megabyte they receive). Give the simple facts, open the door for a return message if the person wants more information, but promise this will be the only message you'll send unless otherwise contacted.

If you receive a direct sale message like this but aren't interested, send a reply saying you aren't interested, but thanks, or just ignore the message entirely. No biggie.

Hey, doesn't all this business about offline deals, cronies, and direct sales suggest we don't really need eBay to buy and sell stuff? Emphatically: *Wrong!* How else might you have met that person that you're now dealing with offline? How else will you meet the next great friend or potential crony, or the next, or the next? How else could you have found a buyer for your item offline or let other sellers know, indirectly, what you're looking for? eBay, that's how. There is so much to see at eBay; so many treasures tucked away that if I just dropped it entirely, I might as well go back to the old ways of collecting and selling. But why would I do that?

SOAPBOX eBay is there to use, not abuse. It is not a public fishing ground for users' e-mail addresses. By becoming a registered eBay user, you acknowledge that you will most likely be contacted by other users as a part of the auction experience or as an involved community member. That's OK—interaction is the whole point behind eBay. But, if you're not a registered and active eBay user, don't even consider trolling the site for user IDs that might be actual user e-mail addresses (some are), then using those addresses for unsolicited spam. In some states, this is considered an offense subject to stiff fines.

chapter 25

And in the End . . .

There is no end. There is only now and the endless future. What you have seen in eBay is the ongoing nurturing of something huge that has taken form and changed the way people feel about the things they buy, the way they buy them, and from whom they'll buy them.

But eBay is much more. What the auction is really all about is you and me and the millions of others who are looking for an oasis away from the physical world of fast talkers in plaid jackets. We have been overloaded with hype, hysteria, promise, and persuasion. Advertisers maintain that we live to shop, and shop to live. That's what their elaborate ad campaigns claim our lives are all about, and sometimes it's easy to begin to believe them—to feel like nothing more than a consumer with an insatiable hunger for what the ads are pushing to feeding frenzy.

But we can only shop for whatever is being sold. The largest and most influential merchants have found the way to tap into our needs, our wants, our fears, and our desires—and then exploit them without conscience. But when those marketing monoliths don't know—can't figure out—what we *really* want, they invent something and convince us this is it. Buy it now or go through life unfulfilled and empty. We are at a disadvantage in the world of persuasive marketing ploys. Can't we just say, *"Enough!"*

And then eBay came along. eBay has grown to be more than just a fancy Web site; it's more than just a place where things are bought and sold. eBay is power and eBay is freedom for each of us. The power is what we bring to the site in our enthusiasm, entrepreneurial drive, and sense of fair play. Although we all want to somehow become insanely successful in our trading, we stop short of manipulation and misdirection of our fellow community members. We have the power of restraint, and we use it judiciously when the big boys won't.

The freedom of eBay is the freedom to set our own agenda and make our own marketplace. There are no marketing directors, focus groups, or demographic studies that we must endure. It's an open air trading post where you and I meet, display our wares, and haggle it out in a fun, playful, and exhilarating environment. Nobody persuades us to buy what we don't want to own, sell what we really want to keep, or believe what we know isn't true. There is no *"tsk-tsk"* of psychological mind-play that exploits our insecurities and talks us out of our hard-earned wages. There are, instead, regular people who have something to sell and are delighted when they find out somebody wants to buy it. No sales quotas, revenue forecasts, or market penetration.

Therefore, eBay is a new beginning because it is a driving force in the new age of e-commerce. eBay has taken the world—and the stock market—by storm. It has outwitted even the most scholarly analysts and market overseers. It has outperformed everyone's expectations, and has withstood the slings and arrows of the Doubting Thomases and prophets of doom. eBay has made more than a splash in the e-commerce sector; it's given rise to an online tidal wave.

Others have come along as copycats and one-night scams, trying to capitalize on and duplicate what they believe makes eBay tick—but it can't be done. Why? Because you and I won't buy it. eBay came along with a spirit, a philosophy, and a respect—a respect for you and me as individuals who deserve a fun and unfettered place to share our passions, hobbies, and ideals. When we make a sale at eBay, we often make a friend, too. And that's probably why the wannabes can't quickly reproduce what eBay has become. eBay wasn't *produced*, it was *grown*, grown from the good intentions of two individuals—Pierre and Linda—and nurtured and shaped by people like you and me who had been longing for just such a place. It's our garden, and we're careful not to trample the sprouts of opportunity.

Most of all, eBay is fun. There's no other way to put it. It's a place to escape. It's a place where good people sell good stuff and have a good time doing it. Your eyebrows will raise and your jaw will drop at some of the amazing, zany, and unbelievable things you'll find on the auction block. And just when you think you've seen it all, you'll find you haven't. eBay has a surprise around every corner.

You've seen a lot of eBay in these pages, you've learned about the ups and downs and ins and outs, but there's clearly more for you to explore. Take the time to fully explore the site, get a better feel for the environment, and watch what the regulars do. eBay is constantly improving and updating, most often inspired by input from its community. If you haven't already, join the community and share in the realization that people make a difference.

But enough of my yakking. I'm just one guy having a good time. Wanna join me?

*   *   *

"Power to the people, right on."

—John Lennon

part 6

Appendixes

appendix A

More Information and Resources

I promised a bunch of tools and references for you throughout the pages you've just read; here they are.

General Information about Auctions

There's certainly a lot more buzz about auctions today than a few years back. Although the online craze is relatively new, it's still good to go back and find out more about the auctions' origin. Then, fast forward to what's happening in auctions today.

Books

Ralph Cassady, *Auctions and Auctioneering*. Berkeley: University of California Press, 1967.

This is an excellent book, though somewhat old, about the history and development of auctions. Sadly, it's been out of print for some time. Check used book stores or your local public library for a copy (that's where I found it). It's worth the hunt.

Daniel J. Leab and Katharine Kyes, *The Auction Companion*. New York: Harper & Row, 1981.

Another great book that gives insight into how auctions work, plus extensive facts on the different auction houses found around the world. It's somewhat out of date, but much of the core information stands the test of time. Sadly, this one is out of print too. Get hunting.

> Charles W. Smith, *Auctions: The Social Construction of Value*. Berkeley: University of California Press, 1989.

This is yet another good read and focuses on many of the details of auctions and those who attend them. Good detail on how auctions shape the cost of goods and services in the global economy. This one's still in print and you can find it quite readily on any of the online bookstores.

Web Sites

Agorics, Inc. (**www.agorics.com**): This is a terrific Web site presented by a company based in Los Altos, California, that provides software development and project management services in the realm of e-commerce and Web solutions. It contains some great information about auctions, gathered from many acknowledged sources. I found a lot of supporting facts on this site and was introduced to some of the other auction books that helped in my research of auction history.

AuctionWatch (**www.auctionwatch.com**): Presented by Omnibot, this is a Web site that offers information and a public forum for everyone and anyone who is interested in online auctions. The discussion groups cover the whole range of online auction sites and the information you can glean from the site regulars is of terrific value. You'll also find special features that delve into different areas of auction interest. They're an eloquent bunch, so mind your manners and use your best netiquette during your visit.

Price Guides and Useful Publications

If you're looking for journals and magazines that cater to your specific area of interest, just visit the magazine rack at your local bookseller. You'll find so many specialty magazines and publications that cover antiques, jewelry, pottery, toys, games, action figures, fast food collectibles, music, movie memorabilia, and just about anything else you could possibly want to buy and collect. I won't even begin to list them here; just go down to your favorite bookstore and "set a spell." *Y'all come back now, y'hear?*

More Info About PCs and Other Gadgets

There's probably more information about PCs and such than you'd care to digest, but here are a few sources that might help you gain some understanding, insight, and motivation. If you're not already very savvy or confident in what you know about PCs, peripherals, and other electronic goodies, do some homework *before* you go shopping. If you don't, you might find yourself succumbing to the wiles of an enthusiastic salesman.

Books

Here are a few books that I found particularly interesting and might be of use if you're kind of new to the PC world.

> John Bear, *Computer Wimp No More: The Intelligent Beginner's Guide to Computers*. Berkeley, CA: Ten Speed Press, 1991.

Yeah, this one's a bit dated and technology has changed an awful lot since it was published. However, it has some good core information about PCs and their use that you'll find still applies today. It's a great guide if you're looking into buying a computer.

> Bill Camarda, *Cheapskate's Guide to Bargain Computing*. Upper Saddle River, NJ: Prentice Hall Computer Books, 1997.

This is a fun little book with a spin I particularly enjoy: it's OK to be cheap. The author does a good job helping you find inexpensive (and free) ways to get the things you want and need for your own personal computing environment. He does a good job of showing you where you can skimp and where you can't. There's even a free CD-ROM included!

> Mary Furlong, *Young@Heart: Computing for Seniors*. New York: McGraw-Hill, 1996.

Well, don't let the title fool you; this book digs down to the bare roots of using a PC and answers all those simple little questions you're too embarrassed to ask. Yes, this is excellent for seniors who want to get comfortable with PCs and get on the Internet (and eBay!), but many experienced (and younger) PC users will find some tidbits of information they'll be glad to have learned, too.

> Faithe Wempen, *Upgrade Your PC in a Weekend*. Rocklin, CA: Prima, 1998.

Real straightforward and easy-to-understand guide to assessing your PC today and your PC needs for tomorrow. Great information for starters who want to spruce up their computing options, including detailed instructions on actual hardware installation. Get out your pocket protectors and little pen-sized screwdrivers.

Web Sites

Here are just a few of the better Web sites I've frequented that deal with PC-related issues.

Build Your Own PC (**www.verinet.com/pc**): This site is a bit outdated and the Web author, Jeff Moe, realizes it. It still has some great information if you want to consider building your own PC, though. Well written and presented, this site could plant the seeds of possibility that you might be able to custom-build a PC to meet your own exacting specifications. Don't get on Jeff about some of the dated material; he knows it needs updating and he shares that he hopes to give the site an overhaul soon.

Dave's Guide to Buying a Home Computer (**www.css.msu.edu/pc-guide.html**): This is a really informative and continually updated site developed by Dave Krauss at Michigan State University. Dave has been teaching courses at Michigan State since 1990 and has decided to publish his material on the Web. You'll learn a lot from Dave's experiences here.

PC Performance and Upgrade Tips (**www.sysopt.com/sphelp.html**): This is a great site if you've been using a PC for a while but want to squeeze even more out of your computing and online experiences. Presented by SysOpt.com (System Optimization Information), this site boasts a bunch of great stuff from enhancing the performance of your CPU to getting faster data transfer from your ISP. There are some great links to PC buying and upgrading sites, too.

Learning More about Web Browsers and the Internet

I know I never went into the intrinsic details of Web browsers and the Internet. Here are some resources that will start you off in the right direction:

Books

Christian Crumlish and Jeff Hadfield, *Netscape Communicator for Busy People*. New York: McGraw-Hill, 1997.

As the back cover puts it, *"The book to use when there's no time to lose!"* A very fast-paced, follow-the-dots approach to using the different components of Netscape Communicator. It does a good job sifting out all the minutiae, giving readers the core competence they'll need to use Communicator quickly.

Dave Johnson, *Internet Explorer 4: Browsing and Beyond.* New York: McGraw-Hill, 1997.

This book approaches the often unruly job of sorting through functions and features of a Web suite and parses them out so you can focus on and master each piece as you like. It's a beginner-to-intermediate level presentation that not only teaches the browser tool but also shows how Web sites are created, leading the reader to some great stopping points on the Web itself.

Cheryl Kirk, *Supercharged Web Browsers.* Rockland, MA: Charles River Media, 1998.

This book is cool in that it takes on the battle over browser accessories and plug-ins and makes sense of the whole matter. From Microsoft ActiveX to Netscape plug-ins, this book helps a reader understand what the fuss is all about and which are the best tools to use for whatever the need might be.

William R. Stanek, *Learn the Internet in a Weekend.* Rocklin, CA: Prima, 1998.

Straight-ahead information about what the Internet is, does, and strives to be. The author gets you geared up with your hardware, ISP, and other accessories that you'll need to step onto the Net. He then takes you on a nice virtual tour of cyberspace, showing you the sights and calling your attention to the key points that will help you understand the Web with greater ease and confidence. If you're brand new to surfing the Net and a little worried about it, hop on the back of William's waxed board and enjoy the ride!

Rob Tidrow and Greg Robertson, *The Essential Netscape Communicator Book.* Rocklin, CA: Prima, 1997.

Learn the ins and outs of Netscape Communicator with this comprehensive book. It not only covers the use of the browser tool, Netscape Navigator, but also covers

the other components of Communicator including Web design tools and e-mail management. Lots o' info in this one.

Web Sites

Netscape Communicator 4.5 Tutorial for New Users (**www-me5.netscape.com/brow-sers/using/newusers/index.html**): Well, why look much further than the official tutorial offered by Netscape itself. It's pretty straightforward stuff that teaches you the different functions and features of this popular browsing software.

The Web Developer's Virtual Library (WDVL): Web Browsers (**www.stars.com/Soft-ware/Browsers/**): Stars.com is a virtual treasure trove of all things cyber. On this particular Web page, you'll find a great rundown on *all* the different Web browser applications. The contributing authors at Stars.com really know their stuff; you should go there . . . *now!*

Internet Safety and Good Practices

Internet safety and privacy are of high concern these days, and rightfully so. Here are some resources I've come across that will open your eyes and help you become more aware of what you can do to further ensure your safety and security on the Net.

Books

Chris Peterson, *I Love the Internet But I Want My Privacy, Too!* Rocklin, CA: Prima, 1998.

This is an informative book that really opens your eyes regarding how much of "you" is out there. In fact, it shows you how much you can learn about yourself without even being online. There are many personal privacy tests that you can conduct to see just how many cyberpeepers there are out there and what they might be looking at.

Brian Pfaffenberger, *Protect Your Privacy on the Internet.* New York: Wiley, 1997.

This book does a great job explaining the need for Internet privacy and how the individual PC user can get it. The author introduces you to privacy strategies and applications that help you make your online travels safer and more worry-free.

> Katherine Murray, *Get Your Family on the Internet.* Rocklin, CA: Prima, 1999

Well, what better way to find safety on the Net than when cruising it in the family station wagon? Although this book is bent toward showing how the Internet can be made safe for families (especially kids), there's excellent information about online safety and privacy that everyone should learn and understand. Plus, there's a lot of fun stuff in here, too, that should appeal to the family-oriented surfers. Check it out if you fit that bill.

Web Sites

There are a lot of homegrown and professional sites that concentrate on the matters surrounding Internet safety on the Web. Here are a couple that I found informative, engaging, and entertaining, too.

Cyberangels Org (**www.cyberangels.org**): You can quickly tell by the name that this is the online home of the Guardian Angels. Regardless of how you feel about this group as an organization, its Web site has a lot of good tips and common sense advice to protect yourself and your family online. Give it a look.

Cybersmarts: Tips for Protecting Yourself When Shopping Online (**www.ftc.gov/bcp/ conline/pubs/online/cybrsmrt.htm**): This is a simple site but it has some great information. It's worth the read.

Junkbusters (**www.junkbusters.com**): With site tag lines like "*Bust the junk messages out of your life*" and *"Master self-defense against privacy-invading marketing,"* you'll know this is a site that serves you. Junkbusters is a privately held corporation devoted to speaking out against spam, cookies, and other unsavory Net garbage that clutters your online world. Lots of great information, tutorials, and free shareware designed to help you take a stand against the flood of useless bits and bytes that want to invade your PC.

HTML Help, Tools, and Tutorials

There's a sea of information out there about HTML and Web design. I won't bore you with a listing that looks like it came straight off Amazon.com. However, here

are a couple of resources that will get you going quickly. If you want more information, just cruise the bookstore, Amazon.com, or your favorite Internet search engine.

Books

More books about HTML and Web design have been written than either you or I could ever hope to read. However, here's one that I recommend to people who are just starting out with HTML, regardless whether they'll use it at eBay or to create their own personal Web site.

> Steven E. Callihan, *Learn HTML in a Weekend—Revised Edition*.
> Rocklin, CA: Prima, 1998.

If you're looking for a start in HTML with enough details and encouragement to make a developer out of you, start with this book. It's a great basic approach to HTML and it proves what I've already told you: HTML is easy.

Web Sites

The Web Developer's Virtual Library (WDVL) (**www.stars.com**): Just three words: Go there now.

The Graphic Station (**www.geocities.com/SiliconValley/6603**): This is a nice site that offers hundreds of little graphics and icons that you can use when you design your super-fancy auction listings.

Beakers Borders, Backgrounds and Graphics (**www.probe.net/~beakers/zborder. htm**): Here's another great site, sporting a whole gob of graphics that you can use to add flair to you HTML designs.

Background Colors (**www.infi.net/wwwimages/colorindex2.html**): A real bare-bones but helpful site that gives you the HTML color codes for all those great shades and hues you see on the Web.

Now there's tons more for you to learn about the Internet and the World Wide Web. What I've provided here is just enough to give you a few more answers and, hopefully, whet your appetite to go beyond that. The more you know and the faster you can use the tools of the Net, the better you'll do in cyberspace, online auctions, or any other electronic endeavor. Learning something new was never this much fun.

appendix B

More HTML Templates

In Chapter 18, when I was showing you how to add some HTML flair to your auction listings, I showed you one design that I used when I auctioned the *It Conquered the World* lobby card. It ended up being a visually fun listing, but it obviously wasn't the only design approach I could have chosen.

Following are a few more styles I could have used, using basic HTML, to design my listing and sell that lobby card.

The Low-Frills Listing

This design still makes use of a bidder hook: the film's tagline starts the listing, but I've also made use of the film's original logo design and a small, eye-catching graphic (taken from the lobby card image and modified using a graphics editing application). After that, I jump into basic text using a no-frills font. I still bring in the image of the lobby card, of course, and you can see that I retained the use of the anchor feature so the bidder can click on the image to jump to a larger version of it stored on my Web site.

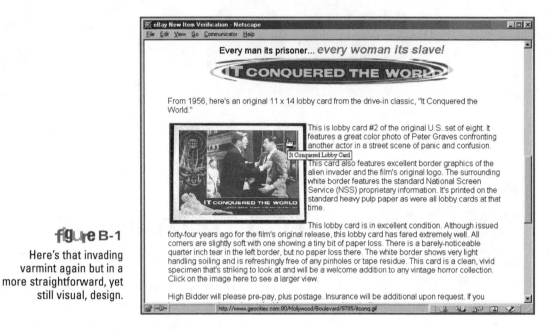

Here's that invading varmint again but in a more straightforward, yet still visual, design.

Here's the HTML code I used to create this listing:

```
<HTML><BODY>

<CENTER>

<FONT SIZE=4 COLOR=BLACK FACE="ARIAL">

Every man its prisoner . . .

<FONT SIZE=5 COLOR=RED><I><STRONG>

every woman its slave!

</I></STRONG></FONT>

<BR>

<IMG ALIGN="CENTER"
SRC="http://www.geocities.com:80/Hollywood/Boulevard/8785/
itconqlog.gif">

<P ALIGN="LEFT">

<FONT SIZE=3 COLOR=BLACK>

From 1956, here's an original 11 x 14 lobby card from the
drive-in classic, "It Conquered the World."

<P>
```

```
<A HREF="http://www.geocities.com:80/Hollywood/Boulevard/8785/
itconq.gif">

<IMG ALIGN="LEFT" HEIGHT=200 WIDTH=275 SRC="http://www.
geocities.com/Hollywood/Boulevard/8785/itconq.gif"

ALT="It Conquered Lobby Card">

</A>

<P ALIGN="LEFT">
```

This is lobby card #2 of the original U.S. set of eight. It features a great color photo of Peter Graves confronting another actor in a street scene of panic and confusion.

```
<P ALIGN="LEFT">
```

This card also features excellent border graphics of the alien invader and the film's original logo. The surrounding white border features the standard National Screen Service (NSS) proprietary information. It's printed on the standard heavy pulp paper as were all lobby cards at that time.

```
<P ALIGN="LEFT">
```

This lobby card is in excellent condition. Although issued forty-four years ago for the film's original release, this lobby card has fared extremely well. All corners are slightly soft with one showing a tiny bit of paper loss. There is a barely-noticeable quarter inch tear in the left border, but no paper loss there. The white border shows very light handling soiling and is refreshingly free of any pinholes or tape residue. This card is a clean, vivid specimen that's striking to look at and will be a welcome addition to any vintage horror collection. Click on the image here to see a larger view.

```
<P ALIGN="LEFT">
```

High Bidder will please pre-pay, plus postage. Insurance will be additional upon request. If you have any questions, please feel free to contact me via e-mail.

```
<P ALIGN="LEFT">
```

Check my eBay

```
<A HREF="http://cgi.ebay.com/aw-
cgi/eBayISAPI.dll?ViewFeedback&userid=dennis_prince">
```

feedback

```
</A>
```

and bid with confidence. Thanks for bidding.

```
</FONT></FONT></BODY></HTML>
```

This time, the listing (and the carrot creature) are well contained within a bordered table design.

The Table-Style Listing

In this design (shown in Figure B-2) I've used some HTML tags that will create tables when displayed. In this case, I've taken the most basic approach to the table tags by creating a single-cell table and then filling it in with a background color, text, and the anchored image. Notice how I also decided to make my usual end-of-listing text smaller; it's kind of like the small print in my ad. I used the *Horizontal Rule* "<HR>" tag to make a nice little separator line between the item description and the small print. You can experiment with text sizes and separators in your listings to emphasize or de-emphasize your words however you see fit.

Of course, this is the simplest table with only a single table cell—it gives the image and text a kind of floating frame. If you like, you could add a left cell and a right cell; one could hold the image and the other could hold the text. Monkey around with it.

Here's the HTML code for this one:

```
<HTML><BODY>

<CENTER>

<P>

<TABLE BGCOLOR=ORANGE ALIGN="CENTER" BORDER="4" CELLSPACING="6"
CELLPADDING="6" WIDTH="75%">
```

```
<TD ALIGN="CENTER">

<P>

<FONT SIZE=6 COLOR=RED FACE="STYLUS">

IT CONQUERED THE WORLD

<P>

<A
HREF="http://www.geocities.com:80/Hollywood/Boulevard/8785/itconq
.gif">

<IMG HEIGHT=200 WIDTH=275 SRC="http://www.geocities.com/
Hollywood/Boulevard/8785/itconq.gif" ALT="It Conquered Lobby
Card">

</A>

<P>

<FONT SIZE=3 COLOR=BLACK FACE="ARIAL">

From 1956, here's a great original lobby card from the drive-in
classic,

<BR>

"It Conquered the World."

<BR>

This film starred Peter Graves, Beverly Garland and Lee Van
Cleef . . .

<P>

<HR>

<P>

<FONT SIZE=-1>

High Bidder will please pre-pay, plus postage. Insurance will be
additional upon request. If you have any questions, please feel
free to contact me via e-mail.

<P>

Check my eBay

<A HREF="http://cgi.ebay.com/aw-
cgi/eBayISAPI.dll?ViewFeedback&userid=dennis_prince">

feedback

</A>

and bid with confidence. Thanks for bidding.

</TABLE></BODY></HTML>
```

The Total Atmosphere Listing

This last example is one where I used a bit more graphic splash, but still held back so as to avoid overworking the design and ending up with a gaudy, slow-loading page. In this one, I decided to unleash a background design of a swirling green alien mist that will actually spill out to the entire page, not just the description area. That sets the atmosphere immediately even before the bidder can scroll down to the description text (see Figure B-3 and B-4).

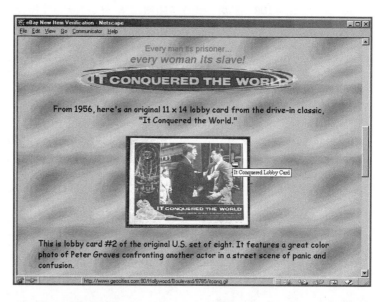

figure B-3

An eerie, other-worldly mist has just covered the city—and your screen. This background sets the stage for ominous things to come.

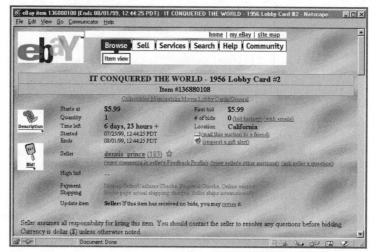

figure B-4

Hey! This green alien atmosphere is everywhere. I hope it's not some noxious fume that will render me docile and easy to conquer.

You have to be careful when you use a full-page background color or image (this one's an image tiled throughout the page); if you choose the wrong color or design, you could obscure or absorb the standard eBay item detail text and your listing will be a mess.

In this listing, I brought back the film's tagline and the original logo. Since I've added a busy background (instead of sticking with the standard white) I brought back the COMIC SANS MS font to increase the readability of the text. And I kept the anchored image of the lobby card.

Here's the HTML code for this design:

```
<HTML><BODY>

<CENTER>

<BODY BACKGROUND="http://www.geocities.com:80/Hollywood/
Boulevard/8785/greenmist.gif">

<FONT SIZE=4 COLOR=RED FACE="ARIAL">

Every man its prisoner . . .

<BR>

<FONT SIZE=5><I><STRONG>

every woman its slave!

</I></STRONG></FONT>

<BR>

<IMG SRC="http://www.geocities.com:80/Hollywood/Boulevard/8785/
itconqlog2.gif">

<P>

<FONT SIZE=4 COLOR=BLACK FACE="COMIC SANS MS">

From 1956, here's an original 11 x 14 lobby card from the
drive-in classic,

<BR>

"It Conquered the World."

<P>

<A
HREF="http://www.geocities.com:80/Hollywood/Boulevard/8785/itconq
.gif">

<IMG ALIGN="CENTER" HEIGHT=200 WIDTH=275 SRC="http://www.
geocities.com/Hollywood/Boulevard/8785/itconq.gif"

ALT="It Conquered Lobby Card">
```

```
</A>

<P ALIGN="LEFT">

This is lobby card #2 of the original U.S. set of eight. It
features a great color photo of Peter Graves confronting another
actor in a street scene of panic and confusion.

<P ALIGN="LEFT">

This card also features excellent border graphics of the alien
invader and the film's original logo. The surrounding white
border features the standard National Screen Service (NSS)
proprietary information. It's printed on the standard heavy
pulp paper as were all lobby cards at that time.

<P ALIGN="LEFT">

This lobby card is in excellent condition. Although issued
forty-four years ago for the film's original release, this lobby
card has fared extremely well. All corners are slightly soft
with one showing a tiny bit of paper loss. There is a barely-
noticeable quarter inch tear in the left border, but no paper
loss there. The white border shows very light handling soiling
and is refreshingly free of any pinholes or tape residue. This
card is a clean, vivid specimen that's striking to look at and
will be a welcome addition to any vintage horror collection.
Click on the image here to see a larger view.

<P ALIGN="LEFT">

High Bidder will please pre-pay, plus postage. Insurance will be
additional upon request. If you have any questions, please feel
free to contact me via e-mail.

<P ALIGN="LEFT">

Check my eBay

<A HREF="http://cgi.ebay.com/aw-
cgi/eBayISAPI.dll?ViewFeedback&userid=dennis_prince">

feedback

</A>

and bid with confidence. Thanks for bidding.

</FONT></FONT></BODY></HTML>
```

The whole point of this appendix is to provide you with a few more templates you can use for your spiffy auction listings. More important, though, is to show how little you have to tweak HTML code—just bringing in a few extra tags—to significantly change the way your listing looks and feels. It's art made simple, and it's fun.

Index